SOURCES OF DRAMATIC THEORY

Volume 1

Sources of Dramatic Theory

Forthcoming titles:

SOURCES OF DRAMATIC THEORY

1: Plato to Congreve

Edited and annotated by

MICHAEL J. SIDNELL
University of Toronto

with

D. J. Conacher, Barbara Kerslake, Pia Kleber,
C. J. McDonough, and Damiano Pietropaolo

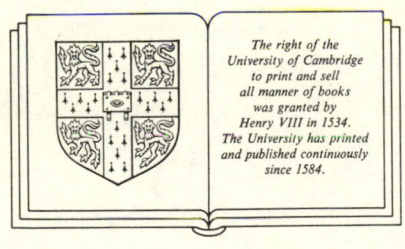

*The right of the
University of Cambridge
to print and sell
all manner of books
was granted by
Henry VIII in 1534.
The University has printed
and published continuously
since 1584.*

CAMBRIDGE UNIVERSITY PRESS

Cambridge

New York   Port Chester

Melbourne   Sydney

Published by the Press Syndicate of the University of Cambridge
The Pitt Building, Trumpington Street, Cambridge CB2 IRP
40 West 20th Street, New York, NY 10011, USA
10 Stamford Road, Oakleigh, Melbourne 3166, Australia

First published 1991

Printed in Great Britain at the University Press, Cambridge

British Library cataloguing in publication data

Sources of dramatic theory.
  1. Drama. Theories
  1. Sidnell, Michael J. (Michael John), 1935–
  808.2

Library of Congress cataloguing in publication data

Sources of dramatic theory / edited and annotated by Michael J.
  Sidnell, with D. J. Conacher ... [et al.].
        p.   cm.
  Includes bibliographical references.
  Contents: v. 1. Plato to Congreve.
  ISBN 0–521–32694–x (v. 1)
  1. Drama. 2. Theater.
  PN1631.S6 1991
  801'. 952 – dc20   90–1564 CIP

ISBN 0521 32694 x hardback

CE

CONTENTS

ACKNOWLEDGMENTS

The following permissions to use published material are gratefully acknowledged:

John Pershing, Hackett Publishing Company, Indianapolis, IN and Cambridge, MA, for the use of G. M. A. Grube's translations in *Aristotle on Poetry and Style* (1958)

Niall Rudd for the use of his translation of *The Art of Poetry* (*Ars Poetica*) published in his *Horace: Satires and Epistles / Persius: Satires* (revised edition, 1979)

The publishers for the use of Andrew Bongiorno's *Castelvetro on the Art of Poetry: an Abridged Translation of Lodovico Castelvetro's Poetica d'Aristotele Vulgarizzata et Sposta* (Medieval & Renaissance Texts & Studies, 29; Binghampton, NY, 1984).

D. J. Conacher thanks Professors Elaine Fantham and Niall Rudd for their help with bibliographical and other matters in connection with the Horace section. Pia Kleber thanks Juris Silarajs for his assistance with the translation of Corneille. The encouragement and support of Ronald Bryden and Brian Parker has been most welcome, as has the material assistance given by Trinity College, Toronto. Ralph Blasting's contribution to this volume not only in systematizing the bibliographical references but with administrative chores and by his cheerfulness has been much appreciated. Michael Sidnell also wishes to express his appreciation of the stimulus afforded by members of his seminar in the Graduate Centre for the Study of Drama at the University of Toronto. He hopes that, when it is completed, this collection of texts will go some way to meeting the needs of *their* students. He also thanks the staff of Cambridge University Press for their resourceful expertise and their constant courtesy and Sarah Stanton, especially, for her vital contributions to the conception and production of this volume.

NOTE ON THE TEXTS

Most of the translations included in this volume have been specially made for it by the editors, as indicated below. The other translations used are: Paul Shorey's of Plato; G. M. A. Grube's of Aristotle; Niall Rudd's of Horace; and Andrew Bongiorno's of Castelvetro. Publication details of these are given in the bibliography. The punctuation and spelling of the originally English texts have been lightly modernized. Whether newly or previously translated, all the texts included here are annotated by the editors of this volume.

Though there has been extensive collaboration among the editors, the primary responsibilities for the notes, commentary and the new translations are as follows:

D. J. Conacher: the introductory note and footnotes to Aristotle's *Poetics*, and to Horace's *The Art of Poetry*

Barbara Kerslake: the translations of, and the introductory notes and footnotes to the selections from d'Aubignac, Racine, and Saint-Evremond, and the passages on *Le Cid*

Pia Kleber: the translation of the selection from Corneille, and the introductory note and footnotes to it

C. J. McDonough: the translations of, and the introductory notes and footnotes to the selections from Donatus, Robortello, and Scaliger

Damiano Pietropaolo: the translations of, and the introductory notes and footnotes to the selections from Giacomini, Giraldi, Grazzini, Guarini, Ingegneri, and Oddi

Michael J. Sidnell: the general introduction; the translations of, and introductory notes and footnotes to, the selections from Lope de Vega, Tirso de Molina, and Torres Naharro; the introductory notes and footnotes to the selections from Castelvetro, Congreve, Dryden, Edwards, Heywood, Jonson, Rymer, Sidney, and Whetstone.

Ralph Blasting compiled the Bibliography.

ABBREVIATIONS

Throughout the volume a system of cross-references has been used to signal and locate passages for comparison. These are in the form of an abbreviation followed by a page number, inside pointed brackets: ⟨Cv/129⟩ refers to the text of Castelvetro on p. 129 of this volume. In the case of Horace's *The Art of Poetry* the line number follows the page number: ⟨Hr/69:180⟩. The abbreviations used are:

Ar	Aristotle	Ig	Ingegneri
Cd	On *Le Cid*	In	Introduction (chapter 1)
Cg	Congreve	Jn	Jonson
Cn	Corneille	Lp	Lope de Vega
Cv	Castelvetro	Nh	Torres Naharro
Db	d'Aubignac	Od	Oddi
Dd	Dryden	Pl	Plato
Dn	Donatus	Rb	Robortello
Ed	Edwards	Rc	Racine
Gd	Giraldi	Rm	Rymer
Gm	Giacomini	Se	Saint-Evremond
Gu	Guarini	Sg	Scaliger
Gz	Grazzini	Sy	Sidney
Hr	Horace	Tm	Tirso de Molina
Hw	Heywood	Wh	Whetstone

Where more than a simple internal reference is required it is supplied in the footnotes.

1

INTRODUCTION

"Theory" is now the usual term for the kind of texts included in this volume though it was not used in this way by any of the authors included here. For the Greeks, who coined the word, it had the sense that it retains of contemplation, of viewing not doing. "Theory" has, in fact, a common etymological root, signifying "see," with the word "theatre." From this it might be surmised that both theory and theatre are modes of contemplation and that theorizing about theatre is thus a distinctly introverted activity. But the theatre is *in* the world as well as a place for observing it; drama never represents the world with complete objectivity and the spectators are never wholly detached observers. Nor, for that matter, has the theory of drama been uninvolved with its practice – on the contrary. So it is fitting that, far from being purely contemplative, the most renowned and influential work of dramatic theory, Aristotle's *Poetics*, is concerned with the *making* of tragedy, not just with its appreciation, and with drama as something *done* and experienced, as well as something contemplated.

Sometimes dramatic theory is dismissed as useless, but it is precisely when it tries to be practically useful that it becomes most contentious. One scenario goes something like this:

PRACTICE (aggressively): What *use* are you?
THEORY (cunningly): Perhaps to consider what use *you* are. (After a moment's silence.) But, tell me, do you know what you're doing?
PRACTICE (insolently): Possibly not, but it works!

In a more civil encounter Practice asks, "Can you tell me how this was done?" Theory, flattered, attempts an explanation and, yielding to temptation, goes on to offer some general rules, which Practice joyfully breaks.

Scientific theories have sometimes been tailored to prevailing moral, political, or religious codes but the historical tendency has been for experimental science to expose contradictions between nature's laws and current understandings of them, or by practical applications to validate existing theories. Since the arts are entirely human productions, theories about them cannot be objectively tested and are therefore more liable to be subsumed under the prevailing orthodoxies. Theologies have often attempted to govern the arts and supply their theory for them and some influential present-day artistic theories have been derived from Marxism. The theory that, to the exclusion of all others and of theoretical discourse itself, attempts to deliver the arts from such subordination holds that artistic works themselves wholly and solely embody whatever principles inform them. Plato seems to be aware of the invincibility of this position when he rules out of order any defense of poetry in the form itself of poetry ⟨Pl/31⟩. Other theories, recognizing that such a claim to full autonomy for the arts would involve theoretical self-contradiction, have acknowledged varying degrees of dependence of larger philosophical or ideological constructs, and have concerned themselves with the defense or elucidation of particular works or with such key issues in the understanding of a specific art as its origins, its present function, the aesthetic principles by which it may be appreciated or judged, and the precepts to be followed in its production. Such theoretical statements have appeared in a variety of forms, from extensive and comprehensive commentaries to short prefaces. Not surprisingly, dramatic theory has often been presented in dialogue form.

Since dramatic theories of the past are the products of their time and place, they are sometimes considered as essentially historical documents. But the history of dramatic theory does not recount a continuous development: many new starts are made in ignorance of what has gone before and certain issues recur so often as to suggest that they are always relevant, despite the particularity of the social and intellectual contexts in which they arise. Some of these recurrent issues are: what it means to represent or imitate something dramatically; how written texts are related to live performances; by what means, in what ways, and to what ends spectators may be affected; how the various contributory arts such as poetry, dance, painting, and music may or should be combined in the theatre; to what degree the actor may be an artistic medium for some other artist such as a playwright or director, or be an interpreter of a role, or be a primary creator; and what constitutes or legitimizes certain dramatic genres and how they are to be distinguished and used.

The intellectual method of treating such theoretical questions as historical ones is comparatively recent. One of its founders was A. W. Schlegel, whose influential *Lectures on Dramatic Poetry* were published in 1812. Up to that time, the interest in theories of the past was almost invariably in their contemporary aesthetic applications. In the sixteenth and seventeenth centuries, Aristotle's *Poetics* and Horace's *Art of Poetry* were treated as active elements in the thought of the times and were often distorted, consciously and otherwise, in the process. In our own century, many once-influential theories have been relegated to history or simply forgotten, but the *Poetics* has been redeployed, both positively and, in some highly significant instances, with a sharp antagonism.[1] Brecht's quarrel with Aristotle, for instance, was an important element in the shaping of his own theory, his plays, and his productions.

By contrast with the modern tendency towards historicism, many commentators in the sixteenth and seventeenth centuries were intent on making Aristotle and Horace, even when they took them as "guides not commanders" ⟨Jn/193⟩, as thoroughly prescriptive (and so as useful) as possible. Whatever else may be said about it, this approach did, at least, try to keep theory in contact with practice. Nor was it an out-and-out abuse of the ancients, for Aristotle is prescriptive in a rather complex way and Horace is clearly so. Stephen Halliwell observes an "affinity between the *Poetics* and various Greek *technai* or didactic manuals which were produced in a variety of fields, perhaps above all in rhetoric, but also in more practical crafts such as painting or sculpture" (1986, 37). But Halliwell insists on "the difference between theoretical and practical prescription, and that the *Poetics* is essentially an exercise in the former not the latter" (p.38). The way in which his interesting argument first posits a distinction between theory and prescription and then gingerly merges them in "theoretical ... prescription" is an illustration of how suspect prescriptiveness has become in modern times.

Theory remote from practice is also suspect, and it was particularly so in 1938, when R. G. Collingwood's *The Principles of Art* appeared. Collingwood, who took up many of the classical issues, was much less worried about being prescriptive than about being "academic." He insisted that he did "not think of aesthetic theory as an attempt to investigate and expound eternal verities concerning the nature of an eternal object called Art, but as an attempt to reach, by thinking, the solution of certain problems arising out of the situation in which artists find themselves here and now." His book, he said, was intended, primarily, to be of "use" to artists (p.vi).

In distancing himself from "academic philosophers" (such as himself) and ranging himself with "poets, painters, and sculptors" (whose "often chaotic" attempts at aesthetic theory were a motive for his own), Collingwood was assuming a rather paradoxical, but by no means unprecedented, role. It may be extravagant to imagine (as the nineteenth-century scholar Teichmüller did) that aspiring Athenian dramatists went to hear Aristotle to learn more about their craft, but it is possible that Aristotle, like Collingwood and many other theorists, wanted to be of some use to makers of plays. His Renaissance commentators certainly did. Robortello and Castelvetro, for example, interpret the *Poetics* very differently but they share with each other and with their contemporaries the assumption that

---

[1] As for instance by Francis Fergusson in his *The Idea of a Theater* ([1949] 1968) and the "Chicago School" (for which see Crane 1952) in a positive way, and by Antonin Artaud in *The Theater and its Double* (1958) and Augusto Boal in *Theatre of the Oppressed* (1976) negatively.

sound theory is a prerequisite of good practice.

The combination of understanding and practical skill was called "art," in a sense that survives today in "the art of medicine" or "state of the art." And the term "art" was also applied to a literary form (related to the modern "guide," "handbook" or "manual") modeled on Horace's so-called *Art of Poetry*.[2] Lope de Vega treated this form with an interesting ambivalence. His *New Art of Making Comedies* undermines the very idea of an "art" that lays down guidelines for the dramatist. He may, indeed, be intimating that "art" is an indefinite but quintessential quality, using the word somewhat in the modern way for certain painted, sculptured, or written works. "Art" in this modern, honorific sense does not usually include ceramics, quilts, chairs, or textbooks, for the production of which some "craft" is required or for which a practical use is intended, and is distinguished from "science" (such as medicine), which is based largely on a body of transmissible knowledge and definite principles.

Lope de Vega's brief theoretical statement is imbued with irony and with an overriding confidence in his achievements, whether they were those of an artist or a crafty entertainer. For Corneille, however, the question of "art" was a vexatious one. He insisted ⟨Cn/235⟩ that the object of drama was pleasure but that "to find this appropriate pleasure and to give it to the audience one must follow the precepts of art and please in accordance to them. It is axiomatic that there are precepts, since there is an art; but it is not established what the precepts are." He formulated the precepts by correlating his own plays with received theory, occasionally finding short-comings in the plays and frequently finding reason in the plays to qualify the theory.

Corneille's antagonist the abbé d'Aubignac called his own attempt at prescriptive theory a "pratique" (which an anonymous English translator rendered as "whole art" ⟨Db/220⟩); in the eighteenth century, Lessing gave the title "dramaturgy" to the series of essays that he had begun with the practical objective of hammering out, in a theatrical context, principles of performance; and, in this century, Brecht chose the crusty Greek word *organon*, meaning – much like "pratique" – an "instrument" for doing something. These titles indicate their authors' ambitions to produce something equivalent to an "art" in the Renaissance sense: a theory of the subject with explicit practical applications.

The works just mentioned are devoted specifically to drama, written and performed, but many of the most comprehensive treatments of drama in the sixteenth century appear as parts of general theories of poetry, or "poetics," in which dramatic poetry is traditionally accorded most atten-tion. Some of these, such as Castelvetro's, are in the form of expositions of

---

[2] The work had acquired the non-authorial cognomen *Ars Poetica* by the time of Quintilian (35–96 A.D.), who refers to it as such.

the (original) *Poetics* that offer to interpret, to complete, to update, and even to correct Aristotle's thought and thus to achieve the status of independent theories; others, such as Scaliger's *Poetices libri septem* are presented as intrinsically independent. As pertaining to drama, the concept of a "poetics," and the word itself, were formerly less awkward than they have since become.[3] Tragedies and comedies were classified as poems, prose drama was widely regarded as an anomaly ⟨Gd/123⟩, and playwrights were called "poets." It was not until the later seventeenth century that the distinction between poet and playwright was regularly made. This verbal distinction not only separates writers of plays from writers in general but also confirms (rather paradoxically) the separation of the writers from the other artists (or "wrights") who contribute to the making of plays.

It should be noted that "poetry" in these earlier contexts does not necessarily exclude theatrical expression: the poet who writes for the theatre is commonly supposed to exercise at least some command of the non-verbal arts of the stage. But the supremacy of the script – the dramatic poem – is assumed by almost all the theorists represented in this volume and, if they address the matter at all, they are mostly vague about the relation between the non-verbal elements of performance and the text. This has since become a prominent issue, as is indicated by the common usage, in English, that distinguishes "drama" (meaning written texts) from "theatre" (implying performance). Considering the root meaning of "drama" as something *done*, this usage is rather inappropriate but what is much more important is that this semantic division of "drama" and "theatre" obscures the basic question of how the semiotics of theatre (which includes non-verbal "languages" of the staging, as well as the words) and its phenomenology (which includes the delivery of the text) may be related.

Castelvetro's clear recognition of a non-verbal language of the theatre is one of several new departures in his theory. It comes about as his ingenious resolution of a difficulty passed down from antiquity concerning the difference between recitation and impersonation. Aristotle, like Plato before him, had distinguished between the narrative (*diegetic*) and dramatic (*mimetic*) modes. Given that the poet speaks in his own voice in the narrative mode, is the dramatic mode to be understood as consisting of speeches assigned to *characters* and delivered by the poet (or rhapsode), or as implying the use of *actors who impersonate* the characters on a stage? The Greek description of the single narrative voice Castelvetro accepts, but the corresponding description of the dramatic, he says, requires a subdivision. To discourse in the form of dialogue he assigns the term "similitudinary" and to drama for performance the term "dramatic." The difference

---

[3] Currently, the term "poetics" is used very elastically: it may refer to the aims of a poet's practice, or to its effects, or be a general theory of literature. Todorov's *The Poetics of Prose* (1977) may be said to be an anti-Scaligerian title.

between them, he says, is that "similitudinary" dialogue is like narrative in being a representation of words and things by means of words alone, while the "dramatic" is a representation of words and things by means of both words and things ⟨Cv/132⟩. This distinction is the theoretical basis for Castelvetro's insistence on performance as essential to the dramatic genre. Many important corollaries follow from it and though some of these (notably the idea of a required "unity of place") found an all-too-ready acceptance, the fundamental premise was virtually ignored.

Castelvetro's idea of a non-verbal dramatic *language* of things is naturalistic to the limited extent that he envisages the representing things as belonging to the same order as the things represented, whenever that can be done: hats by hats, swords by swords, and men by men. But Castelvetro is not interested solely in the *meaning* of theatrical representations. On the contrary, he de-emphasizes the importance of meaning in drama in favor of the sensuous gratification it can afford ⟨Cv/132⟩.

Shakespeare seems to have had much less confidence than Castelvetro in the representation of things by things. The Chorus in his *Henry V*, forestalling criticism, asks the audience to compensate imaginatively for the inadequacy of both the verbal and the material parts of the representation, but the two kinds of imperfection are differentiated. The admission that "four or five most vile and ragged foils, / Right ill-disposed in brawl ridiculous," are a paltry attempt to represent the battle of Agincourt, indicates a real material limitation ⟨Jn/199⟩. But the supposed verbal inadequacy is transcended even in the very admission of it: "Think, when we talk of horses, that you see them / Printing their proud hoofs i' th' receiving earth." We do not, in fact, get mere talk but the lively verbal image of horses. Similar imagery is called upon to present, verbally, the shipping, the battlefields, and the crowds to the mind's eye. With a disarming affectation of modesty, Shakespeare dexterously uses the medium that lies within his control – the words – to compensate for the material deficiencies of the presentation. He seems to share with Scaliger the conviction that, even in drama, "words serve as signs for reality" ⟨Sg/106⟩ and he goes as far as any playwright in meeting Scaliger's demand that "all of the playwright's ideas about the setting, or about the movements, costumes, and gestures of the characters, that are necessary for understanding the story, must be expressed in the lines that are spoken" (Scaliger/Padelford 1905, 117).

Unlike d'Aubignac, who follows him in insisting on the self-containment of the dialogue ⟨Db/224⟩ Scaliger intends to preserve the integrity of the dramatic poem as a literary artefact independent of whatever non-literary means of expression might also be employed. This is in keeping with his insistence on versification, rather than imitation, as the primary and defining characteristic of dramatic (and other) poetry ⟨Sg/108⟩. On this fundamental issue he dissents from Aristotle and precisely and deliberately does what Aristotle is often said to have done: he privileges the written text.

Aristotle's own position is more complex and difficult to interpret. His ranking of "spectacle" as the least important of the six parts of tragedy, with the explanation that it cannot be of the essence since tragedy can be effective in reading, has earned him much opprobrium, particularly in the present century. He stands accused of the original sin of separating text from performance and subordinating the latter (Halliwell 1986, 337ff.). But it should be noted that what Aristotle here called "reading" we would call recitation, and that, though the Greeks read play texts, it was only after printing became common that solitary readers with ideal theatres in their heads became a considerable "audience," and a phenomenon to be reckoned with (as it is by Ben Jonson ⟨Jn/192⟩). Nor is it entirely clear what Aristotle means by "spectacle": whether the whole *mise-en-scène* or only the masks and costumes of the actors – perhaps Copeau's bare stage, on which no clutter of objects was allowed to distract the audience from the concreteness of the verbal presentation,[4] would have seemed to him an absence of spectacle. It is also significant that Aristotle puts the development of tragedy in a theatrical setting, describes a dramatic structure that implies performance and insists that the poet keep the theatre firmly in mind. Nevertheless, Aristotle does, apparently, regard the mature tragic genre (but not necessarily, it should be remembered, comedy or other kinds of drama) as *literature* for the theatre.

According to Aristotle the tragic essence is embodied in a certain kind of imitation of an action of a certain kind, which produces certain effects, notably *catharsis*: "by means of pity and fear bringing about the purgation of such emotions" is a conventionally worded translation of the formulation in the *Poetics* (Dorsch 1965, 39). In Gerald Else's translation, however, this becomes "through a course of pity and fear completing the purification of tragic acts which have those emotional characteristics" (Aristotle/Else 1967, 25). The interpretation involved in this rendering is dubious and it can be aligned with the many interpretations of the sixteenth and seventeenth centuries that locate the pity and fear in the tragic action rather than in the spectators. Scaliger, Castelvetro, and many others after them regard the "purgation" as a *rational* response to the tragic *example* of the potential consequences of these emotions. Analysis is certainly made simpler in this way, though it may be quite wide of the mark: the emotional element can be readily discussed since it supposedly lies in the tragic action itself and the spectators' response, being a rational one, can also be predicted or deduced. This way of interpreting (or perverting) the *Poetics* makes it seem more compatible with a long tradition of didactic theory, and with the almost universally accepted Horatian maxim that the function of drama is to teach and delight ⟨Hr/74:344⟩.

[4] See Copeau 1923.

Among those interpreters who have assumed the reality of a cathartic effect on the spectators there have been major differences. Some have supposed that the spectators feel the pity and fear so intensely that these emotions are evacuated as though by medicinal purgative; some that the specified emotions are purified and remain active in that form as an effect of the tragedy; and some that the tragedy acts as a homeopathic remedy, operating on the spectators like small doses of poison, or the experience of battle on soldiers, leaving them less vulnerable to the enfeebling emotions of pity and fear. In our time, Augusto Boal has adopted the medicinal theory but sees in its operation a means of oppression, a sublimation of the spectators' potential for political action.

Aristotle holds that the cathartic effects of tragedy are produced by the choice of an appropriate subject and, even more emphatically, by its treatment, especially in terms of such structural features as the integrity of the plot and the organization of its incidents in keeping with probability, the changes of fortune visited upon the protagonist, and the uses of reversal and recognition. These will affect the spectators in vital ways, but just how the tragic imitation is supposed to satisfy the spectators' sense of reality or belief – whether, for instance, as an illusion of actuality or as a consciously ritualized enactment – is not made clear in the *Poetics*.

The theorists and commentators of the sixteenth century and later foregrounded this question, partly displacing the Aristotelian criterion of *probability* (within the plot) with complex notions about *credibility*. So d'Aubignac declares that "Considering the action as real, [the playwright] must look for a motive or a plausible reason, which is called a pretext [*couleur*], for these narrations and these spectacles really to have happened in this way. I dare say that the greatest art in writing for the theatre lies in finding all these pretexts" ⟨Db/223⟩. This credibility stems from the choice of subject and from its treatment but is not necessarily, or usually, confined to a likeness to ordinary reality. It can come also from the poet's ability to represent ideal worlds in such a way that they too are believable; for imitation includes the representation of things that do not exist "as if they did, and in the manner they might and ought to exist" ⟨Sg/100⟩.

The credibility of imitations is usually referred to as "verisimilitude," a term that has a range of meanings, even in single texts. Verisimilitude may consist in a successful copying of actuality, in a credible presentation of ideality, or in making a particular representation conform with what is supposed to be typical of the class. Horace's much-quoted advice on characterization is to this end: that young men should be presented in the rashness of their youth, old men as dithering and greedy, and so on ⟨Hr/69:176–78⟩. In this way verisimilitude is achieved with, and by means of, decorum. The playwright, says Torres Naharro, should exercise a decorum that is like the command of a ship: servants will not be made to speak and act like masters ⟨Nh/113⟩. The spectators find such characters credible because they are drawn according to their expectations and these same expectations are thereby strengthened with respect to drama and – very significantly – to real life as well. By making the ought-to-be look lifelike (and therefore possible) drama brings the ought-to-be closer to realization in actuality. Plays written and performed on this understanding, and the judgments of them, tend to conform, of course, with the dominant ideology of their time.

"History" (inclusive of myth) is frequently thought of as a requirement for tragedy and an enabling factor for verisimilitude. By using one kind of truth (such as the names of historical personages and the outlines of known episodes) another, ideal, kind is made credible. Corneille, however, ingeniously argues for the use of history as a means by which the constraints of verisimilitude may be transcended. The marvelous is by definition unlikely but it becomes credible when it can be said to have happened. Moreover, it is more interesting to the audience to be presented with marvels that are thus made credible than with what is credible merely because it is likely ⟨Cn/236⟩. Castelvetro regarded this blending of historical truth and invention in dramatic plots as more difficult than sheer invention, since the poet had to fill in the details of a received story instead of being free to invent details and story together ⟨Cv/137⟩.

Verisimilitude (with its range of meanings) is thought to stem not only from the choice of subject matter (whether historical or otherwise) and from the treatment of the subject with decorum, but also from dramatic structure. George Whetstone scorns the typical English dramatist for failure in all three areas: for grounding "his work on impossibilities" such as monsters; for making "a clown companion with a king" and the "gross indecorum" of using "one order of speech for all persons"; and for inventing plots so loose that they allow for infant characters to grow into men ⟨Wh/166⟩. He does not refer to the "unities" or "rules" as such, but he is making the assumption, common in his time, that in order to achieve verisimilitude it is necessary to adhere to the unities of action, time, and place. If, for example, unity of action is not preserved and the dramatist relies instead on the unity deriving from concentration on an individual character, then the spectators will be confronted with the incredible spectacle of that character going from youth to old age in the space of two hours or so. This would also be a violation of the supposed "unity of time," which theoretically restricts the temporal scope of the action to a maximum of one day, and aims for a minimum disparity between stage time and real time. Again, such a plot would probably involve the need to make the stage represent many different places, with a consequent strain on the credulity of the spectators for whom it is supposedly easier to think of the stage as one location only ⟨Sy/180⟩.

Verisimilitude was the main but not the only argument advanced in favor of the unities. Another source of the neo-classical attachment to them was their supposed provenance from the *Poetics*. Aristotle does, indeed, insist on unity of action ⟨Ar/42⟩, but the idea of a unity of time had its very insecure basis in Aristotle's remark ⟨Ar/41⟩ about tragedy taking place within a revolution of the sun, and, as to unity of place, it was Castelvetro's strict logic about stage illusion that implanted it as a "rule" ⟨Cv/132⟩. Overall the doctrine was riddled with misunderstandings and plain errors and was the occasion of disputes as unproductive as they were tortuous. But one reason for not dismissing the whole discussion of the unities as the product of barren scholasticism is that, right up to the present, dramatic structure has often tended towards just such a concentration of fictional time and space as adherence to the unities produced. Another is that since drama is a medium that combines sequentiality (as in music and speech) with juxtaposition (as in painting or sculpture), the coordination of the temporal and the spatial elements is critical. In the eighteenth century, the question of the differentiations between, or fusions of, the various arts on the basis of their representations of time and space became a central one in the new science of aesthetics but by this time the "rules" were already falling into disrepute and the obvious connection between the new aesthetics and the old precepts was never made.

The doctrine of the unities was foisted on Aristotle by the theorists of the sixteenth century as they tried to formulate their own structural principles. Their basic concept of genre, however, was a genuine inheritance from antiquity and one that has survived (vestigially, at least) up to the present. From the *Poetics* came paradigms in which the structural and attitudinal distinctions between tragedy and comedy corresponded with predispositions of the respectively tragic and comic playwrights and certain effects on the spectators. Furthermore, in Aristotle, these two genres appeared to be ultimately attributable to the basic possibilities of human existence itself, which is experienced or perceived as tragic or comic ⟨Ar/39⟩.[5]

The absence in the *Poetics* of a theory of comedy parallel with that of tragedy was not an insuperable obstacle to the generic duality. The deficiency was (and still is) commonly attributed to the loss of a second book of the *Poetics* and, beginning with Robertello's in 1548, a series of attempts to reconstruct the hypothetical work have been made.[6] Other definitions of comedy – notably the one attributed to Cicero by Donatus

---

[5] In his *On Comedy* (1548) Robortello writes: "Aristotle seems to intimate that both simultaneously arose from nature itself. For he states that since some men were *semnoteroi*, that is rather august and serious, and others *eutelesteroi*, that is light and playful, the former wrote serious productions, that latter light and amusing works and thus two kinds of poetry arose, one serious, the other jesting. That such was the case he proves with an example from Homer, in whom may be seen both natures, the light and the serious." (Translation by C. J. McDonough.)

[6] The most recent work in this vein is Richard Janko's *Aristotle on Comedy* (1986). (In Umberto Eco's entertaining fiction, *The Name of the Rose* [1983] a copy of Aristotle's work on comedy is deliberately suppressed by reactionary clerics, rediscovered, and destroyed.)

⟨Dn/79⟩ – were adduced on the assumption of a fundamental generic duality.

It is interesting to observe how ideas about genre are made to conform with social ideas, as when tragedy is assumed to be fit entertainment for princes, who are capable of suffering it in life, and comedy for commoners, whose harshest misfortunes could be represented in terms of comedy. The reasons given for making tragic protagonists of princely rank also reveal an interesting interplay between social ideas and aesthetics: since princes have further to fall than other men, they are suitable figures for a significant tragic action ⟨Rb/95⟩; since the decisions and falls of princes have consequences that affect many other people, tragedies concerning them will be of wide interest ⟨Sg/101⟩; or, rather subversively and existentially, princes are suitable tragic figures since they are not bound by the laws they make and are therefore free to be self-destructive ⟨Cv/140⟩. Questions about the rank of tragic protagonists – especially about the possibility of tragedy of the common man – continued into the present century.

In Italy in the sixteenth century, strenuous theoretical efforts were made to assert the legitimacy of genres other than tragedy and comedy. The basic Aristotelian division was expanded in order to accommodate modern plays in the pastoral, tragicomic, and other genres. Polonius' command of an elaborate taxonomy of dramatic genres satirizes a pedantic extreme of this development (*Hamlet* 2.2.412).[7] The test case was tragicomedy: whether it had existed among the ancients or was a new but legitimate (or bastard) genre, and how it might include features of both comedy and tragedy, whether separately or mixed, or not at all, and to what effect. Some of the attempts to justify tragicomedy led to new insights about the nature of drama in general, as for instance in Guarini's theory of tragicomedy as a self-conscious fiction ⟨Gu/158⟩. In Spain the Aristotelian duality was evaded by the practical and theoretical development (despite belated but fierce opposition) of the *comedia*, which did not conform with Aristotelian generic categories or their derivatives and which has important implications for theories of genre generally ⟨Tm/211⟩.

One of Sidney's objections to the "mongrel tragicomedy" is that unlike "right" tragedy and comedy, it mingles kings and clowns ⟨Sy/181⟩. But Lope de Vega slyly observes that there was no knowing whether King Philip's irritation at seeing kings in comedy was based on artistic or social criteria ⟨Lp/187⟩. In either case decorum is involved, but the Spaniard does not assume, as the Englishman does, that the social solecism is also an aesthetic defect, and that it will produce emotions that will tend to

---

[7] Polonius' categories are: "tragedy, comedy, history, pastoral, pastoral-comical, historical-pastoral, tragical-historical, tragical-comical-historical-pastoral, scene individable, or poem unlimited." The last two refer not to genre but to plays that respectively do and do not preserve unity of place and time.

neutralize each other. Where Sidney appeals to artistic precepts, Lope de Vega argues from nature, which derives beauty, he says, from variety ⟨Lp/187⟩. But the real force in making tragicomedy acceptable (and even in escaping from the idea of genre altogether) was audience demand. Giving the spectators what they want and allowing them to spend their time in the theatre in ways that best please them often results, it appears, in mixtures that defy generic classification.

Aristotle's brief sketch of the origins and development of tragedy and comedy has been much emulated, with the objective of eliciting the essential significance and function of theatre from the study of its beginnings. But ideas about where theatre *ends* are at least as important as those about where it began. The shows put on in Roman amphitheatres, which included actual deaths as part of the entertainment, may be distinguished from the dramatic art in which all deaths are acted: "acted" in the double sense that something is actually done and that that something constitutes a pretense. The importance of being able to make this distinction between an enacted imitiation and the thing itself is brought out in Philip Massinger's *The Roman Actor* (1626). In the plot of this play a professional actor is dragged into an amorous and deadly theatricalization of actual life. A theatre in which all passions are pretended and no actors die is juxtaposed with an "actuality" in which real passions and real deaths are "staged." Thematically Massinger's play examines the disastrous results, in an extreme case, of the inability to perceive, and the refusal to acknowledge, the differences between theatrical imitation and theatricalized actuality. But the play, being merely a play, belongs unequivocally in the former category, of course, and with this understanding we may perceive a fusion of the pretended and the actual that takes place in a distinctively artistic realm. For us, the actual is the performance itself and the pretended what is represented: for d'Aubignac ⟨Db/224⟩ the pretense lay in the acting, the truth (which might be historical) in the text.

In *The Roman Actor*, as commonly in plays using plays within plays, attention is drawn, teasingly, to the fact that the spectators' attention is given simultaneously to the acting and to what is acted. This doubleness occurs in the interplay between the predetermination of a text, in which everything has been decided, and the freedom of a performance, in which there is something unpredictable in every successive moment. The role of the actor-protagonist is so devised by Massinger that, in the playing of it, it will ultimately be impossible for the spectators to differentiate between an actor acting a role and an actor acting the role of an actor acting a role. But thematically the difference is a matter of life and death. Thomas Heywood, on the contrary, and like many others before and since, cheerfully asserts the theatricality of all existence and hence the vast importance of actors and theatre. This conception of a *theatrum mundi* attributes to the theatre (and the world) the self-reflexivity that some modern literary theorists find in literary and phenomenal "texts."

It has been observed that the notion of the "dramatic" may be almost indefinitely extended "to the television situation comedy or, indeed, to that briefest of dramatic forms, the television or radio commercial" (Esslin 1977, 12–13). But, as Walter Benjamin pointed out, there is "no greater contrast than that of the stage play to a work of art that is completely subject to or, like the film, founded in, mechanical reproduction" (1968, 231). The drama found in the live theatre is quite distinct from the "drama" of cinema and television and the distinction is as significant as the fact that, despite many dire prognostications, the dramatic theatre has survived into the second half of the twentieth century. The theatre in which a playscript is performed remains a distinct and significant artistic form, and this is the form with which the texts in this volume are concerned.

The choice of texts and extracts for this volume has been difficult. The editors have tried to do some justice to closely reasoned and detailed theoretical arguments, even when they have to be extracted from long works, and not to reduce documents to "representative" snippets in an effort to be nominally more inclusive. Even so, some harsh cutting has been required. Also regrettable is that, with the exception of the Jonson selection, extracts from plays have been excluded because the theoretical matter in them is usually too deeply imbedded in the text and structure of the whole work. With much less reluctance, documents that defend or attack the stage without addressing theoretical questions have also been excluded, notwithstanding their historical importance. Plato is allowed (though briefly) his say but thereafter we have assumed that the question of whether or not theatre should be permitted is not a critical one for this volume. Finally it should be noted that though, for convenience, the arrangement of texts is chronological (as it will be in the subsequent volumes), they have been chosen for their intrinsic theoretical interest.

2

PLATO
(429–327 B.C.)

Not until the fourth century B.C. (the century following the great age of Greek drama) do we find any extensive treatment, in Greece, of such subjects as "the arts," including poetry and drama, and of their place in society. Most philosophic speculation before Socrates (Plato's mentor), who lived towards the end of the fifth century, had been concerned with larger matters, such as the nature of the universe. Socrates and the Sophists (his frequent dialectical opponents) were the first Greek thinkers to be primarily concerned with man and his works. Of the thought of Socrates (who wrote nothing) we have only what is attributed to him in Plato's dialogues; of the writings of the Sophists (who were more interested in rhetoric than in poetry and drama) little has remained extant. However, it seems likely from echoes in contemporary dramatists (Euripides, for example, and most notably Aristophanes) that such matters as criteria of poetic excellence, standards of taste, stylistic parody, suitable topics for dramatic competition, and so on, were at least the subject of cultivated conversation in Socrates' and the Sophists' day.

It is perhaps unfortunate and, in some ways, misleading that the first extant serious treatment which we have from the Greeks on the place of the arts in society should be mainly – entirely as far as the dramatic arts are concerned – of a negative and censorious nature. As we shall see, some explanation for this treatment in Plato's *Republic* can be found in the particular contexts in which the discussions arise and, negative though it is, Plato's treatment is of considerable importance. In the first place, it raises, in admittedly extreme form, issues about the social and moral effect of the arts (and particularly of the dramatic arts) which have exercised society up to the present day. In the second place, Book 10 of the *Republic* introduces, perhaps for the first time, the concept of art, and particularly of poetry, as in some sense an imitation of life and of the world around us. Plato's use of the word *mimesis* (imitation) in connection with the arts varies considerably, as we shall see, with the dialectical context of his argument, and his most celebrated exploitation of this "connection" in the *Republic*, Book 10 is one which was possible only within his own metaphysical system. Nevertheless the germ of the long-lived concept of art as imitation of life goes back to one of the passages from Plato's *Republic* printed below.

Plato's shifting use of such words as *mimesis* serves to highlight a feature of this philosopher's dialogues to which readers unfamiliar with them should be alerted. Words which we are inclined to view as terms denoting fixed and clearly defined concepts had, for the most part, not achieved that status at the time when Plato was writing. (Aristotle's usage, in this respect, is quite different.) Plato himself tends to exacerbate this shifting, chameleon-like quality in language by the uniquely dialectical (i.e., basically conversational and argumentative) quality of his discourse. ("Wherever the *logos* leads us, there shall we follow it," as he makes

Socrates say.) Thus words tend not so much to change their basic meaning as to have those meanings undergo various different applications (and even valuations) according to the ever-changing context of the dialectical progression.

The discussion of the arts (*mousike* – which includes the dramatic arts) in the *Republic* arises first in connection with the education of the guardians (who are eventually described as "the philosopher kings") of the ideal state which "Socrates" has been envisaging in order to discover the nature of Justice. Thus it is important to remember that all statements about the arts in Books 2 and 3 of this dialogue are determined by their function of helping to produce the best guardians of the *polis* or state. It has already been decided that each citizen will concentrate on the one task or duty, and that task only, which the state has assigned to him, and this principle of specialization has an important bearing on the treatment of the arts in the guardians' education. Considering solely the moral effect that poets' stories may have on future guardians, Plato's Socrates insists on rigorous censorship of these tales. He goes on, in the passage from Book 3 printed below, to consider the different styles (*lexeis*) of poetic composition and he applies the same criterion (moral effect) with equal rigor. The style described as "imitative" refers here to the dramatic style and it is rejected lest the diversity of imitations involved should distract the guardian from his single and specialized function.

In the second excerpt, which comes from the *Republic*, Book 10, poetry is discussed in rather different terms. In the intervening argument certain conclusions have been reached (about the nature of truth and about the nature of man's soul) which make it possible to question more fundamentally the place of honor which the poet has traditionally held in the state. True being has been shown (in Book 5) to reside in the realm of Ideas, of the single ideal forms ("Beauty," "Honor," "Justice," and so on) which lie behind the many particulars of the world around us; this latter world of appearances, of *phenomena*, then, is merely the reflection of the ideal realm. In their "imitations," the artist and the poet take one step further from truth and reality than the phenomenal world. Secondly, man's soul has been shown (in Book 4) to consist of three parts, the rational, the spirited, and the appetitive; it is now discovered that poetry as a whole and dramatic poetry in particular appeal to the irrational part of the soul and so threaten the dominance, necessary for the soul's just and proper functioning, of its rational element. A clue to the rigorous and categorical nature of Plato's exclusion of poetry from the ideal state in the *Republic*, Book 10, and to the terms (both epistemological and psychological) selected for that exclusion, appears toward the end of the discussion: there, when "Socrates" is made to refer to "the ancient quarrel between poetry and philosophy," Plato reveals, perhaps, the fundamental reason for the exclusion of poets from the ideal state: that the Greeks looked on the poet as a teacher. Plato, it appears, would brook no rival to the philosopher in this capacity. That is why he so categorically demonstrates, in the *Republic*, Book 10, that, in terms of its relation to truth and of its psychological effect, poetry cannot compete with philosophy as a guide to truth and right behavior.

Two other dialogues, the *Ion* and the *Phaedrus*, also reflect the view that the poet has no share in rationally acquired knowledge. Both these dialogues do, however, accord a certain kind of visionary inspiration to the poet: the *Phaedrus* briefly, where "possession by the Muses" is spoken of as one of the useful forms of madness; the *Ion* more playfully but at greater length. In this latter dialogue, the operation of the Muse's inspiration is likened to a magnet from which are suspended a series of rings, first the poet, second the rhapsode or professional reciter (who is also equated with the *hypocrites* or actor), and third the audience or spectator. Neither the poet nor the rhapsode operates by knowledge, or even by technical skill, but by divine dispensation (*theia moira*) or divine power (*theia dunamis*).

These passages referring to the poet's divine inspiration do suggest Plato's recognition that the poet did in fact have his own irrational access to truth, which the philosopher reaches by reason. Even in the *Republic* (at least in the earlier part of the discussion) the poet who accepts the philosopher's restrictions, and embodies "the semblance [or "image," *eikon*] of the good character" in his poems, is found acceptable and useful as preparing the way for the philosopher. It seems unlikely, however, that the *dramatic* poet could ever (for reasons which appear in the passages below) have achieved even this measure of approval from drama's severest ancient critic.

For further reading

Greene 1918; McKeon 1952; Nettleship 1891.

From the *Republic*[1]

BOOK 3

392   "... Is not everything that is said by fabulists or poets a narration of past, present, or future things?"

"What else could it be?" he said.

"Do not they proceed either by pure narration or by a narrative that is effected through imitation,[2] or by both?"

"This too," he said, "I still need to have made plainer."

"I seem to be a ridiculous and obscure teacher," I said; "so like men who are unable to express themselves I won't try to speak in wholes and universals but will separate off a particular part and by the example of that try to show you my meaning. Tell me. Do you know the first lines of the *Iliad* in which the poet says that Chryses implored Agamemnon to release his daughter, and that the king was angry and that Chryses, failing of his
393   request, imprecated curses on the Achaeans in his prayers to the God?"

"I do."

"You know then that as far as these verses,

> *And prayed unto all the Achaeans,*
> *Chiefly to Atreus' sons, twin leaders who marshalled the people,*

---

[1] The following passages (very slightly modified) are from Plato/Shorey 1937. Shorey's translation is based principally on the Teubner edition (Plato/Hermann 1855). The numbers in the margins are conventionally used references derived from the pagination of the "Stephanus" edition.

[2] "Imitation" (*mimesis*): Earlier (at 373b) "Socrates" has used the word "imitators" to include poets and painters as well as actors and others connected with the performing arts. In the present passage, the word "imitation" refers only to "impersonation." Later, in the different dialectical context of Book 10, "imitation" will be given a much broader application. See the introductory note on the dialectical use of this word.

the poet himself is the speaker and does not even attempt to suggest to us that anyone but himself is speaking. But what follows he delivers as if he were himself Chryses and tries as far as may be to make us feel that Homer is not the speaker, but the priest, an old man. And in this manner he has carried on nearly all the rest of his narration about affairs in Ilion, all that happened in Ithaca, and the entire *Odyssey*."

"Quite so," he said.

"Now, it is narration, is it not, both when he presents the several speeches and the matter between the speeches?"

"Of course."

"But when he delivers a speech as if he were someone else, shall we not say that he then assimilates thereby his own diction as far as possible to that of the person whom he announces as about to speak?"

"We shall obviously."

"And is not likening one's self to another in speech or bodily bearing an imitation of him to whom one likens one's self?"

"Surely."

"In such case then, it appears, he and the other poets effect their narration through imitation."

"Certainly."

"But if the poet should conceal himself nowhere, then his entire fiction and narration would have been accomplished without imitation. And lest you may say again that you don't understand, I will explain to you how this would be done. If Homer, after telling us that Chryses came with the ransom of his daughter and as a suppliant of the Achaeans but chiefly of the kings, had gone on speaking not as if made or being Chryses but still as Homer, you are aware that it would not be imitation but narration, pure and simple. . . . "

394 "I understand," he said.

"Understand then," said I, "that the opposite of this arises when one removes the words of the poet between and leaves the alternation of speeches."

"This too I understand," he said, " – it is what happens in tragedy."

"You have conceived me most rightly," I said, "and now I think I can make plain to you what I was unable to before, that there is one kind of poetry and tale-telling which works wholly through imitation, as you remarked, tragedy and comedy; and another which employs the recital of the poet himself, best exemplified, I presume, in the dithyramb ⟨Ar/40⟩;[3] and there is again that which employs both, in epic poetry and in many other places, if you apprehend me."

"I understand now," he said, "what you then meant."

---

[3] The dithyramb was a form of choral lyric containing a large element of narrative. Aristotle tells us that tragedy originated from improvisations by the leaders of the dithyramb sung in honor of the god Dionysus.

"Recall then also the preceding statement that we were done with the 'what' of the speech and still had to consider the 'how.'"

"I remember."

"What I meant then was just this, that we must reach a decision whether we are to allow our poets to narrate as imitators or in part as imitators and in part not, and what sort of things in each case, or not allow them to imitate at all."

"I suppose," he said, "that you are considering whether we shall admit tragedy and comedy into our city or not."

"Perhaps," said I, "and perhaps even more than that. For I certainly do not yet know myself, but wherever the wind, as it were, of the argument blows, there lies our course."

"Well said," he replied.

"This then, Adeimantus, is the point we must keep in view, do we wish our guardians to be good mimics or not?[4] Or is this also a consequence of what we said before, that each one could practice well only one pursuit and not many, but if he attempted the latter, dabbling in many things, he would be mediocre in all?"

"Of course it is."

"And does not the same rule hold for imitation, that the same man is not able to imitate many things as well as he can one?"

"No, he is not."

395   "Still less, then, will he be able to combine the practice of any worthy pursuit with the imitation of many things and the quality of a mimic; since, unless I mistake, the same men cannot practice well at once even the two forms of imitation that appear most nearly akin, as the writing of tragedy and comedy? Did you not just call these two imitations?"

"I did, and you are right in saying that the same men are not able to succeed in both, nor yet to be at once good rhapsodes and actors."

"True. But neither can the same men be actors for tragedies and comedies – and all these are imitations, are they not?"

"Yes, imitations."

"And to still smaller coinage than this, in my opinion, Adeimantus, proceeds the fractioning of human faculty, so as to be incapable of imitating many things or of doing the things themselves of which the imitations are likenesses."

"Most true," he replied.

---

[4] In discussing whether indiscriminately imitative poetry (i.e., drama) is to be admitted as part of the guardians' education, "Socrates" seems to slip into considering whether the guardians *themselves* should be such indiscriminate imitators. This is, however, merely a telescoping of a continuous argument: the basis of accepting or rejecting such imitative poetry is the consideration of its potential effect on the guardians, who, it is implied, will imitate what is imitated in the theatre. Adeimantus is one of the two young friends of "Socrates" who initially challenge him to consider the nature of justice. He and Glaucon (who appears later in this extract) are two of "Socrates'" five interlocutors in the *Republic*.

"If, then, we are to maintain our original principle, that our guardians, released from all other crafts, are to be expert craftsmen of civic liberty, and pursue nothing else that does not conduce to this, it would not be fitting for these to do nor yet to imitate anything else. But if they imitate they should from childhood up imitate what is appropriate to them – men, that is, who are brave, sober, pious, free and all things of that kind; but things unbecoming the free man they should neither do nor be clever at imitating, nor yet any other shameful thing, lest from the imitation they imbibe the reality. Or have you not observed that imitations, if continued from youth far into life, settle down into habits and (second) nature in the body, the speech, and the thought?"

"Yes, indeed," said he.

"We will not then allow our charges, whom we expect to prove good men, being men, to play the parts of women and imitate a woman young or old wrangling with her husband, defying heaven, loudly boasting, fortunate in her own conceit, or involved in misfortune and possessed by grief and lamentation – still less a woman that is sick, in love, or in labor."

"Most certainly not," he replied.

"Nor may they imitate slaves, female and male, doing the offices of slaves."

"No, not that either."

"Nor yet, as it seems, bad men who are cowards and who do the opposite of the things we just now spoke of, reviling and lampooning one another, speaking foul words in their cups or when sober and in other ways sinning against themselves and others in word and deed after the fashion of such men. And I take it they must not form the habit of likening themselves to madmen either in words nor yet in deeds. For while knowledge they must have both of mad and bad men and women, they must do and imitate nothing of this kind."

396

"Most true," he said.

"What of this?" I said, " – are they to imitate smiths and other craftsmen or the rowers of triremes and those who call the time to them or other things connected therewith?"

"How could they," he said, "since it will be forbidden them even to pay any attention to such things?"

"Well, then, neighing horses and lowing bulls, and the noise of rivers and the roar of the sea and the thunder and everything of that kind – will they imitate these?"

"No, they have been forbidden," he said, "to be mad or liken themselves to madmen."

"If, then, I understand your meaning," said I, "there is a form of diction and narrative in which the really good and true man would narrate anything that he had to say, and another form unlike this to which the man of the opposite birth and breeding would cleave and in which he would tell his story."[5]

"What are these forms?" he said.

"A man of the right sort, I think, when he comes in the course of his narrative to some word or act of a good man will be willing to impersonate the other in reporting it, and will feel no shame at that kind of mimicry, by preference imitating the good man when he acts steadfastly and sensibly, and less and more reluctantly when he is upset by sickness or love or drunkenness or any other mishap. But when he comes to someone unworthy of himself, he will not wish to liken himself in earnest to one who is inferior, except in the few cases where he is doing something good, but will be embarrassed both because he is unpracticed in the mimicry of such characters, and also because he shrinks in distaste from moulding and fitting himself to the types of baser things. His mind disdains them, unless it be for jest."

"Naturally," he said.

"Then the narrative that he will employ will be of the kind that we just now illustrated by the verses of Homer, and his diction will be one that partakes of both, of imitation and simple narration, but there will be a small portion of imitation in a long discourse – or is there nothing in what I say?"

397   "Yes, indeed," he said, "that *is* the type and pattern of such a speaker, the more debased he is the less will he shrink from imitating anything and everything. He will think nothing unworthy of himself, so that he will attempt, seriously and in the presence of many, to imitate all things, including those we just now mentioned – claps of thunder, and the noise of wind and hail and axles and pulleys, and the notes of trumpets and flutes and pan-pipes, and the sounds of all instruments, and the cries of dogs, sheep, and birds; and so his style will depend wholly on imitation in voice and gesture, or will contain but a little of pure narration."

"That too follows of necessity," he said. . . .

"And do all poets and speakers hit upon one type or the other of diction or some blend which they combine of both?"

"They must," he said.

"What, then," said I, "are we to do? Shall we admit all of these into the city, or one of the unmixed types, or the mixed type?"

"If my vote prevails," he said, "the unmixed imitator of the good."

"No, but the mixed type also is pleasing, Adeimantus, and far most

---

[5] "Socrates" has already spoken of all poetry as narration (*diegesis*) of some kind, and has then introduced the distinctions of "pure narration," "narrative by imitation" (drama), and "narrative involving a mixture of the two." He is now distinguishing two kinds within this *third* (or "mixed") type. Of these, the one which involves imitations other than that of the good man is to be excluded from the state. Thus even some Homeric epic poetry will, like drama, be eliminated.

pleasing to boys and their tutors and the great mob is the opposite of your choice."

"It is the most pleasing."

"But perhaps," said I, "you would affirm it to be ill-suited to our polity, because there is no twofold or manifold man among us, since every man does one thing."[6]

"It is not suited."

"And is this not the reason why such a city is the only one in which we shall find the cobbler a cobbler and not a pilot in addition to his cobbling, and the farmer a farmer and not a judge added to his farming, and the soldier a soldier and not a money-maker in addition to his soldiery, and so of all the rest?"

"True," he said.

98   "If a man, then, it seems, who was capable by his cunning of assuming every kind of shape and imitating all things should arrive in our city, bringing with himself the poems which he wished to exhibit, we should fall down and worship him as a holy and wondrous and delightful creature, but should say to him that there is no man of that kind among us in our city, nor is it lawful for such a man to arise among us, and we should send him away to another city, after pouring myrrh down over his head and crowning him with fillets of wool, but we ourselves, for our souls' good, should continue to employ the more austere and less delightful poet and tale-teller, who would imitate the diction of the good man...."

BOOK 10

95   "And truly," I said, "many other considerations assure me that we were entirely right in our organization of the state, and especially, I think, in the matter of poetry."

"What about it?" he said.

"In refusing to admit at all so much of it as is imitative; for that it is certainly not to be received is, I think, still more plainly apparent now that we have distinguished the several parts of the soul."[7]

"What do you mean?"

"Why, between ourselves – for you will not betray me to the tragic poets and all other imitators – that kind of art seems to be a corruption of the mind of all listeners who do not possess as an antidote a knowledge of its real nature."

"What is your idea in saying this?" he said.

[6] We are here reminded that the basic "political" reason for rejecting indiscriminate poetic imitation is that it offends against the principle of specialization which, as has been established, is fundamental to the organization, the proper functioning, and, indirectly, to the justice of Plato's ideal state.

[7] In Book 4, where the tripartite nature of the soul – with, ideally, the rational element in charge – has been described.

"I must speak out," I said, "though a certain love and reverence for Homer that has possessed me from a boy would stay me from speaking. For he appears to have been the first teacher and beginner of all these beauties of tragedy. Yet all the same we must not honor a man above truth, but, as I say, speak our minds."

"By all means," he said.

"Listen, then, or rather, answer my question."

"Ask it," he said.

"Could you tell me in general what imitation is?[8] For neither do I myself quite apprehend what it would be at."

"It is likely, then," he said, "that *I* should apprehend!"

596 "It would be nothing strange," said I, "since it often happens that the dimmer vision sees things in advance of the keener."

"That is so," he said; "but in your presence I could not even be eager to try to state anything that appears to me, but do you yourself consider it."

"Shall we, then, start the inquiry at this point by our customary procedure? We are in the habit, I take it, of positing a single idea or form in the case of the various multiplicities to which we give the same name. Do you not understand?"

"I do."

"In the present case, then, let us take any multiplicity you please; for example, there are many couches and tables."

"Of course."

"But these utensils imply, I suppose, only two ideas or forms, one of a couch and one of a table."

"Yes."

"And are we not also in the habit of saying that the craftsman who produces either of them fixes his eyes on the idea or form, and so makes in one case the couches and in the other the tables that we use, and similarly of other things? For surely no craftsman makes the idea itself. How could he?"

"By no means."

"But now consider what name you would give to this craftsman."

"What one?"

"Him who makes all the things that all craftsmen severally produce."

"A truly clever and wondrous man you tell of."

"Ah, but wait, and you will say so indeed, for this same craftsman is not

---

[8] Here Plato seems to be warning us that he is about to talk about "imitation" (*mimesis*) in a way somewhat different from that of his earlier discussion. In the new context, the arts, and especially poetry, are to be considered in relation to truth or "reality," as it has been defined in Book 5 (see introductory note): considered in these terms, we may find that far more than those parts of poetry which involve impersonation may now turn out to be "imitation" and to be unacceptable for somewhat different reasons from those previously advanced – hence the hint, a sentence or so earlier, that Homer, too, may now be subject to rejection.

only able to make all implements, but he produces all plants and animals, including himself, and thereto earth and heaven and the gods and all things in heaven and in Hades under the earth."

"A most marvelous sophist," he said.

"Are you incredulous?" said I. "Tell me, do you deny altogether the possibility of such a craftsman, or do you admit that in a sense there could be such a creator of all these things, and in another sense not? Or do you not perceive that you yourself would be able to make all these things in a way?"

"And in what way, I ask you," he said.

"There is no difficulty," said I, "but it is something that the craftsman can make everywhere and quickly. You could do it most quickly if you should choose to take a mirror and carry it about everywhere. You will speedily produce the sun and all the things in the sky, and speedily the earth and yourself and the other animals and implements and plants and all the objects of which we just now spoke."

"Yes," he said, "the appearance of them, but not the reality and the truth."

"Excellent," said I, "and you come to the aid of the argument opportunely. For I take it that the painter too belongs to this class of producers, does he not?"

"Of course."

"But you will say, I suppose, that his creations are not real and true. And yet, after a fashion, the painter too makes a couch, does he not?"

"Yes," he said, "the appearance of one, he too."

7   "What of the cabinet-maker? Were you not just now saying that he does not make the idea or form which we say is the real couch, the couch itself, but only some particular couch?"

"Yes, I was."

"Then if he does not make that which really is, he could not be said to make real being but something that resembles real being but is not that. But if anyone should say that being in the complete sense belongs to the work of the cabinet-maker or to that of other craftsman, it seems that he would say what is not true."

"That would be the view," he said, "of those who are versed in this kind of reasoning."

"We must not be surprised, then, if this too is only a dim adumbration in comparison with reality."

"No, we must not."

"Shall we, then, use these very examples in our quest for the true nature of this imitator?"

"If you please," he said.

"We get, then, these three couches, one, that in nature, which, I take it, we would say that God produces, or who else?"

"No one, I think."

"And then there was one which the carpenter made."

"Yes," he said.

"And one which the painter made. Is not that so?"

"So be it."

"The painter, then, the cabinet-maker, and God, there are these three presiding over three kinds of couches."

"Yes, three."

"Now God, whether because he so willed or because some compulsion was laid upon him not to make more than one couch in nature, so wrought and created one only, the couch which really and in itself is. But two or more such were never created by God and never will come into being."

"How so?" he said.

"Because," said I, "if he should make only two, there would again appear one of which they both would possess the form or idea, and that would be the couch that really is in and of itself, and not the other two."

"Right," he said.

"God, then, I take it, knowing this and wishing to be the real creator of the couch that has real being, and not a particular cabinet-maker of some particular couch, produced it in nature unique."

"So it seems."

"Shall we, then, call him its true and natural begetter, or something of the kind?"

"That would certainly be right," he said, "since it is by and in nature that he has made this and all other things."

"And what of the carpenter? Shall we not call him the creator of a couch?"

"Yes."

"Shall we also say that the painter is the creator and maker of that sort of thing?"

"By no means."

"What will you say he is in relation to the couch?"

"This," said he, "seems to me the most reasonable designation for him, that he is the imitator of the thing which those others produce."

"Very good," said I; "the producer of the product three removes from nature you call the imitator?"

"By all means," he said.

"This, then, will apply to the maker of tragedies also, if he is an imitator and is in his nature three removes from the king and the truth, as are all other imitators." ...

598   "Then the mimetic art is far removed from truth, and this, it seems, is the reason why it can produce everything, because it touches or lays hold of only a small part of the object and that a phantom; as, for example, a

painter, we say, will paint us a cobbler, a carpenter, and other craftsmen, though he himself has no expertness in any of these arts, but nevertheless if he were a good painter, by exhibiting at a distance his picture of a carpenter he would deceive children and foolish men, and make them believe it to be a real carpenter."

"Why not?"

"But for all that, my friend, this, I take it, is what we ought to bear in mind in all such cases: when anyone reports to us of someone, that he has met a man who knows all the crafts and everything else that men severally know, and that there is nothing that he does not know more exactly than anybody else, our tacit rejoinder must be that he is a simple fellow, who apparently has met some magician or sleight-of-hand man and imitator and has been deceived by him into the belief that he is all-wise, because of his own inability to put to the proof and distinguish knowledge, ignorance and imitation."

"Most true," he said.

"Then," said I, "have we not next to scrutinize tragedy and its leader Homer,[9] since some people tell us that these poets know all the arts and all things human pertaining to virtue and vice, and all things divine? For the good poet, if he is to poetize things rightly, must, they argue, create with knowledge or else be unable to create. So we must consider whether these
9 critics have not fallen in with such imitators and been deceived by them, so that looking upon their works they cannot perceive that these are three removes from reality, and easy to produce without knowledge of the truth. For it is phantoms, not realities, that they produce. Or is there something in their claim, and do good poets really know the things about which the multitude fancy they speak well? ..."

I   ... "Now do not the excellence, the beauty, the rightness of every implement, living thing, and action refer solely to the use for which each is made or by nature adapted?"

"That is so."

"It quite necessarily follows, then, that the user of anything is the one who knows most of it by experience, and that he reports to the maker the good or bad effects in use of the thing he uses. As, for example, the flute-player reports to the flute-maker which flutes respond and serve rightly in flute-playing, and will order the kind that must be made, and the other will obey and serve him."

"Of course."

"The one, then, possessing knowledge, reports about the goodness or the badness of the flutes, and the other, believing, will make them."

"Yes."

9 In *Republic*, Book 10 Plato is particularly concerned to assail the traditional status of the poet as teacher and moral authority in the community. Homer stands at the head of that tradition.

"Then in respect of the same implement the maker will have right belief about its excellence and defects from association with the man who knows

602 and being compelled to listen to him, but the user will have true knowledge."

"Certainly."

"And will the imitator from experience or use have knowledge whether the things he portrays are or are not beautiful and right, or will he, from compulsory association with the man who knows and taking orders from him for the right making of them, have right opinion?"

"Neither."

"Then the imitator will neither know nor opine rightly concerning the beauty or the badness of his imitations."

"It seems not." ...[10]

"And have not measuring and numbering and weighing proved to be most gracious aids to prevent the domination in our soul of the apparently greater or lesser or more or heavier and to give the control to that which has reckoned and numbered or even weighed?"

"Certainly."

"But this surely would be the function of the part of the soul that reasons and calculates."

"Why, yes, of that."

"And often when this has measured and declares that certain things are larger or that some are smaller than the others or equal, there is at the same time an appearance of the contrary."

"Yes."

"And did we not say that it is impossible for the same thing at one time to hold contradictory opinions about the same thing?"

"And we were right in affirming that."

603 "The part of the soul, then, that opines in contradiction of measurement could not be the same with that which conforms to it."

"Why, no."

"But, farther, that which puts its trust in measurement and reckoning must be the best part of the soul."

"Surely."

---

[10] The demonstration of the unworthiness of the arts is based on the tripartite psychology ("the rational," "the spirited," and "the appetitive" or "passionate" divisions of the soul) established in Book 4. "Socrates" now shows that the imitative arts appeal to the irrational and emotional element of the soul and thus militate against its governance by the reason. That part of the argument which concerns the emotional effect of poetry seems directed particularly against tragedy but that is only because it is the most extreme form of imitation, being concerned exclusively with impersonation, often of a particular emotional kind. However, the fact that the epic poet Homer (who, indeed, is described as "first of tragedians") is mentioned three times, shows that this is not specifically an attack on tragedy, and the concluding section of this argument shows clearly that nothing less than a generic exclusion of poetry from the ideal state is intended.

"Then that which opposes it must belong to the inferior elements of the soul."

"Necessarily."

"This, then, was what I wished to have agreed upon when I said that poetry, and in general the mimetic art, produces a product that is far removed from truth in the accomplishment of its task, and associates with the part in us that is remote from intelligence, and is its companion and friend for no sound and true purpose."

"By all means," said he.

"Mimetic art, then, is an inferior thing cohabiting with an inferior and engendering inferior offspring."

"It seems so."

"Does that," said I, "hold only for vision or does it apply also to hearing and to what we call poetry?"

"Presumably," he said, "to that also."

"Let us not, then, trust solely to the plausible analogy from painting, but let us approach in turn that part of the mind to which mimetic poetry appeals and see whether it is the inferior or the nobly serious part."

"So we must."

"Let us, then, put the question thus: mimetic poetry, we say, imitates human beings acting under compulsion or voluntarily, and as a result of their actions supposing themselves to have fared well or ill and in all this feeling either grief or joy. Did we find anything else but this?"

"Nothing."

"Is a man, then, in all this of one mind with himself, or just as in the domain of sight there was faction and strife and he held within himself contrary opinions at the same time about the same things, so also in our actions there is division and strife of the man with himself? But I recall that there is no need now of our seeking agreement on this point, for in our former discussion we were sufficiently agreed that our soul at any one moment teems with countless such self-contradictions."

"Rightly," he said.

"Yes, rightly," said I; "but what we then omitted must now, I think, be set forth."

"What is that?" he said.

"When a good and reasonable man," said I, "experiences such a stroke of fortune as the loss of a son or anything else that he holds most dear, we said, I believe, then too, that he will bear it more easily than the other sort."

"Assuredly."

"But now let us consider this: will he feel no pain, or, since that is impossible, shall we say that he will in some sort be moderate in his grief?"

"That," he said, "is rather the truth."

"Tell me now this about him: do you think he will be more likely to resist and fight against his grief when he is observed by his equals or when he is in solitude alone by himself?"

"He will be much more restrained," he said, "when he is on view."

"But when left alone, I fancy, he will permit himself many utterances which, if heard by another, would put him to shame, and will do many things which he would not consent to have another see him doing."

"So it is," he said.

"Now is it not reason and law that exhorts him to resist, while that which urges him to give way to his grief is the bare feeling itself?"

"True."

"And where there are two opposite impulses in a man at the same time about the same thing we say that there must needs be two things in him."

"Of course."

"And is not the one prepared to follow the guidance of the law as the law leads and directs?"

"How so?"

"The law, I suppose, declares that it is best to keep quiet as far as possible in calamity and not to chafe and repine, because we cannot know what is really good and evil in such things and it advantages us nothing to take them hard, and nothing in mortal life is worthy of great concern, and our grieving checks the very thing we need to come to our aid as quickly as possible in such case."

"What thing," he said, "do you mean?"

"To deliberate," I said, "about what has happened to us, and, as it were in the fall of the dice, to determine the movements of our affairs with reference to the numbers that turn up, in the way that reason indicates would be the best, and, instead of stumbling like children, clapping one's hands to the stricken spot and wasting the time in wailing, ever to accustom the soul to devote itself at once to the curing of the hurt and the raising up of what has fallen, banishing threnody by therapy."

"That certainly," he said, "would be the best way to face misfortune and deal with it."

"Then, we say, the best part of us is willing to conform to these precepts of reason."

"Obviously."

"And shall we not say that the part of us that leads us to dwell in memory on our suffering and impels us to lamentation, and cannot get enough of that sort of thing, is the irrational and idle part of us, the associate of cowardice?"

"Yes, we will say that."

"And does not the fretful part of us present many and varied occasions for imitation, while the intelligent and temperate disposition, always remaining approximately the same, is neither easy to imitate nor to be understood when imitated, especially by a nondescript mob assembled in the theatre? For the representation imitates a type that is alien to them."

"By all means."

"And is it not obvious that the nature of the mimetic poet is not related to this better part of the soul and his cunning is not framed to please it, if he is to win favor with the multitude, but is devoted to the fretful and complicated type of character because it is easy to imitate?"

"It is obvious."

"This consideration, then, makes it right for us to proceed to lay hold of him and set him down as the counterpart of the painter; for he resembles him in that his creations are inferior in respect of reality; and the fact that his appeal is to the inferior part of the soul and not to the best part is another point of resemblance. And so we may at least say that we should be justified in not admitting him into a well-ordered state, because he stimulates and fosters this element in the soul, and by strengthening it tends to destroy the rational part, just as when in a state one puts bad men in power and turns the city over to them and ruins the better sort. Precisely in the same manner we shall say that the mimetic poet sets up in each individual soul a vicious constitution by fashioning phantoms far removed from reality, and by currying favor with the senseless element that cannot distinguish the greater from the less, but calls the same thing now one, now the other."

"By all means."

"But we have not yet brought our chief accusation against it. Its power to corrupt, with rare exceptions, even the better sort is surely the chief cause for alarm."

"How could it be otherwise, if it really does that?"

"Listen and reflect. I think you know that the very best of us, when we hear Homer or some other of the makers of tragedy imitating one of the heroes who is in grief, and is delivering a long tirade in his lamentations or chanting and beating his breast, feel pleasure, and abandon ourselves and accompany the representation with sympathy and eagerness, and we praise as an excellent poet the one who most strongly affects us in this way."

"I do know it, of course."

"But when in our own lives some affliction comes to us, you are also aware that we plume ourselves upon the opposite, on our ability to remain calm and endure, in the belief that this is the conduct of a man, and what we were praising in the theatre that of a woman."

"I do note that."

"Do you think, then," said I, "that this praise is rightfully bestowed when, contemplating a character that we would not accept but would be ashamed of in ourselves, we do not abominate it but take pleasure and approve?"

"No, by Zeus," he said, "it does not seem reasonable."

606   "Oh yes," said I, "if you would consider it in this way."

"In what way?"

"If you would reflect that the part of the soul that in the former case, in our own misfortunes, was forcibly restrained, and that has hungered for tears and a good cry and satisfaction, because it is its nature to desire these things, is the element in us that the poets satisfy and delight, and that the best element in our nature, since it has never been properly educated by reason or even by habit, then relaxes its guard over the plaintive part, inasmuch as this is contemplating the woes of others and it is no shame to it to praise and pity another who, claiming to be a good man, abandons himself to excess in his grief; but it thinks this vicarious pleasure is so much clear gain, and would not consent to forfeit it by disdaining the poem altogether. That is, I think, because few are capable of reflecting that what we enjoy in others will inevitably react upon ourselves. For after feeding fat the emotion of pity there, it is not easy to restrain it in our own sufferings."

"Most true," he said.

"Does not the same principle apply to the laughable, namely, that if in comic representation, or for that matter in private talk, you take intense pleasure in buffooneries that you would blush to practice yourself, and do not detest them as base, you are doing the same things as in the case of the pathetic? For here again what your reason, for fear of the reputation of buffoonery, restrained in yourself when it fain would play the clown, you release in turn, and so, fostering its youthful impudence, let yourself go so far that often ere you are aware you become yourself a comedian in private."

"Yes, indeed," he said.

"And so in regard to the emotions of sex and anger, and all the appetites and pains and pleasures of the soul which we say accompany all our actions, the effect of poetic imitation is the same. For it waters and fosters these feelings when what we ought to do is to dry them up, and it establishes them as our rulers when they ought to be ruled, to the end that we may be better and happier men instead of worse and more miserable."

"I cannot deny it," said he.

"Then, Glaucon," said I, "when you meet encomiasts of Homer who tell us that this poet has been the educator of Hellas, and that for the conduct and refinement of human life he is worthy of our study and devotion, and

607   that we should order our entire lives by the guidance of this poet, we must love and salute them as doing the best they can, and concede to them that Homer is the most poetic of poets and the first of tragedians, but we must know the truth, that we can admit no poetry into our city save only hymns to the gods and the praises of good men. For if you grant admission to the honeyed muse in lyric or epic, pleasure and pain will be the lords of your

city instead of law and that which shall from time to time have approved itself to the general reason as the best."

"Most true," he said.

"Let us, then, conclude our return to the topic of poetry and our apology, and affirm that we really had good grounds then for dismissing her from our city, since such was her character. For reason constrained us. And let us further say to her, lest she condemn us for harshness and rusticity, that there is from of old a quarrel between philosophy and poetry. For such expressions as 'the yelping hound barking at her master and mighty in the idle babble of fools,' and 'the mob that masters those who are too wise for their own good,' and the subtle thinkers who reason that after all they are poor, and countless others are tokens of this ancient enmity. But nevertheless let it be declared that, if the mimetic and dulcet poetry can show any reason for her existence in a well-governed state, we would gladly admit her, since we ourselves are very conscious of her spell. But all the same it would be impious to betray what we believe to be the truth. Is not that so, friend? Do not you yourself feel her magic and especially when Homer is her interpreter?"

"Greatly."

"Then may she not justly return from this exile after she has pleaded her defense, whether in lyric or other measure?"

"By all means."

"And we would allow her advocates who are not poets but lovers of poetry to plead her cause in prose without metre, and show that she is not only delightful but beneficial to orderly government and all the life of man. And we shall listen benevolently, for it will be clear gain for us if it can be shown that she bestows not only pleasure but benefit."

"How could we help being the gainers?" said he.

"But if not, my friend, even as men who have fallen in love, if they think that the love is not good for them, hard though it be, nevertheless refrain, so we, owing to the love of this kind of poetry inbred in us by our education in these fine polities of ours, will gladly have the best possible case made out for her goodness and truth, but so long as she is unable to make good her defense we shall chant over to ourselves as we listen the reasons that we have given as a counter-charm to her spell, to preserve us from slipping back into the childish loves of the multitude; for we have come to see that we must not take such poetry seriously as a serious thing that lays hold on truth, but that he who lends an ear to it must be on his guard fearing for the polity in his soul and must believe what we have said about poetry."

"By all means," he said, "I concur." ...

3

ARISTOTLE
(384–322 B.C.)

Plato never sought to describe poetry as a thing in itself; while he did indicate his view of its relation to reality, his discussions of it were always in connection with something else, for example, its effect on the soul of its creator, or on his audience, or its position in the ideal state. Aristotle, on the other hand, viewed "poetry" – in which he includes all forms of aesthetic creation, what we might call "the arts"[1] – as an objective phenomenon, capable of (and *deserving* of) analysis like any other. For Aristotle believed that, as one commentator puts it: "There is a science whenever there exists a subject matter whose attributes can be expressed in order to gain warranted conclusions concerning the intrinsic nature of the subject."[2]

"Poetry" (including tragedy) is not, of course, a "natural" but an "artificial" object, produced by human beings; therefore the science which investigates it (and which Aristotle called a "productive" science) will be different from the sciences which investigate nature ("the theoretical sciences") and from the sciences investigating practical activities such as "politics."[3] It is, however, much concerned with the relation between natural objects and artistic ones, for Aristotle, like Plato before him, regarded "poetry" as an imitation of nature. How different their views of artistic imitation are (and, consequently, how different their evaluations of "poetry") becomes particularly clear in Chapter 6 of the *Poetics*, where Aristotle speaks of poetry as dealing with universal truths. These differences between Plato and Aristotle arise not so much from the later philosopher's criticism or "correction" of his former master[4] as from his fundamentally different understanding of ultimate reality.

Aristotle believed that everything describable through scientific investigation could be analyzed from four different aspects, which would constitute all that could usefully be said about it. It could be defined in terms of its *final cause* (its *telos*, the purpose for which it exists); in terms of its *efficient cause* (the agent or instrument by

[1] When the words "poetry" and "poetic" are used, in this introductory note and in the footnotes, in the broad sense in which Aristotle and the Greeks generally used them, this is indicated by quotation marks.

[2] Aristotle/Telford 1961, 59. The present editor is indebted, particularly on analytical points, to Telford's excellent commentary, as well as to the seminal teaching and writing of the late R. P. McKeon, to whom Telford likewise expressed his indebtedness.

[3] The science of investigating "poetry" is to be distinguished from the practical sciences insofar as it deals with the work of art as well as with the processes of making it. These two are not, for Aristotle, separate subjects since the work of art is simply a fulfillment of the process.

[4] Humphrey House's "positive," but no more convincing, version of this view is that Aristotle's "whole type of thought was modelled on Plato's, and that even where he most disagreed with his master – his doctrine about Poetry was an instance – he was taking up problems which Plato had propounded" (Aristotle/House 1956, 20).

means of which it achieves its *telos*); its *material cause* (the matter or substance employed in achieving the *telos*); and its *formal cause* (the organization, or structure, which is required for that achievement).[5] This analytical method operates throughout the various parts of the *Poetics* but its application is more complex than may at first appear. A large and complicated subject, such as "the city-state" or "poetry," may be given a generic description in terms of *its* four causes, or aspects; then *each* of these four aspects may, in turn, be examined in terms of *its* four causes, and so on, until an ultimate, or self-caused, principle is reached. Thus the method involves a dynamic process, as layer upon layer of a subject is revealed, requiring more and more detailed investigation. In this process, too, what was, say, the formal cause in one "layer" of investigation may become the final cause of the next.

Not every reader of the *Poetics* will retrace the analytical procedures governing its composition, and only a few preliminary indications of their application can be attempted here and in the footnotes. Nevertheless, forewarned is forearmed. Certain features of the style of the *Poetics* may be easier to understand when it is realized that Aristotle is engaged not in a discursive commentary on "poetry" but in a scientific description of its nature and the nature of one of its major genres.

There are, moreover, one or two corollaries implied in the sort of investigation Aristotle conducts. Since Aristotle is attempting to provide a scientific *description* of "poetry" in general, and of tragedy in particular, it follows that he is not here concerned (as Plato was in the *Republic*) with regulations for its use in the State. Absence of any discussion of censorship on moral or theological grounds, should not, for example, be taken as telling us anything about what Aristotle might have thought of such matters. They were simply not relevant to what he is discussing in the *Poetics*.

A second corollary of Aristotle's "scientific" approach in the *Poetics* would appear to be that his treatment of poetry, and of tragedy in particular, is descriptive rather than prescriptive. Yet this corollary may, perhaps, turn out to be more apparent than real, for the following rather paradoxical reason. It is true, of course, that in this work Aristotle sets out to describe the nature of "poetry" in general, and of tragedy both in general terms and in considerable detail, and that (unlike many of his commentators and imitators) he was not promulgating a set of rules to be followed by prospective tragic poets. Nevertheless it was part of Aristotle's thought that art forms, like organisms in the physical world, went through a period of growth or of evolution until they reached their true nature (i.e., that which best fulfilled their purpose or *telos*), and then stopped.[6] Now it would appear that Aristotle believed that tragedy had indeed achieved "its true nature," perhaps by the time that Sophocles, as Aristotle mentions in this chapter, introduced the third actor. Therefore in his various accounts of how tragic effects are best achieved (as well as of various ways in which tragedies fall short of that goal) Aristotle is drawing on his knowledge of actual Greek tragedies. These idealized descriptions of the way in which the best tragedies are composed, and of shortcomings in less successful ones, cannot help but convey suggestions as to how tragedy *should* (or *should not*) be written. (And indeed Aristotle sometimes slips from the descriptive to

---

[5] See Aristotle, *Physics* 194b16ff. However, as McKeon points out (1941, xxiii): "[In the natural sciences], the formal, efficient and final causes frequently coincide, and physical explanation, therefore, usually consists of stating either the *end* (i.e., the final cause) or the antecedent *necessity* (i.e., the material cause) of a process." Cf., also, Aristotle/Telford 1961, 63–67.

[6] Cf. Chapter 4 and *Physics* 193a36.

the prescriptive, as in Chapter 15 on the presentation of "character.") Nevertheless, the *Poetics* rarely degenerates into a set of specific rules to be followed by the tragic poet. This may be due partly to the fact that the great age of Greek tragic composition was over when Aristotle was writing, but the main reason obviously lies, as already indicated, in the philosopher's scientific approach.

The first five chapters of the *Poetics* define the nature of "poetry," divide "poetry" into its several kinds, and provide explanations in terms of human nature for the origin of these various kinds. In this latter explanation the greatest emphasis is given to the origins of tragedy: here the explanation of "natural" origins blends into a brief summary of tragedy's historical origins and development, a reasonable procedure for Aristotle, since it is a part of his view of nature that everything having a natural basis (including any art form) will go through a process of development until it reaches the form in which it best fulfills its purpose.

"Poetry" in general (what might now be called "the arts") Aristotle describes as a form of imitation. He differentiates the different kinds of "poetry" in terms of their medium (which serves to distinguish, for example, dancing from instrumental music, and both from imitations such as poetry in our sense of the word, which makes use of language alone); in terms of the object imitated (which serves to distinguish tragedy from comedy); and in terms of the *manner* of imitation, which serves to distinguish narrative from dramatic poetry. Even in this preliminary analysis, it is not difficult to see Aristotle's recurrent analytic procedure: imitation is the purpose, the *telos*, the final cause of all "poetry" and the various arts are distinguished from one another in terms of their material, formal, and efficient causes.

Aristotle next seeks an explanation of the human tendency toward imitation and finds it in the natural human delight in learning which he regards as a form of recognition. Similar (though more specialized or diversified) "instincts" gave rise to the various different kinds of arts (e.g., harmony and rhythm, separately or combined, and rhythm, whether by movements or by words, gave rise to instrumental music, singing, dancing, and poetry, in our sense), whereas the different dispositions of poets decided whether they would imitate men better (as in tragedy) or worse (as in comedy) than themselves. And, as already indicated, Aristotle supplements these natural explanations of how the arts came about with a brief illustration of how tragedy began and then gradually developed to reach its natural form. It is implied in Chapter 5 that the comparable developments of comedy would also be indicated were they properly known.

Having defined the nature of creative art and distinguished, in various ways, its different kinds, Aristotle is now ready for the detailed discussion of tragedy which he regards as the most serious and best of these kinds. The discussion begins with the celebrated definition of tragedy in Chapter 6, once again in terms of the four causes. Thus tragedy is described as an imitation of a certain kind of action, using language in certain specified ways, effecting or bringing about the imitation in the dramatic rather than the narrative manner to evoke, and achieve the purgation of, the emotions of pity and fear. These aspects of tragedy (or rather the first three of them, whose proper combination and employment will produce the fourth, the desired end of tragedy) are further analyzed into the six parts of tragedy, two of which (diction and song) belong to the medium employed, one (spectacle) to the manner, and three (plot, character, and thought) to the object of imitation, which is the actions of men and the natural causes from which they arise. Since the plot is established as the first principle (*arche*) or soul (*psyche*) of tragedy, Aristotle devotes the next eight chapters (7–14) to it. He considers first the important matters of logical sequence and organic unity (7–8), and then embarks on a long discussion of the kinds of action to be imitated. In Chapter 9 comes the fundamental distinction between the subject matters (i.e., "kinds of action") of history and of poetry. This is followed (9–14) by a series of fairly technical descriptions of the kinds of action, and of details within such actions, which are most likely to evoke pity and fear, the end, or final cause, of tragedy. These chapters (9–14) are at the very heart of the *Poetics*. For comment on various important features of the discussion, such as Aristotle's observations on recognition and reversal and related matters, the reader is referred to the footnotes below.

Aristotle turns next to the discussion of character, which is second only to plot in importance in tragedy, for character, which defines "what sort of people men are" and which reveals "choice" or "moral purpose" (*proairesis*), has been described along with thought (*dianoia*), as one of the two causes of men's actions. In Chapter 15 Aristotle lists the four requirements of character in tragedy as excellence of moral choice (*proairesis*), suitability to the class of person depicted, verisimilitude or "trueness to life," and consistency. The causal aspects of character are again stressed: just as the events of a plot should exhibit causal sequence (should occur, in Aristotle's phrase, "in accordance with probability or necessity"), so a character's speeches and actions should arise from the sort of person portrayed. This inescapable connection between character and actions (which in turn determine plot) helps to explain why Aristotle introduces here in Chapter 15 (instead of in the chapters devoted to plot) the problem of how to treat "the supernatural," that is, what lies outside this causal connection, in tragedy. It also should serve as a reminder that though Aristotle insists on the primacy of plot over character in tragedy, character is by no means unimportant in Aristotle's (and Greek tragedy's) scheme of things. It is also the case, however, that the Greeks expected little in the way of individualization in their characterizations, and even Aristotle's definition of "character" (*ethos*) in Chapter 6 has indicated only that it is concerned with choice (*proairesis*).

Aristotle turns to the last two elements of tragedy, thought and diction, in Chapter 19. (The intervening chapters, 16–18, which really belong with the chapters on plot, seem misplaced.) As is seen in Chapter 6, thought (*dianoia*) is closely related to character, for both have been called the "causes of men's actions." Aristotle has also said that thought is revealed in speeches concerning general truth, rather than in ones indicating choice (*proairesis*), which concerns character; to these are now added speeches concerned with the arousal of the feelings.[7] That thought is one of the more elusive topics treated in the *Poetics* is partly due to the brevity of the treatment. One scholar observes that, with respect to Greek tragedy, the two concepts character and thought, taken together, really make up what *we* think of as "character."[8] "Diction" is mentioned in this chapter only to be dismissed (as far as a required knowledge of it is concerned) as belonging to another art, that of "delivery" (by actors and rhetoricians).

With Chapter 19 Aristotle has completed his direct discussion of tragedy. However, among the various critical difficulties (*problemata*) discussed in Chapter

[7] Owen (1931, 38) notes that thought, according to Aristotle, also "can be expressed by a 'rhetoric of action'": a good and terse expression for what Aristotle says in the rest of this section on *dianoia*.

[8] See Dale 1969, 143 and 145–46. The observation is suggestive, if not completely accurate, and helps to remind us that the term "character" (*ethos*) as Aristotle uses it connotes rather less than what we think of as being involved in the concept.

25, the question of the relation of the poet's imitation to reality is of particular interest. Nevertheless, this question does not raise, in this context, the sort of metaphysical issues posed in Plato's treatment of imitation. Finally, Chapter 26 gives reasons for regarding tragedy in comparison with epic as the superior mode of imitation. If the comparison seems inconclusive, that may be because epic (in the *Poetics* as we have it) has been described in much less definitive terms than has tragedy.

For further reading

Bremer 1969; Dale 1969; Else 1965, 1969; Friedrich 1983; Halliwell 1986; Janko 1984; McKeon 1941, 1952; Owen 1931; Pickard-Cambridge [1927] 1962; Stinton 1975.

From the *Poetics*[9]

CHAPTER 1

47a Our subject is the art of poetry in general and its different genres, the specific effect of each genre, the way to construct stories to make good poetry, the number and nature of its constituent elements, and all other matters which belong to this particular inquiry.[10] And let us begin as is natural, with basic principles.

The epic, tragedy, comedy, dithyrambic poetry, most music on the flute and on the lyre – all these are, in principle, imitations.[11] They differ in

---

[9] The text is taken from Grube's translation (1958, 3–62). Grube's sub-headings in the text are omitted and his notes are not reprinted here. The conventional marginal numbers have been added for ease of reference.

[10] Aristotle divided the sciences into three kinds: the theoretical (concerned with problems of knowing); the practical (concerned with problems of doing); and the productive (concerned with problems of making). In the last category are included the useful and, most importantly, the fine arts (cf. *Metaphysics* 1025b; *Ethics* 1138–40).

Aristotle's term for the third of these "sciences" was the word with which he begins this treatise: *poietike* (signifying *poietike techne*). Thus Aristotle signals that he intends to treat his subject analytically and scientifically.

[11] In Plato and Aristotle, imitation (*mimesis*) must be understood in terms of its philosophical context. With Plato ⟨Pl/14⟩ the word is used in a variety of ways depending on the dialectical context. It can, for example, mean precise copying of the external world – though, for Plato, this was far from mirroring "reality"; again it can, in other contexts, mean "impersonation": so used, it served to distinguish the work of the dramatic poet, or actor, from that of the narrative poet or reciter.

In Aristotle, *mimesis* becomes a technical term for "the presentation of an aspect of things in a manner other than its natural manner, rendered inevitable by reasons other than its natural reasons" (McKeon 1952, 162). Its meaning does not change, though its context, and so its application, does. Aristotle greatly enriched its use as defining the purpose of the arts, not by rejecting the idea that the arts should accurately reflect reality (for his explanation of the pleasure we get from art is that we recognize the *truth* of its representations) but rather by showing that reality for the artist meant not simply the observable features of the external world, and of men's activities, but the universal truths which underlie them. What this means for the tragic poet becomes clear in Aristotle's accounts of the best kinds of tragic action and of tragic characters. In Chapter 9, in

three ways: they imitate different things, or imitate them by different means, or in a different manner.

Some people imitate and portray many things by means of color and shape (whether as conscious artists or through force of habit); others imitate by means of the voice. So all the arts we have mentioned produce their imitations by means of rhythm, speech, and melody,[12] using them separately or together. For example, melody and rhythm are the two means used when playing the flute or the lyre, or other instruments which may have a similar effect, such as the pipes. The art of dancing uses rhythm only, without melody, yet its rhythmic patterns, too, imitate character, emotions, and actions.

47b   Now the art which imitates by means of words only, whether in prose or verse, whether in one metre or a mixture of metres, this art is without a name to this day. We have no common name which we could apply to the mimes of Sophron or Xenarchus and the Socratic dialogues, and also to any imitations that may be written in iambics, elegiacs, or other such metres. It is true that people join the word poet to the metre and speak of elegiac poets or epic poets, but they give the same name to poets merely because they use the same metre, and not because of the nature of their imitation. The same name is applied even to a work of medicine or physics if written in verse; yet except for their metre, Homer and Empedocles have nothing in common: the first should be called a poet, the second rather a physicist. And if a man should mix all metres, as Chaeremon made his *Centaur* a metrical medley, we must call him also a poet. Distinctions should be made in the manner suggested above.

Certain poetic compositions, such as dithyrambic and nomic poetry,[13] tragedy and comedy, use all the means mentioned: rhythm, music, and metre. They differ because some use them all simultaneously while others use them in turn. These, then, are the differences between the arts, based on the means used in imitation.

CHAPTER 2

48a   Since those who make imitations represent men in action, these men must be superior or inferior, either better than those we know in life, or worse, or of the same kind. For character is nearly always derived from these qualities and these only, and all men's characters differ in virtue and vice. We can see this in painting: Polygnotus represented men as better than life,

particular, we see how completely, and for what reasons, Aristotle's evaluation of artistic imitation contrasts with that of Plato.

12 The Greek word here is *harmonia*, which has been variously translated. Literally, it means "a fitting together, as a musical term ... a satisfying relation between notes" (Aristotle/ Lucas 1968, 58).

13 The *dithyramb* was originally connected with Dionysus and regularly included a substantial narrative element. The *nome*, like the dithyramb, was a form of choral lyric.

Pauson represented them as worse, and Dionysus made them like life. Obviously, these differences also occur in each of the kinds of imitation we have mentioned; they are different because they imitate different models in this way.

The same distinctions can exist in dancing, in the music of the flute or the lyre, and also in prose or in such poetry as is unaccompanied by music. Homer, for example, represents men better than those we know, Cleophon makes them like those we know in life, while Hegemon of Thasos, the first writer of parodies, and Nicochares, the author of the *Deiliad*, make them worse. The same is true in dithyrambic and nomic poetry, for one might represent the Cyclops after the manner of Timotheus or that of Philoxenus. Tragedy and comedy differ in the same way: tragedy imitates men who are better, comedy imitates men who are worse than we know them today.

CHAPTER 3

The third difference lies in the manner in which each of these things is imitated. One may imitate the same model by the same means, but do it in the manner of the narrator either in his own person throughout or by assuming other personalities as Homer does, or one may present the personages one is imitating as actually performing actions before the audience ⟨Pl/16–18⟩.

There are, then, as we said at the beginning, these three differences in imitations: the differences of means, the difference of models, and the difference of manner. In one respect, Sophocles is the same kind of imitator as Homer, for both imitate superior men; in another aspect he is like Aristophanes, for both present their characters in action. That is why their works are called dramas, because they represent men "doing."

The Dorian claim to have originated both tragedy and comedy is based on similarities of words. Comedy is claimed by the Megarians, both by those in Greece who say it had its origin when their democracy was established, and by those in Sicily because their poet Epicharmus was much earlier than Chionides and Magnes. Tragedy is also claimed by certain Peloponnesians. The Dorians say their neighboring villages are called *komai* while the Athenians call theirs *demes*, and that "comedians" were so named, not from the word *komazein* (to revel), but because they were despised in the city and wandered out through the villages. More-over, they say that they express action by the verb *dran*, whereas the Athenians use *prattein*.

So much for the number and nature of the differences found in imitations.

48b

CHAPTER 4

In general, two causes, both inherent in man's nature, seem to have led to the birth of poetry.[14] Imitation is natural to man from childhood; he differs from the other animals in that he is the most imitative: the first things he learns come to him through imitation. Then, too, all men take pleasure in imitative representations. Actual experience gives proof of this: the sight of certain things gives us pain, but we enjoy looking at the most exact images of them, whether the forms of animals which we greatly despise or of corpses. The reason is that learning things is most enjoyable, not only for philosophers but for others equally, though they have but little experience of it. Hence they enjoy the sight of images because they learn as they look; they reason what each image is, that there, for example, is that man whom we know.[15] If a man does not know the original, the imitation as such gives him no pleasure; his pleasure is then derived from its workmanship, its color, or some similar reason.

Next, imitation and melody and rhythm are ours by nature (metre being clearly a part of rhythm); so men were naturally gifted from the beginning, and, progressing step by step, they created poetry out of their random utterances.

Poetry developed in different ways according to men's characters. The more serious-minded imitated the noble deeds of noble men; the more common imitated the actions of meaner men; and the latter wrote satiric verse while the former wrote hymns and encomia. We cannot mention any satiric work before Homer, though there were probably many, but we can begin with his *Margites*[16] and other things of the kind. The iambic metre was introduced because it was particularly suitable to this type of poetry, and such a poem is called *iambeion* to this day, because men used to satirize each other in this metre.

Some of the old poets wrote heroic, others wrote iambic verse. Homer was certainly the greatest writer of serious-minded poetry; he stands alone not only because he wrote well but also because he dramatized his imitations. He was also the first to exhibit the different forms of comedy,

---

[14] Having defined the general nature of poetry (the arts) and its different kinds, Aristotle now turns to the question of how poetry came into being. This he does first in psychological terms (i.e., in terms of man's natural instincts), then in historical terms, at least in the case of tragedy whose origin and development he briefly summarizes. This evolutionary treatment parallels Aristotle's conviction concerning the entelechy of natural growths, for he tells us during this summary that the "many changes" which tragedy underwent "ceased, when it had found its true nature."

[15] This example points to the essential connection between recognition and artistic enjoyment. In the discussion of poetry, and particularly of tragedy, we see how such recognitions involve coming to understand (and so "learning") certain universal truths about the human condition.

[16] The *Margites*: only one brief fragment of this comic epic (probably belonging to the seventh century B.C. and almost certainly not Homer's) has survived.

and he dramatized the laughable, but not the personal satire. His *Margites*
49a bears the same relation to comedy as the *Iliad* and the *Odyssey* do to
tragedy.

When tragedy and comedy were known, men were led by their own
nature to one or the other; one type of man came to write comedies instead
of lampoons, the other type produced tragedies instead of epics, because
these later forms of poetry were more important and more highly esteemed
than the earlier. It is not our purpose here to inquire whether or not
tragedy is now fully developed in its various parts, or indeed whether it is
to be judged in itself or in relation to its audience. That is another question.

Tragedy first arose without deliberate intent, as did comedy also. The
former originated with the leaders of the dithyramb,[17] the latter with the
leaders of the phallic songs which even today remain customary in many
cities. Tragedy developed little by little as men improved whatever part of it
became distinct. Many changes were introduced into tragedy, but these
ceased when it found its true nature. Aeschylus was the first to introduce a
second actor; he also made the chorus less important and gave first place to
the spoken parts. Sophocles added both a third actor and painted
scenery.[18] It is only at a late date that short incidents and the language of
ridicule developed in length and dignity as the satyr-play[19] changed into
tragedy. The iambic trimeter replaced the trochaic tetrameter which had
been used at first because the poetry was then satyric and more closely
related to the dance.

When spoken parts came in, nature herself found the appropriate metre,
as the iambic is of all metres most like ordinary speech. This is proved by

[17] Aristotle's views on the origins of drama, particularly of tragedy, have been much debated
and the literature on the matter is formidable. The more extreme "ritualist" theories, such
as Jane Harrison's, W. Ridgeway's, and Gilbert Murray's, earlier in this century, have now
been abandoned, since they went far beyond the evidence of Aristotle or the tragedies
themselves in seeking to re-create a "Dionysian" ritual form from which tragic structure
developed. On the other hand, reaction from the extravagances of the "ritualists" has also
been extreme: see, for example, Else (1965) and Pickard-Cambridge (1927). Much of the
latter's criticism of the "ritualists" is omitted in the second (1962) edition of his work,
revised by T. B. L. Webster, which purports to offer in its stead a restatement of the ritual
theory, "in a form which is both tenable and viable" (p. 128). For an excellent review of
the whole controversy, and a balanced conclusion, see Friedrich 1983.

[18] Each of these actors, of course, could, and often did, play more than one role. There is
some debate as to what Aristotle means by "painted scenery" (*skenographia*) in this
passage. The painting of the wooden *skene* (which usually represented either a palace or a
temple) may have involved merely decoration (rather than the painting of actual
"scenes"), which also served to suggest perspective.

[19] This pre-tragic "satyric stage" should not be confused with the satyr-play which each
contestant was required to append to the trilogy of tragedies which he entered for the
tragic competition at the Athenian City Dionysia. If we are to believe Aristotle's evidence,
before formal tragic drama was achieved, the pre-tragic choruses were performed by men
dressed as satyrs, Dionysus' "goat-men" followers. The formal satyr-play is attributed to
the invention of Pratinas, early in the fifth century B.C. (a generation after the estab-
lishment of the tragic competition at the Dionysia), possibly as a consciously archaizing
revival of this earlier, now lost, "satyric stage" of tragedy.

the fact that iambic lines occur most frequently in ordinary conversation, whereas hexameters occur but rarely, and then only when we abandon conversational cadences. As for the number of *epeisodia* and the way the other features of tragedy are said to have been elaborated, let us consider these also to have been dealt with, for to discuss them one by one would surely be a lengthy task.

CHAPTER 5

Comedy is, as we said, an imitation of men who are inferior but not altogether vicious. The ludicrous is a species of ugliness; it is a sort of flaw and ugliness which is not painful or injurious. An obvious example is the comic mask, ugly and twisted but not painful to look at.

We know how tragedy changed and who made the changes, but comedy was not seriously pursued at first and its development is obscure.

>b Only in more recent times was comedy produced at public expense; before that it was performed by volunteers,[20] and its various forms had developed before the time of those who are called comic writers and are remembered. We do not know who introduced the masks, the prologues, the several actors, and the rest. Comic plots originated in Sicily (Epicharmus and Phormis), while at Athens it was Crates who first abandoned the lampoon to write comic works with stories and plots of general interest.

Epic poetry resembles tragedy in so far as it is an imitation in verse of what is morally worthy; they differ in that the epic has only one metre and is narrative in form. They also differ in length, for tragedy tries to confine itself, as much as possible, within one revolution of the sun or a little more, whereas the time of an epic is unlimited. This, however, was at first true also of tragedy.

Some parts are common to both; others are peculiar to tragedy. It follows that anyone who knows good tragedy from bad also knows about the epic, as the elements of the epic are present in tragedy, though not all the elements of tragedy are to be found in the epic.

CHAPTER 6

Epic poetry and comedy will be discussed later.[21] Let us now take up the definition of tragedy which emerges from what has been said. Tragedy, then, is the imitation of a good action, which is complete and of a certain

---

[20] Comedy was introduced at the City Dionysia at Athens in 486 B.C.; tragedy, at least according to tradition, in 534 B.C. "Volunteers" (*ethelontai*) are equivalent to our "amateurs," for until comedy was officially recognized, it would not have been granted a chorus by the *archon* in charge of the Festival, and the *choregus* (a wealthy citizen appointed by the *archon*) would not have paid for the expenses of the production.

[21] This promise is only partially fulfilled for epic in Chapters 23 and 24. For arguments for a second book of the *Poetics*, allegedly dealing mainly with comedy, see Aristotle/Lucas 1968, xiii–xiv, and Janko 1984.

length, by means of language made pleasing for each part separately; it relies in its various elements not on narrative but on acting; through pity and fear it achieves the purgation [*catharsis*] of such emotions.[22]

By "language made pleasing" I mean language which has rhythm, melody, and music. By "separately for the parts" I mean that some parts use only metre while others also have music. And as it is through acting that the poets present their imitation, one first and necessary element of a tragedy is the arranging of the spectacle. Then come music and diction, for these are the means used in the imitation. By diction I mean the actual composition of the verses, while the effect of music is clear to all.

Since it is an action which is imitated, it is performed by persons who 50a must have qualities of character and mind, and from them we transfer these predicates to the actions also. Character and thought are the two natural causes of action; through actions men succeed or fail. The imitation of the action is the plot, for this is what I mean by plot, namely, the arrangement of the incidents. Character, on the other hand, is that which leads us to attribute certain qualities to the persons who act. Thought is present in all they say to prove a point or to express an opinion.[23] Every tragedy, therefore, has these six necessary elements which make it what it is: plot, character, diction, thought, spectacle, and music. Two of these elements are the means of imitation, one is the manner, three belong to the objects imitated, and besides these there are no others. We may say that most poets use these elements; every tragedy, in much the same manner, has spectacle, character, plot, diction, music, and thought.

The most important of these is the arrangement of incidents, for tragedy is an imitation, not of men but of action and life, of happiness and misfortune. These are to be found in action, and the goal of life is a certain kind of activity, not a quality. Men are what they are because of their characters, but it is in action that they find happiness or the reverse. The purpose of action on the stage is not to imitate character, but character is a

---

22 Aristotle's celebrated definition of tragedy is given (like any definition of his concerned with "the productive sciences") in terms of the four causes: the formal cause of tragedy (that which gives it its structure) is the imitation of an action of the kind here described; its material cause (what it is made of) is language, suitably embellished; its efficient cause (how it is carried out) is its dramatic (as contrasted with "narrative") form; its final cause (the purposed end, or *telos*) is the *catharsis* (of which more anon) of the emotions of pity and fear (see Aristotle/Telford 1961, 8off.). Of the six formal parts of tragedy to be described in the rest of Chapter 6, two (diction and song) belong to the medium or material of the imitation (i.e., how language is used and "made pleasing"); one (spectacle, i.e., "the visual aspect of the drama, the scenery, costumes, gestures, etc.," Aristotle/Telford 1961, 86) to the manner of the imitation; three (plot, character, and thought) to the objects of imitation. These six parts are then arranged in a hierarchy of importance: plot, character, thought, diction, song, spectacle. Aristotle indicates at the end of this chapter that tragedy can exist and achieve its *telos*, without ever actually being performed.

23 These somewhat terse accounts of character (*ethos*) and thought (*dianoia*) are slightly expanded near the end of this chapter. Cf. also Chapters 15 and 19, where Aristotle has more to say about the deployment of character and thought, respectively, in tragedy.

by-product of the action. It follows that the incidents and the plot are the end which tragedy has in view, and the end is in all things the most important. Without action there could be no tragedy, whereas a tragedy without characterization is possible.[24]

The tragedies of most of our recent poets have no characterization and, generally speaking, there are many such poets. This is the difference, among painters, between Zeuxis and Polygnotus for Polygnotus expresses character very well, while Zeuxis does not express it at all. Moreover, a series of speeches expressing character, well written and well thought-out though they might be, would not fulfill the essential function of a tragedy; this would be better achieved by a play which had a plot and structure of incidents, even though deficient in respect to character. Besides, the most important means by which a tragedy stirs the emotions reside in the plot, namely reversals and recognitions. Another argument is that those who begin to write poetry attain mastery in diction and characterization before they attain it in plot structure. Nearly all our early poets are examples of this.

The plot is the first essential and the soul of a tragedy; character comes second. Pretty much the same is true of painting: the most beautiful colors, laid on at random, give less pleasure than a black-and-white drawing. It is the action which is the object of the imitation; the individual characters are subsidiary to it.

Thought is the third element in tragedy. It is the capacity to express what is involved in, or suitable to, a situation. In prose this is the function of statesmanship and rhetoric. Earlier writers made their characters speak like statesmen; our contemporaries make them speak like rhetoricians. A person's character makes clear what course of action he will choose or reject where this is not clear. Speeches, therefore, which do not make this choice clear, or in which the speaker does not choose or reject any course of action at all, do not express character. Thought comes in where something is proved or disproved, or where some general opinion is expressed.

Diction is the fourth of the elements we mentioned. By diction I mean, as I said before, the use of words to express one's meaning. Its function is the same in verse and prose. Of the remaining elements, music is most important among the features of tragedy which give pleasure. As for the spectacle, it stirs the emotions, but it is less a matter of art than the others, and has least to do with poetry, for a tragedy can achieve its effect even

---

[24] This emphasis on the primacy of the plot is to be very important in Aristotle's subsequent detailed discussion of how the parts of tragedy may best be executed. As the *telos*, or final cause, of the other parts of the tragedy, it will have the lion's share of this discussion. But though Aristotle tells us that it is "possible" for a tragedy to exist without characterization, we should not underestimate its importance in Aristotle's view. It is described a little later in this character as the second most important part of tragedy, and we should remember also that, earlier in this chapter, character and thought have been described as "the two natural causes of action."

apart from the performance and the actors. Indeed, spectacular effects belong to the craft of the property man rather than to that of the poet.

CHAPTER 7

Having now defined these elements, our next point is what the plot structure should be, as this is the first and most important part of a tragedy. We have established that a tragedy is the imitation of an action which is whole and complete, and also of a certain length, for a thing can be whole without being of any particular size. "Whole" means having a beginning, a middle, and an end. The beginning, while not necessarily following something else, is, by definition, followed by something else. The end, on the contrary, follows something else by definition, either always or in most cases, but nothing else comes after it. The middle both itself follows something else and is followed by something else. To construct a good plot, one must neither begin nor end haphazardly but make a proper use of these three parts.

However, an animal, or indeed anything which has parts, must, to be beautiful, not only have these parts in the right order but must also be of a definite size. Beauty is a matter of size and order. An extraordinarily small animal would not be beautiful, nor an extraordinarily large one. Our view
51a of the first is confused because it occupies only an all but imperceptible time, while we cannot view the second all at once, so that the unity of the whole would escape us if, for example, it were a thousand miles long. It follows that, as bodies and animals must have a size that can easily be perceived as a whole, so plots must have a length which can easily be remembered. However, the limit set to length by the circumstances of the dramatic presentation or by the perceptive capacity of the audience is not a matter of dramatic art. If a hundred tragedies were competing at once, the poets would compete with their eye on the water clock, and this they say happened at one time. What is a matter of art is the limit set by the very nature of the action, namely, that the longer is always the more beautiful, provided that the unity of the whole is clearly perceived. A simple and sufficient definition is: such length as will allow a sequence of events to result in a change from bad to good fortune or from good fortune to bad in accordance with what is probable or inevitable.[25]

CHAPTER 8

A story does not achieve unity, as some people think, merely by being about one person. Many things, indeed an infinite number of things, happen to the same individual, some of which have no unity at all. In the

[25] " ... in accordance with what is probable or inevitable": this favorite phrase of Aristotle's (sometimes translated "probable or necessary") is regularly used by him to express causal

same way one individual performs many actions which do not combine into one action. It seems, then, that all those poets who wrote a *Heracleid*, a *Theseid*, and the like, were in error, for they believed that, because Heracles is one person, a story about him cannot avoid having unity. Now Homer, outstanding as he is in other respects also, seems to have perceived this clearly, whether as a conscious artist or by instinct. He did not include in the *Odyssey* all that happened to Odysseus – for example, his being wounded on Parnassus or his feigning madness when the troops were being levied – because no thread of probability or necessity linked those events. He built his plot around the one action which we call the *Odyssey*; and the same is true of the *Iliad*. As in other kinds of imitative art each imitation must have one object, so with the plot; since it is the imitation of an action, this must be one action and the whole of it; the various incidents must be so constructed that, if any part is displaced or deleted, the whole plot is disturbed and dislocated. For if any part can be inserted or omitted without manifest alteration, it is no true part of the whole.

CHAPTER 9

It also follows from what has been said that it is not the poet's business to relate actual events, but such things as might or could happen in accordance with probability or necessity. A poet differs from a historian, not because one writes verse and the other prose (the work of Herodotus could be put into verse, but it would still remain a history, whether in verse or prose), but because the historian relates what happened, the poet what might happen. That is why poetry is more akin to philosophy and is a better thing than history; poetry deals with general truths, history with specific events. The latter are, for example, what Alcibiades did or suffered, while general truths are the kind of thing which a certain type of person would probably or inevitably do or say.[26] Poetry aims to do this by its choice of names; this is clearly seen in comedy, for when the writers of comedy have constructed their plots in accordance with probability, they

(as opposed to random or chance) connections: causal sequence, in the case of actions, and consistency (what one would expect of a certain kind of person in certain circumstances), in the case of moral choices.

[26] This paragraph indicates Aristotle's celebrated and fundamental distinction between poetry, especially tragic poetry, and history. Tragedy imposes a certain pattern on events (and on the relation between character and action) which is not always present (or, if present, not immediately discernible) in the particular events with which history deals. (It should be admitted that Aristotle is thinking of "history" as mere chronicle here.) Thus some kind of explanation, some kind of causal sequence, is always present in tragedy, whose events do not happen by chance (the antithesis of tragedy) but are illustrative of certain universal truths of human experience. These truths *may*, as we see later, underlie certain events in "real life" but it usually requires the selection, adaptation, even "distortions" of the tragic poet to make the universal paradigms appear. Aeschylus' tragic adaptation of the "history" of Xerxes' defeat in *The Persians* is an excellent example of Aristotle's meaning here.

give their characters typical names, nor are they, like the writers of iambic lampoons, concerned with a particular individual.

The tragedians cling to the names of historical persons. The reason is that what is possible is convincing, and we are apt to distrust what has not yet happened as not possible, whereas what has happened is obviously possible, else it could not have happened.[27] However, there are tragedies which use only one or two of the well-known names, the others being fictitious; indeed a few tragedies have no well-known names at all, the *Antheus* of Agathon for example. Both the names and the events of the play are fictitious, yet it is enjoyable nonetheless. It is not, therefore, absolutely necessary to cling to the traditional stories which are the usual subjects of tragedy. In fact, it is absurd to strive to do so, for even the familiar stories are familiar only to a few, yet are enjoyed by all. All this shows that it is the plot, rather than the verse, which makes a (tragic) poet, for he is a poet in virtue of his imitation, and he imitates actions. He is no less a poet if he happens to tell a true story, for nothing prevents some actual events from being probable or possible, and it is this probability that makes the (tragic) poet.

The episodic are the worst of all plots and actions; and by an episodic plot I mean one in which the episodes have no probable or inevitable connection. Poor poets compose such plots through lack of talent, good poets do it to please the actors. As they write in competition and stretch the plot too far, they are thereby compelled to distort the sequence of events.

52a

The object of the imitation is not only a complete action but such things as stir up pity and fear, and this is best achieved when the events are unexpectedly interconnected. This, more than what happens accidentally and by chance, will arouse wonder. Even chance events arouse most wonder when they have the appearance of purpose, as in the story of the man who was responsible for the death of Mitys and was watching a festival at Argos when the statue of his victim fell upon him and killed him. Things like that do not seem to happen without purpose, and plots of this kind are necessarily better.

CHAPTER 10

Some plots are simple, others are complex, just as the actions which they imitate are clearly one or the other. I call simple an action which is one and continuous, as defined above, and in the course of which the change of

---

[27] This passage may seem to contradict both the statement at the beginning of the chapter ("it is not the poet's business to relate actual events") and the statements a little later in the present paragraph which suggest that it is the exception rather than the rule for the poet to deal with "actual events." The explanation may be that by "historical persons" in the present passage, Aristotle is thinking of characters of myth (so Aristotle/Lucas 1968), since the Greeks did not make as sharp a distinction between myth and history as we do. As the treatments by the Greek tragedians show, the events of myth, and their motivation, could be adapted to suit the particular kind of "probable or necessary" sequence which

fortune occurs without recognition or reversal. A complex action is one wherein the change of fortune is accompanied either by recognition or reversal, or by both. These must emerge from the plot structure itself so that they are connected with what has gone before as the inevitable or probable outcome. It makes all the difference whether one incident is caused by another or merely follows it.

CHAPTER 11

Reversal (*peripeteia*) is a change of the situation into its opposite, and this too must accord with the probable or the inevitable.[28] So in the *Oedipus* the man comes to cheer Oedipus and to rid him of his fear concerning his mother; then, by showing him who he is, he does the opposite; also in the *Lynceus* the hero is brought in to die and Danaus follows, intending to kill him, but in the event it is Danaus who dies and the other who is saved.

Recognition (*anagnorisis*), as the name implies, is a change from ignorance to knowledge of a bond of love or hate[29] between persons who are destined for good fortune or the reverse. The finest kind of recognition is accompanied by simultaneous reversals, as in the *Oedipus*. There are, to be sure, other forms of recognition: the knowledge acquired may be of inanimate objects, indeed of anything; one may recognize that someone has, or has not, done something. But the recognition which is most fully part of the plot and of the action is the kind we noted first. This kind of recognition and reversal will evoke pity or fear. Tragedy is the imitation of such actions, and good or ill fortune results from them.

This recognition is between persons. Sometimes the identity of one person is known, and then only one person is recognized by the other; at other times both have to be recognized, as when Iphigenia is recognized by

---

the particular tragedian chose to imitate. The passage has, however, been much debated. See the note on it and the bibliographical references in Aristotle/Lucas 1968, 122.

[28] The important term "reversal" (*peripeteia*) is sometimes confused with *metabasis* or "change of fortune" (in the best tragedies, a change from good fortune to bad) but is quite distinct. Reversal means that the action goes in precisely the opposite direction to that intended by the character or characters concerned or (possibly) to that expected by the audience. Thus, the violent death of the triumphantly returning Agamemnon in Aeschylus' *Agamemnon* is simply a change of fortune, whereas in the two examples which Aristotle gives here the action veers around to the exact opposite of its expected or intended course. Again, it should be noted that a reversal *need* not be central to the action of the tragedy, though Aristotle indicates in the next paragraph that the best kinds of reversals and changes of fortune are those which involve recognitions. However, some tragedies, particularly of Euripides, do have their plots enlivened by several "minor" reversals not of this kind.

[29] I.e., the "recognition" of the person concerned will show that he or she is a friend, not (as previously thought) an enemy, or vice versa. We should note that the word *philia*, here translated "bond of love," is used in this instance in the more restricted sense of "blood relationship"; cf. Aristotle/Else 1967, 349–50. We should also note that there are many kinds of recognition (of fact, of error, and so on) besides "the best kind," which involves the recognition of persons.

Orestes as soon as she sends the letter, but another recognition scene is necessary for her to recognize Orestes.

These things, reversal and recognition, are two parts of the plot. A third is suffering. We have discussed two of the three, namely reversal and recognition. Suffering [*pathos*][30] is a fatal or painful action like death on the stage, violent physical pain, wounds, and everything of that kind.[31]

CHAPTER 12

We have previously mentioned the parts of tragedy in the sense of its qualitative parts. The quantitative sections, on the other hand, into which a tragedy is divided are the following: *prologos*, *epeisodion*, *exodos*, and the choral part, itself sub-divided into *parodos* and *stasima*. These occur in all tragedies; there may also be actors' songs and *kommoi*.

The *prologos* is that whole section which precedes the entrance of the chorus; the *epeisodion* is a whole section between complete choral odes; the *exodos* is that whole section of a tragedy which is not followed by a choral ode. In the choral part, the entrance song (*parodos*) is the first complete statement of the chorus, a *stasimon* is a song of the chorus without anapaests or trochees;[32] a *kommos* is a dirge in which actors and chorus join.

We spoke previously of the parts which must be considered as qualitative elements of tragedy; these are the quantitative parts.

CHAPTER 13

We must discuss next what a writer should aim at and what he should avoid in constructing his plot, how tragedy will come to fulfill its proper function. As already stated, the plot of the finest tragedies must not be simple but complex; it must also represent what is fearful or pitiful, as this

[30] "Suffering [*pathos*]": it is a moot point (and perhaps not a very important one) whether this word (which Butcher translates as "the Tragic Incident") should be regarded as a technical term, i.e., one connoting, in this case, a specific kind (or kinds) of suffering suitable to tragedy and regularly occurring in it. (Aristotle is to describe and evaluate various kinds of such incidents in Chapter 14.)

[31] With the exception of Sophocles' *Ajax* and one or two other slightly more marginal examples, the evidence of extant Greek tragedy has given rise to the view that deaths and deeds of violence were, by convention, kept *off*-stage. This sentence of the *Poetics* suggests, however, that the convention (if such it was) was by no means strictly followed.

[32] In the first part of the *parodos* (at least in older tragedies) there was a "marching-on chant" in the anapaestic metre, before the ode proper began. The *stasimon*, on the other hand, was a steady or continuous song sung by the Chorus after it had become established in the *orchestra* (or dancing-place), and in the action of the play. It has been observed that the definition in the present passage is curiously inexact, since the trochaic metre is found in some *stasima* and the Chorus at *Medea* 1081-115 (which occupies the position of a *stasimon*) is in the anapaestic metre. Nevertheless, there is no compelling reason to entertain, as some commentators have, doubts about the authenticity of this chapter or about its position in the *Poetics*.

is characteristic of tragic imitation. It clearly follows that, in the first place, good men must not be seen suffering a change from prosperity to misfortune; this is not fearful or pitiful but shocking. Nor must the wicked pass from misfortune to prosperity; this, of all things, is the least tragic; nothing happens as it should, it is neither humane nor fearful nor pitiful. A thoroughly wicked man must not pass from prosperity to misfortune either; such a plot may satisfy our feeling of humanity, but it does not arouse pity or fear. We feel pity for a man who does not deserve his misfortune; we fear for someone like ourselves;[33] neither feeling is here involved.

We are left with a character in between the other two; a man who is neither outstanding in virtue and righteousness, nor is it through wickedness and vice that he falls into misfortune, but through some flaw. He should also be famous or prosperous, like Oedipus, Thyestes, and the noted men of such noble families.

A good plot must consist of a single and not, as some people say, of a double story; the change of fortune should not be from misfortune to prosperity but, on the contrary, from prosperity to misfortune. This change should not be caused by outright wickedness but by a serious flaw[34] in a character such as we have just described, or one better rather than worse. This is proved by what has happened: at first tragic poets related any kind of story, but now the best tragedies are constructed around the fortunes of a few families, and are concerned with Alcmaeon, Oedipus, Orestes, Mel-

---

[33] This is the only passage in the *Poetics* in which some explanation is given of the kind of object (i.e., the sufferer) required in tragedy to arouse (in the spectators) the emotions of pity and fear. The evocation of pity and fear, which is the final cause of the plot, determines what kind of tragic sufferer must be chosen. We should note, too, the necessary element of identification by the spectators with the tragic sufferer in the achievement of the second of these emotions in particular.

[34] Aristotle's word *hamartia*, here translated as "a serious flaw," means, basically, "a missing of the mark" and so "a mistake." In the great period of Greek tragedy and in Aristotle's own time the word was used both for an error due to mere ignorance of fact and for moral fault. Earlier didactic and moralizing interpretations of Greek tragedy and of the *Poetics* tended to make the latter meaning the exclusive one and, in reaction, scholarship in the present century (culminating in Bremer's *Hamartia*, 1969) has produced an over-simplification in the other direction. A major part of the modern argument (but see also n. 35, below) has been that in Aristotle's usage the neutral meaning of the word, i.e., "error due to ignorance of fact," is far more common than the sense "moral error" or "moral flaw." However, Stinton (1975) has shown that though the number of Aristotelian usages of *hamartia* meaning "mistake" clearly predominate, the general context of these usages (particularly in the *Ethics*) often has to do with moral calculation so that, in effect, in many of these instances moral error or "morally wrong action" is involved (pp. 222–24). Stinton concludes (pp. 228–31) that *hamartia* may be an error due to ignorance of a fact (Oedipus' case) or an error involving moral judgment, provided only that it not be one due to actual baseness or wickedness (which Aristotle specifically excludes). Stinton allows that *hamartia* can also mean "moral flaw," since "any act due to *hamartia* will have its corresponding disposition" and since, moreover, Aristotle has recommended that "stage-figures [be] given characters conformable to their acts" (p. 236). On this latter point, cf. the similar conclusion in Aristotle/Golden and Hardison 1968 (p. 183).

eager, Thyestes, Telephus, and any other such men who have endured or done terrible things.[35] The best products of the tragic art have this kind of plot structure.

People are therefore mistaken when they criticize Euripides on this very point, because his tragedies are of this kind and many of them end unhappily, for this, as I said, is right. There is convincing proof of this: in the theatre and in dramatic contests such dramas are seen to be the most tragic if they are well performed, and even though Euripides manages his plays badly in other respects, he obviously is the most tragic of the poets.

The double plot, such as we find in the *Odyssey*, where, at the end, the good are rewarded and the bad punished, is thought by some to be the best, but in fact it holds only second place. It is the weakness of our audiences that places it first, and the poets seek to please the spectator. The pleasure provided in this way, however, belongs to comedy rather than to tragedy; it is in comedy that those who, in the story, are the greatest enemies, like Orestes and Aegisthus, are reconciled in the end, walk off the stage as friends, and no one kills anybody.

CHAPTER 14

53b Fear and pity can be caused by the spectacle or by the plot structure itself. The latter way is better and argues a better poet. The story should be so constructed that the events make anyone who hears the story shudder and feel pity even without seeing the play. The story of Oedipus has this effect. To arouse pity and fear by means of the spectacle requires less art and a costly performance. And those plays which, by means of the spectacle, arouse not fear but only amazement have nothing in common with tragedy. We should not require from tragedy every kind of pleasure, but only its own peculiar kind.

As the tragic poet must aim to produce by his imitation the kind of pleasure which results from fear and pity, he must do so through the plot. We must therefore investigate what sort of incidents are terrible or pitiful. Such actions must necessarily occur between people who are friends, enemies, or neither. Between enemies neither the action itself nor the intention excites pity, except in so far as suffering is pitiful in itself. The same is true between people who are neither friends nor enemies. When, however, suffering is inflicted upon each other by people whose relationship implies affection, as when a brother kills, or intends to kill, his brother, a son his father, a mother her son, a son his mother, or some other such action takes place – those are the situations to look for.

It is not possible to undo the traditional stories, the murder of Clytem-

---

[35] It is important to realize, as Stinton (1975, 227) reminds us, that the six heroes mentioned in this passage "are chosen as especially suitable for tragedy simply because of the things they do and suffer" – not because their actions exemplify *hamartia*.

nestra by Orestes or that of Eriphyle by Alcmaeon,[36] but the poet must find ways to make good use of the given situation. Let us clarify what we mean by "good use." The deed can be done, as in the old poets, with full knowledge of the facts, as the Medea of Euripides kills her children. Or it can be done in ignorance of its terrible nature and this recognized later, as the Oedipus of Sophocles killed his father; this action, it is true, lies outside the drama, but it can happen in the course of the play, as with the Alcmaeon of Astydamas or with Telegonus in the *Wounded Odysseus*.[37]

There is still a third way: when someone who intends to do the deed is ignorant of the relationship but recognizes it before the deed is done. There is no further alternative, for one must act or not, either with knowledge or without it.

The worst of all these is to have full knowledge and intend to do the deed, and then not do it; this is not tragic but shocking, and there is no suffering; it is a type never or very rarely used, as when Haemon threatens his father Creon in the *Antigone*. It is better to commit the crime. Better still is to do it in ignorance and to recognize the truth afterwards. Then there is nothing to shock, and the recognition is frightening. Best of all is the last alternative, the way of Merope in the *Cresphontes* where she intends to kill her son but does not do it when she recognizes him, or, as in the *Iphigenia*, where the sister is about to kill the brother, or in the *Helle*, where the son, about to give up his mother, recognizes her.[38]

That is the reason why the subjects of tragedy are, as we said some time ago, provided by a few families. By chance rather than intent, poets found the way to provide these situations in their plots, and this forces them to go to those families which were thus afflicted.

---

[36] Alcmaeon slew his mother Eriphyle when so commanded by his father Amphiaraus. This myth provided plots for various now lost tragedies, including one or more by Sophocles. In the version by Astydamas mentioned a few lines later, it would appear that the playwright had the matricide performed in ignorance of the relationship. As Else observes (1969, 391–92 and n. 86), Aristotle here shows his acceptance of variation (within limits) on traditional myth for the improvement of the tragic effect.

[37] In this lost play of Sophocles, Telegonus, Odysseus' son by Circe, slew his father in ignorance of the latter's identity, when Odysseus mistook him for a hostile intruder.

[38] In Euripides' lost *Cresphontes*, Aepytus, the son of Queen Merope, took his revenge on Polyphontes, the usurper of his father's kingdom, by appearing in disguise and claiming the reward offered for the slaying of himself. His mother was just saved from murdering her disguised son in his sleep (for his supposed slaying of himself) by the intervention of the Paedagogus. For Aristotle to call this situation and the comparable one in Euripides' *Iphigenia in Tauris* (where Iphigenia is saved just in time from the unwitting sacrifice of her brother Orestes), "the best of all" tragic situations seems an inexplicable contradiction of his insistence in the preceding chapter that in a good tragic plot the change of fortune should be from prosperity to adversity. Else's explanation (1969, 420) that here "the essential thing is the *idea* of a *pathos*" and that the actual deed "can be dispensed with," while it may fit his own views on *hamartia*, does not, of course, remove this difficulty. Various commentators (see Aristotle/Lucas 1969, 155) have attempted to mitigate the problem by suggesting that Aristotle is here thinking of a particular scene rather than of the tragic action as a whole but, as Lucas points out, such a scene would be pivotal to the plot and it is difficult to separate the two.

We have now said enough about the arrangement of the incidents and the right kinds of plot.

CHAPTER 15

In expressing character there are four things to aim at. Of these the first and foremost is that the characters should be good. Words and actions express character, as we stated, if they bring out a moral choice,[39] and the character is good if the choice is right. This applies to every type: even a woman or a slave can be good, though the former of these is a weaker being and the slave is altogether inferior. In the second place, characters must be appropriate or true to type: there is a manly character, but it is not appropriate for a woman to be manly or a clever speaker. The third aim is to be true to life, and this is different from being good or true to type. The fourth is consistency. Even if the character represented displays inconsistency as a character trait, he must be consistent in his inconsistency.

Menelaus in the *Orestes* provides an example of a character which is unnecessarily evil; the lament of Odysseus in the *Scylla* and the speech of Melanippe are unsuitable and inappropriate; Iphigenia in *Iphigenia at Aulis* shows inconsistency: her supplication is quite unlike the character she displays later.

In characterization as in plot structure, one must always aim at either what is probable or what is inevitable, so that a certain character will say or do certain things in a way that is probable or inevitable,[40] and one incident will follow the other in the same way.

The solution of the plot should also emerge from the story itself; it should 54b not require the use of the supernatural, as it does in the *Medea* and in the threatened departure of the Greeks in the *Iliad*. The supernatural should be used only in connection with events that lie outside the play itself, things that have happened long ago beyond the knowledge of men, or future events which need to be foretold and revealed, for we attribute to the gods the power of seeing all things. In the incidents of the play there should be nothing inexplicable or, if there is, it should be outside the actual play, as in the *Oedipus* of Sophocles.[41]

Since tragedy is the imitation of characters better than those we know in life, we should imitate good portrait painters. They too render the characteristic appearance of their subject in a good likeness which is yet more

---

[39] "Moral choice" (*proairesis*) or, as Butcher translates it, "moral purpose" is, for Aristotle, the identifying sign of what he means by character (*ethos*).

[40] This requirement of character is a corollary of the passage on "probability or necessity" in relation to action. Insofar as they are dependent on choice, actions (or speeches) must conform with what we would expect that a character of a given kind would be likely to do (or say), or *have to* do (or say), in a given set of circumstances.

[41] There are several "inexplicable" features in the background of the plot of Sophocles' *Oedipus Tyrannus*, e.g., the apparent insouciance of Jocasta about Oedipus' maimed feet.

beautiful than the original. So when the poet is imitating men who are given to anger, indolence, and other faults of character, he should represent them as they are, and yet make them worthy. As such an example of violent temper we have the Achilles of Agathon and Homer.

These things the poet must keep in mind. Besides these, he must also pay attention to the visual and other impressions which, apart from its essential effects, a poetic presentation inevitably makes upon the audience, for frequent errors are possible here also. These are adequately dealt with in my published works.

CHAPTER 16

What recognition is has already been stated.[42] As to its different kinds, the first, least artistic but most frequently used through lack of talent, is recognition by tokens or signs. Some of these signs are congenital, like the spear-shaped birthmark of the Sons of Earth,[43] or the stars which Carcinus used in his *Thyestes*; others are acquired, whether marks on the body like wounds, external possessions like necklaces, or the skiff which was the means of recognition in the *Tyro*. There is a better and a worse way of using these signs; both his old nurse and the swineherds recognize Odysseus by his scar, but the manner of their recognition is quite different. Recognitions deliberately brought about to prove one's identity are less artistic, as are all recognitions of this kind; but those that emerge from the circumstances of the reversal are better, as in the bath scene with Odysseus' old nurse.[44]

The second kind of recognition is that contrived by the poet; it is inartistic for this very reason, as Orestes in the *Iphigenia* brings about the recognition that he is Orestes. The recognition of Iphigenia follows from the letter, but Orestes says himself what the poet, not the plot, requires him to say.[45] This is why it comes very close to the fault mentioned above in the

---

[42] Some commentators find that the account of kinds of recognition is out of place at this point in the *Poetics* and belongs with earlier discussions of recognition, either at the end of Chapter 11 or, possibly, at the end of Chapter 14. After the discussion of character (*ethos*) in Chapter 15, we might expect a further discussion of thought (*dianoia*) with which character is often linked but which is not discussed again until Chapter 19. Indeed the structure of the *Poetics* seems to suffer something of a breakdown at this point. After this chapter on "Kinds of Recognition," the following two chapters (17 and 18) are "a collection of odds and ends concerned mainly with plot," as Lucas has characterized them (Aristotle/Lucas 1968, 182).

[43] This device was used in Euripides' (lost) *Antigone* for Creon's recognition of the son of Haemon and Antigone.

[44] *Odyssey* 19.392ff.

[45] In Euripides' *Iphigenia in Tauris*, the recognition of Iphigenia by Orestes comes about naturally, from the plot, when she reveals the content of the letter which she is intending to send home to her brother Orestes. Aristotle is somewhat captious in his criticism of the self-revelation of Orestes to Iphigenia which follows: this revelation is surely only to be expected (and so in a sense arises from the plot) when Iphigenia's identity has been revealed to him.

case of Odysseus and the swineherds, for Orestes too could have had some tokens with him. The cry of the shuttle in the *Tereus* of Sophocles also belongs here.[46]

55a   The third kind of recognition is through memory: we see one thing and recall another, as a character in the *Cyprians* of Dicaeogenes saw the picture and wept, or the recognition scene in the lay of Antinous, where Odysseus listens to the bard and weeps at his memories, and this leads to the recognition.

Recognition of the fourth kind is by inference, as in the *Choephori*: someone like me has come, there is no one like me except Orestes, therefore Orestes has come. The same applies to Iphigenia in the work of the sophist Polyidus, for it was likely for Orestes to reflect that his sister was sacrificed and that the same thing was now happening to him, or for Tydeus in the play of Theodectes to say that he had come to find his son and was being killed himself. Similarly, in the *Phineidae*, the women, on seeing the place, reflected on their fate: that they were fated to die in this place from which they had been cast out.

There is a further kind of composite recognition based upon a wrong inference by one of the two parties involved, as in *Odysseus the False Messenger*,[47] where one said he would know the bow he had never seen, and the other understood him to say he would recognize it, and thus made a false inference.

Of all these, the best recognition is that which emerges from the events themselves, where the amazement and the surprise are caused by probable means, as in the *Oedipus* of Sophocles and the *Iphigenia*, for it was probable that Iphigenia should wish to send a letter. This is the only kind of recognition which dispenses with contrived tokens and necklaces. The second best is recognition based on a correct inference.

CHAPTER 17

When a dramatist is constructing his plot and elaborating it by putting it into words, he must visualize the incidents as much as he can; he will then realize them vividly as if they were being enacted before his eyes, discover what fits the situation, and be most aware of possible inconsistencies. Let him be warned by the reproach made against Carcinus: in one of his plays no one who did not see the performance was aware that Amphiaraus was

---

[46] According to the myth on which a lost play of Sophocles was based, Philomela, who had been raped and had her tongue cut out, revealed to her sister Procne, by weaving the information on a loom, that the violator was Procne's husband, Tereus. As Lucas says, "the cry of the shuttle," is probably a quotation from the play (Aristotle/Lucas 1968, 169–70).

[47] Nothing is known of this play; in the following lines the text of Aristotle's explanation of his illustration is corrupt and its meaning uncertain.

on his way up from the temple, but the play failed on the stage because the audience resented the inconsistency.

The poet should also, as far as possible, work out the positions and attitudes of the actors in the play. Given equal natural talent, those dramatists who are themselves emotionally affected are most convincing; one who is himself distressed distresses, one who is angry conveys anger most realistically.[48] For this reason, a poet is either highly gifted or unbalanced; the unbalanced poet becomes one character after another, but the man of high gifts retains his critical sense.

;b   In the process of writing, the dramatist must first lay out an outline of the story, even if he has invented it, and then fill it out with incidents. I mean that the outline should be considered as follows, to take the example of the *Iphigenia*: a girl who had been offered in sacrifice mysteriously disappeared; she was established as priestess in another country where the law required her to sacrifice strangers to the goddess; some time afterwards her brother arrived (the fact that the god for some reason had, by an oracle, instructed him to go there does not belong to the outline of the story, and the purpose of the oracle lies outside the plot altogether); on his arrival he is captured and is about to be sacrificed when he makes himself known, either in the manner of Euripides or in that of Polyidus who makes him say, as he naturally would, that not only his sister but himself were fated to be sacrificed. Hence he is saved. The next step is to assign the names and to fill in the incidents. The author must see to it that these incidents belong to his story, as in the case of Orestes, whose madness led to his capture, then to his being saved, since the victim had to be cleansed.

The incidents of tragedy are short, while it is the incidents which give the epic its length. For the actual story of the *Odyssey* is not long: a man has been absent from home for many years, alone and under the eye of Poseidon. The situation at home is that his possessions are being squandered by the suitors, and they plot against his son. He arrives home tempest-tossed; he makes himself known, attacks and kills his enemies, and is safe. That is the essential plot of the *Odyssey*; the rest is incidents.

---

[48] This approving comment on the emotional involvement of the dramatist and the emotional effect of the drama contrasts with Plato's attitude ⟨Pl/21, 30⟩. The similar remark in Horace's *The Art of Poetry* ⟨Hr/67:101ff.⟩ may be derived from this passage of the *Poetics* and the question becomes an important one for such later theorists as Lessing, Hegel, and Brecht. Unfortunately, the precise meaning of the explanatory passage which follows this statement is uncertain. Butcher's somewhat different translation of it goes: "Hence poetry implies either a happy gift of nature or a strain of madness. In the one case a man can take the mould of any character; in the other, he is lifted out of his proper self" (Aristotle/Butcher 1895). It is possible, however, that neither translation brings out clearly enough the contrast between the man naturally endowed (*euphues*) to project himself into his characters, on the one hand, with, on the other, the frenzied, mad, ecstatic man. See the interesting notes by Else (1969, 496–502) and Lucas (Aristotle/Lucas 1968, 177–79).

CHAPTER 18

Every tragedy consists of two parts, the involvement and unraveling. The incidents which precede the beginning of the play, and frequently some of the incidents within the play, make up the involvement, the rest is the unraveling. I mean that the involvement extends from the beginning to the the part which immediately precedes the change to good or bad fortune, while the unraveling extends from where the change of fortune begins to the end. In the *Lynceus* of Theodectes, for example, the involvement includes what has previously taken place and the capture of the child, the unraveling extends from the accusation of murder to the end.

56a There are four types of tragedy, the same number as the elements we mentioned earlier: the complex tragedy, in which reversal and recognition are the whole drama; the tragedy of suffering, like the plays on Ajax or Ixion; the tragedy of character, like the *Phthian Women* and the *Peleus*; and, fourth the spectacular tragedy,[49] like *The Daughters of Phorcys*, the *Prometheus*, and all the plays that are located in the Underworld. One should try to achieve all four kinds or, if not all, most of them and the most important, especially as (tragic) poets are nowadays subject to all kinds of unfair criticism. Each type of tragedy has produced its good poets, but the same man is now expected to surpass all his predecessors in their own specialty.

It is with regard to the plot, more than anything else, that one is justified in calling one tragedy the same as another, that is, two tragedies that have the same involvement and unraveling. Many poets handle the involvement well but the unraveling badly. Both should be mastered.

It is necessary to remember what has already often been mentioned, and not to compose a tragedy with an epic plot structure, by which I mean a plot with many stories, as would be the case if someone were to make the whole story of the *Iliad* into a tragedy. In the *Iliad*, because of its magnitude, the different parts adopt a length appropriate to each, but in tragedies such length is contrary to the concept of the drama. One may prove this by referring to those who have made the whole story of the fall of Troy into a tragedy, and not, like Euripides, parts of that story only, or to those who wrote a tragedy on Niobe, but not in the way Aeschylus did. These writers have been hissed off the stage or at least been unsuccessful, for even Agathon was hissed off the stage for this reason alone.

[49] The text is corrupt at this point; the translation accepts Bywater's (Aristotle/Bywater 1909) conjecture, *opsis*. The kind of plays mentioned might, however, be thought to be ones given to "spectacular effects," to the degree to which such were possible in early Greek theatre (most, if not all, of the plays Aristotle is thinking of here are by Aeschylus). Aeschylus' *Prometheus* plays were set in the distant Scythian and Caucasian mountains; Aeschylus' *Phorcydes* probably concerned Perseus' outwitting of the three eye-sharing maiden sentinels of the Gorgon; and the "plays located in the Underworld" (which would include the *Psychagogoi* and the *Sisyphus*, again by Aeschylus) might also have allowed for spectacle. See Halliwell 1986, Appendix 3.

Yet in their handling of reversals and in simple plots these poets wonder-fully achieve the effect they aim at, for indeed this sort of thing is tragic and satisfies our humane feelings, that is, when a clever but wicked man like Sisyphus is deceived, or a brave criminal is defeated. This is probable in Agathon's sense when he said that many unlikely things are likely to happen.

The chorus must be considered to be one of the actors, an element in the play, and it should take part in the action not as in Euripides but as in Sophocles. In later dramatists the songs are no more part of the story than of another tragedy, so that they are sung as interludes, a practice started by Agathon. Yet what difference is there between singing an interlude and inserting a speech or a whole scene from another play?

CHAPTER 19

We have now discussed the other elements of tragedy, but diction and thought remain to be dealt with. Concerning thought, this should be dealt with in my treatise on rhetoric, for it belongs to that province of study. The expression of thought includes all the effects to be contrived by speech, and under this head come proof, refutation, the rousing of such emotions as pity, fear, anger, and the like, making things appear important or trifling. Now it is clear that in handling the incidents of a drama we must make use of the same rhetorical devices whenever it is necessary to make those incidents appear pitiful, fearful, important, or probable, except for this difference: events on the stage are seen without our being told of them, whereas in a prose speech the events are expounded by the speaker and exist for the audience only through his speech. For what would be the function of an orator if the audience could get an impression of the events he deals with apart from his speech?[50]

In matters of diction, one kind of inquiry deals with the modes of expression. The knowledge of these belongs to the art of delivery, and to the person whose chief art this is: what, for example, is a command, a prayer, a statement, a threat, a question, an answer, or any other possible mode? No serious reproach is made against the poet for his knowledge or ignorance of these things. Would anyone agree with the criticism of Protagoras that Homer was at fault because what he thinks is a prayer is actually a command: "Sing, goddess, of the wrath"? The Sophist says that to order someone to do or not do something (the imperative) is in fact a

---

[50] Text and meaning are uncertain here, and indeed this whole passage on thought (*dianoia*) has been variously interpreted. Aristotle seems to be indicating that speeches involving thought in tragedy (for a description of such speeches, see Chapter 6) should be restricted to ones which express (relevant) matters which cannot be expressed by the action. He may also, as Else suggests (1969, 566), be making an implicit criticism of contemporary dramatic practice of allowing the intrusion of too much rhetoric into tragedy.

command. We may therefore pass over this inquiry as belonging to another art than poetry. ...[51]

CHAPTER 24

59b ... The epic has a special and important feature which allows its length to be greater: tragedy cannot represent different parts of the action at the same time but only that part which is enacted upon the stage, whereas the epic, being narrative in form, can make different parts of the action come to a head simultaneously. ...

60a ... Tragedy should make men marvel, but the epic, in which the audience does not witness the action, has greater scope for the inexplicable, at which men marvel most. The circumstances of the pursuit of Hector in the *Iliad*, for example, would appear ridiculous on the stage, with some actors standing still while Achilles signals to them to keep away, but in the epic this incongruity goes unnoticed. To marvel is pleasant, as can be seen from the fact that everybody adds something in telling a story, thinking to please. ...

What is impossible but can be believed should be preferred to what is possible but unconvincing. The plot should not consist of inexplicable incidents; as far as possible it should contain nothing inexplicable. If this is not possible, the inexplicable should lie outside the part of the story that is dramatized, like Oedipus' ignorance of the manner in which Laius died, and not be in the play itself like the account of the Pythian games in Sophocles' *Electra*,[52] or in the *Mysians* the man who came from Tegea to Mysia without saying a word. It is ridiculous to say that the plot would have been ruined without these incidents. Such a plot should not be chosen in the first place, but if it was chosen and a more reasonable outcome seems possible, the plot is also absurd. ...

CHAPTER 25

60b We turn now to the problems raised by critics and the way to solve them. The following examination will clarify their nature and the classes into which they fall. Since the poet, like the painter and other makers of images, is an imitator, the object of his imitation must always be represented in one

---

[51] Chapters 20 and 21 are concerned with various linguistic and stylistic matters. Chapter 22 continues in the same vein but contains some interesting recommendations (with examples) concerning the use of an elevated style in tragedy. Chapters 23 and 24 are mainly on the epic and only some of the interesting asides on tragedy in the latter are included here.

[52] This account occurs in the lengthy "Messenger Speech" by the Paedagogus in which the false news of Orestes' death in the games is reported to Clytemnestra. It is not clear why Aristotle classes it among "inexplicable incidents," unless it is because the Pythian games did not exist at the time of the dramatic date of the play. The *Mysians* (of Aeschylus), mentioned next, is not extant.

of three ways: as it was or is, as it is said or thought to be, or as it ought to be.

He communicates this by means of language, with the addition, it may be, of rare words and metaphors. We allow the poet many modifications of language. What is right for a politician is not right for a poet; indeed, what is right for a poet is not the same as for any other craftsman.

In poetry itself there are two kinds of flaw, one of which is intrinsic, the other incidental. If a poet chooses a subject for imitation and cannot represent it, that is an intrinsic flaw in his art. But if the mistake lies in the subject as he meant to imitate it and he represents, for example, a horse putting both right feet forward at once, or he makes some other mistake which belongs to the technique of another art – an error in medicine or the like – and this leads to some impossibility in his work, that is an incidental flaw. It is in the light of this distinction that we should seek the solution of critical problems.

First, flaws that are intrinsic in the poetic art. If the poet represents something impossible, it is an error, but he is right if the poetry achieves its own purpose, which has already been explained, if, done in this way, the effect either of the passage concerned or of another part of the poem is more startling. An example of this is the pursuit of Hector. On the other hand, if the poetic purpose can be achieved as well or better without doing violence to the technical correctness concerned, then the passage is wrong, for one should avoid every kind of error where possible. We should ask what kind of flaw it is, whether one of poetic art or an incidental flaw in respect to something else. It is a lesser fault not to know that a hind has no horns than to make a bad picture of it.

Then there is also the criticism that what the poet says is not true. This can perhaps be answered in the words of Sophocles when he said that he made his characters what they ought to be, while Euripides made them what they were.[53] If the representation is not of either of these kinds, the answer may be that this is what men say it is as, for example, in the stories told about the gods: these may be neither better than the truth nor true, and Xenophanes may be right;[54] but that is what men believe. Or perhaps it is not better so, but it used to be so, as in the passage about the arms, where Homer says: "The spears were standing upright on their spikes," for it was then the custom to place the spears so, as today among the Illyrians.

As to whether anything which is said or done is right or not, one should

---

[53] Aristotle is probably relying on tradition in ascribing this now celebrated observation to Sophocles himself. "What they ought to be," does not, of course, imply that Sophocles' characters are morally superior but rather that they are of a kind that characters in tragedy *should* be. Thus Sophoclean characterization, which aimed at capturing the heroic essence of, say, an Ajax or an Antigone, is contrasted with the allegedly more realistic characterizations of Euripides.

[54] Xenophanes, born in about 570 B.C., was a poet and philosopher known for his skeptical and rationalistic criticisms of the traditional mythological depictions of the gods.

not consider only whether that particular statement or action is good or bad, but the character of the person speaking or acting, the other person affected or addressed, the time, the means, and the purpose, as, for example, to realize a greater good or avoid a greater evil. . . .[55]

61b   Generally speaking, we must judge the impossible in relation to its poetic effect, to what is morally better, or to accepted opinion. As regards poetic effect, the impossible that can be believed should be preferred to what is possible but unconvincing. There are, we are told, no such men as Zeuxis painted; true, but he paints them better than life, and the ideal model should be better than the actual reality. The inexplicable in poetry may also be justified by reference to what men say exists; and sometimes, when rightly interpreted, it is found not to be inexplicable at all, for it is also likely that unlikely things should happen.

Contradictions should be examined as is done when refuting an argument, whether the two statements refer to the same thing, in the same relation and in the same sense, so that we can be sure it is the poet who contradicts what he has said in his own person, or that it was contrary to what an intelligent person would assume from what has been said.

It is right, however, to criticize a poet for what is inexplicable or evil whenever these appear without need or benefit; the introduction of Aegeus in the *Medea* of Euripides is inexplicable[56] and the wickedness of his Menelaus in the *Orestes* is unnecessary.

Unfavorable criticisms, then, come under five heads: that what the poet has written is impossible, inexplicable, harmful, contradictory, or artistically wrong. The solutions of these difficulties must be looked for in the ways we have suggested, and these are twelve in number.

CHAPTER 26

One might be at a loss to know whether epic or tragic imitation is the more worthy. For, the argument runs, if the less vulgar art is the better, and that art is less vulgar which appeals to a better audience, it very obviously follows that the art which does everything by impersonation is vulgar. For it is the realization that their audience does not understand unless they make additions of their own which leads the tragic actors to indulge in every kind of gesticulation, like second-rate flute players who whirl themselves around when they imitate discus throwing, or drag their chorus leader about when they are playing Scylla. And so tragedy is a vulgar art.

[55] The passage here omitted is almost entirely concerned with the use of the Greek language.

[56] Aegeus arrives at a singularly opportune moment both for the plot of the play (he promises Medea the refuge she has been seeking) and for the theme (his childlessness reminds the audience, and perhaps Medea herself, of how much a king values offspring). But Aegeus' entry is viewed as *alogos* (here translated "inexplicable") by Aristotle because it does not arise naturally from anything which has preceded it in the plot.

So, too, the older actors looked upon their successors, as when Mynniscus called Callipides an ape because of his exaggerated acting; and the same opinion is held about Pindarus. As these two kinds of actors are to one another, so tragedy is to the epic. The epic, they tell us, is directed to a more select audience who do not need these antics, whereas tragedy is directed to an inferior audience. And if it is vulgar, it is obviously less worthy.

Now in the first place this criticism does not apply to the tragedy, but to the acting, for a rhapsode too can overdo the gestures when reciting epic, as Sosistratus did, and so can a singer in a contest, as did Mnasitheus of Opuntium. Moreover, not every kind of gesture is to be deprecated – one would not condemn the dance – but only those of worthless men, as Callipides was blamed, and other actors are today, for acting the part of women in a base manner. Then again, tragedy can achieve its effect without any kind of gesture, just as the epic can. You can tell what kind of a tragedy it is by reading it. It follows that if tragedy is superior in other respects, it is not necessarily subject to this weakness.

In the second place, tragedy contains all the elements of the epic – it can even use epic metre – and besides these, it has the important elements of music which stirs us to pleasure most vividly, and of spectacle. Indeed, it has vividness both in the reading and the performance. And it fulfills the purpose of its imitation in a smaller compass. The more compact is more pleasing than that which is spread over a great length of time. Imagine someone giving the *Oedipus* of Sophocles as many verses as the *Iliad*!

Epic imitation has less unity; indeed, any epic provides the subject matter for several tragedies. If an epic poet chooses one story, either he must present it briefly and his poem comes to an abrupt end, or he follows the length proper to his metre and his subject is watered down. The epic contains several actions – and both the *Iliad* and the *Odyssey* have many such parts with a length of their own, even though those two poems are constructed in the best possible way and are the imitation of one action as far as an epic can be.

If, then, tragedy excels in all these ways and also in its artistic function, for no art must arouse just any kind of pleasure but only that which is appropriate to it, then tragedy achieves its purpose better and is superior to the epic.

So much for tragedy and the epic, their kinds and their elements, the number and differences of these, the causes of success and failure, the problems raised by critics, and their solution.

4

HORACE
(65–8 B.C.)

What we know as *The Art of Poetry*, a title given to the work by Quintilian (*Institutes of Oratory* 8.3.60) in the first century A.D., was originally an epistle addressed to the Pisones, probably L. Calpurnius Piso and his two sons,[1] ostensibly to give advice to the latter as aspiring young poets. Horace often adopted the letter-writing style for what are essentially moral or literary essays in verse, and *The Art of Poetry*, probably written late in the poet's life, is the longest of these. Whether it was intended primarily as practical advice to contemporary young poets or as a serious critical treatise on poetry has long been hotly debated. The relaxed tone, the almost indiscernible structure, and perhaps even the "limitations" of the work tend to suggest the former and certainly it is a mistake to view it as a kind of Roman version of Aristotle's *Poetics*. Nevertheless, there is one puzzling feature of the work which suggests that its author may have had a cultural context other than the Roman one and perhaps a more general intention in mind.

A considerable portion of *The Art of Poetry*, indeed by far the largest part of it which deals specifically with poetic composition, concerns dramatic writing and productions. Yet, as a leading authority has observed of the period in which Horace was writing, "We certainly know enough of the Augustan literary scene to assert that interest in drama was slight."[2] Stranger, still, a considerable part of the advice in this section of *The Art of Poetry* concerns the writing of satyr-plays, which figure chiefly as a relatively minor element in fifth-century performances of Greek tragedy ⟨Ar/40 n.19⟩. There were, to be sure, revivals of the satyr-play (presumably apart from its original *raison d'être* as an appendage to serious tragic performances) in the first and second centuries B.C., and there is some evidence that satyr-plays continued to be written until the second century A.D.[3] Nevertheless, there is no evidence (though it is not an impossibility) that satyr-plays were ever performed at Rome, either in the Augustan period or at any other time. This disproportionate concern with drama and with the satyr-play has been taken as an indication that Horace is taking over "a Greek literary world" along with "a traditional Greek literary form" (deriving ultimately from Aristotle) which he shaped "into the form

---

[1] See, among various scholars who argue for this identification (and for the dating of *The Art of Poetry* late in Horace's life which follows from it), Dilke 1958; cf. also Syme 1980. For a survey of views on this and related problems, see Brink 1963, 217ff.

[2] Williams 1964, 193. See also Williams 1968, 345ff., for further discussion of the problems raised by the passages on drama in *The Art of Poetry* in view of the actual state of dramatic composition and production (as far as we can ascertain this) in the Rome of the Augustan Age. Cf. also Fantham 1984.

[3] See Sifakis 1967, 124–26. Cf. also Latte 1925, esp. p. 7.

of a practical letter from a poet to two would-be poets."[4]

Horace's concern in *The Art of Poetry* with literary-critical discussions and especially with dramatic genres more associated with Greek than with contemporary Roman culture raises the question of the influence of Aristotle's *Poetics* on his work. Renaissance critics often tended to identify Aristotelian and Horatian critical views, sometimes expounding and expanding on critical "nuggets" in *The Art of Poetry* by reference to allegedly relevant passages in the *Poetics*, of which they regarded Horace as the adaptor and interpreter, sometimes conflating the two works into a single literary-critical theory.[5]

Nevertheless, though there are many passages in *The Art of Poetry* which seem to echo passages in the *Poetics*, the echoes are often dim and the differences more striking than the similarities. These differences are due in part to the differences between Horace's epistle and a formal philosophical treatise, in part to the very indirect nature of the influence of Aristotle's work on Horace. Such teachings of Aristotle as did reach Horace probably reached him in the form of literary-critical and rhetorical treatises, some of them adapting various aspects of Aristotle's *Poetics* and *Rhetoric* composed in the Peripatetic and Alexandrian schools; modern scholars, unlike those of the Renaissance, think it unlikely that Horace had the philosopher's work before him. Moreover most of the Horatian "precepts" which had the most influence on Renaissance and later theory (such as the emphasis on the didactic function of poetry, the insistence on "decorum" and propriety in all aspects of poetic composition, the necessary blend of *ars* and *ingenium* in the making of poetry, and the "five-act" rule) lack any clear precedent in Aristotle's pronouncements.[6]

The peculiarly Horatian flavor of *The Art of Poetry*, despite its indebtedness to "the tradition," sets it apart from other treatises on poetry and drama. This is due to the fact that, as has been frequently observed, Horace employs the immediacy and concrete imagery of the poet in the expression of his critical ideas and precepts. One scholar who has commented on the lyric manner of this epistle's juxtapositions of images suggests that it is for this reason that *The Art of Poetry*, though it does not lack a logical development, so stubbornly resists formal analysis.[7] This difficulty has not, to be sure, prevented *all* commentators from attempting such analysis, but the wiser among them have contented themselves with an account of the major divisions of the poem, and have left the reader to rely on the poet to lead him, by subtle and unobtrusive transitions, from one topic to another within these larger divisions.

For further reading

Brink 1963; Dilke 1958; Fantham 1984; Grimal 1968; Herrick 1946; Latte 1925; Pickard-Cambridge 1968; Sifakis 1967; Syme 1980; Tracy 1948; Williams 1964, 1968.

---

[4] See Williams 1964, 193 and 195. For a fuller discussion of these points, see also Williams 1968, 341–45.
[5] See the excellent monograph by Herrick (1946), pp. 106ff.
[6] Other Horatian precepts (as will be noted below) do, however, clearly stem, directly or indirectly, from Aristotle's *Poetics*.
[7] See Grimal 1968, 10–11. Cf. also Brink 1963, ch. 1: "Has *Ars Poetica* a Structure?"

The Art of Poetry[8]

Suppose a painter decided to set a human head
on a horse's neck, and to cover the body with coloured feathers,
combining limbs so that the top of a lovely woman
came to a horrid end in the tail of a deep-black fish –
when invited to view the piece, my friends, could you stifle your
    laughter?
Well, dear Pisos, I hope you'll agree that a book containing
fantastic ideas, like those conceived by delirious patients,
where top and bottom never combine to form a whole,
is exactly like that picture.
                      'Painters and poets alike
10 have always enjoyed the right to take what risks they please.'
I know; I grant that freedom and claim the same in return,
but not to the point of allowing wild to couple with tame,
or showing a snake and a bird, or a lamb and tiger, as partners.[9]

Often you'll find a serious work of large pretensions
with a purple patch or two deliberately sewn on
to give a vivid and striking effect – lines describing
Diana's grove and altar, or a stream which winds and hurries
along its beauteous vale, or the river Rhine, or a rainbow.
But here they are out of place. Perhaps you can draw a cypress;
20 what good is that, if the subject you've been engaged to paint
is a shipwrecked sailor swimming for his life? The job began
as a wine-jar; why as the wheel revolves does it end as a jug?
So make what you like, provided the thing is a unified whole.

Poets in the main (I'm speaking to a father and his excellent sons)
are baffled by the outer form of what's right. I strive to be brief,
and become obscure; I try for smoothness, and instantly lose
muscle and spirit; to aim at grandeur invites inflation;
excessive caution or fear of the wind induces grovelling.
The man who brings in marvels to vary a simple theme
30 is painting a dolphin among the trees, a boar in the billows.
Avoiding a fault will lead to error if art is missing.

The poorest smith in the area round Aemilius' school
will render nails in bronze and imitate wavy hair;

---

[8] The text is from Horace/Rudd 1979. Revisions of this text made for this edition by its
translator have been incorporated here.

[9] Renaissance critics sometimes compared this passage to Aristotle's discussion of "the
marvelous" and the ways in which it may be introduced into poetry ⟨Ar/58⟩; see Herrick
1946, 7. The comparison is superficial, at best.

the final effect eludes him because he doesn't know how
to shape a whole. If I wanted to do a piece of sculpture,
I'd no more copy him than I'd welcome a broken nose,
when my jet black eyes and jet black hair had won admiration.

You writers must pick a subject that suits your powers,
giving lengthy thought to what your shoulders are built for
40 and what they aren't. If your choice of theme is within your scope,
you won't have to seek for fluent speech or lucid arrangement.
Arrangement's virtue and value reside, if I'm not mistaken,
in this: to say now what has to be said right now,
postponing and leaving out a great deal for the present.

The writer pledged to produce a poem must also be subtle
and careful in linking words, preferring this to that.
When a skilful collocation renews a familiar word,
that is distinguished writing. If novel terms are demanded
to introduce obscure material, then you will have
50 the chance to invent words which the apron-wearing Cethegi[10]
never heard; such a right will be given, if it's not abused.
New and freshly created words are also acceptable
when channelled from Greek, provided the trickle is small. For why
should Romans refuse to Virgil and Varius what they've allowed
to Caecilius and Plautus?[11] And why should they grumble if I succeed
in bringing a little in, when the diction of Ennius and Cato
showered wealth on our fathers' language and gave us unheard of
names for things?[12] We have always enjoyed and always will
the right to produce terms which are marked with the current stamp.
60 Just as the woods change their leaves as year follows year
oa (the earliest fall, *and others spring up to take their place*)[13]
so the old generation of words passes away,
and the newly arrived bloom and flourish like human children.
We and our works are owed to death, whether our navy

[10] "The apron-wearing Cethegi": the Cethegi were an old Roman family; "apron-wearing" refers to the custom of earlier days of wearing a broad waist-band, rather than the tunic of Horace's day, beneath the toga. Thus Horace is referring, by a characteristically concrete image, to Romans of the olden days.

[11] The contemporary Augustan poets Virgil and Varius are being compared with the earlier comic poets Caecilius (d. 168 B.C.) and Plautus (251?–184 B.C.) in the matter of using Greek words.

[12] Ennius was an early Roman poet (239–169 B.C.) who wrote epics, tragedies, and satires. Though his work has not survived except for fragments, it was very influential on later Roman language and literature. Cato the Censor (234–149 B.C.) was sometimes said to have founded Latin prose style with his work *On Agriculture*, the first of its kind in Latin literature.

[13] The italicized words have been supplied as a conjecture by the translator.

is screened from the northern gales by Neptune welcomed ashore –
a royal feat – or a barren swamp which knew the oar
feeds neighbouring cities and feels the weight of the plough,
or a river which used to damage the crops has altered its course
and learned a better way. Man's structures will crumble;
so how can the glory and charm of speech remain for ever?
70 Many a word long dead will be born again, and others
which now enjoy prestige will fade, if Usage requires it.
She controls the laws and rules and standards of language.

The feats of kings and captains and the grim battles they fought –
the proper metre for such achievements was shown by Homer.[14]
The couplet of longer and shorter lines provided a framework,
first for lament, then for acknowledging a prayer's fulfilment.
Scholars, however, dispute the name of the first poet
to compose small elegiacs; the case is still undecided.
Madness handed Archilochus her own missile – the iambus.
80 The foot was found to fit the sock and the stately buskin,[15]
because it conveyed the give and take of dialogue; also
it drowned the noise of the pit and was naturally suited to action.
The lyre received from the Muse the right to celebrate gods
and their sons, victorious boxers, horses first in the race,
the ache of a lover's heart, and uninhibited drinking.
If, through lack of knowledge or talent, I fail to observe
the established genres and styles, then why am I hailed as a poet?
And why, from misplaced shyness, do I shrink from learning the trade?
A comic subject will not be presented in tragic metres.
90 Likewise Thyestes' banquet[16] is far too grand a tale
for verse of an everyday kind which is more akin to the sock.
Everything has its appropriate place, and it ought to stay there.
Sometimes, however, even Comedy raises her voice,
as angry Chremes[17] storms along in orotund phrases;
and sometimes a tragic actor grieves in ordinary language –

[14] The metres Horace refers to are: the dactylic hexameter used for epic poetry; the elegiac couplet (hexameters alternating with pentameters) originally used for laments and encomia, later for didactic and erotic poetry as well; the iambic pentameter used for invective verse (both personal and political). Iambic metres were also used, though not exclusively, in the spoken parts of tragedy and comedy.

[15] "The sock," referring to the low slipper worn by Greek comic actors, and "the stately buskin," to the high boot worn by tragic actors (though not until the Hellenistic period), are typical Horatian short-hand for comedy and tragedy, respectively.

[16] Thyestes' banquet was the hideous dinner consisting of Thyestes' own children, served by his brother Atreus.

[17] Chremes was a typical stock character, "the angry father," of Greek New Comedy and Roman comedy.

Peleus and Telephus (one an exile, the other a beggar)[18]
both abandon their bombast and words of a foot and a half
when they hope to touch the listener's heart with their sad appeals.[19]

Correctness is not enough in a poem; it must be attractive,
oo leading the listener's emotions in whatever way it wishes.
When a person smiles, people's faces smile in return;
when he weeps, they show concern. Before you can move me to tears,
you must grieve yourself ⟨Ar/55⟩. Only then will your woes distress me,
Peleus or Telephus. If what you say is out of character,
I'll either doze or laugh. Sad words are required
by a sorrowful face; threats come from one that is angry,
jokes from one that is jolly, serious words from the solemn.
Nature adjusts our inner feelings to every variety
of fortune, giving us joy, goading us on to anger,
10 making us sink to the ground under a load of suffering.
Then, with the tongue as her medium, she utters the heart's emotions.
If what a speaker says is out of tune with his state,
the Roman audience, box and pit, will bellow with laughter.
A lot depends on whether the speaker is a god or a hero,
a ripe old man, or one who is still in the flush and flower
of youth, a lady of high degree, or a bustling nurse,
a roaming merchant, or one who tills a flourishing plot,
a Colchian or an Assyrian, a native of Thebes or Argos.

Writers, follow tradition, or at least avoid anomalies
20 when you're inventing. If you portray the honoured Achilles,
see that he's tireless, quick to anger, implacable, fierce;
have him repudiate laws, and decide all issues by fighting.
Make Medea wild and intractable, Ino tearful,[20]
Ixion treacherous, Io a roamer, Orestes gloomy.[21]
If you are staging something untried and taking the risk

---

18 Peleus, the father of Achilles, suffered exile on two occasions earlier in his life. Telephus
    was a Mysian king who appeared in Euripides' (lost) tragedy of that name disguised as a
    beggar.
19 Some Renaissance commentators and theorists attempted (see Herrick 1946, 86) to relate
    this passage to Aristotle's distinction ⟨Ar/38⟩ between tragedy and comedy in terms of
    their objects of imitation ("better" or "worse" men, respectively). But Horace is concerned
    here with the *styles* appropriate to each genre and to the characters presented therein.
20 Medea slew her own children in vengeance against her unfaithful husband, Jason. Ino,
    nurse to the infant Dionysus, and driven mad by Hera, was a byword for many unjust
    sufferings.
21 Ixion, a byword for treachery, was punished by Zeus by being tied to an eternally
    revolving wheel in Hades. Io, an Argive maid beloved by Zeus and turned into a cow by
    him to disguise her from the vengeful Hera, was pursued across two continents by a gad-
    fly sent by Hera. Orestes, Agamemnon's son, dispossessed of his patrimony until he ful-
    filled Apollo's orders and slew his mother and Aegisthus, had good reason to be gloomy.

of forming a new character, let it remain to the end
as it was when introduced, and keep it true to itself.

It's hard to embody general traits in particular characters.
You'd be well advised to spin your plays from the song of Troy
130 rather than introduce what no one has said or thought of.
If you want to acquire some private ground in the public domain,
don't continue to circle the broad and common track,
or try to render word for word like a loyal translator;
don't follow your model into a pen from which
diffidence or the laws of the genre prevent escape;
and don't begin in the style of the ancient cyclic poet:
'Of Priam's fate I sing and a war that's famed in story.'
What can emerge in keeping with such a cavernous promise?
The mountains will labour and bring to birth a comical mouse.
140 How much better the poet who builds nothing at random:
'Tell, O Muse, of the man who after Troy had fallen
saw the cities of many people and their ways of life.'[22]
His aim is not to have smoke after a flash, but light
emerging from smoke, and thus revealing his splendid marvels:
the cannibal king Antiphates, the Cyclops, Scylla, Charybdis.[23]
He doesn't start Diomédes' return from when Meleager[24]
died, nor the Trojan war from the egg containing Helen ⟨Ar/44–45⟩.[25]
He always presses on to the outcome and hurries the reader
into the middle of things as though they were quite familiar.
150 He ignores whatever he thinks cannot be burnished bright;
he invents at will, he mingles fact and fiction, but always
so that the middle squares with the start, and the end with the middle.

Consider now what I, and the public too, require,
if you want people to stay in their seats till the curtain falls
and then respond with warmth when the soloist calls for applause:
you must observe the behaviour that goes with every age-group,
taking account of how dispositions change with the years.
The child who has learnt to repeat words and to plant his steps
firmly is keen to play with his friends; he loses his temper

---

[22] This is a shortened version of the opening verses of Homer's *Odyssey*.
[23] These are monstrous figures appearing in the so-called "Deep Sea Tales" of Homer's *Odyssey*.
[24] "Diomedes' return" (from the Trojan War) may have been the subject of a lost epic poem. Horace's point is that a proper treatment of this subject would not include everything from the time of the death of Meleager, who died before the Trojan War began.
[25] Helen, the daughter of Leda and of Zeus, who mated with Leda in the form of a swan, was allegedly born from an egg. (Euripides pokes fun at this legend in his *Helen*, vv. 21 and 257–58.) Again the point is that an account of the Trojan War should not contain everything in the life of the one whose beauty was said to have been its cause.

60 easily and then recovers it, changing from hour to hour.
The lad who has left his tutor but has not acquired a beard
enjoys horses and hounds and the grass of the sunny park.
Easily shaped for the worse, he is rude to would-be advisers,
reluctant to make any practical plans, free with his money;
quixotic and passionate, he soon discards what he set his heart on.
Manhood brings its own mentality, interests change;
now he looks for wealth and connections, strives for position,
and is wary of doing anything which may be hard to alter.
An old man is surrounded by a host of troubles: he amasses
70 money but leaves it untouched, for he's too nervous to use it;
poor devil, his whole approach to life is cold and timid;
he hopefully puts things off, is faint in hope, and shrinks from the future.
Morose and a grumbler, he is always praising the years gone by
when he was a boy, scolding and blaming 'the youth of today'.
The years bring many blessings as they come to meet us; receding,
they take many away. To avoid the mistake of assigning
an old man's lines to a lad, or a boy's to a man, you should always
stick to the traits that naturally go with a given age.

An action is shown occurring on stage or else is reported.
80 Things received through the ear stir the emotions more faintly
than those which are seen by the eye (a reliable witness) and hence
conveyed direct to the watcher. But don't present on the stage
events which ought to take place within. Much of what happens
should be kept from view and then retailed by vivid description.
The audience must not see Medea slaying her children,
or the diabolical Atreus cooking human flesh,
or Procne sprouting wings or Cadmus becoming a snake.[26]
I disbelieve such exhibitions and find them abhorrent.
No play should be longer or shorter than five acts,[27]
90 if it hopes to stage a revival 'in response to public demand'.
Don't let a god intervene unless the dénouement requires
such a solution; nor should a fourth character speak.
The chorus should take the role of an actor, discharging its duty
with all its energy; and don't let it sing between the acts
anything not germane and tightly joined to the plot ⟨Ar/57⟩.
It ought to side with the good and give them friendly advice,

---

[26] Procne was turned into a nightingale while being pursued by her unfaithful husband
Tereus, for slaying their son, Itys. Cadmus was the mythical founder of Thebes. He and his
wife Harmonia were eventually turned into serpents.
[27] Though the number of episodes varied in Greek tragedy, a rule of five acts (including
prologue and exodus) was established for Roman tragedy. It did not obtain for comedy.
See Wilkins' instructive note and references ad loc. (Horace/Wilkins 1896).

control the furious, encourage those who are filled with fear.
It ought to praise the simple meal which is not protracted,
healthy justice and laws, and peace with her open gates.
200 It ought to preserve secrets, and pray and beseech the gods
that good fortune may leave the proud and return to the wretched.
The pipe (which was not, as now, ringed with brass and a rival
of the trumpet, but rather slender and simple with not many openings)
was once enough to guide and assist the chorus and fill
with its breath the rows of seats which weren't too densely packed.
The crowd was, naturally, easy to count because it was small,
and the folk brought with them honest hearts, decent and modest.
When, thanks to their victories, the people widened their country,
extending the walls around their city and flouting the ban
210 which used to restrain daytime drinking on public occasions,
a greater degree of licence appeared in tunes and tempo.
(What taste was likely from an ignorant crowd on holiday,
a mixture of country and town, riff-raff and well-to-do?)
Vulgar finery and movements augmented the ancient art,
as the piper trailed his robe and minced across the stage.
The musical range of the sober lyre was also enlarged
while a cascading style brought in a novel delivery,
and the thought, which shrewdly purveyed moral advice and also
predicted the future, came to resemble the Delphic oracles.[28]

220 The man who competed in tragic verse for a worthless he-goat
later presented as well the naked rustic satyrs ⟨Ar/40⟩.[29]
Rough (yet still in earnest) he tried his hand at joking;
for the crowd which, after the rites, was in a drunken holiday mood
had to be kept in their seats by something new and attractive.
However, to make a success of your clownish cheeky satyrs
and achieve a proper transition from heavy to light, make sure
that no god or hero who is brought onto the stage
shall, after just being seen in regal purple and gold,
take his language down to the plane of a dingy cottage,
230 or in trying to keep aloft grasp at cloudy nothings.

[28] On this interesting but, in the context, puzzling comment on musical accompaniment in the theatre, see Williams 1968, 336ff. Williams argues that the passage is more applicable to the contrast between the musical situation in the fifth and sixth centuries B.C., respectively, in Greece, than to the situation at Rome in Horace's time.

[29] Tragedy takes its name from this prize of a goat (*tragos*) which was competed for at the Athenian City Dionysia, established in 534 B.C. The satyr-play was invented by Pratinas early in the fifth century B.C., probably to recall the earlier, ritualistic antecedents of tragedy, at least if Aristotle's sketchy account of those antecedents is sound. This rough burlesque of tragic solemnity (in which the members of the Chorus were dressed as satyrs) became a required addition to the three plays with which the tragic poets competed at the festival.

Tragedy thinks it beneath her to spout frivolous verse;
and so, like a lady obliged to dance on a public holiday,
she'll be a little reluctant to join the boisterous satyrs.
If *I* ever write a satyr drama, my Pisos, I shan't
confine my choice to plain and familiar nouns and verbs;
nor shall I strive so hard to avoid the tone of tragedy
that it might as well be the voice of Davus or brazen Pythias,
who has just obtained a talent by wiping Simo's eye,[30]
as of Silenus[31] – guardian and servant of the god in his care.
40 I'll aim at a new blend of familiar ingredients; and people
will think it's easy – but will waste a lot of sweat and effort
if they try to copy it. Such is the power of linkage and joinery,
such the lustre that is given forth by commonplace words.
Fauns from the forest, in my opinion, ought to be careful
not to go in for the dandy's over-emotional verses,
or to fire off volleys of filthy, disgraceful jokes,
as if they came from the street corner or the city square.
Knights – free-born and men of property – take offence
and don't greet with approval all that's enjoyed by the buyer
50 of roasted nuts and chick-peas, or give it a winner's garland.

A long syllable after a short is named iambus.
Being a quick foot, he ordered iambic verses
to be called 'trimeters', in spite of the fact that six beats
occurred in a pure iambic line. At a time in the past,
so as to reach the ear with a bit more weight and slowness,
he was kind and obliging enough to adopt the stately spondees
and share the family inheritance – though never going so far
in friendship as to relinquish the second or fourth position.
Iambus rarely appears in Accius' 'noble' trimeters,
60 and his all too frequent absence from the lines that Ennius[32] trundles
onto the stage leaves them open to the damaging charge
of hasty and slapdash work or else of professional ignorance.
It isn't every critic who detects unmusical pieces;
so Roman poets have enjoyed quite excessive indulgence.
Shall *I* therefore break out, and ignore the laws of writing?
Or assume my faults will be seen by all, and huddle securely
within the permitted range? Then I've avoided blame;
I haven't earned any praise. My Roman friends, I urge you:

[30] Davus, Pythias, Simo: these are characters (a slave, a wily slave-girl, and a rich man, respectively) from Roman comedy.
[31] Silenus, the eldest of the satyrs, was a regular character in satyr-plays.
[32] Accius (170–80 B.C.) and Ennius (239–169 B.C.) were Roman poets whose works (no longer extant except for fragments) included tragedies based on Greek models and a few on Roman themes.

get hold of your Greek models, and study them day and night.
270 To be sure, your forefathers praised the rhythm and wit of Plautus.[33]
On both counts their admiration was far too generous,
in fact it was stupid – assuming that you and I know how
to tell the difference between clumsy and clever jokes,
and discern correctness of sound with the aid of ear and fingers.
We are told Thespis discovered the genre of the tragic Muse
which was never known before; he carried his plays on a wagon
to be sung and acted by men who had smeared lees on their faces.[34]
After him came Aeschylus,[35] introducing the mask
and lordly robe; he laid a stage on lowish supports
280 and called for a sonorous diction and the wearing of high-soled boots.[36]
Old Comedy followed, winning a lot of acclaim;
but its freedom exceeded the proper limit and turned to violence
which needed a law to control it. The law was obeyed, and the chorus
spoke no more having lost its right of scurrilous insult.
Our own native poets have left nothing untried.
They have often been at their best when they have had the courage
to leave the paths of the Greeks and celebrate home affairs
with plays in Roman dress, whether serious or comic.
Latium now would be just as strong in her tongue as she is
290 in her valour and glorious arms if the patient work of the file
didn't deter our poets each and every one.
Children of Numa,[37] condemn the piece which many a day
and many a rub of the stilus have not smoothed and corrected
ten times over, to meet the test of the well-pared nail

Because Democritus[38] holds talent a greater blessing
than poor despised technique and debars a poet from Helicon[39]
unless he's mad, many no longer cut their nails
or beard; they make for secluded spots and avoid the baths.
For a man will surely acquire the name and esteem of a poet

---

[33] Plautus (251?–184 B.C.) composed comedies based on Greek New Comedy.
[34] Thespis, the winner of the goat-prize at the first City Dionysia, is often called the father of
tragedy, though the "discovery" was not quite as abrupt as Horace's statement here
might suggest. For the "lees", see below, p. 80, n. 9.
[35] Aeschylus (525/4–456 B.C.) was the earliest of the three great Greek tragedians.
[36] It is now believed that these high-soled boots were not worn until several centuries after
Aeschylus, in the Hellenistic and Roman theatres. See Pickard-Cambridge 1968, 204ff.
[37] Horace may be addressing his advice here both to the particular descendants of Numa (the
Piso family to whom this epistle is directed) and to the Romans generally, since they too
are often referred to as the descendants of Numa.
[38] Democritus was a fifth-century B.C. Greek philosopher known mainly for his atomic
theory. He did, however, write a (now lost) work on poetry of which little is known. The
view ascribed to him here introduces the antithesis between *ingenium* (here translated
"talent") and *ars* ("technique") which became so common in later theory.
[39] Helicon is a mountain in Boeotia, in Greece, which was regarded as sacred to the Muses.

oo if he never allows the scissors of Licinus near his head –
a head which three Antícyras couldn't cure.[40] And me?
Like a fool I banish madness by taking springtime sedatives.
No one could put together better poems; but really
it isn't worth it. And so I'll play the part of a grindstone
which sharpens steel but itself has no part in the cutting.
Without writing, I'll teach the poet his office and function,
where he can find his resources, what nurtures and shapes him,
what is correct, what not; what is right and wrong.
Moral sense is the fountain and source of proper writing.

10 The pages of Socrates' school will indicate your material;[41]
once that is provided, words will readily follow.
First be clear on what is due to your country and friends;
what is involved in loving a parent, brother, or guest;
what is the conduct required of a judge or member of senate;
what are the duties imposed on a general sent to the front.
Then you will give the proper features to every character.
The trained playwright, I say, should turn to life and behaviour
for dramatic models – and as a source of living speech.
A play with attractive moral comments and credible characters,

20 but wholly lacking in charm and poetic force and finish,
sometimes pleases the public and holds its interest better
than lines devoid of content – mere melodious wind.
The Muse bestowed on the Greeks talent and also the favour
of eloquent speech; they craved for nothing but admiration.
Roman children learn by doing long calculations
how to divide the *as* a hundred times.[42] 'Very well then,
young Albanus: five twelfths – we subtract one of them,
what's the remainder? Come on, hurry up!'

'A third, sir.' 'Splendid!
You'll look after your money! Now *add* a twelfth to make it –'

30 'A half.' But when this craze for coppers, this verdigris,
has formed on our hearts, how can we hope to fashion poems
fit to be oiled with cedar and stored in polished cypress?

The aim of a poet is either to benefit or to please
or to say what is both enjoyable and of service.
When you are giving advice, be brief, to allow the learner
quickly to seize the point and then retain it firmly.

---

[40] Licinus is unknown. Antícyras, in Phocis in Greece, produced hellebore, used in the treatment of madness.

[41] Socrates himself made a point of not committing his teachings to writing. Horace is doubtless thinking of Socrates' followers, most notably Plato, who immortalized Socrates' teachings in his (written) dialogues.

[42] The *as* was a Roman coin of very low denomination.

If the mind is full, every superfluous word is spilt.
Make sure that fictions designed to amuse are close to reality.
A play should not expect us to take whatever it offers –
340 like 'child devoured by ogress it brought alive from her belly'.
The senior bloc refuses plays which haven't a message;
the haughty young bloods curl their nostrils at anything dry;
everyone votes for the man who mixes wholesome and sweet,
giving his reader an equal blend of help and delight.
That book earns the Sosii money; it crosses the ocean,
winning fame for the author and ensuring a long survival.

There are, of course, certain mistakes which should be forgiven.
A string doesn't always sound as mind and finger intended
[when you want a bass it very often emits a treble],
350 nor does a bow invariably hit whatever it aims at.
In a poem with many brilliant features I shan't be offended
by a few little blots which a careless pen has allowed to fall
or human nature has failed to prevent. Where do we stand, then?
If a copying clerk persistently makes the same mistake
in spite of numerous warnings, he is not excused; if a harpist
always misses the same note he causes laughter.
So for me the inveterate bungler becomes a Choerilus,[43]
whose rare touches of goodness amaze and amuse me; I even
feel aggrieved when Homer, the pattern of goodness, nods.
360 Sleep, however, is bound to creep in on a lengthy work.

A poem is like a picture. One will seem more attractive
from close at hand, another is better viewed from a distance.
This one likes the gloom; this longs for the daylight,
and knows it has nothing to fear from the critic's searching eye.
That pleased once; this will please again and again.

My dear Piso major, although your father's voice
and your own good sense are keeping you straight, hear and remember
this pronouncement: in only a limited number of fields
is 'fairly good' sufficient. An average jurist and lawyer
370 comes nowhere near the rhetorical power of brilliant Messalla,
nor does he know as much as Aulus Cascellius; still,
he has a certain value; that *poets* should be only average
is a privilege never conceded by men, gods, or bookshops.
When, at a smart dinner, the orchestra's out of tune,

---

[43] Alexander was said to have given the epic poet Choerilus a gold piece for every good line
he wrote, a total of seven pieces! See Horace, *Epistles* II.1.233.

or the scent is heavy, or poppyseeds come in Sardinian honey,
we take it amiss; for the meal could have been served without them.
It's the same with a poem, whose *raison d'être* is to please the mind;
as soon as it misses the top level, it sinks to the bottom.
A man who is hopeless at field events avoids the equipment,
80 keeping his ignorant hands off shot, discus and javelin,
for fear of giving the crowds of spectators a free laugh.
The fellow who is useless at writing poetry still attempts it.
Why not? He's free, and so was his father; his fortune is rated
at the sum required of a knight; and his heart's in the right place!

You will compose and complete nothing against the grain
(you have too much sense and taste). If you do write something later,
be sure to read it aloud to the critic Tarpa, and also
to your father and me. Then hold it back 'till the ninth year',
keeping your jotter inside the house. You can always delete
90 what hasn't been published; a word let loose is gone for ever.

Before men left the jungle, a holy prophet of heaven,
Orpheus, made them abhor bloodshed and horrible food.
Hence he is said to have tamed rabid lions and tigers.
It is also said that Amphion, who built the city of Thebes,
moved rocks by the sound of his lyre and led them at will
by his soft appeals. This was the wisdom of olden days:
to draw a line between sacred and secular, public and private;
to bar indiscriminate sex, and establish laws of marriage;
to build towns and inscribe legal codes on wood.
00 That is how heavenly bards and their poems came to acquire
honour and glory; after them Tyrtaeus and Homer
won renown, for their verses sharpened the courage of men
to enter battle. Song was the medium of oracles, song
showed the way through life. By means of Pierian tunes[44]
a king's favour was sought, and an entertainment devised
to close a season of long work. So don't be ashamed
if you love the Muse's skill on the lyre and Apollo's singing.

Is it a gift or a craft that makes outstanding poetry?
I fail, myself, to see the good either of study
10 without a spark of genius or untutored talent.
Each requires the other's help in a common cause.
The Olympic athlete who strains to breast the finishing tape
worked and suffered a lot as a boy, sweating and freezing,

---

[44] Pieria in Thessaly was particularly associated with the Muses.

leaving wine and women alone. The piper competing
at Delphi was once a learner and stood in awe of his teacher.
Is it enough to proclaim 'I'm a marvellous poet!
The last one home is a cissy; I hate to lag behind
or admit I'm utterly ignorant of something I never learnt.'

As an auctioneer attracts a crowd to bid for his goods,
420 a poet with large estates and large sums invested
encourages toadies to come and obtain something for nothing.
If he's also the sort who knows how to serve delicious dinners,
who will sponsor a shifty and penniless client or come to his rescue
when he's up to his neck in a lawsuit, then *I'll* be very surprised
if the lucky fellow can tell a true friend from a sham.
When you have given someone a present, or plan to do so,
and he's pleased and excited, never invite him to hear any verses
you have written. He'll shout 'Fine! Lovely! Oh yes!'
He will turn pale at this, at that he will squeeze a tear
430 from his loyal eyes; he will jump to his feet and stamp the ground.
Just as those who are hired to come and wail at a funeral
say and do, if anything, more than the truly bereaved,
so the fake is more visibly moved than the real admirer.
When kings are keen to examine a man and see if he merits
their trust, we are told, they make him submit to the test of wine,
plying him with a succession of glasses. So if *you* compose,
make sure you are not deceived by the fox's hidden malice.

When you read a piece to Quintilius he'd say 'Now shouldn't you alter
that and that?' If you swore you had tried again and again
440 but couldn't do any better, he'd tell you to rub it out
and to put the lines which were badly finished back on the anvil.
If, instead of removing the fault, you chose to defend it,
he wouldn't waste another word or lift a finger
to stop you loving yourself and your work without a rival.
An honest and sensible man will fault lines that are feeble,
condemn the clumsy, proscribe with a black stroke of the pen
those which haven't been trimmed, prune pretentious adornment,
where a place is rather dark insist that light be admitted,
detect ambiguous expressions, and mark what ought to be changed.
450 He'll be a new Aristarchus;[45] nor will he say 'Why should I
annoy a friend over trifles?' For such 'trifles' will lead
to serious trouble when he is greeted with laughter and hisses.

---

[45] Aristarchus was a critic of the second century B.C. famous for his commentaries on Homer.

As with the man who suffers from a skin disease or jaundice
or religious frenzy caused by the lunar goddess's anger,
sensible people are wary of touching the crazy poet
and keep their distance; children unwisely follow and tease him.
Away he goes, head in the air, spouting his verses;
and if, like a fowler watching a bird, he happens to tumble
into a pit or a well, however long he may holler
60 'Somebody! Help!' no one will bother to pull him out.
If anyone does bring help and drops him down a rope,
'How do you know', I'll say, 'he didn't throw himself in
on purpose, and doesn't want to be *left* there?' I'll add the tale
of the poet of Sicily's death – how Empedocles, eager to join
the immortals, leaped into Etna's inferno (thus catching fire
for the first time). Dying is a poet's right and privilege.
To save him against his will is tantamount to murder.
He's done it before; and it's not as if, when you hauled him up,
he'd become human and cease to yearn for a notable death.
70 One wonders why he persists in writing poetry. Is it
a judgement for pissing on his father's ashes, or has he profaned
a gruesome place where lightning has struck? He's certainly mad,
and like a bear that has managed to smash the bars of its cage
he scatters everyone, cultured or not, by the threat of reciting.
For he firmly grips the person he catches, and reads him to death.
The leech never lets go the skin till he's full of blood.

5

DONATUS
4TH CENTURY A.D.

Translated below is all that remains of the treatise *De Comoedia et Tragoedia*, attributed to Donatus, the Latin grammarian and expert on rhetoric. This extant fragment (which concerns comedy only) has exercised an influence on the theory of comedy that continues to be felt up to the present.[1] Together with Evanthius' *De Fabula*,[2] Donatus' treatise was well known to scholars (and their pupils) during the Middle Ages and, even after the rediscovery of Aristotle's *Poetics*, it remained a key document, much used and quoted by writers on comedy in Italy, Spain, France, and elsewhere in Europe. The importance of the fragment may be gauged from the fact that it was usually printed in the editions of Terence's plays that appeared frequently during the Renaissance.

The work probably mediates some of the views on comedy of the Peripatetic school of philosophy, of which Theophrastus, in succession to Aristotle, became the head. Thus the definition of comedy attributed vaguely to "the Greeks" (5.1)[3] may derive ultimately from Theophrastus. Here, as in Aristotle's remarks on comedy in the *Poetics*, but more specifically, the genre is defined by features that implicitly distinguish it from tragedy: by the contrast between the social status of the characters in comedy and tragedy, and that of the *mise en scène*. The division of the comic plot into the four parts (see 7.1–7.4) of *prologus*, *protasis*, *epitasis*, and *catastrophe*, which bequeathed a technical vocabulary to Renaissance theory, probably originated with Theophrastus. This development was undoubtedly influenced by Aristotle's statement on "tying" (*desis*) and "untying" (*lysis*), which were fundamental to his idea of unity of action in tragedy ⟨Ar/56⟩.[4] Thus within Donatus' schema (in reality a threefold division, for the *prologus* is no longer linked with the dramatic action), the *protasis* is conceived as presenting a critical situation which is then intensified in the *epitasis* before its final resolution in the final section, the *catastrophe*. This division does not depend on a formal structure determined by the interventions of a Chorus and the emphasis is less on the idea of change than on the increasing tension produced by the comic situation.

---

[1] See Blanchard 1983, 63 and n.128, for a discussion of the structure of Menander's plays, using divisions employed by Donatus.

[2] We know from Rufinus that Evanthius, a grammarian active in the early part of the fourth century A.D., wrote a commentary on Terence and introduced it with a discussion entitled *De Fabula*. How this became incorporated with Donatus' commentary is not known. The text of *De Fabula* can be found in Donatus/Wessner 1962–63, 1:13–22 and the fullest modern treatment of Evanthius is Cupaiulo's (Evanthius, ed. Cupaiulo, 1979).

[3] The section/paragraph numbering in the introductory note and in the translated text below is that of Donatus/Wessner 1962–63, 1:22–31.

[4] See Webster 1950, 178–9. On the influence of this schema on later theorists, see Herrick [1950] 1964, 116–29.

Donatus asserts the didactic function of comedy and implies that the moral lessons reflected in it would, by some means, be absorbed by the audience. There is no discussion, in the fragment, of the nature of the pleasure derived from comedy, of the immediate impact of the play on the audience nor, more basically, of what constitutes the comic, but a definition of comedy endlessly repeated by Donatus' successors is given in the quotation from Cicero: "an imitation of life, mirror of manners, image of truth."[5]

For the rest, Donatus assembles here a variety of miscellaneous information about many aspects of comedy, including the etymology of the word, brief remarks on its historical development, the classification of various types of comedy based on subject matter, characterization, and matters to do with performance such as the costuming of actors and the use of musical accompaniment.

For further reading

Beare 1950; Blanchard 1983; Brink 1971; Cicero 1960; Curtius 1953; Duckworth 1952; Herrick [1950] 1964; Preminger, Hardison, and Kerrane 1974; Webster 1950.

The fragment from *On Comedy and Tragedy*

5.1 Comedy is a [form of] drama containing the various designs of public and private individuals' desires. Through them people learn what is useful in life and what, on the other hand, ought to be avoided. The Greeks defined comedy as follows: "Comedy is an episode of private affairs, which contains no danger."[6] Cicero defined comedy as the imitation of life, the mirror

5.2 of manners, and the image of truth. Because songs of this type were initially performed in the villages of Greek society (like the festivals celebrated at crossroads in Italy), with a small measure of speech intermingled, which used to amuse the people during the changing of the acts, comedy according to an ancient convention took its name *apo tes komes* ⟨Ar/38⟩, that is from the actors' performance of the life of men who live in villages, because of their insignificant circumstances, and not in royal courts, like the

5.3 characters of tragedy. Comedy, because it is a poem composed to imitate

5.4 life and to resemble manners, consists of gesture and speech. The first inventor of comedy among the Greeks is uncertain. Among the Romans, it is known that Livius Andronicus was the first to discover comedy, tragedy

5.5 and national drama.[7] He,[8] with some justification, declares comedy to

---

5 Donatus' quotation is the only source for Cicero's definition. Ziegler (Cicero, ed. Ziegler 1960, 4.13) speculated that it might have occurred in a non-extant portion of *De Republica*. On the image of the mirror in literature, see Curtius 1953, 336 and n.56.

6 Webster (1950, 179) notes that the definition (which Donatus cites in Greek) may mean merely "a formed sequence of private affairs involving no disaster." Photius glossed the word *perioche*, which is used here, as being equivalent to *peripeteia*. If this is accepted, then the definition could be "a change in private affairs involving no danger."

7 In 240 B.C. Livius presented, in Rome, adaptations of plays by Sophocles and Euripides, while he drew his comedies from Greek New Comedy. See Duckworth 1952, 39–40.

8 Probably a further reference to Cicero; see Blanchard 1983, 412, n.12.

mirror everyday life. For just as we gaze into the mirror and easily acquire the outlines of reality through the image, so, while reading comedy, we very easily observe the imitation of life and manners.

5.6   The motive for the origin of comedy came from foreign states and customs. When the Athenians wished to preserve the propriety of Attica and brand those who were living an immoral life, they happily and enthusiastically came from every corner to villages and crossroads and there named individuals and broadcast their vices. From this custom the

5.7   name was put together and it was called comedy. These compositions were first performed in pleasant meadows. Prizes were offered to induce the wits of the educated to write and gifts were also offered to actors, that they might be more willing to use the pleasing intonation of the voice to gain sweet praise. They received a goat as a gift, as it was considered an animal harmful to vines. From the goat tragedy also derived its name. Some, however, have preferred to derive tragedy's name from the [Greek] word for the lees of oil, a watery liquid, [that is] as if [it came] from the word

5.8   "trygodia."[9] Since these games were being played out by the actors in honor of father Bacchus, the actual composers of comedies and tragedies also started to worship and venerate the propitious power, as it were, of this god. A commendable reason for this practice existed. For the compositions, though primitive, were produced in such a way that it was established that through the songs the praises and glorious deeds of

5.9   Bacchus were celebrated and made known. Then by degrees the reputation of this art increased. Thespis was the first to bring these writings to everyone's notice and later Aeschylus followed the example of his predecessor and enriched it.[10] Horace speaks about them in his *Art of Poetry* ⟨Hr/72:275–88⟩ ...

6.1   "Drama" is a general term; its two main parts are tragedy and comedy. If the subject matter dealt with Roman affairs, the tragedy was called a *praetexta*. Comedy, however, has many forms: *palliata*, *togata*.[11] The last-named took its name from the lowliness of the theme and the worthless-

6.2   ness of the actors, who performed on the stage or platform, not with a buskin or a slipper, but bare-footed. Another reason for the name was that the play did not deal with those matters which concern characters dwelling in towers or upper stories but with people occupying a low or humble

---

9   This etymology is based on the Greek word *tryx*, meaning "wine-lees." As one of the explanations of the word "tragedy," Evanthius (*De Fabula* 1.2), reports that, before Aeschylus' invention of masks, actors used to smear wine-lees on their faces.

10   The translation renders Leo's emendation substituting "locupletauit" for the corrupt "publicauit."

11   The *fabula palliata* referred to adaptations of Greek comedy (the *pallium* was the mantle Greeks wore for everyday use), and *fabula togata* and *tabernaria* (see Donatus' definitions at 6.5 below) to native Latin comedy. The *fabula Atellana* was a type of farce; Rhinthon of Tarentum (early 3rd century B.C.) wrote plays that treated tragic themes in a comic way. See Beare 1950, 256–58.

5.3 position. Tradition holds that Cincius Faliscus was the first to perform comedy using a mask; in tragedy, it was Minucius Prothymus.[12]

5.4   The title of every comedy is taken from four circumstances in all: name, place, deed, and result. [The titles] *Phormio*, *Curculio*, and *Epidicus* [derive] from a name; from a place come the *Andria*, *Leucadia*, and *Brundisina*. From an action [arise] the *Eunuchus*, *Asinaria*, and *Captivi*, and from the issue [of

5.5 the action] the *Commorientes*, *Crimen*, and the *Heautontimorumenos*. There are three forms of comedies: the *palliatae* refer [to comedies presented in] Greek dress; the *togatae*, called by some *tabernariae*, require the toga as dress according to the kind of characters. The *Atellana* [comedies] are composed with wit and jokes and contain only the refinement associated with ancient times.[13]

7.1 There are four divisions in comedy: *prologus*, *protasis*, *epitasis*, and *cata-*

7.2 *strophe*. The *prologus* is the first speech, deriving its name from the Greek *protos logos* ["first speech"] and it is an address that comes before the actual composition of the play (*ho pro tou dramatos logos*). There are four types of *prologus*: *sustatikos*, which commends, where the poet or the story is recommended; *epitimetikos*, which criticizes, where a rival is cursed or the audience thanked; *dramatikos*, which relates to the plot, which sets out the theme of the story; *miktos*, mixed, which contains all of these. Some have

7.3 claimed that a prologue and an introduction differ in that the former is so defined when the poet vindicates himself or the play is recommended, but

7.4 when the plot is the sole subject, it is an introduction. The *protasis* is the first act of the comedy, where part of the plot is explained, but the rest is kept secret to hold the audience in suspense. The *epitasis* is the complication of the action and it is through its refinement that the plot has coherence. The *catastrophe* is the unfolding of the story, by which its outcome is established.

8.1 In most dramas the names of the plays were presented before those of the poets; in some, however, the poets' names precede those of the drama. The difference in this procedure has the sanction of antiquity. For when the dramas were first brought out, their titles were read aloud before the poets were named, to prevent them from being deterred from writing because of any hostility. However, when the poet had acquired a reputation by publishing many plays, the names of the poets again took precedence, so

8.2 that the plays might gain attention through the poets' names. It is clear that dramas were produced and took their name from the various festivals.

---

12 The Latin may mean no more than that they were the first Roman actors.

13 The meaning of the phrase "uetustatum elegantias" is unclear and the notion of old-fashioned refinement, which seems to be indicated, runs counter to what is known from the tradition and the extant fragments of the *fabula atellana*, a popular kind of rustic farce, developed from early times in Campania. See Beare 1950, 129–40.

For the *curule aediles*[14] superintended four kinds of festivals in their public office. The Megalesian were consecrated to the great gods, whom the Greeks call *megalous* ["great"]. The funeral games were instituted to divert the people, while the procession decreed for a burial to honor a nobleman was being fully drawn up. The plebeian games were offered for the welfare of the people. The Apolline games were devoted to Apollo.

8.3 On stage two altars were usually set up: one to Bacchus on the right, and on the left one to the god in whose honor the games were being held. So Terence in the *Andria* [1.726] says: "Take some branches from the altar

8.4 there." Ulysses is invariably represented wearing a cap, because on one occasion he feigned madness (he wanted to conceal his identity so that he would not be recognized and compelled to go to war) or on account of his unique wisdom, under whose protection and defense he greatly benefitted his allies (for his particular excellence was a mental disposition for constant deception). Some recall that the inhabitants of Ithaca wore the cap,

8.5 for example, the Locrians. The characters of Achilles and Neoptolemus wore diadems, although they never held royal scepters. The proof adduced for this argument is that they never entered into an oath of alliance with the rest of Greece's young men to wage war against the Trojans and were never under Agamemnon's command.

8.6 Old men in comedy are dressed in white clothing, because that shade was thought to be most venerable. Young men are assigned clothes of various colors. Slaves in comedy are clothed in a short dress on account of the poverty of the past or that they may move more easily. Parasites appear in clothes wrapped around them. A man in a happy state is assigned a white garment, whereas a person in distress is given a worn-out dress, a rich man clothing of dark red and a pauper one purple-red in color. A soldier is dressed in a dark cloak and a girl in a costume from abroad. A pimp uses a cloak of many colors and a whore is given a golden-yellow

8.7 dress to denote her greed. *Syrmata* [theatrical robes with a long train] derive their name from the fact that they are trailed, a feature introduced by the extravagant Ionians. The same garments worn by grieving characters signify a lack of care for themselves due to neglect.[15] Embroidered

8.8 curtains [*aulaea*] are spread out on stage. This decorated embroidery was brought to Rome from the court of Attalus. Instead of these a later age adopted smaller curtains [*siparia*]. It is a curtain associated with the mime, which is set up before the people while the acts of the story were being changed.[16]

---

[14] The *curule aediles* were so called from their use of the *curule* or official chair. They administered the public games as part of their wider duty of urban administration at Rome.

[15] Beare (1950, 176–87) discusses the evidence of Donatus in his chapter on "Costumes and masks."

[16] At the death of Attalus III of Pergamum, in 133 B.C., his kingdom was bequeathed to Rome; on the relation of the *aulaeum* to the *siparium*, see Beare 1950, 259–66.

The actors delivered the dialogue, whereas the monologues were com-
3.9 bined with melodies composed not by the poet but by a musical expert.
Within individual songs not everything was performed using the same
melodies. The melodies were often varied, as is indicated by those who
inserted three numbers in comedies. These three convey "change of music
10 in the song."[17] The name of the composer is placed at the beginning of the
11 drama after the names of the author and actors. Songs of this type were
played on pipes, so that on hearing these many in the audience could tell
what drama the players were about to present, before the title preceding
the play was announced to the spectators at all. They were performed on
pipes of the same length [i.e., on the right and on the left] and on pipes of
different length.[18] The pipes on the right with their sombre tone foretold a
serious speech in comedy; the pipes on the left with the lightness of their
tone pointed to a joke in the comedy. When the drama was marked to be
presented with the left and with the right, a mixture of jokes and serious
matter was intimated.

[17] In his preface to *Adelphi* (Donatus/Wessner 1962–63, II:5, 1.7) Donatus states that the
letters DV stood for *diuerbium* (speech) and were placed after the names of the actors at the
beginning of the scene, while other parts were marked with MMC (*mutatis modis cantata*),
as they were to be sung with frequent changes of music. See Beare 1950, 212–13, 221.
[18] On the pipes, see Beare 1950, 160.

6

FRANCESCO ROBORTELLO
(1516–1568)

Robortello's detailed commentary on Aristotle's "difficult and obscure little book," as he called the *Poetics*, was a pioneering work of interpretation, one that exerted an enormous influence for many decades after its appearance in 1548. Out of Aristotle's spare remarks Robortello elaborated a dramatic and poetic theory, which was faithful to the original in associating the pleasure in tragedy with the perception of the formal qualities of the work, derived "from the appropriate and well-crafted imitation of men's manners, speeches, and actions" (1548, 321).[1] But for Robortello the pleasure is clearly a means of expressing useful doctrines in the most persuasive manner. This usefulness is closely associated with verisimilitude in art, and in his various discussions of plot, characterization, and speeches, truth to nature emerges as a recurrent issue. Tragedy that achieves verisimilitude teaches the spectators how to draw solace and support amid the disasters of their own lives, by recalling that similar misfortunes are the common fate of mankind.

For Robortello, the mission of poetry and drama is so to manipulate the thoughts and feelings of a fit audience, defined as an intellectual élite with appropriate expectations, that they will adopt or avoid certain courses of action. And since the audience response is governed by diction and language, above all, it is not surprising that he assigns a dominant position to rhetoric in his commentary. The comparison of tragedy with rhetoric is pervasive: in the insistence, for example, that the prologue and epilogue of tragedy are related to the play in a manner analogous to the *exordium* of a speech (p. 205); in discussions of the differences in the ways the topic of recognition is treated in oratory and poetry (p. 113); or in the mass of excerpts gathered from various ancient rhetorical treatises to illustrate his points. Thus, the commentary is consistent with Robortello's dedicatory letter to Cosimo I de' Medici, in which he also emphasizes the close links between rhetoric and dramatic (and other) poetry (p. iii). In this respect, as Robortello was well aware, he was following in the tradition of antiquity, when these arts were commonly seen as having the common purpose of arousing an emotional response in the audience.

The much shorter treatise *On Comedy* was part of Robortello's larger design to supply commentaries on a number of genres (including satire, epigram, and elegy), using "the method of Aristotle." Since Aristotle, he supposed, must have written a poetics of comedy, his disciple would make good its loss with a work that incorporated every remark on comedy in the *Poetics*. Where this procedure left gaps, Robortello adapted to comedy Aristotle's systematic and detailed analysis of tragic drama. On this basis, for example, the Aristotelian terms of "tying" and

---

[1] Page references (in parentheses in the introductory note and in the margins of the translation) are to the 1548 Florence edition of Robortello's text.

84

"untying" are applied to the comic plot, and Aristotle's short statements on characters in tragedy are used to reconstruct the qualities of the comic character.

For further reading
Beare 1950; Herrick, 1946; Weinberg 1952.

From his commentary on Aristotle's *Poetics*

1 Before attempting to unravel the fabric of this small treatise, it seems necessary to inquire into the nature of the poetic faculty and the power it has, the goal set for it, and the subject matter out of which it accomplishes its task. This final item should be treated first, for everything else will rather conveniently follow from it. The material basis, as it were, for the poetic faculty is discourse, as it is for all other activities that revolve around discourse. ... From among these each branch arrogates one kind: the demonstrative, truth; dialectic, the probable; rhetoric, persuasion; sophistic, what is probable, the kind that possesses verisimilitude; poetry, the false or the fabulous. This is the nature of the discourse poetry uses.

There are two types of discourse, one that is said to originate from the mouth, while the other springs from the depths of the heart and the recesses of the mind, or, if I may use the Greek terms ..., one resides in expression [*prophorikos*], the other in conception. The demonstrative appropriates "its demonstration from thought" [*apodeixin apo endiathetou*],
2 for everything it adduces is considered and weighed. All the others produce their syllogisms, arguments, sophisms, and stories, respectively, from expression [*apo prophorikou*]. ... From the foregoing, in my view, the nature of discourse available to each faculty for disposition, poetry's included, is quite clear. Since, then, poetry takes as its matter fictional and mythical discourse, clearly poetry's province is to shape myth and fiction in a suitable manner and no other art more properly devises fiction than poetry. ... To speak briefly: in poetic fictions false principles are taken up as true and from them are drawn true conclusions. There is no reason for anyone to think that all stories relate to poetry. For poetry speaks only of those things which are or could be or what long-standing opinion among men holds to exist. But it does not fabricate or name particular things which do not in fact exist, for since poetry strives above all to imitate, it can only imitate what exists and what performs some action. But if someone counters this with Cerberus and his three heads, the triune chimera and the rest of Hell's prodigies, I have already stated that poetry speaks also about those creatures which men reckon to exist, and poetry maintains as much of its power in these matters as if it were treating entities which exist in reality. Now it has been made plain enough, in my view, what subject matter the poetic mode has: discourse which is fictive, or mythical and full

of fictions. I have sufficiently explained how poets are to shape their fictions and what mythical material they should adopt or avoid.

Now it seems to follow ... that I should say something about the purpose of this mode. To a careful observer, poetry focuses all its power to create delight, although it is also useful. In human society there is no greater pleasure worthy of a noble-minded man than that which is perceived in the mind and thought. It frequently happens that things strike awe and terror into men, as long as they exist in their own nature. Yet when they are set outside nature and represented in a way close to it, they give great pleasure. No one looks without shuddering at the ferocious face of a lion or a bull striking with his horn or a slithering snake. But the same creatures, described in words or realized in stone or bronze or painted in colors, are viewed with pleasure. On the same principle, men enjoy sculpture in marble or bronze, painting, poetry, and all discourse which deals with description. What other end, then, shall we say the poetic mode has than to give delight by representation, description, and imitation of all human actions, every emotion, and every thing, living or inanimate? And since this imitation and representation occur through language, we hold that the end of poetry is discourse which imitates, just as in rhetoric it is language that persuades. Cicero's excellent remark about comedy can be applied to poetry as a whole, namely that it is the imitation of life, the mirror of manners, and the image of truth ⟨Dn/79⟩. That discourse may create a representation of the world is quite evident from the following train of reasoning, which is absolutely correct and quite unassailable. Thought receives images from objects. The mental images are expressed in words and speech. It can be inferred, then, that the representation of everything is brought about by language, written or spoken. The language of poetry does not represent the inner dispositions of virtues or vices but the very actions which result from any state. As this state lies hidden in the mind and is not available to our vision, it can only be represented by

3 actions, which everyone can perceive and judge. But representation belongs not only to poetry but also to the stage. There are, however, differences between the two. For actors have the ability and power to imitate and represent character, and emotions, roles, and actions of men so as to achieve plausibility and to persuade the audience and the spectators. The poet exercises all his power merely in expressing and describing the morality of men, so that he creates, as it were, a silent representation set in language. The actor, however, achieves a representation which is spoken and expresses what is to be represented by means of voice, speech, expression, and gesture, even though the actor's art is obviously dependent on poetry.

Poetry and acting are both concerned with making the minds of the readers and listeners, respectively, disposed to receive the image of the object they are trying to represent. For representation or action on the stage unites in some way the image of the thing represented and enacted with the thought and imagination of men, as if it joins the entity itself with thought. Representation of this kind has great power in moving and inflaming men's minds to anger and fury, then in recalling them to kindness and assuaging them, in stirring them to compassion, weeping, and tears, as well as to laughter and joy. To complete its imitation properly, poetry needs no supports drawn from elsewhere, such as notes, songs, metres, mime, and expression, and all the other devices which can be called theatrical. Nevertheless, it sometimes uses notes, masks, and gestures and many other procedures; they greatly assist in introducing all kinds of affection and distress into men's minds. It is for this reason that Aristotle very clearly declares ⟨Ar/37⟩ that notes, verses, and suchlike are a part or means of the poetic mode. . . .

But I return to the representation, which discourse creates. Not everyone can introduce representation into the listeners' minds. Nothing is more difficult to achieve than that men, on hearing something, should grasp it in their thoughts, as if they saw it with their own eyes. Only an educated, wise, sharp, and clever man can do this, a man who can clothe himself in ways that are foreign to him and take up the role of different men, as if he has forgotten his own existence. . . . Just as there are various poetic declamations and imitations, so they confer upon mankind usefulness of many kinds. For if one proclaims and imitates the virtues and praises of some outstanding man, people are spurred on to virtue. If, on the other hand, vices are portrayed, men are strongly deterred from them and are repulsed by a greater force than if one used any other exhortation. But if the representation and depiction of grisly and dangerous events is produced on stage, it reduces man's mindless effrontery and rashness. But if events that merit compassion are played out, the minds of the audience are moved to feel kindness and compassion. In brief: every imitation and poetic recital allied with action enlivens, softens, presses, incites, moves, and inflames men's souls. . . .

3   What differentiates tragedy and comedy arises from their subject matter. For since tragedy is engaged in the imitation and representation of the disasters and miseries of a king or some hero, it imitates above all men of outstanding type. By choice it unfolds the predicament of prominent people, since a greater degree of compassion is excited from their character than if the catastrophe of obscure and lowly people were passed in review. Comedy represents the somewhat insignificant and trivial actions of men. . . .

9   It is quite clear that men are driven to imitation from that fitting and forceful power of the faculty of the imagination. Young children mimic voices and actions, bird calls, and the sound of animals. . . . No animal does this except man and this distinguishes him from the beasts. It is for this reason that Aristotle here ⟨Ar/39⟩ remarks that men differ from other

creatures. .... Thus he teaches that one should proceed from some universal thing, which he has gradually inferred and observed from many individual items. For example, if one states that a lion is a four-footed animal, large, sandy-colored, with a mane, has small ears, longish tail, curved claws, short legs, is agile and swift, he could not have documented these details, had he not previously seen a lion and later, from the thought he had retained in his mind, described its shape and size in discourse, which represented the actual lion. Obviously, therefore, he teaches by imitation. The pupil who listens to the teacher has either seen a lion previously or will see one in the future. If he has seen it before, he recognizes its depiction in the man's language and learns it. If he sees it at some later date, he had heard about it, remembers its description, and observes that the characteristics he has heard about are present in the lion. He perceives in his [teacher's] words a kind of imitation of that creature. By this method he learns. It is, therefore, clear what Aristotle meant in stating that man learns through imitation. ....

30   The second reason is expressed in the words "the pleasure that all men take in works of imitation" ⟨Ar/39⟩; for, although men are very adept at imitation, unless some also felt pleasure in such imitation, they would not have pursued representation with any success. The next reason Aristotle adduces to show poetry's origin is a natural one; it is drawn from the end of poetry, for men derive pleasure from imitation. For poetry has a double end as its goal, and one is prior to the other. Imitation comes first and pleasure is second. Both, of course, are natural, for men are born with an aptitude for imitation and have been endowed by nature to derive pleasure from imitation or from matters given expression by representation. .... Aristotle argues ⟨Ar/39⟩ *a maiori* as follows: if men look with pleasure even upon horrible subjects in painting and sculpture, how much greater their pleasure will be when they contemplate the action of poetry, in which there is imitation, though not imitation of dreadful events. For poetry does not express or place before our eyes actual slaughter, wounds, and disgusting dismemberment, as Horace pointedly warned ⟨Hr/69: 185–87⟩ in his *Art of Poetry*. ....

What is the reason the two imitative arts of painting and sculpture represent fearful and horrible things but that the imitative art of poetry and the art of acting do not? One could easily answer this by stating that in the arts of painting and sculpture the imitation is, as it were, silent and lifeless; they do not portray the object of representation in the same nature and substance. But in poetry and on the stage, although there is imitation, just as in painting and sculpture, it is alive and almost identical, with this one exception, that it does not arise from the same things, for if it did, there would not be imitation. ....

46   He states ⟨Ar/41⟩ therefore that comedy is an imitation of persons who are inferior. .... Men are called wicked because of their vices. But not

all vices and faults are equal; some are rather trivial, others more serious. Even though comedy, then, has wickedness as its subject matter, that is man's vice, yet it does not include all vice but that aspect of it which is so unseemly that it provokes laughter rather than outrage or sympathy. The nature of this I can easily summarize: the unseemly includes both destructive and non-destructive parts. The former, according to Aristotle's *Rhetoric* Book 2[8.9], comprise blows, beatings, lack of food, bodily afflictions like old age and diseases. These inflict pain on the victim and arouse compassion in the spectator. Non-destructive elements bring to the victim not pain but embarrassment and shame. Aristotle defines the nature of these in *Rhetoric* Book 2[6.2–4]: "Shame," he says, "is a pain and mental discomfort that results from wrongdoing, because of which one must submit to disgraceful censure, for example, to desert one's position in the battle line or to throw away one's shield." ... Cicero's distinction in *De Oratore* Book 2[58.237], where he talks about the orator's wit, is fine and to our point. For he says that wretchedness does not invite laughter, for we tend to pity men in that state; indeed, it is the height of cruelty to try and get a laugh from someone else's misery. Extremely disgraceful and criminal acts arouse indignation and are meant to be crushed by a greater force.

7 Therefore, somewhat unseemly behavior excites laughter. ...

0   The third difference between epic and tragedy consists in the matter of length and space of time; for representation in tragedy does not exceed an imitation of events over a longer time than a single circuit of the sun ⟨Ar/41⟩. The words of the Greek text [*mian periodon heliou*] can appear ambiguous. Do they mean what is commonly termed by the mathematical astronomers a natural day or an artificial one? I would imagine that Aristotle meant the latter. The reason is this. Tragedy is an imitation of a single action, which is brought to a conclusion as soon as possible. The poet would not intermingle in his story anything which occurs in an epic, a poem of very great length, and his entire imitation is related to his audience. So it is eminently reasonable that there is an imitation of an action which is apparently completed in one day.

For at night men rest and enjoy their sleep; they do nothing and do not converse about anything. That these statements of mine are very accurate, anyone may observe from the writings of the ancients. To facilitate this, I shall attempt to lay down the rule using the *Oedipus Tyrannus* of Sophocles. He portrays the people of Thebes performing sacrifice in the morning to avert the gods' anger, for a plague had attacked the city. King Oedipus comforts them, telling them to cheer up; he will do everything which can appease the gods. Thus he has sent Creon to Apollo's oracle and is quite surprised that he is taking so long. While Oedipus is speaking, they see Creon approaching. Here one may observe Sophocles' care as a poet in writing this genre of poetry. Since he realized that the imitation of a tragic action must be completed in a day, he is continually hastening towards the end and reporting events close on the heels of the last. For if he had not entertained this consideration, what reason would he have for representing this timely arrival of Creon, with no intervening period of time? A little later it is possible to observe Sophocles with great aplomb hastening to the ending. For since he needed Tiresias to explain Apollo's oracle, Oedipus says he has already sent Creon to him. And while announcing this very fact, he [Sophocles] causes Tiresias to arrive. A little later when he represents Jocasta in conversation with Oedipus, relating how Laius was killed and how certain information needed the verification of the slave who had escaped unharmed (he was living as a shepherd tending the flocks of the king on the outskirts of the city), the slave had to be summoned. Therefore Sophocles interposes as much of a delay as suffices. For while Oedipus is talking with the messenger who has come from Corinth, the slave arrives and during his interrogation of the slave about all the details he had in the meanwhile heard from the messenger, Oedipus suddenly perceives the entire picture. In all these places, although a delay may be interposed, it is possible to see the poet hastening with great skill to complete his imitation of the tragic action in one day. ... My remarks about tragedy should also be applied in every way to comedy; for it completes its imitation in the same time as tragedy.

53   ... If anyone asks the nature of Aristotle's opinion about tragedy, my answer is that he thinks that the two emotions of pity and fear are purged when it is performed and seen ⟨Ar/42⟩. For when men are present at performances and they hear and see actors speaking and performing those things which closely approximate truth itself, they generally feel pain, fear, and compassion. The result is that when they themselves experience what all men must, they suffer less pain and fear. For it is unavoidable that the person who has never been troubled by any disaster will later undergo more violent grief, should any adversity happen to him unexpectedly. Further, men do not often experience genuine pain or fear. However, when poets in the performance of their tragedies present characters and events that merit great sympathy and the justifiable dread of everyone, even a sage, men learn the nature of those things which properly arouse compassion and grief and which produce fear. Finally the audience and the spectators receive from tragedy the supreme benefit that, since all people are subject to the same fate and nobody is immune from disasters, men endure with greater ease any misfortune that happens to them and support themselves with the very powerful consolation of recalling that the same disaster has occurred to others. ...

58   ... The end of imitation in tragedy is action, for tragedy imitates actions. The plot contains actions; therefore the plot is the end and the greatest of all the parts of tragedy. At this point one may object and assert that the end of tragedy is not to imitate actions but men themselves, as is obvious. But I would think that the answer must be that tragedy does indeed imitate men,

but not merely insofar as they are men, but insofar as they are men of action. Again a somewhat more pointed objection may be that the end of tragedy is apparently not the imitation of actions but rather the expression of the happiness or unhappiness in men's lives. To this the reply must also be that the life and happiness of men depend on actions and it is termed happy or not according to the manner in which a person has performed honorable or base deeds. Thirdly, another may state as an objection that the end of tragedy is not the imitation of actions but of men's characters, for it attempts to express them at every turn. To this I would like to say in response that in tragedy character is expressed, not by itself but through actions. For the nature of character is later discerned from them. But in the first instance tragedy does not try to effect the expression of character but an imitation of men in action, who are for that reason happy or not. ...

It must be noted, as we have also stated above, that the imitation in tragedy is viewed in two ways: insofar as it is dramatic and is performed by actors or insofar as it is a product of the poet's pen. If you understand it as the latter, we say that the primary end of tragedy is to imitate through written discourse the state of mind and character of men. From this description it can be seen whether men are happy or not. If you take it as the former (Aristotle always so takes it, when he talks about imitation), we say that the greatest and most powerful end is action itself, from which men are determined to be happy or unhappy. In the writing and imitation of the poets the following order is established: if one follows nature, there results character, which determines happiness or unhappiness. In the dramatic acting of actors as they recite, there arises action, from which issues happiness or unhappiness.

In tragedy the greatest end is that which expresses happiness or unhappiness very closely, in itself, instantly, and, as they say, directly. But if the imitation of tragedy is understood as it is acted on the stage (Aristotle always understands it so), it is the action itself that creates a very close and immediate expression of happiness or unhappiness. ...

36   Aristotle intimates ⟨Ar/45⟩ that it is the poet's function to procure a true action or to invent one. If the action he arrogates is true, he does not recount how it happened but how it could or ought to have happened. But if he devises it himself, he must invent according to the possible (I may so

37 render *to dynaton*) or necessary, or the probable and the verisimilar. ... But at this point there arises another question. When Aristotle states that a poet departs from the truth on condition that he invents nothing contrary to the possible, the necessary, or the verisimilar, his statement does not seem to be true and it can be shown by many arguments and examples. Homer and the poets wrote that the gods ate ambrosia and drank nectar; that the gods were wounded, like Venus; that the gods lived among mankind; that a way lay open to the gods of the underworld, as in Virgil; that the Cyclops and Sirens existed; that clouds spoke, as in Aristo-

phanes. . . . To this I reply that poets fashion and invent their fictions in two ways, either in matters according to nature or in matters contrary to nature. The latter case can also be divided in two ways, either in matters which have been already accepted by the opinion of people, or in matters never previously heard or narrated by another. If it happens according to nature, it is set within the will and authority of all writers, provided that probability and necessity [to eikos and anagkaion] are preserved. If it is contrary to nature, this is nobody's prerogative and it is altogether not permissible, but one may compose fictions only from a paralogism. Matters are above all spun from a paralogism, whenever false matters are taken as true. . . . To continue with the examples above: if the gods dine on ambrosia and drink nectar, this is contrary to nature, but it is drawn from a paralogism, because it has been so received into people's opinion. . . . The case is the same in all the remaining cases, although tragedy and comedy do not admit fictions of this kind, even if man's opinion has established them. It is for this reason that Horace states ⟨Hr/69: 187–88⟩ in his *Art of Poetry*: "Procne must not be turned into a bird or Cadmus into a snake. Whatever you thus show me, I disbelieve and abominate."

This reason can be adduced: in tragedy and comedy there is an imitation of men performing some action according to nature. The epic admits some things, such as the stories about Circe, the Sirens, and the Cyclops. These are not included in tragedy, because it is not produced by description [di'appangelian], that is, by a report, as the epic is. In a narration, many events can be related, however marvelous [thaumasta] and contrary to the belief of men, which otherwise cannot be performed by actors on stage in front of spectators. Thus the same situation prevails in comedy, although comedy does not admit even the incidents that tragedy does, like conver-
88   sations with gods, whether conducted from a machine or in other ways. I am speaking now about New Comedy, for all these things were admitted by Old Comedy. To the question why New Comedy did not allow them, I would imagine the answer must be that it rejected all fiction and began to express only the base actions of men. Therefore epic admits more than tragedy, tragedy more than comedy, while the latter admitted no fiction at all, except "what is necessary and probable" [to anagkaion kai eikos]. . . .

93   At this point one could object to Aristotle as follows: Aristotle, in his desire to prove that poetry is concerned with universals, stated ⟨Ar/46⟩ that this was clear from the procedure of the comic poets, who in addition to inventing plot and action also provide names. This is true for the actions in comedy but the case is otherwise in tragedy, where real names are retained. So Aristotle does not seem to have proved to his satisfaction that poetry deals with universals, because it imposes names. Aristotle replies that all these things are utterly true, but it is no accident that in tragedy the true names of characters are preserved. For since tragedy contains the imitation and the portrayal of people in action, the matter, as enacted,

must not only be verisimilar and probable, but also true, and there must be expressed the true names of the actual characters, who first carried out the action in fact. For there is no reason for anyone to believe that the plots of tragedy were the poets' inventions; they were clearly taken from the greatest calamities which happened to heroes and kings. For this reason, a little later Aristotle says that the plots of tragedy are few, for incidents of this kind are rare. What is the reason for the retention of true names in tragedy? Tragedy has as its goal the movement of two of the mind's greatest emotions, pity and fear. It is much more difficult to arouse these feelings than the others which provoke a more pleasant reaction, such as hope, laughter, and suchlike. For men are naturally inclined to pleasant things and are averse to unpleasant ones. They cannot easily be driven to feel grief. They must therefore know that the incident happened in that way before. But if the plot of a tragedy contains an action which did not occur and is not true but is an invention, based on verisimilitude, of the poet himself, it will perhaps move the audience's sensibility but certainly not as much. For we feel pleasure in verisimilitude, a delight that derives altogether from the fact that we know it is grounded in the true. Since generally verisimilitude shares in the true, it has the power to move and be convincing. Aristotle, therefore, argues *a maiori* thus: if incidents based on verisimilitude move us, true ones will move us much more. The former arouse us, since we believe that it was possible that the incident happened in this way. True matters move us because we know that they did happen as represented. Whatever power, then, resides in the verisimilar is taken over completely from the truth. ....

8   From certain words which have been set out in defining tragedy, Aristotle now deduces another precept of the following kind. A tragic
9   action must entail compassion and terror. This follows from our previous statement that in the performance of tragedies two of the mind's greatest emotions, pity and fear, are purged. In this text Aristotle, then, sets out two points, first the precept I have set out, then how each one is produced separately, so that pity is properly evoked and fear inspired. ... Both emotions cannot always coexist in a single matter but sometimes one of the two is separated. Examples from tragedies will be able to make this clear. In Euripides' *Iphigenia*, the slaughter of foreigners causes fear. In the *Ajax* of Sophocles the gods cast madness over men and this certainly produces terror and fear. Both are present in the *Oedipus*: inasmuch as Oedipus lacks foresight and is guided by fate, his descent to great disaster excites fear. For no one has ever taken adequate caution against fate's force through intelligence. On the other hand, with the loss of his eyesight he becomes utterly pitiable, though he had previously been extremely fortunate and highly placed. This produces pity. In the *Electra* there is only the element of pity. .... Aristotle dwells on the interrelationship of pity and fear in the *Rhetoric*, Book 2[8.12]. Here he states that Amasis shed not a

tear when he saw his son being dragged off to his death but he did weep at the sight of a destitute friend begging, because this aroused compassion but the former event struck terror. Whenever dread attacks and seizes the human mind, it drives out all compassion, for this feeling affects the mind before anything frightful is brought on. ... Both pity and fear must be present in tragedy. ...

113   The recognition we are presently discussing seems to be especially a characteristic of the tragedians, as can be illustrated in the case of Oedipus when the question is raised whether or not he killed his father Laius or whether or not he slept with his mother Jocasta. My answer is that poets pose these questions in a different way from that used by orators. Firstly, in poetry the person who is the subject of the inquiry is unaware of his actions, whereas with orators the person is fully aware but denies them. Secondly, in tragedy, that person voluntarily investigates the matter and its present status, because he hopes that he will be freed from all suspicion, like Oedipus in Sophocles' play. In the case of orators, the defendant avoids every attempt to investigate the crime, because he knows he did it. In tragedy if anyone is convicted on the evidence for the crime, people are amazed at how he acted in ignorance, driven by fate. When anyone is convicted of a crime before orators and judges, he takes it badly that it has been uncovered by his opponent's shrewdness and no amazement is aroused in the case. In tragedy, the person deserves to be excused or pitied because he acted in ignorance, whereas in the courts he merits punishment because he is discovered to have acted infamously in committing the crime. Furthermore, in tragedy, a reversal attends the discovery of whether the person committed the act or not, whereas when the deed is established in the courts, it does not, for the entire dispute seems to have been brought to an immediate end at that point, so that there is no need for further inquiry. Finally orators draw their arguments from what is probable, which are almost all from outside the case, cleverly devising conjectures based on the upbringing, disposition, and nature of the accused or the defendant. They either prove the crime or not. Tragedians produce recognition from signs which are in the subject matter itself, thus in the case of Sophocles' Oedipus, from the scar and the crippled feet,[2] from the crossroads and the retinue, and many others.

129   In tragedy ... poets must have as their aim the arousal of pity and fear, yet these emotions are aroused not by words that induce tears or fear or by

130   acts of savagery and horror but rather by the actual characters, around whom the tragedy revolves. For an incident might perhaps be in itself cruel, arouse compassion, and further be expressed in language that elicits tears, but because it happens to a man of bad character, it fails to stir pity. The character, therefore, and not the event, causes this, the character who

---

[2] Robortello's text as printed has *humore pedum*; for this translation this is assumed to be a misprint for *tumore pedum*.

is the victim of some calamity. In my view, it might be best to group the three types of actions unsuitable for tragedy. Firstly, the fall of a good man into unhappiness, then the attainment of happiness by a man of evil and dishonest character, and finally a reprobate's descent into misery. ... It remains that only one way of creating a tragedy is permissible, namely one that arises from the fate and action of some wretch who lies midway between the extremes of the good and the bad. ... Clearly, a man who commits an offense, yet does so in ignorance, has to be placed at a point
32   midway between the good and the bad. ... There is one other requirement in this type of action and in the tragic character under discussion: the offense should be great and detestable and the character should fall from the pinnacle of happiness to the deepest misery. For if the offense is negligible or the unhappiness not great enough, it will inevitably follow that the compassion aroused is also inconsiderable. But the element of compassion must be the greatest possible in order that it may have a greater effect and arousal on the minds of the audience. ...
42   The uncultivated and ignorant crowd of men, led by feeling and opinion rather than by intelligence, knowledge, and skill, invariably disagrees with what is right and approved by discriminating men. Poets once used to pander to the tastes of the mob and composed the kinds of stories they thought could be acceptable to it, and abandoned the art, which proposes a guideline for writing properly. For art demands that the two greatest emotions of the mind, pity and fear, about which we have spoken in the definition of tragedy, must be purged by the performance of tragedies. Men, however, who are more easily inveigled by pleasures and delights, often shun disastrous and tragic events, because they are unpleasant. Accordingly, they demand a happy ending to the action, to prevent terror and pity from causing them perpetual anguish and oppression and allowing their return to the happiness they felt before. ...
46   ... At this point someone perhaps may wonder why Aristotle says pleasure is felt from tragedy. For if tragedy arouses pity and fear, two emotions reckoned bad, how do they give pleasure and what is the pleasure that affects the audience? It is as if events, which occasion mourning and grief, conferred gaiety and pleasure. What balanced man would ever make such claims? But I answer that the pleasure taken from tragedy is the product of imitation. The great power this has to divert the mind can be sufficiently understood from the fact that even dreadful things, if presented to us portrayed in an imitation, produce delight and pleasure. ... This then is the nature of the pleasure derived from tragedy. Similar to this is that pleasure emanating from comedy, inasmuch as it contains an imitation. Comedy then gives delight, because it presents a joyous imitation of men's ridiculous actions, while tragedy does so by artfully representing mankind's sadness, grief, and catastrophe. Which of the two confers the greater pleasure? I would venture to say the pleasure of tragedy

is much greater, for it penetrates our minds more deeply, is a rather rare occurrence in our experience, and a greater force is generated by that representation. Therefore, our knowledge of the greater difficulty involved in expressing this imitation causes us to admire it the more, if it has been carried off, and to experience greater pleasure. ...

167   Goodness in a character should not be considered in itself in some simple way but on account of the things in which it is present. For the same manners, which elicit praise in one person, may not be praiseworthy in another. As examples, I may cite Nestor, Socrates, an honest man or woman, an honest slave, anyone who among his kind is honest. But if this man is compared with another, he is less virtuous; indeed, he can be called dishonest, so great is the dissonance and chasm that exists in morals according to the persons involved. Take some slave who is not a thief. In a slave this will constitute the highest virtue and goodness; in the case of an outstanding man and a hero, it would be no praise. Weaving, embroidery, and spinning are praised in a woman, but not in a man. ... Therefore the praise appropriate for people of lower rank is no longer praise, if it is attributed to people high on the social scale. ... Aristotle's view is that the attribution of a wife's goodness to a man diminishes it. If a slave's character is assigned to a king or some nobleman, he will be able to be seen not only as worse but wicked. Thus it is evident that what constituted goodness in a slave is a vice in a king. Therefore a wife is virtuous, if she is chaste, modest, silent, and dutiful to her husband. A good slave is loyal, industrious, compliant, and obliging to his lord. A king is good, if he is just, alert, and discharges his duty towards his subject people. ... The second requirement in character is that it should be appropriate. Bravery is a supreme virtue but if attributed to a woman, and if a poet portrays a brave woman, who is like Achilles as represented by Homer, it will not be seen to suit her. ...

181   Aristotle supplies another precept which refers to the theory of depicting manners; it is drawn from certain assertions that have been proved earlier: ... that comedy imitates "worthless people" [ton phauloteron]; the other, however, is that tragedy imitates more outstanding people. Repeating this conclusion, Aristotle draws from it a particularly necessary precept of the following nature. Since tragedy imitates "better people" [beltionon], it must be observed that in describing manners, the poet should represent them in as appropriate and refined a way as possible. This will happen, if he does not look piecemeal at the manners of the character he is portraying and imitating, but at nature herself and the perfect model for manners, whose description must be undertaken. So that if he wants to imitate a person quick to anger, he would look not at the man he intends to represent but to nature and the absolute model of anger. If the character is to be portrayed as brave and just, he should turn his attention on to the model for bravery

and justice. This procedure was observed with precision by Homer, especially in Agamemnon, Ulysses, Nestor, and Achilles. . . .

23   The third component of tragedy, as stated above, is thought, called *dianoia* by Aristotle ⟨Ar/57⟩ and all the other Greek rhetors. . . . From this point one may recognize that poetry follows rhetoric and must be assigned a secondary position. In addition, it is more characteristic of rhetoric than poetry to consider "the thoughts expressed in speeches" [*tas dianoias ton logon*]. For rhetoric expresses the natural speech which is our natural endowment. Poetry, however, takes a speech expressed in rhetorical terms, produces it in a metrical arrangement, and tries to make it similar to a rhetorical speech. The power of rhetoric above all assumes the task of appropriately shaping thought so that it instructs one to speak as the dignity of the theme demands. Important and pleasant thoughts must be devised and simultaneously be arranged and filled out. Otherwise the speech would be like a very ancient picture drawn in a limited number of colors. It is not enough to produce the thought. Care must be taken over its ending and rhythm. The gravest defect in thought is lightness, for weight and dignity are required. The former quality may be found in thought, if it expresses matters appropriately and includes many elements at the same time. Relevant to thought, then, is everything which is produced to signify, prove, or refute anything. . . . The poet almost never produces thought in a naked and unadorned way but he always clothes it in some dress. . . . In the text Aristotle says ⟨Ar/57⟩ there are five parts or functions of thought: to prove, refute, stimulate emotions, amplify, and play down. Obscure points are proved and opposing and contrary forces are resolved. Stimulation refers to the audience's minds. Spare and slight matters are enlarged, great and important issues are diminished. It is the duty of both poet and orator to effect these things, for they fall under the conversation which all men

24 share. Aristotle, in Book 2 of the *Rhetoric* [2.20–25], provides topics for corroborating and refuting arguments and proves his entire case with numerous examples drawn from the poets, because the latter use them no less than the orators. . . . An orator strives to arouse these emotions the more easily to persuade. . . . The poet does so to gain his particular goal, which is to drive men's feelings into different emotions, whatever may be the nature of the material in the subject matter he is treating and representing. . . .

7

JULIUS CAESAR SCALIGER
(c. 1484–1558)

The writing of the *Poetices libri septem* occupied most of the last decade of Scaliger's life and the appearance in 1561 of this highly systematic theory of poetry and drama set the seal on his vast reputation as an interpreter of Aristotle, theorist, and critic. The first four of the seven books of the *Poetices* are concerned with theory; the next two are essentially practical, containing critical judgments on a variety of authors, ancient and modern; and the final book constitutes an appendix of sorts to the first six. The work was so fundamental to the dramatic and poetic theory of the late sixteenth and early seventeenth centuries that allusions to Aristotle were, in fact, often allusions to Scaliger. In England, Sidney and Jonson were both deeply influenced by the Scaligerian mediation of Aristotle.

Scaliger begins his treatise with a detailed defense of poetry, especially against the Platonic charge that poets pose a moral danger to society. For Scaliger, poetry is a given of nature that can help man attain happiness (*beatitudo*) and is no less vital than the study of philosophy; further, the creative and inspired poet can reveal what is hidden from others, and his god-like activity is superior to all other human pursuits. Scaliger's exhaustive taxonomy of the constituents of poetry, however, makes it clear that the imaginative power (*ingenium*) of the poet must be tempered by knowledge and mastery of the art that the *Poetices* attempts to codify.

Scaliger's theory of poetry is decidedly didactic. While he does not deny the value of imitation, he rejects the idea that it may be an end in itself. Imitation, he says, has for "its further end, instruction" (1.1.1).[1] The instruction is intended to achieve the practical result of stimulating virtuous actions by means of the pleasurable lessons embodied as examples in the work. Like Robortello before him, Scaliger lays heavy emphasis on verisimilitude as the aspect of imitation that contributes most to the persuasiveness of the work.

The poet, says Scaliger, has to have certain abilities that enable him to achieve the required impact on his public and so fulfill the task of poetry (3.25.113). Poetry itself is seen pre-eminently as an art of discourse and one of its essential characteristics for Scaliger (who dissents in this respect from Aristotle) is metre. Defining poetry as a verse art, Scaliger divides it (1.3.6) into three large groups: the first works of simple narration, as exemplified by the didactic poetry of Lucretius; the second a variety of dramatic forms; and the third a "mixed" group including epic and other genres. By far the most detailed treatment is reserved for epic and drama, especially tragedy. Though he cites Aristotle's definition of tragedy, Scaliger modifies it by adding details of his own (1.6.12) and ultimately demands that it teach, move, and delight (3.97.144), that is, that it adopt the goals so often proposed for

---

[1] The reference is to the book, chapter, and page numbers in Scaliger [1561] 1964. In the text below the location of the beginning of each extract is so indicated.

rhetoric. He qualifies Aristotle's theory in appearing to give character primacy over plot in tragedy. He tends clearly towards an idea of conventionalized characterization and, like many of his contemporaries, he makes the social rank of the characters the line of demarcation between tragedy and comedy.

In his discussion of comedy Scaliger is briefer. He records his objections to Donatus' definition, attributed to "the Greeks" (Dn/79), as inadequate and offers one of his own (1.5.11). He also introduces a new structural category, *catastasis*, that Jonson, among others, found useful. Scaliger's view of comedy may also be gauged from his unconventional downgrading of Terence's plays as insipid and his praise for the vitality and genius of Aristophanes.

For further reading

Beare 1946; Blanchard 1983; Euripides (ed. Seaford) 1984; Ferraro 1971; Hall 1945, 1948; McPherson 1971; Montgomery 1979; Somville 1975; Weinberg 1942, 1961; Donatus/Wessner 1962–63.

From *Poetices libri septem*

1.1 The necessity, origin, use, goal, and manner of discourse

All human activity is included in the category of necessity, utility, or pleasure, but the power of expressing these things in language was bestowed by a certain nature, established from the start or later with the advance of time. For man, whose accomplishment was to depend on the branches of knowledge, could not have done without that instrument which inevitably made him participate in knowledge of the world. Moreover, discourse is, as it were, the conveyer of the spirit, which, by the possibility of communication it offers us, allows political gatherings to take place, cultivates the arts, and establishes bonds of intelligence between man and society. For we have to ask others for things we lack, order the doing of what has not been done, prohibit, propose, dispose, decide, and abolish. This was the nature of discourse at its start. But soon its use and usefulness were increased with the addition of dimensions, prescriptions, and outlines to this primitive and incomplete entity. From this emerged a fixed law for discourse. Finally there occurred the discovery of ornament, like a dress or some item of clothing so that the matter, permeated with form and spirit, might sparkle. Just as on an undefined body geometry imposes sides, angles, and straight lines and masters of harmony also add measures which the Greeks call "rhythms," so a law first added to uncouth discourse what writers on the subject have termed rules. ... Refinement of this kind, or, as it were, defensive armor protected the soldier to meet any necessity or it clothed the senator with the utility a toga could provide; similarly, a more elegant cloak adorned a rather smart citizen and gave him pleasure. Therefore, discourse had ends little different from these. Necessity produced discourse to facilitate the investigation of truth among philosophers, but speech was cultivated by wise politicians for its utility and it was pleasure that introduced it into the theatre. Philosophical discourse, circumscribed by the confined ambit of argumentation, was appropriately terse and on a level with the nature of the subject being explained. However, in the forum or among soldiers, it could be more expansive depending on theme, place, time, and people; this expertise was called oratorical.

The third mode has two kinds, not very dissimilar; they possess a shared matter in their common form of exposition and much embellishment. However, they differ in that the credibility of one is unerring; it professes and produces the truth, weaving its discourse out of a rather simple thread. The other adds fictive events to the true or imitates the truth with fiction, with greater splendor however. But both types, as stated, would have performed the function of narrative equally. However, it happened that the name of history was applied only to the former, because it was satisfied by the movement of discourse that simply explained what had happened.

The latter type received the name of poetry because it not only reproduced with words things which actually exist, but also represented things which did not exist, as if they did, and in the manner they might and ought to exist. It is for this reason that imitation is the foundation of all poetry. This is the intermediate end which leads towards the ultimate goal, which is to teach while giving pleasure. For the poet also teaches and not only gives pleasure, as certain people used to think. ...

I.5.II Comedy

... On the subject of comedy, the grammarians have presented false information in stating that, because it is a poem grounded in imitation, it consists entirely of gesture and speeches. But surely comedy exists nonetheless even when it is read silently. Further, gesture belongs only to those who read aloud, but not everybody who reads does so aloud. It has already been often stated that imitation is the end of all poetry. Accordingly, we must define comedy as follows: it is a dramatic poem, full of intrigue, happy in its outcome, in a style accessible to the people. The following definition for the Roman playwrights is untenable: "Comedy is an episode involving ordinary people and civil affairs, with no danger" ⟨Dn/79⟩. In the first place, this definition is applicable to other non-dramatic poems, which can be performed with a simple narrative. Further, in comedy danger is ever present, otherwise the outcomes would be extremely dull. For what is danger if it is not the approach or the onset of threatening catastrophe? In addition, there are not merely perils, but even losses for pimps, rivals, slaves, and masters, as in the *Asinaria* and *Mostellaria*.[2]

Even the masters themselves are roughly handled. Furthermore, the

---

[2] Two comedies of Plautus (born c. 255 B.C.), the Roman playwright who adapted his works from the New Comedy of several Greek dramatists.

praetextatae should not on this definition be termed comedy, for they do not deal with private citizens. Finally the definition includes mimes and dramatic satire. At Athens, Crates did away with metre and was the first to present comedy in prose ⟨Ar/41⟩.

11 **Tragedy**

Tragedy, like comedy, is fashioned on portraits from human life, though it differs from comedy in three ways: in the status of its characters, in the nature of the circumstances and affairs that happen in them, and in the outcome. These three differences necessarily entail a difference in style. In comedy, characters like Chremes, Davus, and Thais are of low extraction and are drawn from villages.[3]

The beginnings are somewhat chaotic, the endings happy; the language is drawn from that of ordinary life. In tragedy, there are kings and princes from cities, fortresses, and castles. The start is rather calm but the outcome is horrible. The language is majestic, refined, and far removed from everyday speech. It shows nothing but anxiety, fears, threats, exiles, and death. Tradition has it that Archelaus, King of Macedon, the confidant and patron of Euripides, asked the poet to write a tragedy about him. Euripides replied that he hoped to heaven that disaster of that magnitude would not befall him.

Tragedy derived its name from the type of drama performed in honor of the god to whom a goat was sacrificed. The winners, presented with the goat, then offered it as an act of worship to the god. It is a matter of record that tragedy began to be performed during the vintage. ...

... Here is the definition offered by Aristotle ⟨Ar/41⟩: "Tragedy, then, is the imitation of a good action, which is complete and of a certain length, by means of language made pleasing for each part separately; it relies in its various elements not on narrative but on acting; through pity and fear it achieves the purgation [catharsis] of such." At this point I do not wish to oppose this definition other than by appending my own. Tragedy is an imitation through actions of the fate of a famous person, unhappy in its outcome, in stately language in poetic metre. The addition of song and music are not, according to the philosophers, of the essence of tragedy. For tragedy would only have existed on stage; without that, tragedy would not have existed. As for Aristotle's phrase that tragedy must "possess magnitude" ⟨Ar/41⟩, this was established to differentiate it from epic, which is sometimes lengthy, though not invariably, as is seen in the work of Musaeus.[4]

Further, the word *catharsis* is by no means useful for any subject matter whatsoever, as is the case for "magnitude." In this context "magnitude"

---

[3] Chremes, Davus, and Thais are characters in Terence's comedies, *Adelphi, Andria, Phormio,* and *Eunuchus.*

[4] Musaeus was a fifth-century A.D. Greek poet and grammarian.

means a happy medium, for the expectation of the audience cannot be sated with a few verses. The audience comes together for the express purpose of exchanging the tedium of countless days for several hours' diversion. Prolixity is also unsuitable when you are moved to deliver the witticism of Plautus [*Menaechmi* 882]: "My back aches from sitting, my eyes from watching."

1.9.15   **The parts of comedy and tragedy**

... The legitimate parts [of comedy] are those without which the play cannot exist and by which it must be contained. The *protasis* is the part where a summary of the action is laid out and narrated without revealing the ending. This is a procedure requiring some subtlety, since it always keeps the audience's mind in suspense and anticipation. If the outcome is announced at the start, the play becomes somewhat dull. Although one grasps everything from the plot, nevertheless the *protasis* contains a brief intimation so presented that it does not so much satisfy the imagination as fire it. The *epitasis* is the part where confusion is set in motion or directed. The *catastasis* contains the activity and the crux of the plot, where the situation is drawn and embroiled in the storm of fortune. This component has not been noticed by many but it is essential. *Catastrophe* is the transformation of the intrigue which has been stirred up into a calmness not anticipated. To these parts was added, as we have stated, a prologue, which certain critics attribute only to Latin playwrights.

... An act is so called from the actions undertaken by all, because the entire genre is "dramatic" [*dramatikon*]. It is part of the plot containing different actions to match the difference of the parts, as we have stated. They are designated in an order which encloses them with the number five and it is inappropriate for there to be more or less than five ⟨Hr/69:189⟩. They are marked off from one another by the appearance of some new character. Afterwards, one may find a different procedure. Donatus says that the same character does not make more than five entrances on stage, though this is incorrect.[5] Immediately in the *Andria* itself Davus shows that this is not the case. ...

A scene is part of an act, in which two or more people converse. It begins sometimes with the entry of all the players and at other times with that of one person only, who then discovers someone else from the preceding scene. A scene is concluded when everybody leaves or occasionally when only one individual makes an exit. So that if there were three characters, the two persons remaining would constitute a scene. Sometimes a single character is left on his own for the next scene.

---

[5] See *Andria, praefatio* 2.3 (in Donatus/Wessner 1962–63, I:38.17–39.11); *Adelphi, praefatio* 1.4 (in Donatus/Wessner 1962–63, II:4.7–14); Beare 1946; Blanchard 1983, 43–50.

18 **The parts of tragedy**

Tragedies also are divided into almost the same parts as comedy. I mean the *protasis* and the rest, likewise acts and scenes. *Protasis* and *catastrophe* do not differ in type but in manner. For both are full of activity. *Catastrophe* added death or exile to those disorders. However, it was common for both to have on occasion an outcome mingled with sadness and happiness. For, in the *Asinaria*, *Casina*, and *Persa*, one may find happy and sad people at the same time. One finds even a soldier who is severely punished.[6]

A comedy was written about him, nonetheless. For if the outcome of comedy is happy and a soldier is the subject of a comedy, the soldier ought to have a happy ending. Similarly, in the *Antigone*, a mother and an adulterer are killed; but the young maidens dance with joy. So in Euripides' play also, the demise of Eurysteus alone fills the hearts of many with joy. In tragedy, however, new acts are not always constituted by a new character, as may be observed in many cases. . . .

20 **Characters in comedy**

. . . A character has been given more than one definition. . . . A character is a fictive living entity placed on stage, who imitates an actual one. We have described an actual character in its proper place. The nature of a man I placed in his character and in his fortune. In this way we comprehend his mental state and the reason for this disposition in every sex and condition. It imitates by name, body, character, words, deeds, feelings, and deportment. I say "a living entity" to distinguish it from fictive places, which also represent actual places. "A living entity" is a universal term by which I can include even frogs. . . . So too clouds, birds, wasps, and other things. Why should they not be accepted as characters? They are given speeches, arguments and plans.[7]

The same holds for ghosts in the shapes of the dead which are introduced in place of the actual body of Polydorus in Euripides and that of Darius by Aeschylus.[8]

. . . Characters are distinguished in comedy on the basis of their circumstances, profession, duty, age, and sex. Circumstances I call the state of every lot, for it is, as it were, a kind of trade where Fortune acts as the artisan: a slave, a freedman, a freeman, the father or the son of a household, a virgin, a bachelor, a husband. A profession is the condition whereby a person undertakes some act for the business of living: a soldier, his servant, farmer, pimp, banker, whore, merchant, or sailor. Duty in comedy is much different from the way philosophers see it. For they

---

6 The *Asinaria*, *Casina*, and *Persa* are *fabulae palliatae* of Plautus. At the conclusion of his *Miles Gloriosus*, the *miles*, Pyrgopolynices, is flogged as an adulterer.

7 Scaliger is referring to the choruses of the *Clouds* (423 B.C.), *Wasps* (422 B.C.) and *Birds* (414 B.C.) of Aristophanes.

8 The ghost of Polydorus, the son of Priam and Hecuba, delivers the opening speech of Euripides' *Hecuba*; Darius appears as a ghost in Aeschylus' *Persae* (681f.).

do not separate duty from virtue. In comedy a pimp exclaims that he is doing his duty, when he corrupts young people ... Here then duty is the right to act which pertains to all conditions. Age is the measurement of life, varied according to the change imposed by growth: infancy, boyhood, puberty, the age of youth, moderate age ... followed by old age and then dotage or extreme old age, which comic writers call "headed for the grave."[9]

For these various names are suited, taken from the countryside or the towns. Slaves are usually called Davus, Syrus, or Sosia. ...

1.16.24 **Characters in tragedy**

It is right that in tragedy the characters of kings, generals, soldiers, and messengers assume no other nature than the one supported by reality. The Greeks, however, establish some characters so far from the seriousness that tragedy demands that they appear ridiculous. However, for the sake of fullness, I have decided that not even these should be omitted. All characters should possess dignity and stature. ...

3.1.80 **The division of things**

As previously stated, poetry is an imitation. Four questions must be asked: first, the object of imitation, followed by the why, thirdly, the end of imitation, and fourthly, the manner. ... Let us now see what we should imitate. Everything which concerns us is divided between words and reality. Words, as we have already stated, make up the parts and the matter of discourse, their arrangement and their lay-out provide, as it were, their form, but we will take it up again. As for reality, it is the end of discourse and words serve as signs for reality. For this reason, it is from reality that they receive their form by which they are what they are. ...

3.25.113 **On the four virtues of the poet**

... Since the orators of early times acted only with a view to affect people, their attempts at persuasion were uncouth. Poets, however, aimed exclusively to entertain, by whiling away leisure hours by the sole means of alluring songs. Later both borrowed from the other the element each lacked. Tradition holds that Isocrates was the first to add rhythm to discourse in its early stages, although scholars who have more carefully sifted the matter itself among the literary evidence have given that honor to Thrasymachus, whose efforts were further advanced by Gorgias.[10]

---

[9] Plautus, *Miles Gloriosus* 628.
[10] Isocrates (436–338 B.C.), an Athenian orator, speech-writer and pupil of Gorgias, was a careful stylist who paid particular attention to rhythm in prose. Thrasymachus (fl. 430–400 B.C.) is best known from the portrait by Plato in the *Republic*, Book 1. Gorgias of Leontium, a fifth-century B.C. rhetorician, was "clever at speaking" according to Plato (*Symposium* 198c) and was noted for his prose style.

Finally the Isocrates already mentioned provided the finishing touch. To the rhythms and the tone of the poets was added at a later date the vital principle; when they were transferred from the countryside to the city, they incorporated short stories to point a moral and maxims to impart advice. Horace gave perfect expression to this idea with his verse: "the person who commingled the useful with the delightful won the applause of all" ⟨Hr/74:343⟩ so that poetry's total force may be completed under two heads: teaching and imparting pleasure. Both of these goals were attained by poets who related events that were rather close to reality and were always consistent with themselves, and who took pains to season everything with variety. For nothing is more unfortunate than to sate the audience before is is satisfied. For what kind of banquet is it which produces disgust instead of pleasure? The third quality is what I call liveliness. ... This quality you will find in few poets. It is a certain energy found not only in themes but also in language, which drives even an unwilling listener to pay attention. The fourth quality is pleasantness, which draws the lively energy of that vividness away from the roughness which so often accompanies it, to a specified balance. Let these stand as the most important attributes of a poet: skill, variety, liveliness, and pleasantness.

44 Tragedy and comedy

Tragedy, though similar to this epic poetry, differs in this respect, that it seldom admits characters of low rank, such as messengers, merchants, sailors, and their kind. Conversely, powerful people are never found in comedy, except in a few cases, such as Plautus' light-hearted treatment in the *Amphitryo*. ...[11]

... Tragedy and comedy share the same mode of representation but their arrangement and themes are different. The themes of tragedy are sublime and dreadful, such as the commands of monarchs, slaughters, suicides, exiles, bereavements, parricides, incests, fires, battles, blindings, tears, wailings, complaints, funerals, funeral orations, and dirges. Comedy includes jesting, banquets, weddings, drinking, cunning slaves, drunkenness, old men deceived and cleaned out of their cash. ...

45 ... Tragedy is completely serious. Certainly genuine tragedy is. Some of them were satyr-plays, which differed little from comedy apart from the serious demeanor of certain characters, such as Euripides' *Cyclops* ⟨Gu/151⟩.[12]

All is wine and jokes, with an ending so happy that all Ulysses' companions are freed. Only the Cyclops loses his eye. ... Many comedies have

---

[11] In the *Amphitryo* of Plautus, Jupiter appears in the guise of Amphitryo, a great commander.
[12] The *Cyclops* is the only surviving satyr-play. It was written c. 410 B.C.; see Euripides, ed. Seaford, 1984.

endings that are unhappy for some, such as Plautus' *Miles*, *Asinaria*, *Persa*, and others. Several tragedies are no less happy. In Euripides' *Electra* many people experience joy, if we discount Aegisthus' murder. In both the *Ion* and the *Helen* the outcome is joyful. Aeschylus' *Eumenides* contains tragic material in the slaughter and the avenging spirits, yet its structure is closer to comedy. The start brings joy to the guard but it distresses Clytemnestra on account of her husband's arrival. The murder follows with the consequent happiness for Electra and Orestes. The outcome is happy for everyone, Apollo, Orestes, the people, Pallas, and the Furies, so that previous statements that an unhappy ending is a property of tragedy goes by the board, provided that it contains within the body of the work frightful events.

Since plots are quarried from history, care must be taken not to deviate much from it. But early poets were by no means scrupulous about this. For Aeschylus followed Greek history in fixing Prometheus to a rock but he invented his death by a thunderbolt to bring his tragedy to an end on this note. For there would have been nothing dreadful at the end but only at the start when he was fixed to the Caucasus. Some tell that Hercules drove away the eagle, others that it was killed by arrows and that Prometheus was freed by Jupiter, because he had warned the god not to sleep with Thetis, for she would bear a son greater than his father. Even Euripides invented material about Helen which published stories strongly opposed. They reproached Euripides with having brought onto the stage criminal and infamous women. What is more loathsome than Phaedra, Jocasta, Canace, and Pasiphae, whose immorality caused people to become worse? In reply Euripides held that he had not depicted invented women but such women as had existed.[13]

Further, histories themselves must be done away with, if all wickedness was to be suppressed; it was for this reason that comedies were valued, because through knowledge of them the vices mentioned in them were condemned, especially in cases where a miserable death fell to women who had led an immoral life. There are two kinds of thoughts and tragedy as a whole must be supported by both, for they constitute, as it were, the columns and pillars of the entire structure of tragedy. An example of a short and simple thought is: death rewards the good. The second type is colorful and extended; thus the previous statement can be recast as follows: Do not think that the good perish; their soul, immortal in itself, flies away from these miseries to the abode from where it had set out. ... The events themselves must be so drawn out and arranged that they approximate the truth as near as possible. The play should not present such a spectacle that the audience is awe-struck or excited (a fault that

---

[13] Aristophanes (*Frogs* 850, 1042–43) states that Euripides had introduced onto the stage women such as Phaedra and Stheneboea; cf. *Frogs* 1078–81.

critics state Aeschylus continually committed); it must be a vehicle for teaching, stirring the emotions, and giving pleasure. We are delighted by joking, which is comedy's domain, or by serious matters, if they are somewhat close to reality, for most of mankind spurns lies. Thus I am displeased by the battles or carnage that is completed at Thebes within a space of two hours. A skilled poet does not order matters so that someone travels in the twinkling of an eye from Delphi to Athens and from Athens to Thebes. So in Aeschylus, Agamemnon is killed and buried very quickly, so quickly that the actor scarcely has time to breathe. Hercules' action in throwing Lichas into the sea gains no one's approval, as it cannot be represented without doing violence to truth.[14] ...

46 The division of things

Everything which exists is indicated by the naming of the thing. But of these things some are primary, others are images of them. The former are an ox, a man, an oak-tree; pictures or expressions of other kinds are images of them. More refined and sharp observation reveals that some of these images derive from art in their entirety. Others nature claims completely for herself. Some are intermingled, where art has added some element to nature. For instance, only imitations which are immaterial are realized by art, like dances, since they are executed through the deportment and motion of the body alone. Nature provides no material for these; an ape belongs entirely to nature's riches. In her domain the shape of mankind was molded. Hybrid are those whose matter art has borrowed from nature and made her own by the imposition of some form. This occurs in many ways. Some are obvious, such as painting, statuary, works made from marble or casting. Others are not so clear to the common people but they do not escape the educated. For if nature had provided a horse for carrying, then to be sure threshers imitate a horse, when they carry straw on their poles to the hay-lofts. Further, a house seems a kind of copy of a cave. When men first observed caves hollowed out by nature and they had enjoyed their advantages, at the start they set out to excavate rocks for their own use; then they also hit on the idea of stories. The largest part of the arts, therefore, consists of imitation. ... The paramount consideration is that all imitation is undertaken for some end. For the ancients set up statues to honor the memory of those who had performed a remarkable exploit, so that by such examples later generations would be inspired to perform equal deeds. Therefore no imitation exists for itself. All art looks outside itself at what is profitable for someone. For a sword is not made for its own sake but to protect its owner. On this basis, it is sufficiently clear that all our language is nothing but an image. For the names themselves are the ideas of things. ... All those arts for which discourse is an

---

14 See Sophocles, *Trachiniae* 600–812.

instrument are created by imitation. But imitation not of a single mode, since not even things [are single]. For one description is simple, such as "Aeneas is fighting." Another adds means and circumstances, such as "with a sword," "armed," "on horseback," "angry." Here there is also the external form of the warrior, not simply the action. Thus the addition of the circumstances results in a still fuller and more muscular imitation of place, emotion, occasion, time, speech, and outcome. From this spring (apart from the consistency and fineness of the delineation) shadow, light, the withdrawal and advancement of parts, force, and efficacy. Since therefore all of these things are created through the poet's industry, Aristotle caused the end of poetry to reside completely in imitation and he attributed it as particular to man alone of all living things ⟨Ar/39⟩. But since he never abandoned this kind of opinion once it had been posited and endlessly repeated, he led us into two absurdities. The first is when he made not only poetry in general, but also its species, epic, common to the mimes of Sophron and to the dialogues of Alexamen of Teios, written in prose, about philosophy. The second absurdity occurred when he stated that if Herodotus' history was bounded in verse, it would still be history. The first absurdity is such that he has made epic a type of prose. But this is not the case concerning history. For it will not be history, but an historical poem. On these grounds, imitation is not the goal of poetry; it is learning accompanied with pleasure, by which the character of minds may be brought to right reason; that by them man may attain perfect action, which is called beatitude. But if the goal of poetry is imitation alone, anyone who creates an imitation is a poet. Even the character of Socrates in the dialogues, even an orator will become a poet in the personifications [prosopopoeiae]. Plato too in his Laws will be a poet, where he excludes the poet from his laws. Even in trade the merchant will be a poet, when he explains his master's orders in his own words. Further, when an epic writer introduces a character, he will be a poet; when he speaks in his own person, he will not be a poet. At the same time, the Iliad will be a poem when it is made up of fictional characters, but it will not be, when the person [speaking] is Homer. ... It must be stated that the poet's goal is to give instruction and pleasure; that poetry plays a part in the administration of the commonwealth, which is contained, although with a different appearance and condition, under the legislator. For the ordinances issued in legislation and exhortations delivered by politicians and governors of the people are specific and distinct works of poetry and they will be furnished with certain delights in order to educate the state. Wherefore any statement that poetry is so closely connected with sophistry that it is the proper function of poetry to embellish a lie is not true. For deception stole in later and blended itself with the simplicity which had arisen when poetry had. For at its beginnings the poets of comedies proclaimed the unvarnished truth, just as everything had been carried out, done, and performed. Later, invented matter, which the audience would never have listened to in earlier times, won more acceptance because of the novelty of the themes. This approval made fictional matter possible on the stage. Thus the same people were very wrong, when they wrote that it was a property of discourse to signify the necessary truth. For since not every-thing is necessary and the language for everything is known, not all discourse is necessary. Truth, as we stated elsewhere, is an adjusting of ideas to those things of which they are ideas. A property of discourse, therefore, is to signify. ... [Poetry] does not arise from imitation (for not every poem is an imitation), nor is everyone who imitates a poet. It does not arise from a fiction and a lie. For poetry does not lie or the poetry which deceives always does so. Therefore the same thing would be poetry and not poetry. In short, there is imitation in all language, because words are the images of things. The goal of poetry is to teach with pleasure.

47 **Does the poet teach morality or actions?**
... What then does the poet teach? Actions which proceed from the passions of the mind we call "conditions" [*diatheseis*]? Or does he teach the means by which we may emerge as such people that the possibility of right conduct may arise and there may begin a method to avoid evil deeds? Aristotle was of the following opinion. Since a poem was analogous to the education of citizens, which leads us to happiness, and happiness was defined as nothing other than perfect action, the poem will by no means lead us to imitate their characters but actual deeds. He is perfectly correct and our opinion is no different. Aristotle's additional thought, however, is rather less suitable, for he asserts that tragedy cannot exist without action, whereas it can without mental states. For the moment I interpret *ethos* as the actual characters; for the tragedians of his era wrote plays almost devoid of character [*aetheis*]. Thus the painter Zeuxis expressed no character in his works; Polygnotus was the supreme painter of character [*ethnographon*]. But if character [*ethos*] is a disposition toward action and it is excluded from the actions of tragedy, everything will happen by chance or turn out utterly at random. For Orestes once murdered his mother. In this case there was no characterization [*ethos*], for his action was out of character. But Aegisthus did act characteristically, as did Polymestor, Pylades, Euclio, Pseudolus, Ballio, and Davus. Thus we should not ask whether the poet teaches character [*ethos*] or actions [*pragma*], but whether he teaches mental dispositions [*diatheseis*] or their consequences. For although many things happen out of character, they do not transpire without a state of mind. This is the question to be posed and it is answered by the statements above. The poet teaches states of mind through actions so that we may embrace the good ones and imitate them to guide our

conduct, and to reject the evil ones in order to refrain from them. Action, then, is a means of instruction; a state of mind is what we are taught that we may act. In a play, the action is, as it were, the model or the means, while the state of mind is the goal. But in the case of a citizen the action will be the end, the disposition will be its form. ...

8

BARTOLOMÉ DE TORRES NAHARRO
(c. 1485–c. 1520)

Torres Naharro was born in Spain and may have died there but the middle part of his career was spent in Rome. There he was a member of the very large Spanish community that must have provided the greater part of the audience for his plays. These were first published in 1517, in Naples, as part of the volume that constitutes, in effect, Torres Naharro's collected works. The modest or optimistic title of this collection is *Propalladia*, which signifies that the volume is only the beginning of a (literary) "temple" in honor of Pallas Athene.

The introduction to *Propalladia* is remarkable as a very early instance of a theoretical statement by a playwright who writes with no knowledge of Aristotle's *Poetics* to aid or trouble him. Torres Naharro does indicate that he is familiar with such classical authorities as Cicero, Horace, and Donatus, but though he may have known their works at first hand, his allusions to them here are derived from the introductory notes to the plays of Terence by the Belgian scholar and printer Jodocus Badius (c. 1461–1535). Badius' *Praenotamenta*, designed for young scholars, appeared in more than thirty editions of Terence, the first published before 1500, others following regularly through the early decades of the sixteenth century. A letter addressed to Badius by an unknown author, and printed in the first edition of *Propalladia*, recommends Torres Naharro and his work to the famous scholar.

Much more important than his rather bored allusions to classical authorities are Torres Naharro's sturdily independent observations on *comedia*, which is, for him, an apparently general term for a play and so an anticipation of later Spanish usage, as also is his use of the word *jornada*, which he explains in a theatrically pragmatic way.

Torres Naharro's simple and incisive distinction between two kinds of comedy is based on his own strikingly avant-garde plays, of which nine are extant. Prime examples of the distinction he makes are *Tinellaria*, a slice of the life "below stairs" in an ecclesiastical palace and something of an exposé, done with great realism in multilingual dialogue, and *Ymenea*, in which he uses a fictional, borrowed plot to pit love against honor in a way that anticipates the plays of Lope de Vega. Both as playwright and as theorist, Torres Naharro is a provocative and highly original writer.

For further reading

Sánchez Escribano and Porqueras Mayo 1972.

III

From the Introduction to *Propalladia*[1]

... It seems to me less harmful to present to you from my own hands this admittedly inferior thing than to wait for it to find its own way to you in an uncorrected and corrupted form; the more so since most of these little pieces already circulate outside my control and against my wishes.

I have called them *propalladia*, from *prothon*, which signifies the first, and *Pallades*: that is, the first element of a Palladium, to distinguish these works from those that may be added after more mature study. Since it is to be spiritual nourishment it seemed to me that I ought to arrange this book in the manner of bodily nourishment: that is, offering you initially, by way of a first course, a few little tidbits, such as the occasional poems and verse epistles etc.; and for main course the more substantial fare of the comedies; and, similarly, for dessert a few other little things, as you shall see.

As far as the comedies – the main course – are concerned, I think I ought to give you an account of my views about them, not in the presumption that I am an expert, but to offer you my opinion until there is a better one available. Comedy, according to the ancients, is "concerned with the changes in the individual citizen's fortune and is not a matter of life and death," by contrast with tragedy which is "concerned with a change for the worse in the fortune of a noble character."[2] And, according to Tully ⟨Dn/79⟩, "comedy is an imitation of life, a mirror of custom, an image of truth." And, according to the poet Acro, there are six kinds of comedy: *stataria, pretexta, tabernia, palliata, togata, motoria* ⟨Dn/80⟩;[3] and [a comedy] has four parts: *prothesis, catastrophe, prologus, epithasis* ⟨Dn/81⟩;[4] and as Horace requires ⟨Hr/69:185–90⟩, five acts and, above all, a decorum that should be carefully preserved etc. All of which takes longer to tell, it seems to me, than it is necessary to hear.

Since I have given others' opinions, I would now like to give my own. And this is what I have to say: that comedy is nothing more or less than an artful construction of remarkable and ultimately happy events, enacted in

---

[1] This appears to be the first English translation of this document. In the opening sentences of his Introduction (for which he uses the formal, latinate term *Prohemio*), Torres Naharro humbly, but not at all obsequiously, compares his works with the first produce of a poor farmer, and the effort in making them endure with the process of tanning.

[2] The quotations are from Badius.

[3] Acro, or Helenius, was a Roman grammarian of the second century A.D. His commentaries on Terence and Horace have been lost. Torres Naharro is quoting Badius.

  Stataria and *motoria* are categories of comedy also used by Robortello and probably derived from Badius. As the names imply, the first are those (e.g., Terence's *Andria*) meant to be performed in a quiet manner; the latter (e.g., Terence's *Eunuchus*) boisterously. The *pretexta* (or *praetextata* – from the use of the *toga praetextata* or purple-banded official dress) is comedy on historical Roman themes; the *tabernia* (or more properly *tabernaria*) concerns low life, as in taverns; the *palliata* (from *pallium* or cloak), like the comedies of Plautus and Terence, depicts scenes from Greek life; the *togata* (from *toga*) depicts scenes from Italian life.

[4] The terms derive from Donatus but their order is muddled (possibly by the printer) by the placing of *prologus* third rather than first, and *catastrophe* second rather than last.

dialogue.[5] The division of comedy into five acts seems to me not only good but very necessary, although I call them *jornadas*[6] because they seem to me more resting places than anything else, by means of which the comedy may be better understood and played.[7]

As to the number of characters who should be introduced, in my opinion there should not be so few that the entertainment is dull, nor so many as to create confusion. Although more than twenty characters are introduced in the *Tinellaria*, because the subject of the comedy could not be treated with fewer, the optimum number ⟨Hr/69:192⟩, I would say, is six to twelve characters.

Decorum in comedy is like the command of a ship, something that a good writer of comedies should keep in mind. Decorum is an appropriate and acceptable development of the subject: giving everyone his due, avoiding improprieties, and making use of whatever is proper, so that the servant neither says nor does what pertains to the master nor vice versa; presenting what is sad in sad tonalities and what is happy happily, with all the care, diligence, and finesse possible, etc.

How comedy came to be so called is a very confusing matter, since there are so many opinions. As to the kinds of comedy, it seems to me that for us, speaking in terms of the Spanish language, two are sufficient ⟨Rb/92⟩: realistic comedy and fictive comedy.[8] Realistic means the truthful presentation of something really seen and documented. *Soldadesca* and *Tinellaria* are examples. Fictive comedy concerns fantasized or imagined things which look true but are not. *Seraphina* and *Ymenea*, etc. are examples. As to the parts of comedy, two are again sufficient: preamble and plot.[9] If you find that there is more to be said about either the kinds of comedy or the parts of comedy, [well and good. Writers] of discretion may add and subtract freely.

---

5 The ambiguous phrase "por personas disputado" might mean either that comedy is in the form of "dialogue between characters" or that it is "acted by players," but it appears that there is no distinction here between dramatic form and theatrical performance and that both these meanings are implied.

6 Gillet suggests that here, for the first time in Spanish, Torres Naharro is using the words *actos* and *jornadas* to mean act divisions and that the applicable sense of *jornada* is not "day's work" or "day's journey" but the period of rest at the end of the day.

7 The ambiguous verb *recitar* (an Italianism) could mean "declaim" but probably means "act" or "perform." The idea is that the players, as well as the audience, are refreshed by the breaks between acts.

8 The Spanish terms for the two kinds are *a noticia* and *a fantasía*. A *noticia* denotes observation from actuality (in Torres Naharro's practice so close that *Tinellaria* might even be called "naturalistic"). *Fantasía* has the connotations of musical elaboration of a theme and Torres Naharro clearly intends a closer resemblance to actuality than is connoted by the English word "fantastic."

9 The Spanish terms are *introito* (preamble) and *argumento* (plot). The first is a structural element (as in liturgical usage) and, in the light of Torres Naharro's practice, might be described as a piece of theatrical business designed to seize the audience's attention. *Argumento* combines some of the senses of theme, development, and plot. Elsewhere Torres Naharro uses *argumento* to mean exposition or preliminary synopsis.

You will find, moreover, some Italian idioms in my works, especially in the [realistic[10]] comedies. I have made use of [such idioms] having due regard for the place in which and the audience for which [the plays] were played. Some such [idioms] I have eliminated, others left alone, since they do not have the effect of diminishing our Spanish language but of making it richer. However this may be, I beg you to forgive the ineptness that arises from my ignorance and to give thanks to God for what, in your opinion, I have managed to accomplish, for: "God dwells in us, we conspire with the heavens and inspiration comes from on high."[11]

[10] The Italian idioms occur in those plays cited as examples of realistic comedy (*comedia a noticia*) and it appears likely that the words "*a noticia*" were accidentally omitted at this point.

[11] Ovid, *Ars Amatoria* 3.549–50.

9

ANTONFRANCESCO GRAZZINI ("IL LASCA") (1503–84)

A founding member of the *Accademia degli umidi*,[1] an editor, dramatist, poet, *novelliere*, and polemicist, Grazzini was a staunch defender of modernity against slavish adherence to neo-Aristotelian precepts. His *commedie erudite* ("erudite comedies"),[2] as well as his popular farces, capture the mercantile milieu of Renaissance Florence with lively realism and in language as vital as Machiavelli's in *La Mandragola*.

Grazzini's *The Witch* (*La Strega*) was written in 1546–47 but it was not published until 1582, and not acted in his lifetime. The prologue was probably written much later than the play, perhaps as late as 1574 (Grazzini/Plaisance 1976, 26–37). This was a time of crisis for the *commedia erudita*, which was overshadowed by the increasing professionalization of the theatre: by lavish *intermezzi* for the aristocracy, and by the *commedia dell'arte*, which, with its highly trained performers, was quickly establishing itself as the popular comic form.

The survival of the *commedia erudita*, according to Grazzini, depended on a realistic evaluation of audience demands and the abandonment of pedantic and antiquarian approaches to the composition of comedies and the theatre. In the prologue to *The Witch*, Grazzini advocates a middle course between the entertainments of the court theatre and those of the *piazza*. His aim is a form of drama that captures the contemporary spirit of mercantile or middle-class life. From his awareness of the requirements for performance and its social context come his most important insights.

For further reading

Goggio 1943; Hathaway 1962; Nagler 1964; Rodini 1970.

The Witch: "Dialogue instead of Prologue"

Speakers: *Prologue* and *Plot*

They enter suddenly from either side of the perspective and, pretending not to see one another, start reciting at the same time until *Prologue* says:

[1] "The Academy of the Clammy Ones": like other members of this fancifully named Florentine academy, Grazzini, who was one of the founders, adopted a nickname – "Il Lasca" (the Roach). The academy's purpose was to restore to its former glory the Tuscan dialect (the *volgare*), which had been the language of Dante, Petrarch, and Boccaccio and which had been overshadowed by scholarly reverence for the classics.
[2] The "erudite comedies" were so called to distinguish them from such popular entertainments as the *commedia dell'arte*. Modeled on the plays of Plautus and Terence, preceded

"Who is this ill-mannered creature?"; from *Plot*'s reply they continue the
dialogue to the end.

Prologue and *Plot* together:

PROLOGUE: God save you, most honorable spectators.

PLOT: May God give you a good day, most noble spectators.

PROLOGUE: We are here to recite for you ...

PLOT: Bonifazio, a citizen of Florence ...

PROLOGUE: Who is this ill-mannered creature?

PLOT: What is this saucy fellow up to?

PROLOGUE: You, there! Who are you and what are you looking for?

PLOT: And what are you doing here? And how dare you ask?

PROLOGUE: I am the Prologue, and have come to address these gentlemen
and knights.

PLOT: And I am the Plot, come to address these gallant and fair ladies.

PROLOGUE: Are you not aware that the Prologue enters always before the
comedy? Better go back inside and let me have my turn first.

PLOT: You are the one who should return inside, good-for-nothing
that you are, and let me perform my duties.

PROLOGUE: You are as unpleasant and loathsome as ever.

PLOT: And you are pretentious and rude.

PROLOGUE: If I have this privilege and superiority, why do you want to
steal it from me?

PLOT: It's yours without reason, for you have nothing to do with the
comedy, and the comedy can easily be done without you. You
are an after-thought, added to the comedy not because you are
needed, but for the convenience of the author or of those
responsible for staging the comedy. You are good only to bring
forth their excuses; without me nothing can be done.

PROLOGUE: Nevertheless, though I am not needed, I'm always summoned
on the scene and this is a sign that I'm much loved and admired
by the people; and if truth be told, the greater part of the
comedies, especially modern ones, can be done without you as
well. So, don't give yourself airs, for in these comedies the
authors introduce some characters in the first scenes of the first
act who reveal in their dialogue what has happened before and
what is to come after. This is one of these comedies and follows
this rule.

PLOT: We might as well not have come at all, then.

PROLOGUE: Yes, you should have; but I must at least tell these most

---

by a prologue and divided into five acts, and taking character stereotypes from Greek New
Comedy and Roman comedy, the *commedie erudite* were usually a minor pursuit of men of
letters and scholars, performed by amateurs in aristocratic residences.

courteous spectators the name of the scene, the title of the comedy, and the name of the author.

PLOT: If that is all you are required to do, you should have stayed home. In the first place, the scene is easily recognized as Florence; don't you see the cathedral, you ox! In height, in breadth, in beauty, and majesty it surpasses all other buildings in the universe. The name of the comedy is written there, above; and knowing or not knowing the name of the author is irrelevant. So, you see: you should have stayed home.

PROLOGUE: And is it not a good thing to praise and glorify the spectators, while claiming humility for our efforts, so as to make them reasonably disposed towards us?

PLOT: It matters little, or nothing.

PROLOGUE: And should we not at least ask them to keep a calm and grateful silence, so they will be attentive and mild?

PLOT: They are all useless remedies. We need more than that.

PROLOGUE: What the devil do we need, then?

PLOT: The comedy must be cheerful, fanciful, witty, funny, beautiful, and well acted.

PROLOGUE: Where can you find, today, such comedies and such actors?

PLOT: You must know what you want and where to look; and this you can do by commissioning from men who are practical, wise, and who understand.

PROLOGUE: Well, now! Let us see how this comedy will fare.

PLOT: This one is not the work of princes or lords and is not presented in ducal palaces or lordly manor; nor is it accompanied by such pomp in scenery, perspective, and *intermezzi* as we have been seeing lately; nor can it be recommended to anyone, it being the work of private persons in the company of honorable youths and lovers of virtue.[3]

PROLOGUE: And what do you mean by that?

PLOT: Merely that it should, in this respect, be forgiven.

PROLOGUE: On the contrary! It should be commended, for it is neither right nor lawful nor appropriate for vassals and subjects to compete with their lords and masters.

PLOT: So it seems to me, but that is not enough; I also maintain that comedies that are neither good nor beautiful are like certain older and ugly women: however hard they try, by dressing up in silks and gold, garlands and pearls, polishing and dolling up their faces, to look young and beautiful, so much more ugly they appear.

PROLOGUE: There's no doubt that the rich beauty of the *intermezzi* repre-

[3] Grazzini and the other members – "honorable youths" – of the *Accademia degli umidi* were not members of the aristocracy but of the middle or mercantile class. See Rodini 1970, 7.

senting mostly nymphs, cupids, gods, and demi-gods casts a shadow over the comedy and makes it appear poor and ugly.

PLOT: Indeed! Especially when on the scene you see an old man and a parasite, a lover and a servant, a widow and a soldier: what verisimilitude! What decorum!

PROLOGUE: But there's nothing to be done! That's the way of the world. We must get used to these new customs.

PLOT: And what great customs they are! We used to see *intermezzi* in the service of the comedy; but now we see comedies in the service of *intermezzi*. What do you say to that?

PROLOGUE: I see it the way you do, but neither you nor I can reform the wits of today.

PLOT: I know who is to blame for this!

PROLOGUE: Who?

PLOT: It is the pedants into whose hands Italian, Tuscan, vernacular, and Florentine poetry has fallen.

PROLOGUE: Alas! Once Giovanni della Casa, Annibal Caro, and father Varchi[4] died, our language ...

PLOT: was left without guidance.

PROLOGUE: You are forgetting the academy.

PLOT: Oh, I like that one! If you really want to hear me out ...

PROLOGUE: Come now! Let's drop this argument and return to the comedy.

PLOT: Our comedy may not have such rich ornaments of scenery or *intermezzi*, but it has a beginning, a middle, and an end so distinct one from the other that they can be easily recognized; nor will you find in our comedy such spiteful and tiresome speeches, such long-winded and vexing arguments, such limp and tasteless recognitions as are plentiful in other comedies.

PROLOGUE: Does it not follow the decorum, the art, and rules which are proper to comedy?

PLOT: What do I know about that? But it will be agreeable and merry.

PROLOGUE: That's not enough. Don't you know comedies are an image of virtue, an example of customs, and mirror of life ⟨Dn/79⟩?

PLOT: You are as old-fashioned and unbecoming as the Baronci:[5] today we no longer go to see comedies so that we can learn to live but for pleasure, sport, delight, and to while away melancholy and thus find enjoyment.

PROLOGUE: You might as well summon the *zanni*.[6]

PLOT: They would perhaps be more pleasing and so would their

---

[4] Defenders of Tuscan as a literary language.

[5] The "Baronci" were a Florentine family made notorious, by Boccaccio in his *Decameron*, for their ugliness.

[6] The *zanni* (from which the English "zany" is derived) were the early performers of the *commedia dell'arte*.

playful and pleasing comedies delight more than our own grave, learned, and wise ones.

PROLOGUE: The author wishes to present good manners, and makes his principal aims gravity and teaching for so the rules of art demand.

PLOT: Enough said about art! You've bored me to death with your art. True art is pleasure and delight ⟨Cv/131⟩.

PROLOGUE: And would you leave profit behind?

PLOT: He profits better who is pleased and delighted; and I have already told you that we no longer make comedies with this purpose in mind. Those who wish to learn good manners and Christian life should not go to comedies for it; rather, they should read a thousand good books and go to sermons and sacred readings, not only during Lent, but every Sunday throughout the year and be grateful to God for it.

PROLOGUE: We have no time to retire into the vestry, and this is not the proper place; but I still say that it is necessary to follow the ancient rules as stated by Aristotle and Horace.

PLOT: You must be dreaming, brother! Aristotle and Horace lived in and knew their own times. Ours have changed: we have other customs, another religion, and a different way of life. That is why we must make comedies in a different mode. In Florence, life is not like it was in Athens or in Rome: we have no slaves here, nor have we any use for adopted children. There are no scoundrels who sell women nor do the soldiers of today, when sacking a city, run off with little girls in swaddling clothes to raise as their own daughters and give them a dowry. They are careful to steal as much as they can and should fortune put into their hands maidens or married women they will take their virginity and honor if they can't hold them up for good ransom.

PROLOGUE: We should not blame scholars and men of letters if they follow the rules of art when composing their inventions and fables.

PLOT: Will you never give up on this doctrine, on these rules! Your scholars and rulemongers muddle the ancient and modern, the old and the new and their compositions are always niggardly, dry, cold, and so constipated that they please no one; and as we have a thousand times witnessed almost everyone has had his fill and is tired of them.

PROLOGUE: You say that; learned men are of another opinion.

PLOT: You would have these most beautiful and most honest gentlewomen, who've come here to be delighted and amused, sit there astonished and confused listening to some pedant's ugly fable with all its sermonizing that will make no one laugh or cry.

PROLOGUE: But these gentlemen, lords, and knights will be satisfied in recognizing the art and rules of comedy.

PLOT: You are showing your age! These gentlemen, these nobles and knights have not come here to look and listen to a comedy.

PROLOGUE: Why are they here, then?

PLOT: To see and contemplate the great beauty, the infinite charm and divine grace of these most beautiful, most honest damsels, ladies, and matrons. The comedy will pass by unseen to their eyes and ears.

PROLOGUE: In the name of God, I would always follow the opinion of those who know.

PLOT: That would be well done; but you follow the opinion of those who think they know: sophists and grammarians. But look, here they come.

PROLOGUE: It's time for us to clear this place and return inside.

PLOT: Yes! We have chattered long enough.

The end.

10

GIAMBATTISTA GIRALDI ("CINTHIO") (1504–73)

Much of Giraldi's[1] prolific theorizing had its origin in his defense of his own work. When, for example, his tragedy *Orbecche* (a remodeling of Seneca's *Thyestes*) was first produced in 1541, he was accused of such violations of classical precedent as: a tragic plot not based on historical events but created by the author; the division into five acts preceded by a prologue; the use of the current vernacular; and the death of the protagonist on stage. Giraldi responded with *An Address by the Tragedy of Orbecche to the Reader* (1541), a work much cited in arguments about the propriety of death on stage. His next tragedy, *Dido* (1543), was also attacked: for introducing gods on the stage, which was thought to be forbidden by Aristotle; for excessive length; for employing too many characters; for violating the rules of decorum; for using verse rather than prose; for dividing tragedy into acts and scenes; and for not following the model of the perfect tragedy, Sophocles' *Oedipus Tyrannus*. This time Giraldi replied with his *Letter on Tragedy* (1543), a point-by-point refutation in which he propounded his favourite theme: the necessity of catering to the audience and of adapting classical forms to the taste and customs of the time.

In his three treatises *On the Composition of Romances*, *On the Composition of Comedies and Tragedies*, and *On the Composition of Satires for the Stage*, Giraldi attempted his most comprehensive theoretical statement. In *On the Composition of Comedies and Tragedies*, which was published in 1554 (though Giraldi claimed that it was written much earlier), he espouses what could be called an evolutionary theory of drama, maintaining that "things in their beginning are not perfect and our diligence is necessary to develop them to their suitable end and perfection." Thus, the Romans improved on the Greeks and Giraldi's own generation can improve on the Romans. He was quite willing to justify any departure from Aristotle's *Poetics* on the grounds that the playwright must serve the audience of the time; moreover, the ancients, he maintains, broke their own rules.

Hence we find the Prologue to his *Altile* (written c. 1543) claiming that if the ancients were alive they too would have served the audience as he has with respect to what he calls "tragedy with a happy ending" ("tragedia di lieto fine"), or tragicomedy. His advocacy of this genre was Giraldi's most original contribution to dramatic theory. Departing from Aristotle (and perhaps under the influence of Terence), Giraldi insists that the double plot is necessary for the happy ending; an ending in which virtue triumphs and vice is punished, with the wicked and virtuous characters relegated to the appropriate plot. The best play, in his view, is one in which a reversal of fortune unties the knot and reveals the operations of a Christian Providence.

[1] From Giraldi's custom of referring to himself, in his poetry, as "Cinzio" he came to be known as "Cynthio" or "Cinthio" in Elizabethan England and is still often referred to thus.

For further reading

Bilancini 1890; Gilbert 1940; Herrick [1955] 1962; Horne 1962; Lucas 1984; Weinberg 1961.

Prologue to *Altile*[2]

It is certain that all that exists is generated, corrupts, will alter and change, either in whole or in part; and that man is in the world to choose, in accordance with his free will, where he will turn his mind. This is why our poet[3] believes that the rules of tragedy are not so firm that they forbid him to depart from what is prescribed in order to serve the age, the spectators, and subject matter as yet untouched by either ancient or modern poet. . . . If, therefore, he has relied on himself and departed from ancient usage (as by having me appear[4] on stage before the characters in the tragedy), he has considered that our age and the tragedy that is just now being born demand it. But I think I have seen many among you furrow your brows on hearing the simple word "tragedy," as though you were about to hear nothing but weeping. Be cheerful, for the events of today will end happily; tragedy need not be so miserably ominous that a happy ending might not be possible. Such was the *Ion* of Euripides and his *Orestes*, *Helen*, and *Alcestis* and also *Iphigenia*, and many others on which I will remain silent. But if it should displease you to call it a tragedy, you may, at your pleasure, call it a tragicomedy (a name which is used in our language),[5] for it shares with comedy its ending, which after much travail ends with much happiness. In this, our *Altile* (named after the queen on whose travails the play is based), and you witness how much fickleness guides human affairs, and

---

[2] Translated from Weinberg's edition of the Prologue to "Altile tragedia di M. Gio. Battista Giraldi Cinthio nobile ferrarese. Con privilegi, Giulio Cesare Cagnacini, 1583," in Giraldi/ Weinberg 1970–74, 1:489–91. This translation is a selection from the Prologue, omitting only the description of the scene and the presentation of the characters. In 1543 Giraldi published the text of *Orbecche*, which had received its first performance at the court of Ercole II in Ferrara in 1541. In the dedication of *Orbecche* he mentions the existence of three other tragedies, *Dido*, *Cleopatra*, and *Altile*. *Altile* was to have received its premiere in April 1543, but this was prevented by the death of Flaminio Ariosti, who was to have played the title role. Although the Prologue to *Altile* may have been written as early as 1541, there is no evidence on which to base such a conjecture. See Horne 1962, 17–18; Giraldi/Weinberg 1970–74, 1:637.

[3] Giraldi is referred to as "our poet" by the dramatic persona of the Prologue as he addresses the audience and presents the play.

[4] A reference to the fact that this Prologue is different from the part of the play so named in Greek drama. Here, it has the same function as in Terence: to address the audience explaining the poet's intention and introduce the characters.

[5] The term "tragicommedia" has been in use in Italy since at least 1519. In that year the celebrated Spanish novel *Celestina*, by Fernando de Rojas, has been published in Italian under the title *Celestina, Tragicomedia de Calisto e Melibea novamente tradocta de lingua Castigliana in italiano idioma* (Venice). See Herrick [1955] 1962, 67.

that a wicked soul will not find joy through evil doings and that (in spite of all opposition from fraud and deception) what is ordained in Heaven by the Supreme Mover that holds everything in his ineffable Providence, must needs unfold.

From *On the Composition of Comedies and Tragedies*[6]

1 On the similarities between comedies and tragedies

Comedy and tragedy, then, have this in common: they imitate an action; but they are different in that the latter imitates an exalted and royal action, while the former imitates a civic and popular one, although Aristotle himself said ⟨Ar/41⟩ that comedy imitated the worst actions. However, he did not mean that it was an imitation of depraved and wicked actions, but those which are less exalted, which are worse with respect to their nobility than royal ones. . . .

Now . . . these two sorts of plays are, with respect to the instrument of their imitation, in parts similar and in others not. Tragedy and comedy imitate with smoothly flowing speech, that is, in verse (which was called metre by Aristotle) and not in prose, and neither can be commendably composed without verse. Verse is a part of the body of tragedy and comedy as a whole, and when it is lacking they cannot but be deficient and crippled; and if in ancient times, after the Greeks, there were some who wrote them in prose ⟨Ar/37⟩, it was because in their beginning things are not perfect, and our industry and diligence is necessary to develop them to their suitable end and perfection. If writing in prose was not reproached then, because they did not know better, now that they [comedy and tragedy] have taken on a proper form, it cannot but be reproachable not to write them in verse ⟨Hr/66: 89–91; Sg/108⟩.

These two types of plays are dissimilar in that tragedy, in addition to verse, resorts to chant and movement of the body; the former (that is, chant by human voices) was called melody by Aristotle, while the latter he called rhythm (that is, movement of the body measured against the chant). In our times comedy uses neither of these, because, while melody and metre are suitable to tragedy with respect to their choruses, they cannot be suitable to comedy, which does not have them [choruses] in our times, as it did not in Roman times . . . .

In addition to all the aforesaid things which they have in common, these two types of play have also a common end: to introduce good morals; but in this shared end they are different, because comedy has no terror and no pity (and in it there are no deaths or terrible events, rather with pleasure and mirthful wit it seeks its end); and tragedy, whether of happy or

[6] The original text is from Giraldi/Crocetti 1973.

unhappy ending, by means of wretchedness and horror purges the souls of their vices and leads them to good morals.

2 On plot

... although the plot is common to both tragedy and comedy, some hold nonetheless that the tragic plot is to be taken from history, while the comic plot can be invented by the poet. Such difference can be, it seems, explained with good reason, which is: that comedy must make recourse to civic and popular actions and tragedy to royal and exalted ones; to private citizens in one case and kings and persons of high rank in the other; and since the latter are in the public eye, not to have heard of any singular action as soon as it is performed by them seems to lie outside the bounds of verisimilitude. Therefore, tragedies being numbered among exalted actions because of the persons who give rise to them, it seems unlikely that they could be brought onto the stage without some prior knowledge. Private events, on the other hand, can easily be invented, because in general they seldom go beyond their households, and are soon forgotten. In this case the poet can therefore have a wider field in which to invent what he wants, and to invent new plots for the stage. But even though this argument seems reasonable, nevertheless I still maintain that, as is the case of comedy, tragic plots can also be invented by the poet .... [For] since the power to move the passions is based solely on an imitation which does not stray from the verisimilar, and since the passions cannot be moved without the joining together of numerous speeches in a becoming way, it seems to me that it is within the power of the poet to move the tragic passions as he will in a tragedy of his own invention, the action of which he invents in accordance with natural customs and which stays within the range of what usually happens or might happen. The invented action, because it is new to the souls of the spectators and can thus command more attention, can move the passions more easily towards the introduction of good morals. The spectator, aware that the action about to be represented can only be known through the representation, as soon as he has tasted the fable and thinks that it might be ingeniously constructed, concentrates his attention in order not to lose one word. And this might be the reason that led Aristotle (when he allowed us the inventing of plots) to say that, among those that are taken from history, the least known are more pleasing and effective ⟨Ar/46⟩. Although horror and pity are determined by the effect of the plot they are nonetheless without any power unless the genius of the poet expresses them in delightful and effective words. That an invented plot has this power was shown by the experience of my *Orbecche* (such as it is) every time it was performed: not only the new spectators (allow me, Messer Giulio,[7] to point out the truth to you, not in self-praise, but to

---

[7] Giulio Ponzoni was Giraldi's pupil and played Oronte in the first production of *Orbecche*. The treatise on the composition of comedies and tragedies is addressed to him.

confirm my present argument with the latest example) but even those who had seen it every time, could not contain their sobs and tears. . . .

Now, whether true or invented (and I am of the opinion that either can be most suitable), the plot in tragedy is always an imitation of an exalted action, while in comedy it is an imitation of a civic and popular one. But if both are to turn out to be deserving of praise, the poet must concentrate on the knot and the resolution of the action which he wants to imitate, and by "knot" I mean the texture or the composition of the play, and by "resolution" the explanation of it. The resolution must be such that, once the play ends, the soul of the listener, or the reader, must be left in such a state of contentment that he may wish for nothing more: something which, according to Aristotle ⟨Ar/50⟩, among the Greeks Euripides failed to do, and likewise in his comedies (it seems to me) Plautus among the Latins . . . .

3 The tragedy of the double plot

In this part it is to be advised that, although tragedies of double plot are not much admired by Aristotle ⟨Ar/49⟩ (although some would have it otherwise), this [structure] is worthy of no less praise [than the single plot] in comedy: the plots of Terence have shown this admirably. The double plot I call that which has in its action diverse sorts of persons in a similar situation, as two lovers of different understanding, two old men of differing nature, two servants of contrasting morals, and so on, as we can see in the *Andria* and other fables by the same poet, where it is clear that these similar persons of contrasting morals add much grace to the knot and resolution of the plot. I believe that if this were to be imitated in tragedy by a good poet, who tied the knot so that the unraveling would not create confusion, the result would be no less pleasing (with due respect as always to Aristotle) than in comedy . . . .

Now, since in both instances nothing is imitated but the action, and since the action of comedy is popular and does not have terror or pity, it does not present as much difficulty in the choice of persons as does tragedy: especially since it allows the representation not only of honest citizens, but servants, parasites, prostitutes, cooks, pimps, soldiers, and all sorts of common persons that live in the city. Tragedy must show more consideration. It should, however, be known that, in this regard, regal and great actions can be of three types: about good persons, persons of intermediate morals, or wicked persons. But the actions that are suitable to tragedy must be sought out with a view that this kind of plot is composed all of terror and pity: for the sake of good morals the poet must therefore choose to imitate actions that can produce this effect of good morality. . . .

4 Actions suitable to comedy and tragedy

Now, leaving others to do as they please, let us return to our purpose: as great and royal persons are suitable to tragedy, so are popular persons suitable to comedy, as we said above. Their actions are different and, although both have the same end of introducing good morals, they achieve it in different ways. With horror and compassion, showing us what we must avoid, tragedy purges us of the perturbations which have been incurred by the tragic characters. Comedy, on the other hand, by proposing to us that which we must imitate, shows us the way to a good moral life, by means of passions, restrained sentiments mixed with games, with laughter and playful sayings. Among the ancients there were different types of tragedies and comedies; but of the different types of comedy it is not necessary to say anything now other than that in our own day the good ones are only of one type, those modeled on Ariosto.[8] Tragedies can be of two types: one ends in misery, while the other one has a happy ending, although in its management of the action it does not depart from the terrible and compassionable, for without these good tragedies cannot be made. . . .

. . . although Aristotle says that this [use of a happy ending in tragedy] is to cater to the ignorance of the audience, and since he has others to defend him, I have deemed it better to satisfy the listener with some lesser excellence (if the opinion of Aristotle is to be accepted as better) rather than with a little more greatness to displease those for whom the play is staged. There is little to be gained by writing more praiseworthy plots that are odious when performed. Terrible plots with unhappy endings (if they are abhorrent to the souls of the spectators) are better suited to the printed page, those that end happily to the stage.

5 Death on the stage

Nonetheless, the events of these less proud tragedies must be given birth in such manner that the spectators are in a suspended state between horror and compassion until the end, which, because it turns out to be happy, leaves them all consoled. This suspense must be managed by the poet so that the spectator is not always in the dark with respect to the plot; rather, the action must be conducted so that the plot is unraveled gradually, thus making the spectator feel that the end is coming but leaving him uncertain as to the outcome. For the greater satisfaction and instruction of those who listen, in this sort of plot, those who are responsible for the turbulent events suffered by the characters of middle rank are punished or made to die. Euripides did this in the *Children of Hercules* in which Eurystheus is killed, and Sophocles in his *Electra* in which Aegisthus is killed. And following their example, I had Astano die in my *Altile* and Gripo in the *Selene*, and both at the time in which, because of their wickedness, they thought

---

[8] Under the direction of the epic poet and dramatist Ludovico Ariosto (1474–1533), the court of Ferrara, Giraldi's birthplace, had been staging classical plays since the late fifteenth century. Ariosto's versification of his own plays was a precedent supporting Giraldi's assertion that drama must be written in verse.

themselves happier than all the rest: for the spectator feels an astonishing pleasure on seeing the crafty deceived and taken away, and the wicked, powerful, and unjust overthrown.

These deaths are introduced not to arouse commiseration but for the sake of justice: therefore they should take place off-stage. The spectators hear the voices of the dying from behind the scenes or learn about their deaths through the narration either of a messenger or a character chosen by the author for this purpose. The use of messengers to narrate the death when the action of the plot demands it occurs not only in tragedies with a happy ending, but also in those that end miserably. Such deaths, however, must be without cruelty which, in plots that are deserving of praise, must always be far removed from the characters who give rise to horror and compassion. I believe that this is what Horace meant ⟨Hr/69: 185⟩ when he commanded that Medea should not kill her children on stage .... Horace did not intend to forbid the use of suitable deaths on the stage, only that we must avoid those that are accompanied by cruelty, especially since Aristotle said that the deaths, the torments, the wounds that, through error, afflict blood relatives are well suited to tragic compassion if performed in full view of the audience. Although, as far as I know, there may be those whose interpretation of Aristotle's *en to fanero* differs from mine and from that of Paccio and Valla before me.[9] But in truth (as Horace himself says ⟨Hr/69: 180–81⟩) things that are heard move our spirits more slowly than things that are seen. Therefore, narrated events are less horrible and pitiable than those that are seen. ...

6 The tragedy with a happy ending

You should know that tragedies of happy endings like intricate knots best, and are to be more praised when double rather than simple. This is not true of tragedies that end miserably, which are better simple and not double. ... With respect to both the argument and the distribution of characters, therefore, tragedies that end miserably are more similar to the *Iliad*, while those that end happily are more similar to the *Odyssey*; and with these two compositions, it seems, Homer intended to give us examples of both kinds of tragedy, as in the *Margites* he gave us the example of comedy, ⟨Ar/39⟩, which was less censurable in his times. We can see, therefore, the extent to which these who have said that the *Iliad* gave us the example of tragedy while the *Odyssey* that of comedy have been deceived: both give us the example of tragedy; the former of tragedy that ends unhappily, the latter of tragedy that ends happily. Likewise, they were also mistaken in their opinion that a tragedy with a happy ending could not be made. And though we have said that wicked persons do not arouse compassion or

---

[9] *en to fanero* = on the stage. But Aristotle does not combine this with injuries done to friends and relatives. Giorgio Valla and Alessandro Pazzi de' Medici had translated Aristotle's *Poetics* into Latin.

horror, I would not want you to believe that they cannot give their name to the tragedy, and this was commendably done by the ancients, as is shown by Seneca's *Medea* and *Thyestes* and others like them. The title of the tragedy is often taken from the characters who give rise to the events of the play, even though these characters may not be suitable to arouse compassion and horror, not having been introduced for this end, because, as we have said, horror and pity are aroused not by wicked persons but by those of middle rank.

7   Reversal and recognition

Recognition, then, is nothing other than the coming into knowledge of something which was unknown; and through this knowledge enemies are turned into friends, those who are happy become unhappy, and, with respect to tragedies with a happy ending, those who are unhappy become happy. We can see, therefore, that if the recognition is to be effective, it must be accompanied by this change in the condition of the soul: for from the soul spring the perturbations, the horrors, the compassion, and all other things suitable to bring about a change of state in the person. This recognition, which is connected to reversal, is thought by Aristotle to be worthy of praise above all others, because more than anything else it moves the souls of the spectators. Sometimes it is so overpowering that, overcome with pity and fear, the spectators faint; as it happened, Messer Giulio, to your own Guerriera, who, during the performance of our *Orbecche*, on seeing the head of Oronte (the character whom you played), fell down as if dead, no less than if she had seen you dead in reality. . . .

Reversal and recognition are not limited to tragedy but (if we can broaden our concern) pertain also to comedy. But in comedy it comes about differently, because recognition, or reversal, never arouses horror or compassion: rather, through them, persons who are perturbed are brought to tranquility and happiness, but without a change in fortune (with respect to the happiness or unhappiness of their state) from better to worse, or vice versa. The characters do not change their social status, but whereas before they were perturbed and sad, they are now happy and tranquil, for the end of comedy is to conclude the action in such a way that none of the characters remain in a troubled state: and this is done through the most appropriate reversal and recognition. . . .

LUDOVICO CASTELVETRO
(1505–71)

Castelvetro's position as one of the most influential critics of his age was due partly to his immense erudition and his knowledge of ancient and modern languages, partly to his polemical vigor. The latter was such that he had to live in exile from his native Italy after being condemned by the Inquisition in 1560 for doctrinal deviance. A major feature of Castelvetro's theory is his insistence on intended performance as a defining characteristic of the dramatic genre; and one of his key insights is that drama (in performance) uses a language of things, as well as of words ⟨In/6⟩. As to his assertion that pleasure is drama's primary purpose, Saintsbury found reason to rejoice and shudder, he said, "at the audacity of a critic who in the mid sixteenth century calmly says: 'What do beginning, middle and end matter in a poem provided it delights.'"[1]

That Castelvetro should have been responsible for the promulgation of the third of the so-called "unities" is ironic in view of the pedantries later associated with them. His advocacy of "unity of place" arises from his (illusionistic) ideas about the staging of plays rather than from formal, literary considerations. The limitation of the stage representation to one place leads, for Castelvetro, to the "unity of time," while the only truly Aristotelian unity – that of action – he finds least important.

Like Scaliger, Castelvetro is quite prepared to contradict and extensively supplement Aristotle. His *Poetics of Aristotle, Translated into the Vernacular and Explicated*[2] is not only, he says, a scholarly work that pays attention to Aristotle's text (especially the neglected passages) and to the work of earlier commentators; it is also an attempt to construct a whole poetics that will be of service to both poets and critics. The fact that Castelvetro's is the first major commentary on Aristotle to be written in a modern language itself demonstrates his concern, shown throughout, with the contemporary applications of his theory.

Maintaining that plays are intended primarily for the "rude multitude," who are incapable of understanding the subtle arguments of philosophers and whose main reason for theatre-going is to be entertained, Castelvetro contradicts all those who attempt to dignify dramatic art by attributing to it a didactic function in relation to a refined audience ⟨Rb/84⟩. But he does not belittle the art of the poets who write for a popular theatre. On the contrary he has great admiration for those who possess that power of invention which enables the creation of credible plots based on "the everyday happenings that are talked about among the people, the kind that resemble those reported in any one day's news and histories." Not being deceived by the illusion but fully conscious that it is one, the spectators derive pleasure from,

---

[1] Saintsbury [1902–04] 1934, II:87.
[2] *Poetica d'Aristotele vulgarizzata e sposta*, first published in Vienna in 1570. A second edition appeared in Basel in 1576.

and feel admiration for, the work in which the resemblance[3] to actuality is closest – and this is what the poet strives for.

Castelvetro makes a crucial and un-Aristotelian distinction between fact (or history) and fiction (which, in the case of tragedy, is based on fact). "Truth," he says, "existed by nature before verisimilitude[4] and the thing represented before the representation," so "verisimilitude depends wholly upon truth." The credibility of drama lies in the accuracy with which poetry mirrors history, or with which it makes fiction just as believable as fact – often in both at once. But, as is seen at the beginning of the selection below, one of the basic problems for poetics, according to Castelvetro, is that since we do not know what history is, in the first place, the status of the verisimilitude that depends on it is also obscure.

For further reading

Barilli 1984; Bray 1931; Charlton 1913; Della Volpe 1973; Gilbert 1940; Saintsbury 1905; Spingarn 1908b; Weinberg 1952, 1961.

From *Poetics of Aristotle, Translated into the Vernacular and Explicated*[5]

I.1 Poetry and history

If Aristotle or another had written a proper treatise on the art of history – and the art of history should logically have been written before the art of poetry – poets and critics would have found the ideas in Aristotle's brief *Poetics* more useful in composing and judging poetry than they have or they might even have dismissed them as superfluous. . . . The soundness of this view will be clearly demonstrated, unless I am deceived, by the following considerations. Truth existed by nature before verisimilitude[6] and the thing represented before the representation. But since verisimilitude depends wholly upon truth and looks upon it as its model and precisely the same relationship exists between the representation and the thing represented, and since we cannot attain a right knowledge of dependent and reflecting things unless we first possess a knowledge of the things they depend upon and reflect, it necessarily follows that we cannot acquire the faculty of making right judgments about the adequacy and fidelity of representations and probabilities unless we first possess an accurate and exhaustive knowledge of the things represented and the truth. Then since history is the recital of memorable human actions that

---

[3] On the translation of *rassomiglianza* see note 7, on p. 131, below.
[4] On the use of this word see note 6, below.
[5] The text is from Castelvetro/Bongiorno 1984.
[6] Bongiorno (1984, 329n., I.3.1) notes that "'Verisimilitude' translates *verisimilitudine*, which will also be translated 'probability.' *Verisimile* and *verisimilmente* will be regularly translated 'probable' and 'probably.'" The idea of "probability" implied in this usage should not be confused with the Aristotelian idea of "probability" (having to do with the internal structure of tragedy), which Castelvetro, like many of his contemporaries, did not grasp.

have happened and its distinguishing mark is truth, and poetry the recital of memorable human actions that may happen and its distinguishing mark verisimilitude; and since, again, history is a thing represented and poetry, as will be shown hereafter, a representation, no art of poetry so far written can possibly offer a complete and accurate knowledge of poetry because we still lack a complete and distinct knowledge of history, and future arts of poetry will continue to be less than serviceable as long as the art of history remains imperfectly known. . . .

I.9 History and the arts and sciences not fit subjects for poetry

Poetry is the image and imitation[7] of history. And just as history consists of two principal parts, matter and language, poetry likewise consists of those same two parts. But the two parts are not identical in both. The matter of history is not supplied by the historian's genius but by the course of earthly events or by the manifest or hidden will of God, and its language, though supplied by the historian, is that of men engaged in ordinary discourse. But the matter of poetry is invented and imagined by the poet's genius, and its language is not that of ordinary discourse, since men do not address one another in verse, but is ordered metrically by the poet. Now though the matter of poetry must resemble the matter of history, it must not be identical with it; if it were it would not be its image or imitation, and not being that it would be the production of a writer who had shirked the labor of invention and consequently had given no proof of the acuteness of genius that the invention would have required. For this reason he would merit no praise . . . .

[The good poet's] function is by the exertion of his intellectual faculties to imitate human actions under fortune's sway as they truly are and through his imitations to provide pleasure for his audiences, leaving the discovery of hidden truths of natural and contingent things to the philosopher and the student of the arts, who have their own way, and one quite different from that of the poet, of offering the world profit and pleasure.

But there is another and more obvious reason why the arts and sciences cannot supply matter for poetry. It is that poetry was invented for the sole purpose of providing pleasure and recreation, by which I mean to provide pleasure and recreation to the souls of the common people and the rude multitude, who are incapable of understanding the rational proofs, the distinctions, and the arguments, all of them subtle and nothing like the talk normally heard among the unlearned, which philosophers make use of in

---

[7] Bongiorno translates both *rassomiglianza* and *rappresentatione* as "imitation" and treats the verbal forms of these words similarly. Gilbert, who made the same choice, noted that "resemblance," the English equivalent to *rassomiglianza*, had "lost the flexibility and breadth of meaning it once possessed" and chose "imitation" as the conventional translation of the Greek *mimesis*, which is Castelvetro's point of departure (1940, 311n.20). But "resemblance," meaning something like a copy of the original, may best convey Castelvetro's own ideas.

their investigations of the truth of things and students of the arts in constituting the arts; and, not understanding them, it is only natural that they should hear them with annoyance and displeasure, for we are all naturally annoyed beyond measure when others speak of matters exceeding our intellectual reach. And so if we conceded that the arts and sciences could supply proper matter to the poets, we should be obliged to concede also either that poetry was not invented to give pleasure or that it was not invented for the ignorant, but that its purpose was to teach and its only audience persons disciplined by the study of letters and exercised in disputations. That these views are false will be proved in the pages that follow.

Now since poetry was invented for the pleasure and recreation of the common people, its subjects must be things suited to their understanding and therefore capable of giving them pleasure. Such things are the everyday happenings that are talked about among the people, the kind that resemble those reported in any one day's news and histories. . . .

I.17 The modes of imitation reconsidered

It is now time for me to set forth my own views on the subject under discussion, for I am not satisfied with what has been written by others. Words and things or, better, the images of words and things stored in the memory are manifested in one of three ways: with words alone in place of both words and things, with words and things in place of words and things, and with words and things resembling (not reproducing) words and things. The first of these modes is called the narrative, the second the dramatic, and the third the similitudinary. Plato and Aristotle seem not to have recognized the third of these modes but only the first two . . . .

The dramatic mode which, as we have said, represents things with things and words with direct words, differs from the narrative mode in a number of ways. (1) It represents words and things with words and things, whereas the narrative mode represents things with words only and represents direct utterances with indirect. (2) It is more restricted in space, for it cannot represent places remote from one another, as the narrative mode may do, which in this respect need observe no restrictions of any kind. (3) It is more restricted in time, for, unlike the narrative mode, it cannot represent actions that unfold over different periods of time. (4) It may represent only things visible and audible, whereas the narrative deals with both the visible and the invisible, the audible and the inaudible. (5) It stirs the emotions more effectively than the narrative. (6) The narrative mode is able to give a better and fuller account of things, even of those peculiarly apt to stir the emotions, for owing to the difficulty of representing actions in a lifelike manner, murders and other such actions, which are difficult to represent with dignity, are never represented on the stage but are more fittingly made to occur behind the scenes and are then reported by a messenger ⟨Sy/181⟩. (7) The narrative mode can relate in a few hours the occurrences of many hours, and in many occurrences of a few, whereas the dramatic mode represents actions in the time in which they would naturally occur and can neither spread a few actions over many hours nor crowd many actions into a few. Hence the performances of tragedies and comedies, which are species of dramatic poetry, must not last so long as to cause hardship to the audience, nor must a play represent more actions than those that could have filled the space of time it is made to cover, the dramatist being, as we have said, under constraint to have due regard for the physical needs of the people, who after a certain number of hours must leave the theatre to attend to the human need for food, drink, sleep, etc. (8) The narrative mode treats things that have actually happened and those that have not happened but are within the realm of the possible, whereas the dramatic mode represents only imaginary things that may happen. This restriction is due not to its inability to represent actual happenings but to the tradition which has come down to us from the ancients, who seem not to have employed the dramatic mode for any stories except those of the poet's own invention. Hence the custom prevalent in some localities of representing the Passion of Our Lord or other histories dramatically is in violation of this tradition. . . .

II.4 Poets not imitators in Aristotle's sense

. . . I therefore find it difficult to believe with Aristotle that the first poetry was spontaneous or unpremeditated ⟨Ar/39⟩, for nothing can be produced spontaneously but by those who have had long practice of the necessary art and have formed the habit of it. . . . We may therefore conclude that the imitation which is natural to men is one thing and the imitation required by poetry another. For the imitation which is natural to men and is implanted in them from childhood, the imitation through which they acquire their first knowledge, for which they all have a stronger aptitude than the other animals, and in the exercise of which they consequently take pleasure – such imitation consists in nothing but in copying models supplied by others and doing exactly as they do without knowing why. But the imitation required by poetry not only does not copy models set before it or duplicate something already made without knowing why it has been so made, but rather makes a thing in every way distinguishable from any made before that day, and, so to speak, creates a model for others to copy. To do this the poet should know perfectly the reason why he does what he does and should devote time and thought to discovering the subtlest reasons for the procedures he is called upon to follow. So true is this that it can be affirmed in all confidence that the imitation peculiar to poetry is not truly and properly imitation, and should not and cannot rightly be given that name, but is and should and may be called a contest between the poet and the dispositions of fortune or the course of human events to determine which will invent the complex of human actions that in the hearing will be judged to be the more marvelous and the more abundant source of pleasure. . . .

III.1 The definition of tragedy

. . . Now it is the duty of the wise and discerning lawgiver to proscribe all arts, crafts, and practices that may in some fashion harm the citizens and corrupt their moral habits. Hence Plato, who believed that the example set by tragic personages might produce these evil effects in them by making them pusillanimous, cowardly, and compassionate, would forbid the representation of tragedy in his republic ⟨Pl/29⟩ fearing that if the citizens saw and heard men whom they held in high esteem doing and saying things that are usually said and done by the compassionate, the timorous, and the pusillanimous, they might take comfort and forgive themselves their own compassionateness, timorousness, and pusillanimity and, seeing that men in high places, such as kings, are not unlike themselves, learn from their example to be moved more than is suitable by those passions. To keep his readers from believing on the authority of Plato that by writing on the art of tragedy he was constituting an art that would harm the citizenry by corrupting their moral habits, Aristotle refutes him in a few words, saying that the effect of tragedy is the exact opposite of that which Plato deplores. Tragedy, he contends, by being frequently enacted on the stage, i.e., by frequently exposing men to scenes of a kind to excite their pity, fear, and pusillanimity, will fortify them against these weaknesses and thus make the pusillanimous magnanimous, the timorous brave, and the compassionate severe, which explains how with the emotions of pity and fear as a means tragedy purges and expels those very emotions from the hearts of men.

Let us now try to ascertain what Aristotle's exact meaning may be, for his own words are few and somewhat obscure: few, because as we have said more than once the *Poetics* is no more than a collection of notes to be utilized in the writing of a larger work; obscure, because he was perhaps restrained by reverence from refuting his master in plain words. We shall understand him better if we consider one or two analogies. A certain quantity of undiluted wine is stronger than a like quantity of the same wine that has been diluted with a great deal of water and thus exceeds the other wine in quantity; but the treatment it has undergone has made it watery and has robbed it of all its former strength. Again, a father will love his children more and be more solicitous of their welfare if he has only a few, say one or two or three, than if he has a great many, say a hundred or a thousand or even more. Thus men's pity and fear will be stronger and more distressing if concentrated on a few piteous and terrible events than if diffused over many. This explains why tragedy, through which we witness piteous and fear-inspiring events more frequently than we otherwise might, will weaken our emotions of pity and fear by causing us to diffuse them among a great variety of actions. Of this phenomenon we receive palpable proof from our experience in times of plague, when we are moved to pity and fear by the first three or four victims but later remain unmoved when the dead are counted in the hundreds and the thousands. In like manner, at their baptism of fire soldiers are terrified by the din of muskets and harquebuses and are moved to great pity by the wounded and the dead; but they later return to the field with composure and cease to be moved to great pity by their wounded and dying comrades.

These are very strong arguments, but perhaps not strong enough to warrant the repeal of Plato's law, for they do not contemplate the evils that Plato sought to proscribe. This will become clear if we consider that in tragedies we have on one hand actions arousing pity and fear and on the other characters undergoing piteous and terrifying experiences. Tragic characters are of two kinds, brave and faint-hearted, and tragic actions are also of two kinds, those of rare and those of frequent occurrence. If the character who suffers is courageous and patient, his example will instill courage and patience in the souls of others and purge them of pity and fear; if he is faint-hearted and weak, his example will make the spectators even more timorous and compassionate, and will confirm them in their fear and pusillanimity. ... As for the tragic incidents, the most piteous and most terrifying are those of rarest occurrence. Those of frequent occurrence move us less and seem to purge human hearts of pity and fear by their very frequency. There are two reasons for this. (1) Seeing ourselves untouched by many calamities all about us we gradually lose our fear of them and bring ourselves to believe that having spared us so often in the past God will continue to spare us in the future. (2) Calamities which occur frequently and involve many do not affect us as very terrible and consequently as very piteous even if we are certain that having struck down so many others they will one day descend upon us. And this, as we have seen, is how men learn to respond to great dangers in times of plague and on the field of battle. ...

III.2 The qualitative parts of tragedy

... Aristotle may also be said to have discovered[8] the six qualitative parts of tragedy by following a different course. An action, he may have reasoned, cannot be represented without a stage, performers, and costumes, and these together constitute the qualitative part known as the spectacle. Of the performers, some represent the action by dancing, others by singing, still others by playing musical instruments, and the rest by speaking. We thus have two more qualitative parts, melody (dance, song,

[8] Castelvetro has reviewed the first three of Aristotle's six qualitative parts of tragedy in their usual order (plot, character, thought) and in a conventional way. He now reverses the order of the six, *beginning* (as Aristotle did not) from performance.

and music) and language. Speech and action reveal men's moral traits, and these constitute a fourth qualitative part known as character. The chief function of language is to express the thought of men in action. It is clear, therefore, that there is a fifth qualitative part, thought, which manifests more plainly than any of the others whether the action is happy or unhappy. Without an action there can be no tragedy – it is, as it were, the soul of tragedy. The action, then, is the sixth qualitative part of tragedy and is called the plot . . . .

III.5   The plot and its eight requirements

Aristotle has shown that the qualitative parts of tragedy are six in number and has ranked them in the order of their importance. He now ⟨Ar/43⟩ undertakes to show how each of these parts is to be fashioned if we would have a proper tragedy. Beginning with the plot he says that to be a well made thing of its kind a plot must meet eight requirements: it must be a whole; it must have magnitude; it must have unity; it must be possible; it must not be episodic, i.e. it must not contain any superfluous and useless episodes; it must be marvelous; it must be complex; it must represent suffering. Some of these requirements are explicit and some implicit in the definition of tragedy. . . .

III.5b   It must have magnitude[9]

. . . A plot may be considered in two ways, as something that may be apprehended by the intellect alone, without the aid of the media that convey it to the senses, and again as something conveyed to the senses by the media of imitating and to be apprehended by both sight and hearing, or by the hearing only. The magnitude of a plot may be considered in the same two ways. Reserving consideration of the magnitude of plots of the first[10] type to a later page, we observe that the magnitude of plots that are apprehended by both sight and hearing should be equal to that of an actual event worthy of being recorded by history; for since the imaginary action from which the plot is formed represents words directly with words and things with things, it must of necessity fill as many hours on the stage as the imaginary action it represents would have filled or would fill in the world if it had actually occurred or were to occur there. Hence we may say that the magnitude of an imaginary plot considered as something that can be apprehended by the senses should equal that of the event it represents, and that it stands in the same relation to that event as, say, a portrait to its original when the latter's dimensions are preserved. Now a plot that is

[9] Having just reviewed the first requirement of plot – that it should be whole – Castelvetro now goes on to the second.

[10] Castelvetro's basic division is between the plots of works intended purely for reading and those intended for performance of some kind. The second category includes epics and other works intended to be heard, as well as plays intended for the stage.

apprehended by sight and hearing must not exceed twelve hours, as we have argued elsewhere in support of Aristotle. This limitation holds for both tragic and comic plots. ...

III.5c It must have unity

... A tragic or comic plot should contain a single action, or two so interrelated that they may be accounted one ⟨Gu/158⟩, and of one person rather than of a whole people, not because it cannot by nature hold more, but because the limitations of time (twelve hours) and place under which the tragedies and comedies are performed will not permit the representation of many actions or of a single action of a whole people, and quite frequently not even of the whole of a single action if it is somewhat long. This, not Aristotle's, is the principal and most compelling reason why tragic and comic plots should contain only a single action of a single person or two actions that may be accounted one because of their interdependence. ...

III.5d It must be possible

The fourth requirement of the plot is that it be possible ⟨Ar/45⟩. It is well to note that this requirement is more important than any of the other seven or than all of them combined, for the quality of possibility in a plot is, as it were, its substance, the other qualities being its accidents, or, again, its matter, which comes first by nature while the rest come after and attach themselves to it. ...

Its subject being what has happened, history need not contemplate either the probable or the necessary but only the true. Poetry on the other hand, whose subject is the possible, establishes the possibility of what it represents by contemplating not the true but the "probable or the necessary" ⟨Ar/45⟩. If, for instance, a man with a wound in the head will probably die of it if he lives an irregular life, then death is for him a possibility, and the poet may without impropriety introduce it into his plot. ... But possible incidents are not always the only kind found in a plot. In my opinion, in fact, they are never the only kind found in the plots of tragedies and epic poems. The plots of these two types of poetry are always developed from something that has actually happened. It is comic plots that always exclude all types of incidents except those that are possible and have never happened. The plots of tragedy and epic poetry must of necessity be based upon incidents which we have classified as things happening to a particular person and are known only in summary form. The story of Orestes, who, accompanied by Pylades and with his and Electra's help, slew his mother, is a suitable one for tragedy and epic poetry, for though the matricide is a historical occurrence we lack all precise knowledge of how it was committed.

Why tragedy and epic poetry may legitimately share with history the recital of things that have actually happened is clear to the point of demonstration. The actions proper to tragedy and epic poetry cannot be simply human actions; they must be the magnificent actions of royal personages. And if they are such, it follows that they must be the known actions of kings who have lived and whom we know to have lived, for no poet may legitimately invent a king who never lived and attribute some action to him; and though he tells of a kind who once lived and is known to have lived he may not legitimately attribute to him an action that was never his. ... Hence all plots fashioned by tragic and epic poets are and ought to be based upon events that can be called historical, though Aristotle is of different opinion. ...

The comic poet invents both the universal form of his plot and its particulars, and since every detail of the whole is of his own invention and nothing that has actually happened is any part of it, he may without impropriety give and is in reason bound to give his characters names of his own choosing. These characters, who perform actions that have never happened, must be private persons, the kind of persons whose actions are quite unknown and are never transmitted to posterity by history or oral tradition. A poet who represents only actions and characters of this kind cannot be accused of falsifying either history or tradition. And if he wishes to be known as a true poet – as an inventor – he is bound to invent every constituent of his comedy, which he is in position to do since private characters and actions constitute his only matter. ...

III.5f It must be marvelous

The sixth[11] requirement of the plot is that it must be marvelous ⟨Ar/46⟩. Tragedy has been defined as the imitation of an action that is not only magnificent, complete, etc., but composed of incidents capable of arousing pity and fear. And since such incidents owe their effect primarily to the element of the marvelous in them, we could not neglect to speak of the marvelous, which engenders and intensifies pity and fear, without thereby forfeiting a full knowledge of those two emotions, which are among the principal elements of tragedy. ...

We now proceed to a discussion of ... the type of marvelous occurrence that intensifies pity and fear. To understand the matter fully we must first divide the marvelous into three classes, according as it is met (1) in irrational animals and insensible objects, (2) in men doing some horrible deed deliberately, or (3) in men doing some horrible deed accidentally against their will. These last are of two kinds, (a) those who do some horrible deed by following the very ways which they believe are least likely to lead to it and (b) those who are deceived into doing one against their intentions. ...

---

[11] Castelvetro has just reviewed the fifth requirement for the plot: that it must not be episodic.

III.5g It must be complex

The seventh requirement of the plot ⟨Ar/46⟩ is that it be complex and not simple. A complex plot is one consisting of two different or, rather, contrary constituents, happiness and misery or misery and happiness. A simple plot is one in which happiness or misery prevails throughout. ...

I call the plot "simple" when, like that of *Oedipus the King*, it contains only one reversal of fortune, though the reversal may also be from misery to happiness. My definition differs from Aristotle's in that a simple plot is for me not one without a reversal but one containing a single reversal, as against two or three. ...

III.6 Recognition and its means

Aristotle maintains ⟨Ar/47⟩ that "the best type of recognition is that which occurs at the same time as the reversals." His use of the phrase "at the same time" indicates that the recognition he has in mind is the recognition of persons which brings with it a reversal from happiness to misery, eliminating the subsidiary type, such as that between Orestes and Electra.[12] Why Aristotle should pronounce the first of these two types of recognition far superior to the second is quite clear; but when he says, as he does soon after, that it is also superior to every other type, and especially to the discovery of deeds, we cannot understand his preference unless it is justified by other reasons than those that he himself adduces. To prove that the recognitions in question and the consequent reversals from happiness to misery are the most suitable to tragedy, Aristotle says that they arouse pity and fear and that they make the agents happy or unhappy. Yet the discovery of an unknown deed and the consequent reversal in actions of the type suitable to tragedy are neither more nor less effective than the type of recognition and reversal praised by Aristotle for arousing pity and fear and making for happiness or misery.... It is not for the reasons given, then, that the recognition of persons is the most suitable to tragedy, but because ignorance of persons is a rarer thing than ignorance of deeds. For people do not commonly lose the ability to recognize other members of their own families, and when they do, or are made unable to recognize them by some accident, it is almost a miracle that out of the thousands of men and women in the world the deed of horror should involve two members of the same family who are unknown to each other. And it is no less a miracle that they should finally recognize each other by chance and thanks to words and things never intended to effect a recognition. These are the reasons why the recognition of persons is superior to all other types. ...

---

[12] In Sophocles' *Electra* the recognition (of Orestes and Electra) moves the plot towards the murder of Clytemnestra but the recognition does not itself involve a reversal causing tragic suffering.

III.11 Happiness and misery as ends of tragedy and comedy

The end of tragedy is happiness or misery, but not happiness or misery of every kind, for as we shall see these differ according as they are produced by tragic or comic incidents. The happiness produced by tragedy is the kind a person knows when he himself or some one dear to him is saved from death or is released from suffering or avoids a fall from the rank of royalty. Tragic misery, on the other hand, is restricted to the kind a person knows when he himself or someone dear to him suffers death or is plunged into suffering or falls from the rank of royalty. The happiness produced by comedy is the kind a person knows when he has succeeded in putting an end to the scorn to which he himself or persons dear to him have been subjected, in blotting out some disgrace which had been thought inefface-able, in recovering some lost person or thing dear to him, or in achieving the satisfaction of amorous desire. Comic misery, on the other hand, is restricted to the misery a person knows when he himself or some one dear to him is made the object of mild scorn, suffers some mild disgrace or the loss of a few possessions, is thwarted in love, or is otherwise made somewhat unhappy.

Why cannot comedy and tragedy have the same kind of happiness or misery as their ends? The answer is to be sought in the differences between tragic and comic agents. Tragic agents are royal personages. They are high-spirited and haughty, and what they desire they desire immoderately. If they suffer or think they suffer an injury they neither seek redress from the magistrates nor possess their souls in patience, but settle their own accounts as their passions dictate, vengefully slaying persons closely or distantly related to them by blood, and sometimes in desperation even turning their hand against themselves. Being of royal rank, which is held to be the summit of human felicity, and enjoying the power to avenge personal injuries, they are never made the objects of even mild scorn or derision and are neither ruffled by the loss of a few possessions nor even subjected to such loss by others. Their habitual good cheer is not augmen-ted by a marriage or the satisfaction of amorous desires, for they may truly be said to live in perpetual nuptials and in continuous amorous pleasures and therefore cannot rise to a happy state unless they have first fallen from their former felicity or at least have been in clear danger of doing so. On the other hand they cannot know unhappiness unless they are plunged into misery or fall from their high estate in truly memorable fashion.

Comic agents, on the other hand, are faint-hearted. They are in the habit of obeying the magistrates, of conforming to the laws, of submitting to injuries and losses, and of seeking redress for the loss of honor or posses-sions from the authorities and their ordinances. They never take matters in their own hands, nor resort to the slaying of strangers, kinsmen, or themselves for the reasons that such measures are resorted to by kings. Being poor and of low condition, they need not fall from a former felicity before they can rise to a happy state, for their happiness is far from total and can be augmented by a moderate stroke of good fortune, such as a desired marriage and the like. On the other hand they may be made unhappy by the loss of a few possessions or some mild abuse. These are the reasons why the happiness and unhappiness which are the ends of tragedy differ from those which are the end of comedy.

If I am asked why comedy cannot deal with the rise of a private person to a throne, of which some instances are recorded in history, I reply first that a plot of this kind is appropriate to tragedy and not to comedy and that for the reasons already given it could not properly be invented outright but would have to be taken from history, and secondly that performances of it would give little pleasure in republics and even less in monarchies: in republics because men who love freedom and are determined to preserve it cannot desire that their fellow-citizens witness the example of a private person usurping a throne, and in monarchies because being jealous of their royal state kings guard against setting before the common people and private citizens examples of actions that might awaken in them the desire to overthrow the monarchy and establish a new order. Kings, in fact, invariably forbid the public performances of tragedies, for they know that the common people rejoice at the misfortunes of the great, and tragedies are never performed except among people who are not subject to a single ruler. The end of tragedy, then, is either happiness or misery. But since in tragedy whose end is happiness the royal personage is normally exposed to some great peril, this type of tragedy produces pity and fear as well as happiness, so that the happiness, as we shall show, is not without an admixture of unhappiness. It remains true, however, that the tragedy best fitted to arouse pity and fear is the one that has misery for its end. The end of tragedy, then, is happiness or misery, the kind of each that we have described as suitable to tragedy. . . .

III.12 Plots and their emotional effects

Aristotle has established that the tragic plot must be complex. But since many complex plots do not contain and do not imitate piteous and fear-inspiring actions, he now adds ⟨Ar/47⟩ that the complex plot proper to tragedy "must imitate incidents that arouse pity and fear." Now whether a tragedy must be composed only of incidents that arouse those emotions is a question that I will not consider further at this point, but it seems to me certain that Aristotle has not yet proved his contention, though he assumes that he has. Aristotle set out to contradict Plato, who had contended that tragedy undermines the people's moral habits. With this purpose in mind he withholds approval from every type of tragedy but that which, in his opinion, effects the moral improvement of the people, purging their souls of pity and fear by the actions of these emotions in the manner we described earlier and he is so intent on contradicting Plato that he fails to notice that he contradicts opinions he himself advanced on earlier pages. For if poetry was invented principally for pleasure and not utility, as he demonstrated in discussing poetry in general, why would he have us go to tragedy, which is a species of poetry, principally for its utility? Why not go to it principally for pleasure and disregard utility, of which, if we follow his earlier counsel, we should either take no account whatever or not so much that we should reject every kind of tragedy that cannot provide it? Then, too, Aristotle restricts himself to a single kind of utility, namely the purgation of pity and fear. Yet if utility is not to be ignored, there are other kinds of tragedies that could be performed for the people's edification, as, for instance, those that represent the good as rising from misery to happiness or the bad as falling from happiness to misery, both of them examples that could reasonably confirm the people in the pious opinion that God watches over the affairs of men and that He is especially solicitous about His own, protecting them and confounding both His enemies and theirs. . . .

III.14 Tragic character

Aristotle now ⟨Ar/49⟩ inquires into and discovers the nature of the tragic person, i.e., the kind of person who by falling from happiness to misery or rising from misery to happiness will most effectively arouse the emotions of pity and fear. His procedure is first to divide all persons into three groups, the pre-eminently good, the extremely wicked, and the ordinarily virtuous, and then to show that the common people are not moved to pity and fear when the pre-eminently good and the extremely wicked fall from happiness to misery or rise from misery to happiness, but only when persons of ordinary virtue fall from happiness to misery. He therefore concludes that the truly tragic person is the person of ordinary virtue represented as falling from happiness to misery. . . .

. . . I am unable to understand why the fall of a man of very holy life from happiness to misery should not arouse pity and fear; why it should not, in fact, arouse greater pity and fear than the fall of a man of ordinary virtue, for those whose lives are not of a holiness comparable to his, as the lives of the common people generally are not, are more terrified and dismayed by the sufferings of one better than themselves than by those of one of their own kind. The experience of such a fall would fill them with the fear that they may well be visited by a similar misfortune, bringing before their minds the Gospel text, "For if they do these things in a green tree, what should be done in the dry?" [Luke 23.31] And who shall be pitied if not the saintly man who falls into misfortune? For if we are moved to pity by those who suffer unjustly, who deserves misfortune less than the man of most saintly life? None assuredly, and the representation of a supremely saintly man falling from happiness to misery should not therefore have been rejected as incapable of moving audiences to pity and fear. Yet Aristotle asserts that the fall of such a man does not fill us with pity and fear but with indignation against God, which is a blasphemous state of mind. To which I reply that if we are filled with indignation against God it does not follow that we are not also filled with pity and fear. The indignation does not extinguish the pity and fear. When, for example, a person of ordinary virtue is unjustly injured by some one, we feel indignation against the latter, but do not for that reason fail to be moved to pity and fear by the undeserved suffering of the injured man. Who is there that does not hate Phaedra, the false accuser of Hippolytus to his father, and is not at the same time moved to pity and fear by Hippolytus' death, which is a consequence of that accusation?

At this point someone may protest, "I concede to you that the fall of a man of holy life from happiness to misery will move people to pity and fear if you will concede to me that it will also move them to indignation against God. But that indignation is blasphemous, and to avoid it we must eschew the kind of reversal involving that kind of person and renounce all the pity and all the fear that it might generate." To which one may briefly reply that the common people, who believe that God rules the world and watches over all individual things, exercising a special care over each, believe also that He is just in all His actions and makes all things redound to His own glory and to the good of His faithful servants. . . .

It is to be borne in mind, then, that just as we are moved to pity and fear by the fall of a just man because seeing misfortune overtake one who is like ourselves or better and therefore deserves it less than we we realize that misfortune may one day overtake us, so we are similarly moved by the rise of a bad man from misery to happiness, for the spectacle brings to mind the possibility that we may one day suffer the same pains that he inflicted upon his innocent contemporaries, the possibility, that is, of another baseborn villain rising to the lordship of our city and cruelly subjecting us, though innocent of wrongdoing, to oppression and persecution. Thus if we consider the persons who should or may be considered, we may conclude that the rise of a bad man is no less capable of moving to pity and fear than the fall of a just man. . . .

IV   Comedy

We shall now say a few words on the subject of the ludicrous, and we shall do so for two reasons: to gain a clearer understanding of the doctrines which Aristotle has set forth so succinctly in one brief note, and to discover, it may be, principles of which he makes no mention. Laughter is provoked by pleasurable things apprehended by the senses or the imagination. These may be divided into four classes. (1) We are pleased to see, for the first time or after an absence, persons who are dear to us, or acquire or recover things which we value highly. The persons who are dear to us are our fathers, mothers, children, lovers, friends, and the like. Hence fathers and mothers embrace their children with laughter and rejoicing, and little children, on their part, run to their parents with joyous laughter. Lovers, too, embrace one another with laughter. The things that are dear to us are honors, public offices, jewels, possessions, good tidings – in short everything that becomes ours after we have desired it long or ardently. (2) Deceptions, as when a person is made to say, do, or suffer what he would not say, do, or suffer unless he were deceived. Such deceptions are a source of very great pleasure to us and move us to laughter. The cause of this laughter is the sin of our first parents, which so corrupted our nature that we take pleasure in the ills of others as we do in our own good fortune. And no human ills delight us more than those which proceed from the faculty peculiar to man, namely, the reason; for when others are deceived in our presence we assume that we are superior to them, and superior in the very faculty which makes man akin to God and sets him far above all other creatures. ... (3) The third class of things that give us pleasure and provoke our laughter consists of wickedness of soul and physical deformities, together with the actions of which they are the cause. But we laugh at them only when they appear to us under the guise of other things, for then we may pretend that not they but these things are the real causes of our laughter. For, as we have already said, our nature has been so corrupted by the sin transmitted to us by our first parents that we take pleasure in the defects of our fellow men either because the knowledge that many others are also imperfect offers us assurance that we are not as imperfect as we believed, or because the recognition in others of defects of which we are free enhances our self-esteem and fills us with pride and joy. ... (4) The fourth and last class of pleasurable things that move us to laughter consists of all the things having to do with carnal pleasure, like the privy parts, sexual intercourse, and the memories and representations of both. ...

RICHARD EDWARDS
(1524–66)

Richard Edwards, who lectured in logic at Christ Church, Oxford, came to enjoy a considerable reputation as a musician, playwright, and poet. In 1561 he became Master of the Children of the Chapel Royal, in which office he was schoolmaster, choirmaster, acting-coach, and deviser of entertainments put on by the Children.

In 1566, Queen Elizabeth was present at a performance of Edwards' *Palamon and Arcite*, produced by him at Christ Church. This play has not survived. Nor have others that he wrote in his youth and which were said by his friends to surpass those of Plautus and Terence. Edwards' one extant play is *Damon and Pithias*, which may have been played before the Queen in 1564.

Damon is remarkable for the careful construction of its complex plot in the course of which Damon falls into the clutches of Dionysius of Syracuse, is falsely accused of spying, and is condemned to death. In order to give Damon the opportunity to return home and set his affairs in order, his friend Pithias offers himself as a hostage who, if Damon fails to return, will die in his place. At the climax of the play, Pithias is about to be executed, Damon returns in the nick of time, each vies to save the other, and the tyrant Dionysius, profoundly impressed by this ultimate sincerity, not only reprieves them both but becomes a candidate for inclusion in their bond of friendship.

When *Damon and Pithias* was printed (possibly not for the first time) in 1571, it was described on its title-page as an "excellent comedy . . . . Newly imprinted, as the same was showed before the Queen's Majesty, by the Children of Her Grace's Chapel, except the Prologue that is somewhat altered for the proper use of them that hereafter shall have occasion to play it, either in private or in open audience. . . ." The Prologue is one of the earliest examples of an attempt at dramatic theory by an English playwright. Edwards' idea of "tragical comedy" and his use of the term derive from Renaissance Latin drama and he may have been the first to apply it to a play in English.[1] He has not arrived at the idea of "tragicomedy" as the hybrid genre that Guarini would passionately defend ⟨Gu/149⟩ and that Sidney, along with many continental theorists, would dismiss ⟨Sy/181⟩ as a contemptible "mongrel." What, for him, makes the play "tragical," is that it is based on history and is serious (to the point of involving mortal danger to the protagonists). The exemplary values of tragedy and its affective power (in contrast to mere philosophy) are not alluded to in the Prologue, but are clearly thematized in the

---

[1] Nicholas Grimald (1519?–1562?), who was Edwards' contemporary at Christ Church, had called his *Christus Redivivus* (1540), a "tragic comedy, sacred comedy, sacred and new." The play was in the long tradition of adaptations of Terence's dramaturgy to biblical themes. *Apius and Virginia* by "R. B.," also described on its (1575) title-page as a "tragical comedy," is a play on a classical and moral theme written at about the same time as *Damon and Pithias*. See Ristine 1910 and Herrick [1955] 1962.

play. The good, philosophical councilor, Eubulus, fails to moderate the tyrannical behavior of his master, and another philosopher is thoroughly corrupted by becoming a courtier. But Damon and Pithias achieve an unpremeditated success through the *enactment* of their "tragedy." As Dionysius confesses:

> My heart this rare friendship hath pierc'd to the root,
> And quenched all my fury. This sight hath brought this about,
> Which thy grave counsel, Eubulus, and learned persuasion, could never
>   do.
>   [To Damon and Pithias]
>   O, noble gentlemen, the immortal gods above
> Hath made you play this tragedy, I think for my behoof.   (vv. 1666–70)

Edwards' insistence on the historical and geographical particularity of the tragedy is a prudent disclaimer of any specifically contemporary and local criticism, and it also defines tragedy as something played out in real life before it is represented on the stage. But his idea of dramatic decorum obviously does not exclude the mixture of "mirth and care," tragic and comic matter, and his use of satirical subplots is further reason for calling the play a comedy. It is possible, too, that Edwards, like his acquaintance and fellow-playwright Nicholas Grimald, regarded the happy ending as inherently comic, though many sixteenth-century theorists ⟨Gd/126⟩ vehemently insisted that happy endings were appropriate for tragedies and that to suppose otherwise was a vulgar error.[2] Not everyone ends happily in *Damon and Pithias*, however, and though Edwards does not mention it, this mixture of good fortune for the virtuous, misery for the vicious was frequently taken, in the sixteenth century ⟨Gu/153⟩, as an essential feature of tragicomedy, legitimized by Aristotle's remark ⟨Ar/50⟩ on double endings.

For further reading

Armstrong 1958; Bradner 1927; Herrick [1950] 1964, [1955], 1963; Kramer 1968; Ristine 1910

Prologue to *Damon and Pithias*

On every side, whereas I glance my roving eye,
Silence in all ears bent I plainly do espy:
But if your eager looks do long such toys to see,
As heretofore in comical wise were wont abroad to be,[3]
Your lust is lost,[4] and all pleasures that you sought
Is frustrate quite of toying plays. A sudden change is wrought:
For lo, our author's Muse, that masked in delight,
Hath forced his pen against his kind, no more such sports to write.
Muse he that lust[5] (right worshipful) for chance hath made this change
For that to some he seemed too much, in young desires to range:

---

[2] Grimald gives this opinion in his "Epistle Dedicatory" to *Christus Redivivus*.
[3] "wont abroad to be" = once widely current.
[4] "lust" = wish, pleasure, desire.
[5] "Muse he that lust" = Think what he will.

In which, right glad to please, seeing that he did offend,
Of all he humbly pardon craves: his pen that shall amend.
And yet, worshipful audience, thus much I dare avouch:
In comedies the greatest skill is this: rightly to touch
All things to the quick, and eke to frame each person so
That by his common talk you may his nature rightly know.
A roister[6] ought not preach, that were too strange to hear,
But as from virtue he doth swerve, so ought his words appear.
The old man is sober; the young man rash; the lover triumphing in joys;
The matron grave; the harlot wild and full of wanton toys;
Which all, in one course, they no wise do agree,
So, correspondent to their kind, their speeches ought to be.
Which speeches, well pronounced, with action lively framed,
If this offends the lookers on, let Horace then be blamed,
Which hath our author taught at school, from whom he doth not swerve,
In all such kind of decorum to observe ⟨Hr/68:156⟩.
Thus much for his defence, he saith, as poets erst have done,
Which heretofore in comedies the selfsame race did run.
But now, for to be brief, the matter to express,
Which here we shall present is this: Damon and Pithias,
A rare example of friendship true, it is no legend lie,
But a thing once done, indeed, as histories do descry,
Which, done of yore in long time past, yet present shall be here,
Even as it were in doing now, so lively it shall appear:
Lo, here in Syracuse, the ancient town, which once the Romans won,
Here Dionysius' palace, within whose court this thing most strange was
    done,
Which matter, mixed with mirth and care, a just name to apply,
As seems most fit we have it termed a Tragical Comedy,
Wherein talking of courtly toys, we do protest this flat,
We talk of Dionysius' court, we mean no court but that,
And that we do so mean, who wisely calleth to mind
The time, the place, the authors[7] here most plainly shall it find.
Lo, this I speak for our defence, lest of others we should be shent;[8]
But, worthy audience, we you pray, take things as they be meant,
Whose upright judgement we do crave, with heedful ear and eye,
To hear the cause and see th'effect of this new Tragical Comedy.

6 "roister" = swaggerer.
7 The "authors" are the persons who performed the deeds here dramatized.
8 "shent" = blamed.

13

GIAMBATTISTA GUARINI
(1538–1612)

Guarini's theory of tragicomedy as a hybrid form with its own set of rules is inextricable from the controversy over his pastoral tragicomedy *Pastor fido* (*The Faithful Shepherd*). The *Compendium of Tragicomic Poetry*[1] was written primarily as a defense of the play, which, even before it was first published in 1589, had become a test case of the legitimacy of tragicomedy. Giason de Nores,[2] called it "a monstrous and irregular composition" because it mixed the high tone of tragedy with the low tone of comedy, thus violating the supposed rules of unity and verisimilitude. The play, which used musical settings within the dialogue, was also sharply criticized for its excessive lyricism. These features, combined with its Arcadian setting, with mysterious caves and sacrificial altars, in which white-robed shepherds perform allegorical dances and are rescued from certain death by magical herbs, led some of Guarini's detractors to label it a string of madrigals, rather than a drama (Perella 1973, 3).

Pastor fido was often reprinted in the first decades of the seventeenth century, and even though the play may have been performed only once in the author's lifetime, its influence on the development of pastoral drama and tragicomedy was immense. In England this was felt in *The Faithful Shepherdess* (1610) by John Fletcher, whose justification for writing a pastoral tragicomedy was taken almost verbatim from Guarini's *Compendium*:

> A tragicomedy is not so called in respect of mirth and killing, but in respect it wants death, which is enough to make it no tragedy, yet brings it near it, which is enough to make it no comedy, which must be a presentation of familiar people, with such kind of trouble as no life to be questioned; so that a God is as lawful in this as in a tragedy, and mean people as in a comedy. (Fletcher [1610] 1893, 321.)

The 1601 edition of Guarini's *Compendium of Tragicomic Poetry* marks the climax of a long and heated debate about tragicomedy. Started by Giraldi's *Treatise on the Composition of Comedies and Tragedies* (1554) ⟨Gd/121⟩, this debate had been preoccupied with two main issues: the role and function of catharsis, and the use of the double plot. Much of the theoretical discussion on catharsis focused on finding ways to *reinforce* pity rather than to purge it away. Guarini himself asks: "what need do we have today to purge terror and compassion through tragic sights since we have the most sacred precepts of our religion which teaches through the Gospels?"

---

[1] The *Compendium* was so called because it was a compilation of two previous works which Guarini had published under the titles *Il Verato I* and *Il Verato II*. (Verato was a famous actor of the time.)

[2] For a discussion of the de Nores–Guarini controversy, see Perella 1973, 7–10, and Weinberg 1961, II: 1074–1106.

Even more emphatically, Guarini seeks in the *Compendium* to prove that *Pastor fido* respects the rule of unity. His main strategy is to examine what he calls the "instrumental" and the "architectonic" ends of tragicomedy, arguing that this new form of drama is not a juxtaposition of comic and tragic elements but is analogous to natural or man-made hybrids and alloys ⟨Tm/210⟩, and thus distinct from its parent elements. Its instrumental, or mechanical, end is to mix elements of tragedy and comedy, but only after these have been tempered in order to remove from comedy its excessive lewdness and from tragedy its excessive savagery. The architectonic, or functional, end is to purge the listeners of melancholy. The rule of unity is respected because, although tragicomedy draws on elements of comedy and tragedy, it is a form with a single end: the purgation of melancholy. Thus, like his contemporary Lorenzo Giacomini ⟨Gm/173⟩, Guarini creatively misinterprets Aristotle in proposing a new and Christian kind of catharsis.

For further reading

Della Valle 1973; Doran 1954; Fletcher [1610] 1893; Gilbert 1940; Greg 1906; Hathaway 1962; Herrick [1950] 1964, [1955] 1962; Hirst, 1984; Perella 1973; Spingarn 1908b; Weinberg 1961.

From *Compendium of Tragicomic Poetry*[3]

From what has already been said it should not be difficult to judge in which species of poetry *Pastor fido* belongs: it is a mixture of tragic and comic poetry, and if both of these are dramatic, it necessarily follows that it also is dramatic. But it seems that it is more difficult to understand the skill with which two very different sorts of poems have been brought together to make a third that is well ordered and without defects, for it seems impossible that a tragic poem, which is all tears, could ever mingle so well with a comic one, which is all laughter, without offense to art. This difficulty is compounded by the fact that every poem, insofar as it is a single[4] poem, is all the more perfect . . . . This excellent quality [of unity of action] has been commended by all good teachers of this art, and it must seem scandalous when any poem is deprived of it. And, if tragedy and comedy, even when separate, can easily fall into this defect of not possessing unity, what will become of the third species, which cannot be presented or considered unless it is multiple. In truth, in every species of poetry unity is a very important and necessary attribute because the form, which gives being to all things, is one; moreover beauty is nothing but the harmonious and consonant union of all the parts. How then can a fable composed of two, not only different, but contrasting fables, preserve unity and be good? . . .

---

[3] *Compendio della poesia tragicomica, tratto dai duo Verati, per opera dell'autore del Pastor Fido, colla giunta di molte cose spettanti all'arte*, Venice: Ciotti, 1601. The present translation is from the text in Brognoligo 1914.

[4] "single" = possessing unity of action.

There are two ways in which it can be said that *Pastor fido* does not preserve the rule of unity: first, because of the two forms of comedy and tragedy; and secondly, because it has more than one subject, as do all the comedies of Terence.[5] In order to make our argument more clear and expedient we shall use our own works and shall call the first [way] with its usual name of "mixed," while the second we shall call "grafted." With respect to the first, we should bear in mind that a tragicomedy is not composed of two complete plots, the one a perfect comedy and the other a perfect tragedy, joined together in such manner that they can be separated without damaging each other or themselves. Nor should it be believed that it is a tragic story corrupted with the lowliness of comedy, or a comic plot contaminated with the deaths of tragedy, for this would not be a good composition. Whoever sets out to make a tragicomedy does not intend to compose separately a tragedy and a comedy, but of these two to make a third, perfect of its own kind, but which takes from both of them those several parts that can best remain together with verisimilitude. Therefore, when judging it, one should not confuse the terms "mixed" and "double," as do those of little understanding[6] who do not realize that nothing can be mixed unless it is one, and if the parts contained in it are not mixed in such a way that they cannot be recognized separately. . . .

Tragedy and comedy have performance in common, plus all the rest of the stage machinery as well as rhythm, harmony, finite length, dramatic plot, verisimilitude, recognition, and reversal. By "in common" I mean that they make use of the same things, although there are some differences between them in the way they make use of these things. Other qualities are so peculiar to each of them that not only do they vary in practice, as do the already mentioned ones, but differentiate the species in such a way that they are its identifying characteristics. There is no doubt that should anyone attempt to transfer either of them in its entirety into the confines of the other, using in tragedy that which belongs to comedy alone or vice versa, he would make an improper and monstrous plot. The point, however, is to see whether these specific differences are so contrary to each other that a third species of poetry, legitimate and reasonable, cannot be formed.

These specific differences are proper to tragedy: persons of high rank, serious actions, terror, and pity; and these to comedy: private persons and affairs, laughter, and witty remarks. As to the first, I acknowledge, follow-ing Aristotelian doctrine, that persons of high rank are appropriate to tragedy and those of low rank to comedy; but I deny that it is contrary to nature and to the art of poetry in general to introduce persons of high and

---

[5] On the justification of the use of the double plot in comedy, and also in tragedy, by reference to Terence, especially the *Andria*, see Herrick [1950] 1964, 89ff.

[6] Giason de Nores had criticized *Pastor fido* for mixing two plots. See Herrick [1955] 1962, 137.

low rank together in one plot. Was there ever a tragedy that did not have more servants and persons of similar rank than characters of great consequence? Who unties the beautiful knot in the *Oedipus* of Sophocles? Not the king nor the queen, not Creon nor Tiresias, but two servant herdsmen. Therefore it is not contrary to the nature of the stage to mix persons of high and low rank, not only in a mixed poem as is tragicomedy, but in a pure tragedy; and, if we were to ask Aristophanes, also in a comedy, for he mingled gods and men, citizens and countrymen, and even introduced animals and clouds to speak in his plots. As far as great and small events are concerned, I cannot understand why it is improper that they should be in the same play, which may not be purely tragic, when they are sensibly inserted. Can it not be that some charming incidents might occur between serious events? And are these not frequently the cause of the happy resolution of dangerous situations? Furthermore, do princes always sit in majesty? Do they never deal in private matters? Certainly they do: why then cannot a high-ranking person appear on the stage when he is not engaged in matters of great importance? Euripides did this in his *Cyclops* in which he mixed the grave danger of death facing Ulysses, a tragic person, with the drunkenness of the Cyclops, which is comic ⟨Sg/106⟩.[7] Among the Latins, Plautus did the same thing in his *Amphitryon*, in which the persons of high rank, not only Amphitryon but also the king of the gods, are accompanied by the laughter and jests of Mercury. It is not contrary to reason, then, that persons of high rank can coexist in the same play with events of not so great importance. I might say the same thing about laughter and pity, which are comic and tragic qualities respectively: indeed, they do not seem to me so contrary that they cannot, albeit in different circumstances and characters, appear together in the same plot. On reading in Terence the case of Menedemus, who willingly mortified himself because of the harshness with which he behaved towards his son, who can fail to be moved to pity and, like Chremes (who could not hold back his tears), weep over it? But even in the very same play[8] there is laughter at the cunning with which the crafty Siro ridicules and deceives the already mentioned Chremes. I say, then, that in the same play there can be pity and laughter, though not happiness and sorrow. Therefore, the total sum of this contradiction can be reduced to one single difference, that is, the terrible, which can never occur except in a tragic plot, nor can anything comic ever mingle with it, because the terrible is always the result of serious and sorrowful representations: where it is found, there is no room for laughter and sport.

---

[7] In this satyr-play (the only one extant), the essentially serious Homeric matter of the encounter with the Cyclops, who eats some of Odysseus' comrades before the hero escapes, is burlesqued by Euripides, particularly in the satyr chorus and the figure of the drunken Silenus.

[8] *Self-Tormentor (Heautontimorumenos)*.

All of the things mentioned above could be brought forward in defense of tragicomic poetry. But I do not wish to avail myself of them, and am happy to leave to tragedy its royal characters, its serious actions, the terrible and the miserable; and to comedy, its private persons and affairs, its laughter and jests as the specific differences between them. I will grant, for the present, that one may not enter into the jurisdiction of the other: but does it follow from this that, because they are different in species, they cannot mix together to form a new poem? Certainly it cannot be said that this is contrary to the use of nature and even less so to that of art. Now, to begin with nature: are not the horse and the ass two different species? Certainly, yet from their union a third species is produced: the mule which is neither one nor the other. The same can be said of the mule born of the union of the dog and the wolf which is neither dog nor wolf. The same can be said of the "third nature," which springs from the pheasant and the rooster, the fox and the dog, and of many other things reported by Aristotle in his books *On the Generation of Animals*, in which he cites the proverb, much hackneyed in his day, that Africa has always something new to offer, assigning the cause to the various unions of animals of different species which, due to the lack of water, are forced to go the same place to quench their thirst.[9] But perhaps it could be objected that these third natures are born of the mingling of the seeds and not of the bodies, and that they are works of nature and not works of art, as are the works which interest us.

Let us therefore turn to works of art and their hybrids, which are made of solid bodies but are different in their natures. Bronze is made from copper and tin, and the bodies of both of them enter into their mingling, but their natures are fused together in such manner that the hybrid which results from their mixture is neither tin nor copper. Sulphur and nitre, along with the carbon as a third, enter into the making of gunpowder: all three are complete in their nature and different in their accidentals, yet gunpowder is neither the one nor the other. Now, someone might argue that these examples are not suitable because the results are obtained through fire, which changes the quality of those substances in such a manner that it might be called a natural process, which is not true in poetic mixtures which are completely dependent on the skill of their maker and not on the intervention of nature. Let even this be granted, and let us speak of painting which is the blood-cousin of poetry: does painting not make diverse mixtures of its colors without employing any other means? The same can be said of music which came into being at the very same birth with poetry: does it not mingle the diatonic with the chromatic, and the chromatic with the enharmonic, and with each other what the Philosopher [Aristotle] calls "harmonies"? Yet, it is the single work of a composer. But those who wish to object further might reply that while the

---

9 "Libya is always bringing forth something new" (*On the Generation of Animals* 2.2.746b7).

painter works with colors and the composer with voices, the poet sets in motion human affairs and persons. Let even this be granted and in the end a mixture may be found that is so similar to a poetic mixture that there is no difference between them, except for that which is known to exist between the real and the fictional. This is very appropriate in our case, in which the representation is almost the same as the thing which it represents, poetry being nothing other than the imitation of the verisimilar.[10] But have we not said earlier that poetry deals with actions and persons? Let us therefore give an example involving actions and persons. Do not Marcus Tullius ⟨Dn/79⟩ and Horace ⟨Hr/72: 286–88⟩ say that comedy is the mirror of social relations? An example from social relations shall be given. Does not Aristotle say ⟨Ar/41, 46⟩ that tragedy is made of persons of high rank and comedy of ordinary men? Such is the state. Now, are not its citizens human persons and its acts of government human actions? And if these, which occur in the real world, can be mixed, cannot poetic art, made by those who operate in the world of fiction, also be mixed? Where only the few have the exercise of power, is it not wielded only by the great? And where the common people have the exercise of power, is it not wielded by the plebeians? And are not these contraries? Yet they conjoin in a single mixture. Furthermore, is tragedy not the imitation of the great and comedy of the humble? And are the humble not the opposite of the great? Why cannot poetry mix them if politics can? . . .

The writer of tragicomedy takes from tragedy its great persons but not its action, its verisimilar but unhistorical plot, its stormy emotions somewhat attenuated, its pleasure but not its sadness, its danger but not its death; from comedy he takes laughter that is not lewd, its modest pleasures, its fictional knot, its happy reversal, and above all the comic order, of which we will speak in its proper place. All these parts, when modified in the manner we have just outlined, can stand together in a single play, especially if they are seasoned with their own decorum and the manners which are appropriate to them. . . .

A new doubt may arise here as to what in actual fact is a tragicomic mixture; to which I would answer that it is the moderate tempering of tragic and comic pleasure in order to prevent the listeners from falling into the excessive melancholy of tragedy or the excessive lewdness of comedy. From this results a poem of the most excellent form and composition which not only fully corresponds to the complexity of human nature, which consists entirely in the tempering of the four humors ⟨Jn/197⟩,[11] but is also much nobler than simple tragedy and simple comedy: it does not

---

[10] Having defined tragicomedy as the imitation of a fictional action, Guarini uses "verisimilar" to indicate the quality of the fiction which is wrought (imitated) into drama.

[11] The medical theory of humors holds that health and temperament in human beings are determined by the balance of the four humors – blood, phlegm, black bile and yellow bile – and their corresponding emotions. (See below, p. 197, n.15.)

inflict on us such horrible and inhumane sights as atrocious events, blood, and deaths, while, on the other hand, it does not render us so dissolute in our laughter that we sin against the modesty and decorum of the well-bred man. And truly, if today poets knew well how to make a tragicomedy, for it is not an easy thing to do, no other type of play should be put on stage, for tragicomedy includes within it all the good parts of dramatic poetry and rejects the bad ones. It can be a source of delight for men of different taste, temperament, and age, which is neither true of comedy nor of tragedy, both of which sin by falling into excess. For this reason many great and wise men today abhor the one and have little regard for the other.

But it seems to me that my task will not be completed if, after having made known the parts of tragicomedy, which are, so to speak, the forms that make it a well-ordered and good form of poetry, I should fail to do the same for its end. Now, since its plot is mixed, someone might legitimately ask what its end should be, whether tragic, comic, or mixed. This cannot be done without much difficulty for each form of art has its own end towards which it moves; where a form of art has two ends, one is always subordinate to the other in such a manner that it moves only towards its principal end. Let us grant that tragicomedy is a reasonably mixed form: what does it attempt to do? What is its end?

... Does it want tears or laughter, since both cannot be had at once? ... These questions cannot be answered until we have determined the ends of tragedy and comedy respectively. Now, in order to understand this, it should be known that each form of art has, in addition to the principal end of which we have spoken above, another end. The first is that by means of which the artist, as he works, introduces into the matter at hand that form which is the end of the work of art; while the other is that for the use and benefit of which he brings the work to completion. ... One of these ends we shall call "instrumental" and the other, with Aristotle's own term, "architectonic"; and both of these we find in tragic and comic art.

Let us begin with comedy: its instrumental end is to imitate those actions of private men which, because of their defects, move us to laughter; this is Aristotle's notion. The architectonic end, however, is not found in Aristotle, for in the treatise on *Poetics* which has come down to us, there is no examination of comedy, and so we must assume that he assigned an end to comedy as he did to tragedy. But from the end [i.e., the instrumental one] which he did assign to comedy, we can conjecture what the architectonic end might be, since this is the model the artist sets before himself. Therefore, when we consider comedy's origins in Bacchic festivals, and its drunken nature and phallic license; and, furthermore, when we see that Aristotle himself distinguishes it from tragedy, assigning plebeian persons and laughter as its specific differences, it seems to me that it can have no other end than that of purging the soul of those passions which are produced in us by private and public worries. It purges melancholy, which is such a harmful emotion that it often causes men to go mad and kill themselves . . . .

Tragedy, on the contrary, calls back the wandering and relaxed soul and, has, therefore, vastly different ends, both of which have been explained by Aristotle in the *Poetics*, where, with respect to this, he defines tragedy as more fortunate than comedy. The first, or instrumental end, is the imitation of some horrible and miserable event; the second, or architectonic end, is the purgation of pity and terror. If we wish to lay our hands on what we are seeking, it is very necessary to understand how this purging takes place. I am aware that this is one of the most difficult passages in all of the *Poetics* of Aristotle. I intend, therefore, to treat it with great modesty towards those who have been among the first men of their time and who, in my opinion, have rather obscured it than made it clear. Everything in this passage that raises serious doubt can, it seems to me, be reduced to two points. The first point is the reason for which Aristotle wishes man to rid himself of compassion which is, as Boccaccio says,[12] such a human thing. In truth, it is very reasonable or, rather, necessary, to purge terror, a disordered emotion which corrupts the virtue of fortitude. But who can divest himself of pity without at the same time divesting himself of humanity? For this alone tragedy would deserve to be abhorred as a scandalous and violent spectacle. The second point is: how can it be that terrible things purge fear, since it does not appear that choleric matters are appropriate to purge anger but rather intensify it, and likewise the phlegmatic and other humors? Therefore, the sight of horrible and frightening things would only intensify the emotion of fear in those who are timid by nature. Yet some say that becoming accustomed to the sight of horrible things, such as blood, wounds, and deaths, renders the soul fearless, and from the soldier's example conclude that in similar fashion tragedy purges terror ⟨Cv/134⟩.[13] . . . but this does not fortify the soul, nor does it purge the fear of death. That this is true can be seen from observing soldiers in battle: although they see blood every day, few of them will stand their ground without turning their back on seeing that the peril of death is not in the hands of fortune but those of a stronger enemy who has overcome them. The bravery of the few who resist and hold their ground does not come from their habitual witnessing of horrifying and violent sights, but from their being acustomed to an honorable, virtuous, and praiseworthy aim.

I come now to compassion, of which it can be said that continued exposure to scenes arousing compassion might consume it. But I cannot see how anyone can rid himself of this emotion without divesting himself of his humanity, which is the same as becoming cruel; nor can I see how Aristotle can condone this, having himself taught us in his *Ethics* that we

[12] "Umana cosa è l'aver compassione degli afflitti": the opening line of the *Decameron*.
[13] See Hathaway 1962, 268–70.

must feel compassion for our friends when some evil befalls them [1171a–b]. These, then, are the difficulties which must be solved before we can properly understand how tragedy purges.

Before proceeding any further, it should be known that the term "to purge" has two meanings .... Tragedy does not purge its emotions in the stoic manner, by eradicating them completely from our heart, but by mitigating them and reducing them to that good proportion which can serve virtuous habit; rather, it uses one emotion as medicine for another, for it is far from being the case that all fears are corrupt, and there are some that are natural incentives to virtue, as is the fear of infamy. Likewise pity is not all good, for if it does not keep within its customary limits, it passes over into tenderness and softness and thus weakens those of good spirit. These two emotions, therefore, need to be purged, that is, tempered to virtuous mixture, and this is done by tragedy. But if the "purging" is considered to be an effect of the purging agent, we will say that these emotions are purged in the first sense, the good being used as a means to wipe out and altogether eradicate the bad. Now, if fear and compassion purge emotions similar to them, and some feelings of fear and compassion are good while others are not, we must therefore determine what in tragedy does the purging and what is purged; hence it will appear that it is not repugnant to their nature to purge or be purged.

Beginning with terror I say that, since man has two lives, one of the intellect and the other of the senses, he should fear two deaths from which, as Aristotle is witness, terror mostly springs. What, then, is the purging terror of tragedy? It is the terror of inner death, which, excited in the soul of the listener by the image of the thing represented, and because of the similarity of one fear with the other, draws unto itself like a magnet the evil sinning emotion. ... The whole function of tragedy, then, consists in this: by representing the terrible which can accompany the death of the soul, it teaches us to have no fear of the death of the body and imparts in us the power of justice. For this reason we see tragic protagonists who, although tormented in spirit, do not feel the torments of the body and show no fear of death. The wicked, therefore, have no place in tragedy for they have killed within themselves the sense of reason.

But let us turn to examples. What is the source of Oedipus' sorrow in the *Oedipus* of Sophocles, the queen and model of tragedies? After his recognition of parricide and incest, what is the source of the unhappy king's sorrow? The loss of his kingdom? Of his country? In having fallen from the state of majesty and become, from a king, a pauper? No. But although these are the greatest blows that can befall a person so nobly born, he does not feel them; rather, he begs to be led out of the city as soon as possible, leaving the kingdom, through his legal, if not natural death, to Creon. Nothing torments him but his incest and parricide, for he sees himself as having fallen into such abhorred sins that, because of his sense of inner justice, before committing them he would rather have killed himself. He is so afflicted by this horror and infamy that he forgets all other injuries. This grief is such that he does not feel the loss of his eyes or his country, nor his regal scepter: he speaks of his inner suffering, as though he felt neither external pain nor loss. Such a spectacle forces us to acknowledge our own shortcomings and clearly shows, to those who greatly fear death, that in human nature there are things more horrible than death. And even if death is to be feared, we should fear only the death of the soul, for the death of the body is unfelt in comparison with it. . . .

Tragedy is a fable, and within the limits of a fable, its aim is not to teach virtue, but to purge those two perturbations of the soul that are an obstacle to fortitude, a virtue both noble and necessary to all human acts. Let us now move on to the feeling of compassion, which is nothing other than sorrow for the suffering of others. This suffering, however, can be of two sorts: of the body or of the soul, from which spring the two kinds of compassion, good and bad. The good kind is present when we grieve over someone who feels afflicted in his soul because he has indulged in too much bodily pleasure. The bad kind is present when we grieve over someone who afflicts his body in order to achieve peace in his soul. . . . We should not, therefore, have pity for the suffering of the body, when this suffering is just; rather we should have pity for the fault, which, when acknowledged and felt by the sinner, becomes the penance for his sin. The first weakens the spirit of him who takes pity while the second fortifies it . . . . Which sort of compassion should be purged and which is the sort that purges, can be understood from what we have just said. . . .

. . . If laughter, which is repugnant and contrary to the two emotions named above, should enter into the mixture, the species will be corrupted. Furthermore, when the end is changed the form will also be changed, for where there is laughter there can be no terror and pity – these are contrary emotions and one will destroy the other. If laughter corrupts tragic form, what sort of poem will result when laughter is found in a subject that is not base and plebeian but partakes of those parts of tragedy which are not contrary to the ridiculous? Not a tragedy, for the form of tragedy will be destroyed as a result of laughter, but neither a comedy, which cannot admit a noble subject, but is limited to representing the defects of cowardly men who are fit for laughter. What can the poem be other than a third participant in those comic and tragic qualities which can be united to-gether? What will be its end? We have finally come to the resolution of that difficulty which has moved us to such long discourse.

I say, therefore, that tragicomedy, like the others, has two ends: the instrumental, which is the form resulting from the imitation of comic and tragic matters mingled together; and the architectonic, which is to purge the soul of the evil affection of melancholy, an end which is entirely simple and entirely comic and which cannot have anything in common with tragedy. Since the effects of purging [in tragicomedy and tragedy] are truly opposite – one gladdens and the other saddens, one leads to relaxation and the other to constraint, which are contrary movements of the soul for one moves from the center to the periphery while the other moves in the opposite direction – it may be said that in the dramatic mode these are contradictory ends. ... But the instrumental end can be mixed, since tragedy has many parts which, when stripped of the terrible, have the virtue of producing, together with the other comic parts, comic pleasure. Therefore, since Aristotle allows pleasure in tragedy ⟨Ar/50⟩, pleasure easily agrees with pleasure. And what is tragic pleasure? The imitation of the serious action of an illustrious person with new and unexpected accidents. Now, if we remove terror but leave only the danger, invent a new plot with new names, and alleviate everything with laughter, we will be left with pleasure of imitation, which will be potentially, but not actually, tragic: only the shell of tragedy will remain and not the emotion, which is the terror that is to be purged and which can only be induced by all the tragic parts ....

By its very nature tragedy is not pleasing to many people since not all of them need such purging. And since times change, so customs change with them. ... And truly, if public performances are meant for the listeners, then poems must also keep changing in accordance with changing times and customs. And to come to our own age, what need do we have today to purge terror and compassion through tragic sights since we have the most sacred precepts of our religion which teaches through the Gospels? Those horrible and cruel spectacles are superfluous, and it does not seem to me that in our age one should introduce a tragic action for any end other than to provide delight.

On the other hand, comedy has fallen into such tedium and scorn that unless it is accompanied by the marvels of the "intermezzi"[14] there is hardly anyone who will put up with it. That excellent poem, which was once accustomed to crown its makers with glory, has been contaminated and reduced to this vile state by mercenary and sordid persons who have traveled with it here and there for most vile pay.[15] In order to raise comic poetry from such a wretched state and make it appealing to the unwilling ears of modern audiences, the makers of tragicomedy, following the example of Menander and Terence who raised comedy to a serious level of decorum and respect, have endeavored to mix with the pleasing parts of comedy those parts of tragedy that can be united with it in order to achieve the purgation of sadness. ... But to conclude, finally, with that which it was my first intention to prove: should anyone ask what the end of

---

[14] Performed between acts, the "intermezzi" were spectacular entertainments and often allegorical representations of the nobility. For the 1595 performance of *Pastor fido*, Guarini wrote verses for the five *intermezzi* glorifying the house of Gonzaga.

[15] The professional players of the *commedia dell'arte*.

tragicomedy is, I will say that it is to imitate with the resources of the stage a fictional action which is a mixture of those parts of tragedy and comedy which can unite with decorum and verisimilitude in a single dramatic form whose end is to purge by means of delight the sadness of the listeners. Hence, the imitation, which is the instrumental end, is mixed, for it is the representation of comic and tragic parts mingled together; but the purging, which is the architectonic end, is single for it unites the two qualities in one purpose, that of freeing the listeners of melancholy.

14

SFORZA ODDI
(1540–1611)

Sforza Oddi, a professor of jurisprudence, wrote three plays: *The Strife of Love and Friendship*, *The Living Dead*, and *The Prison of Love*. This last was performed, in 1590, by Oddi's students at the University of Pisa. Little known today, *The Prison of Love* was both critically esteemed in its time and very popular. It went through twenty-two printings between 1590 and 1634.

Oddi's three plays are highly developed examples of the sub-genre *commedia grave* ("serious comedy"), which was characterized by a sentimental mixture of pathos, romance, and broad comedy and which he modified, chiefly in simplifying the romantic plot and in appropriating for comedy the aristocratic rank and sensibility that were usually associated with tragedy. The debate between Comedy and Tragedy in the Prologue to *The Prison of Love* is a defense of this modern type of comedy, which was thought by purists to be an improper hybrid genre.

Sforza Oddi was indebted to Giraldi's conception of tragedy with a happy ending ⟨Gd/122⟩ and to Vincenzo Maggi's pietistic theory, which held that the chief aim of both comedy and tragedy was to arouse a Christian *caritas*. This meant, for tragedy, not the purgation of terror and pity but the enhancement of pity through terror, and, for comedy, not the distancing of misfortune through ridicule, but its acceptance through the example of such self-sacrificing protagonists as Erminia in *The Prison of Love*. The Prologue to this play is addressed to courtiers, whose aristocratic sensibility, as Comedy declares, is a source of the play and its refined moral and aesthetic judgment.

For further reading

Clubb 1973; Corrigan 1934; Hathaway 1962; Herrick [1955] 1962, 1965; Sanesi 1954.

Prologue to *The Prison of Love*[1]

"AUTHOR'S PROLOGUE IN DEFENSE OF THIS AND TWO OTHER COMEDIES"

TRAGEDY: If this proud scene and this noble crown are not unjustly usurped from me, I hope today to see my almost fallen honors rise again, and feel the air quiver with sighs and tragic sobs,

---

[1] Translated (apparently for the first time into English) from Oddi 1591: *Prigione d'amore*.

with the frenzy of Hercules or Aramante; and to break those marbled hearts with the ancient miseries of Hecuba, Sofonisba, or Rosmunda.[2] But who is this, so merry and laughing, coming out to disturb my dreadful preparations?

COMEDY: I, who have delighted you often with the sweet strife of love and friendship or the cheerful error of the living dead,[3] have come to delight you once again, gentle spectators, with a lovers' prison; and with unheard manner of pleasure brimming with affection, to these generous lovers I will today be a mirror of their lives and loves.

TRAGEDY: Oh usurper of others' honors! Who are you that with my glorious name do try to adorn yourself? I am the rightful heir of such high tribute and from the beginnings of the world have been a true mirror to emperors and kings; you force me to call you but a mendacious and rash braggart.

COMEDY: If you should but deign to disclose your reasons for such high censure, I will attempt to prove that I am as worthy as you of such high title, most noble queen of poetry; and that today, I, Comedy, am with you and with the whole world pleasant and modest; while you, Tragedy, strike horror and admiration in the auditors.

TRAGEDY: Answer this: how dare you, in the presence of this illustrious crown, compete with me by claiming to be the mirror of human affairs? From the time of your birth, already with your first milk, you claimed as your own the worst defects of the people. That is why you are proclaimed from the public theatres and are shunned by noblemen's quills and modern writers, and from such ignominious exile you have bought your way back only with your clowning. Did not the prince of sciences himself, who wrote so highly of me, prescribe for you such narrow confines, as you well know, limited to bringing laughter to the plebeians by representations of some stupid and unbecoming human activity?

COMEDY: If at first I was abused by satirical and legendary Greece[4] it's through no fault of mine; and if the great Peripatetic gave me the ridiculousness of the human folly of others ⟨Ar/41⟩, it was rather to keep it from your greatness and majesty than to reserve it solely to me and my low rank. Besides, laughing at the human follies of others may teach us to be wise when we can

---

[2] These tragic protagonists appear in Seneca's *Hercules Furens*; *Hecuba* (1543), by Ludovico Dolce; *Sofonisba* (1515), by Giangiorgio Trissino (who also wrote a commentary on Aristotle's *Poetics*); and *Rosmunda* (1525), by Giovanni Rucellai.

[3] Oddi alludes to the plots of his previous two comedies.

[4] Oddi alludes to the Bacchic origins of Greek comedy and to Aristophanic Old Comedy.

recognize, as though in a mirror, our own follies and so correct them; but it does not matter to me that the narrow role given to me by old Greece was broken by the new, and expanded in such manner that the great Rome, with its large empire, dressed me in its official *toga* and *praetexta* ⟨Dn/80; Nh/112⟩[5] to tell the amorous adventures of its knights and senators.

TRAGEDY: This pomp of yours was brief; it fell with ancient Rome, and lies now in the proud ashes of her empire.

COMEDY: If I fell with her, and you fell with me, my queen, after many centuries we are both like young phoenixes reborn: you, more full of terror and majesty, I more cheerful and graceful than ever.

TRAGEDY: This rebirth was most fitting to me, for, with the very same example of the ruins of Italy and Rome, I've become a mirror to Princes so that they should not unduly value greatness and empires. Therefore, with pity and tears at the miseries of others I perturb and purge their emotions. But why do you usurp that which ancient Rome cannot render to you and abuse, in place of waggish tales, noble tales of love full of heroic virtue to move the emotions and tears of your audience? Which teacher taught you this?

COMEDY: Reason herself: that same reason which the New Greek and Latin states understood better than ancient Greece.

TRAGEDY: You'll never be able to prove this.

COMEDY: Now you'll see: are there not three ranks of fortune among the peoples of the world? The mighty who consider themselves to be happy; the wretched, who are so miserable they think they'll never rise again; and those of middle rank who are not perturbed by this or that face of fortune, either because of their virtue or the mediocrity of their state?

TRAGEDY: That is so.

COMEDY: Now, let's leave aside the last ones, for they need neither my teaching nor yours. You are a mirror to the first ones, and, conversely, I'm a mirror to the second. ... From both extremes of fortune we both call upon the citizens to be happy with civil moderation. It must be confessed then that, nobly renewed as I am, I, no less than you, can attain the virtuous aim of consoling and profiting the wretched and miserable persons as well as the commonwealth; and this is something I could not have done by

---

[5] The *fabulae togatae* were Roman comedies with an Italic plot and setting, as contrasted with the *fabulae palliatae*, with Greek plots and settings. These categories derive from *toga*, the national tunic worn by Roman citizens, and *pallio*, a small cape worn by Greeks. The *toga praetexta* was the official dress of high-ranking Roman citizens and *fabula praetexta* thus came to designate tragedies of Italic, as contrasted with Greek, plots and settings.

following the Peripatetic rule and staying within the boundaries of the ridiculous.

TRAGEDY: Do you want, then, to deprive yourself of the cheerfulness and ridiculousness that makes you so attractive to the people?

COMEDY: My ingenious practitioners know how to mix the good examples of a serious plot full of virtue, with many jests and pleasant speeches. Those who listen to me attain both profit and delight, as was rightfully said by my Latin [mentor] when he ⟨Hr/ 73:333–34⟩ mixed the useful and the delightful.

TRAGEDY: I like that; but who gave you license to usurp from me, as you often do, compassion and those other emotions that are rightfully mine, to try and make your plots almost tragic?

COMEDY: In the bitterness of tears hides the sweetness of delight; and, since I want more than ever to delight, I often make a charming mixture of tears and laughter; and the bitterness of tears makes more cheerful the sweetness of laughter.

TRAGEDY: You speak well, but the perturbing of emotions is more suitable to the mighty than to those of middle rank.

COMEDY: My lady, who is willing to restrain the natural pity of a man who weeps and pains at seeing and listening to the ruin, not only of a prince, but one his own equal or inferior, nay, even a dear and beloved dog? ...

TRAGEDY: ... But it must be said that this setting, when compared to the real presence and beauty of these gracious ladies, although it is appropriate, is not enough; and it seems to me, now that I gaze first upon the one and then the other, that this is overcome by the majestic charm of their smiles.

COMEDY: If I could not equal the merit of such great beauty with an appropriate setting, I have compensated for this blemish by making myself more beautiful with what is most beautiful in their souls; and, therefore, these most gentle spirits will recognize and will confess that, whatever you and I, my lady, produce that is good and gracious, springs from those bright fountains of translucent splendor and radiates from those blazing suns, their eyes.

TRAGEDY: This is all true; but how will you unravel this new plot?

COMEDY: So that I will not deprive the listeners of the delight in what is new, I will not reveal my plot, but I will tell you this: a lady of this court is possessed of such virtue and gracious heart, that in order to free her brother and her lover from prison, she locks herself away in it and dies and thus, with such amorous imprisonment,[6] frees both.

---

[6] The plot of *The Prison of Love* centers around Lelio and Erminia, twin brother and sister. Erminia is in love with Lelio's best friend, Flaminio, but the Duke has promised her to

TRAGEDY: She strikes this bargain by dying? You must have more than my excellent skill to end this happily!

COMEDY: Listen to those who are beginning to talk, and with the height of your intellect, you will understand. Come let us retire that way.

another. Rather than consent to this marriage Erminia runs away. Lelio is ordered to find her on pain of death. Erminia returns disguised as her brother, takes Flaminio's place in prison and drinks the poison intended for Flaminio. But, contrary to what Comedy tells the audience, Erminia does not really die, since the "poison" is actually a sleeping potion. She awakens to be forgiven by the Duke, and both her lover and her brother are saved.

15

GEORGE WHETSTONE
(c. 1544–1587)

Best known for his verse biography of the dramatist and critic George Gascoigne, Whetstone was also a translator, anthologist, and story-teller, whose writings are animated by his belief in edification through history, social criticism, and literature. For the playwright himself to publish his unacted play, as Whetstone did in 1578 with *Promos and Cassandra*, was unusual in sixteenth-century England but is in keeping with the critical attitude Whetstone displays in the dedicatory epistle, addressed to a kinsman, in which he discriminates sharply between the essential utility and pleasure of drama and the abuses to which it is subjected by uncouth contemporary playwrights. Sidney may have been indebted to Whetstone (who was better informed in this respect) in his later attack ⟨Sy/179⟩ on the abuses of the stage. Like Richard Edwards ⟨Ed/147⟩ before him and Sidney afterwards, Whetstone is much concerned with the decorum of dialogue and characterization; with how certain characters should be made to speak and act, and with whom associate, according to their social rank and type. He also has firm ideas about dramatic structure, though he uses the theory then current in Italy rather informally. He does not specify the unities as such but heaps scorn on the "impossibilities" on which, in violation of the unities, the plots of English plays are founded. More surprisingly, he makes no claims for the legitimacy of tragicomedy – he does not even use the word – though *Promos and Cassandra* is a notable example of the genre.

Whetstone's division of his play into "two comedies" results in a tragic Part One in which Promos, the unjust official, enjoys Cassandra's body and, breaking his corrupt bargain, executes her brother. Part Two brings the comic conclusion in which Promos is exposed, agrees to marry Cassandra, and is saved by her. Her brother is found to be still alive, after all. Both parts introduce low-life matters into the serious action but with a decorum that keeps them at a distance. The "two comedies" constitute, in effect, a single play in ten acts (but shorter than Shakespeare's longest) in which the mood changes markedly between the two parts.

Whetstone found his plot in Giraldi's collection of stories, *Hecatommithi*, but made no use of Giraldi's own dramatization of the story. Shakespeare was heavily indebted to *Promos and Cassandra* for his *Measure for Measure* and may be assumed, therefore, to be familiar with the issues raised in Whetstone's dedication.

For further reading

Bullough 1958; Herrick [1955] 1962; Izard 1942; Ristine 1910.

Promos and Cassandra: from the "Epistle Dedicatory"[1]

... I divided the whole history into two comedies for that, decorum used, it would not be conveyed in one. The effects of both are both good and bad: virtue intermixed with vice, unlawful desires (if it were possible) quenched with chaste denials: all needful actions, I think, for public view. For, by the reward of the good, the good are encouraged in well-doing: and with the scourge of the lewd, the lewd are feared from evil attempts:[2] maintaining this my opinion with Plato's authority. Naughtiness comes of the corruption of nature and not by reading or hearing the lives of the good or lewd (for such publication is necessary) but goodness, saith he ⟨Pl/20⟩, is beautiful by either action.[3] And to these ends, Menander, Plautus, and Terence, themselves many years since entombed, by their comedies in honor live at this day. The ancient Romans held these shows of such price that they not only allowed the public exercise of them but the grave Senators themselves countenanced the actors with their presence; who, from these trifles, won morality as the bee sucks honey from weeds. But the advised devices of ancient poets, discredited with trifles of young, unadvised, and rash-witted writers, hath brought this commendable exercise in mislike. For, at this day, the Italian is so lascivious in his comedies that honest hearers are grieved at his actions: the Frenchman and Spaniard follow the Italian's humor: the German is too holy, for he presents on every common stage what preachers should pronounce in pulpits. The Englishman in this quality is most vain, indiscreet, and out of order: he first grounds his work on impossibilities; then in three hours runs he through the world, marries, gets children, makes children men, men to conquer kingdoms, murder monsters, and bringeth gods from heaven, and fetcheth devils from hell. And, that which is worst, their ground is not so unperfect as their working indiscreet; not weighing, so the people laugh, though they laugh them (for their follies) to scorn.[4] Many times, to make mirth, they make a clown companion with a king;[5] in their grave counsels they allow the advice of fools; yea, they so use one order of speech for all persons: a gross indecorum, for a crow will ill counterfeit the nightingale's sweet voice – even so affected speech doth ill become a clown. For, to work a comedy kindly, grave old men should instruct, young men should show the imperfections of youth, strumpets should be lascivious, boys unhappy,

---

[1] The text is from the 1578 edition.

[2] "with the scourge of the lewd, the lewd are feared from evil attempts" = the [spectacle of the] punishment of the wicked makes the wicked fearful of attempting wicked deeds.

[3] Whetstone is here misinterpreting Plato.

[4] "their ground is not so unperfect as their working indiscreet; not weighing, so the people laugh, though they laugh them (for their follies) to scorn" = the basis of their work is not so imperfect as the way they carry it out. They care for nothing except to make the people laugh, even though what the people are scornfully laughing at are the follies of the writers themselves.

[5] "clown" = ignorant and lower-class – often rural – character. ⟨Sy:181⟩.

and clowns should speak disorderly: intermingling all these actions in such sort as the grave matter may instruct, and the pleasant delight; for, without this change, the attention would be small, and the liking less ⟨Hr/73:333⟩.

But leave I this rehearsal of the use and abuse of comedies, lest that I check that in others that I cannot amend in myself. But this I am assured: what actions soever passeth in this history, either merry or mournful, grave or lascivious, the conclusion shows the confusion of vice and the cherishing of virtue. . . .

16
ANGELO INGEGNERI
(1550–1613)

Ingegneri's varied career as a stage director and producer took him from his native Venice to Rome, to Ferrara (where the pastoral, which Ingegneri, along with Guarini, defended as superior to both comedy and tragedy, reigned supreme), to Turin and Vicenza. In Vicenza, he was responsible for the production of Sophocles' *Oedipus Tyrannus*, in an Italian translation, which opened Palladio's "Teatro Olimpico" in 1586.

The first Italian producer and director to publish systematic dramatic theory, Ingegneri left a body of work that included also two plays, political treatises, and a voluminous correspondence with his patrons and his friends, including Torquato Tasso. Ingegneri's pastoral play, *The Dance of Venus* (*Danza di Venere*), was staged in Parma in 1583, and his tragedy, *Tomiri*, was published in Naples in 1607. Although *Tomiri* conforms with the rigorous rules set out in his treatise *On Mimetic Poetry and the Manner of Representing Scenic Fables*, it is pervaded by the Senecan exploitation of horror that, in his theory, Ingegneri condemns, as offensive to "the eye, covetous of delight."

Not surprisingly, given his experience as a stage director, Ingegneri's theory is eminently practical. According to him, poets who write for the stage should be guided by such requirements as probability and social decorum, which must be respected if credibility is to be achieved; settings that are natural meeting-places; dialogue appropriate to the rank of the characters and always advancing the action; as close correspondence as possible between the duration of the action and the time taken by performance; and a general conformity with the "reason of verisimilitude and decorum." His insistence that plays should preserve a rigorous internal logic, coupled with his assertion of the superiority of the pastoral over all other forms of drama, strikes a somewhat paradoxical note.

For further reading
Hathaway 1962; Toffanin 1920; Weinberg 1961.

From *On Mimetic Poetry and the Manner of Representing Scenic Fables*[1]

... It is clear that if there were no pastorals we could say that the use of the stage would be all but lost and, consequently, stage poets would be in a desperate situation, for their compositions are written to be represented, and if this [rejection of pastoral plays[2]] were to persist we would not find an author willing to put together even one hundred verses ⟨Gu/149⟩. The damage to civil life would be great, but I will not dwell on that. I will say, however, that there are not many poets who are as good at epics as they are at drama. Consequently, [without pastorals] the good lessons that we find in skilled and well-mannered poets would be fewer; nor will I be silent on the fact that the human soul, in need at times of relaxation and recreation, lacking that supplied by the stage, would turn in a short time to a source which is less virtuous, lacking in honor and unprofitable.[3] ... Tragedies (leaving aside the fact that there are few which can be read that do not show important and inexcusable shortcomings which often make them unstageable) are sad spectacles and the eye, covetous of delight, adapts badly to them. Some hold them to be of ill omen and so they spend neither time nor money on them. Finally, because they are imitations of royal actions and personages (and today's conventions require a pomp in scenery and costumes other than sufficed in Sophocles' time to represent the poor king of Thebes, insulted by his brother-in-law and threatened by a soothsayer), they must needs resort to the royal treasury, which is wisely put aside by today's princes for the preservation of their states and the security of their subjects.

In fifty years not one [tragedy] has been suitably represented: and to do so would require very rich companies, as in Venice; generous academies, as in Vicenza; and wonderful theatres like the Olimpico.[4] We are left, then, with pastorals which, in a rustic and verdant setting and with costumes more delightful than sumptuous, are most sweet to the sight; likewise they are pleasant to the ear and the intellect because of their gentle verse and

---

[1] From *Della poesia rappresentativa e del modo di rappresentare le favole sceniche* (Ingegneri/ Marotti 1974). This is a new translation of selected passages from the first part of Ingegneri's treatises, which is devoted to questions of dramatic structure; the second is concerned with the staging of plays.

[2] Ingegneri is arguing against the late Giason de Nores, who had denied the legitimacy of Guarini's pastoral tragicomedy *Il Pastor fido* and was one of those who condemned tragicomedy and pastoral drama in general as hybrid modern forms and monstrous travesties, because all precepts of verisimilitude, propriety, and proportion are neglected in their composition. See Weinberg 1961, II:1074–78.

[3] Ingegneri is referring to the performances of the *commedia dell'arte*, which he thought vulgar, and which, as he says "have lowered the standards of comedy" to a level of obscenity.

[4] Designed by Andrea Palladio and opened in 1586, the Olimpico embodied the architectural principles of Vitruvius, notably in its semicircular orchestra and elaborate *frons scenae* in the Roman style.

delicate speech which while not incapable of tragic gravity ... can also admit most suitably some humorous actions, and, introducing on the stage girls and honest women, can give rise to noble emotions like those of tragedies, which is not permissible in comedy. In conclusion, as a middle ground between the two types of poems they [pastorals] are a source of delight and the marvelous, be they with chorus or without, with *intermezzi* or without ....

... the action, which according to the masters of the art can embrace the duration of the natural day, that is to say twenty-four hours ⟨Ar/41; Cv/132⟩, would be worthy of the highest praise were it to last the same period of time as it takes to represent it, that is, four or five hours. This is due to the fact that the stage is obliged in certain ways to allow the actors, as well as the scenery, many things which are far removed from the real in order to achieve a level of the credible which can give rise to emotional effects; nonetheless, the closer to reality the above-mentioned things are, the more effective they are in stirring up the emotions ....

The characters, according to my judgment, should never be more than a dozen ⟨Nh/113⟩ and they should all be necessary and (so to speak) so functional in the plot that, should one of them – any one at all – be removed, the plot would fall apart. As far as the number is concerned, it is clear that a multitude of characters poses difficulties of representation: in order to take precautions against the thousand possible encounters which might give rise to confusion in the representation, it is necessary for actors to double and, in some instances, to triple; and when there are more than ten or twelve parts, it is almost impossible to find as many actors as are needed. To this we must add that the new spectator, if he wishes better to follow the plot, must know the actors individually by their unique skills[5] and must remember the name and condition of each one of them; this cannot be accomplished properly when there are so many as to generate confusion in the mind. The same explanation will demonstrate that characters which are not necesssary or functional are not a good idea because they will give rise to much more intrigue in the unraveling and create impediments to the science [*notizia*] which is proper to the stage.

The poet is free to create these characters according to his judgment, as long as he follows what we have just observed with respect to their number and necessity. He must, however, be careful to come as close as possible to the manners, ancient or modern, of the place which is being represented; and if they are fictional, they must be drawn with gentle and good graces, without partaking of anything cruel or loathsome. In the case of historical

---

[5] In this passage Ingegneri starts out by discussing the maximum number of characters that a good play should have. However, he does not seem to follow this argument to its logical conclusion, but shifts his focus from characters to performers. "Characters" translates *personaggi*, "actors" translates *recitanti* and *istrioni*.

tragedy, based on events which have occurred in reality, they [the characters] should be the same ones as in the original story, with the addition of as many as are necessary to unravel the plot in a proper manner: these must never become leading characters nor should any horror or pity befall them. When there are real persons who can move the desired passions, I hold it to be a great error to resort to fictional characters to do so; in such cases neither the real nor the fictional will move them, and this is true especially in cases where pity is thought to be increased by these means, which, rather than multiplying, divide it. A further error is caused by changing the historical events significantly: however verisimilar and possible the additions, the action, which is supposed to be historical, becomes a fable and loses credibility and is of little efficacy.

... Now we come to the fable, and it seems to me that the first thing to take into account is that the stage on which the performance is to occur must represent a place in which the unfolding events must take place due to a certain necessity or good probability; likewise it must be a meeting-place for the persons who engage in dialogue. Those who make it otherwise badly serve the cause of decorum and verisimilitude: therefore I deem it very important that the poet refrain from introducing casual characters without any purpose, unless this casual introduction masks a purpose and serves as an artful aid in the unraveling. Nor is it fitting to try, as some have done, to avoid the first disaster [an improbable location] by falling into the second, which is probably worse: that is, to give vain reasons of having selected such a place as more conducive to privacy, as opposed to their [the characters'] own homes or dwellings, as though public places are more private than closeted rooms. Finally it is wise to heed this warning: the more likely the entrance of any character on the boards the better and more graceful the scene. And if it be possible to unravel the proceedings in a manner such that the events, which are to take place in the public square or street or Royal Palace (which in tragedy is probably the most likely of all settings), could not possibly take place anywhere else, and such that the characters could not be or – each in turn – are prevented from being found anywhere else: this, I believe is the way to the highest perfection of art and the way to absolute honor for all participants. ...

17

LORENZO GIACOMINI
(1552–99)

Lorenzo Giacomini spent most of his life in Florence, where his contributions to the intellectual life of the city were mostly through his involvement in the three Florentine academies. In one of these,[1] in 1586, he read his short treatise *On Purgation in Tragedy*, singling out this crucial topic, rather than attempting to deal with the whole of the *Poetics* (which he had translated in 1573). A generation earlier, Robortello had interpreted catharsis as a homeopathic process through which the body rids itself of the emotions of pity and fear by being subjected to the experience of them in tragedy ⟨Rb/93–94⟩. Disputing Robortello's interpretation, Vincenzo Maggi[2] had proposed that such emotions, which he considered desirable in a Christian society, could be used to purge the sinful passions of wrath, lust, and avarice (Toffanin 1920, 89–92).

Giacomini discusses three schools of thought on this controversial subject of catharsis and develops his own homeopathic theory, justifying it by reference to classical medical texts as well as to Aristotle's argument in the eighth book of the *Politics* on the effects of Phrygian music. He concludes that catharsis is really the physical expenditure of emotion and that weeping draws off excessive vapors from the mind and thus lightens it of its burdens.[3]

For further reading

Gilbert 1940; Hathaway 1962; Herrick 1946; Maggi and Lombardi 1550; Spingarn 1908b; Toffanin 1920; Weinberg 1961.

---

[1] The *Accademia degli alterati* (Academy of the Intoxicated) was one of several fancifully named literary societies founded in sixteenth-century Florence with a view to fostering the Tuscan vernacular as a literary language. Plays written in the vernacular were presented by members of the academies.

[2] See Maggi and Lombardi 1550. The Latin paraphrase of Aristotle was by Lombardi, the commentary by Maggi. See also Hathaway 1962, 214ff.

[3] His contemporary Giovanni Della Casa reports a similar view: "As I once heard it said by one of our neighbours, a man to be depended upon, men often have as much need of tears as they have of laughter. He used to say that this was why grim plays, which were called tragedies, were first compiled, and the purpose of them when they were recited in the theatres, as was done in those days, was to move to tears all those who felt the need of them. In this way, by weeping, they were cured of their disorders" (Della Casa [1558] 1958, 41).

From *On Purgation in Tragedy*[4]

... the end of the poet, as poet, is to construct the poem with honest reason, and the end of the tragic poet to follow the idea of art in giving shape to tragedy, which, like any other poem, can be used to many ends, the consideration of which, due to his motives, is proper to the statesman who forms or governs the city. To gain a clear understanding of all this, let it be known that since every doctrine aims to some end, poetic doctrine, because it is still an art, gazes upon its own end, which is the poem itself, as melody is the end of the musician, the statue of the sculptor, painting of the painter, and health of the doctor. And "poem," in its strictest meaning, we define as "an imitation, with fabulous speech, in verse, of human action (in the term 'action' we include also the emotions and internal operations), made according to poetic art, and aiming to purge, to teach, and to give repose or noble entertainment."

In this definition the imitation of a human action is the form, and by imitation we mean to give form to something that is not real, or with regard to its unreality, in the likeness of something that could be true or believable. The material cause is language, in the same manner as color is to the painter and marble to the sculptor. The efficient cause is the poetic art of man. The ends, according to Aristotle, will be purgation, teaching, rest from the vexations and troubles of life, and finally the amusement of the spirit in the man of understanding, which is the cheerful and perfect appreciation of the excellence of the work; and any or more of these, according to the diverse sorts of poems. ...

... But to understand better what is the purgation of tragedy, it must be understood ... what exactly is meant by purgation, which seems to pertain to the body and to the body's humors. The act of healing is performed either through contraries or through the use of purgative medicines which stir those humors which cannot by themselves move. This type of healing is called "catharsis" by the Greeks, that is to say, purgation, and any medication which has such virtue is said to be a purgative, and works not as a contrary or enemy of the humor but as a friend and ally. That is why rhubarb or aloe or black hellebore, once ingested in the stomach, circulating in the limbs, their virtue which has been stirred by native heat, due to a natural similitude of choleric, phlegmatic, or melancholic humor, has the power to attract such humors to themselves, as a magnet attracts iron and amber straw, not only from the nearby veins but from the remotest parts of the body (with the contribution of course of that natural virtue which expels noxious substances) and bring them to that place where they are spreading their virtue, or to the stomach, from which burdened nature is expelling them. ...

---

[4] Translated from *De la purgazione de la tragedia*, in Weinberg 1970–74, III:345–72.

... tragedy pleases through teaching the action which is being represented, since learning is a pleasurable activity by nature; it pleases through astonishment by showing the incredible as probable; it is delightful for its imitation, which allows for a syllogism between one thing and another; it delights with the nobility of its thoughts and the charm of its metaphors, the sweetness of its rhyme, the sweetness of its music, the celebration of the dance, the magnificence of the sets, the splendor of the majestic costumes, the consideration of the poet's skill in the disposition of the fable, in the digressions, the recognitions, peripeties, traditions, thoughts, of the fable.

These pleasures can be suitably accompanied by three others, albeit somewhat external and remote. The first is that, since compassion is an act of virtue, and since every operation stemming from virtue or similar to it is by nature pleasant, so in this manner can the compassion of tragedy bring delight. Likewise, as Aristotle is witness, honor also brings delight, almost as a sign to the one honored, of his own virtue; and in friendship, the friend who has given benefit derives more pleasure than he who has received. The other is that it [tragedy] makes us realize that we are free of such violent misfortunes, which cannot but bring us pleasure and joy. The last one comes from learning healthy historical lessons, and principally among these, that kings and princes sometime fall into calamity and ruin, and that the true happiness of mortals is to live with virtue and aspire to the most high, immortal, and unique Being. These many pleasures surpass that little pain that our sensitive part derives not from tears, but from painful objects, even if feigned. We therefore discover that tragedy is profitable not only for its purgation, but for its teaching and for its amusement of the soul and its relaxation, which are the four ends of music, and therefore of poetry, as assigned by Aristotle [*Politics* 1341b].

... The doubt that must be removed, however, is this: how can a tragedy with a happy ending, moving from misery to happiness, effect such purgation without representing some sorrowful deed from which compassion can spring? The answer is not difficult, and after that our reasoning is come full circle. We say that even such a tragedy [with a happy end] contains terror and pity, because the evil which is near and seemingly inevitable is considered by the soul to be present, and as such it moves us to compassion. Iphigenia, who, because of a barbarian law, is ready to kill her estranged brother, is likely to move us to pity no less than if she had killed him ⟨Gu/155⟩;[5] and the apparatus of the instruments of miserable death so near in action, either true or represented, move us to compassion as much as the representation of death which has taken place and which can be represented at times with such great suffering and horror, with such withdrawal of spirits from the principle of life, that would negate

---

[5] Euripides' *Iphigenia in Tauris* was often cited as a classical precedent for tragedy with a happy ending. Guarini would also approve death averted and, in England, John Fletcher defined tragicomedy as "the danger not the death."

compassion and tears and induce only stupor and that senselessness of which Dante said: "I could not weep, so turned to stone inside was I" [*Inferno* 33.49]. Because of this, Aristotle was to call plots of this type excellent ⟨Ar/41⟩, even though earlier ⟨Ar/49–50⟩ he had said that during competitions the people held stories with miserable ends to be more tragic.

18

SIR PHILIP SIDNEY
(1554–86)

In *The Defence of Poesy*[1] Sidney addressed the major issues of poetic theory with a comprehensiveness, learning, and power entirely without precedent in England, where it became a rich source for later discussions of poetry. In the European context it looks rather different: a masterful synthesis and penetrating critique of current thought, adopting the conventional Horatian standard of instruction and delight, drawing on Italian and other theorists, and, above all, using the inspiration of Neoplatonism to take issue with Plato's objections to poetry.[2]

One of Sidney's great claims for poetry is that, far from being merely "wordish," it creates images so substantial as to constitute "a speaking picture" and "a second nature." Of his many examples of this power, the following is particularly interesting in relation to drama:

> Anger, the Stoics said, was a short madness. Let but Sophocles bring you Ajax on a stage, killing or whipping sheep or oxen, thinking them the army of Greeks, with their chieftains Agamemnon and Menelaus, and tell me if you have not a more familiar insight into anger than finding in the schoolmen his genus and difference. (p. 19)[3]

If this is a tribute to the power of stage presentation it is only so in a very special sense since, in Sophocles, the episode is narrated. For Sidney the effect of the speech would seem to be the realization of the image in the theatre of the mind.

Not accepting Plato's view of the scope of poetic imitation, Sidney finds a special excellence in the real poets who "to imitate borrow nothing of what is, hath been or shall be but range, only reigned with learned discretion, into the divine consideration of what may be and should be" (p. 12). Astronomers, mathematicians, philosophers, historians, physicians, even metaphysicians, are "Actors and Players" (p. 8) of nature's text, says Sidney, but the poet is not:

> Only the Poet, disdaining to be tied to any such subjection, lifted up with the vigour of his own invention, doth grow in effect into an other nature:

[1] Two separate editions were published in 1595, though the work was written c. 1590. The first, unauthorized, printing was for H. Olney with the title *An Apologie for Poetrie*. This was followed some six months later by an edition printed for William Ponsonby with the title *The Defence of Poesie*. The Ponsonby edition is the basis for the present selection.

[2] There are many echoes in the *Defence* of English, French, and, especially, Italian discussions of poetry, notably of Minturno's *De Poeta* (1559) and Scaliger's *Poetices libri septem* (1561). Spingarn asserts that "there is not an essential principle in the *Defence of Poesy* which cannot be traced back to some Italian treatise on the poetic art" (1908b, 257–58). For detailed notes on sources and analogues see Dowlin 1944, Gilbert 1940, Myrick 1965, Sidney/Shepherd 1965, and Sidney/Smith 1904.

[3] The references (in brackets in the introductory note, in bold in the text) are to the actual (unnumbered) pages of the Ponsonby edition.

in making things either better than nature bringeth forth, quite anew, forms such as never were in nature, as the Heroes, Demigods, Cyclops, Chimeras, Furies, and such like .... (p. 9)

The playwright, as poet, enjoys this creative liberty, but only in the verbal realm. To bring unnatural forms onto the stage would be to violate its decorum and even its essential character, as Sidney understands it.

In dismissing the charge that poetry is lies, he incidentally defends theatrical convention with the mocking question: "What child is there that coming to a play and seeing 'Thebes' written in great letters upon an old door doth believe that it is Thebes?" (p. 41).[4] But he nevertheless castigates playwrights for their absurd departures from a supposed realism inherent in the "unities" of time and place, which he regards as canons of dramatic art.

Until he arrives at the first passage printed below, Sidney has little to say about drama in the *Defence*. He takes tragedy to be a self-evidently noble and useful genre (though he ranks it below heroic poetry) and, in passing, praises plays by Aeschylus, Sophocles, and Terence for representing virtues, passions, and vices "so in their own natural states, laid to the view, that we seem not to hear of them but to see through them" (p. 19). But when he actually focuses on drama it is to illustrate, very scornfully, the abuse of poetry, of dramatic form, and of the theatre by English playwrights. This may be Sidney's oblique response to *The School of Abuse* by Stephen Gosson,[5] an attack on the theatre presumptuously dedicated to Sidney. Sidney's eloquent account of the origins, modes, effects, and values of poetry sharply contrasts with Gosson's narrowly moralizing attitude but, though he praises the dramatic genres, he by no means defends the contemporary stage or its playwrights.

Sidney admits to a limited experience of the theatre and there is no hint that he has any enthusiasm for it. This may be connected with his insistence that poetry, at best, conveys images of virtue in action and that, far from being inimical to real action, or a substitute for deeds, it is "the companion of the camps" (p. 45) and conducive to the good conduct of soldiers. For Sidney poetry plays a vital role on the stage of the world but a dubious one, it appears, in the theatre.

The *Defence* was written in 1580 or thereabouts, some four years after Burbage opened The Theatre. Before it was published – not until 1595 – there had occurred the great efflorescence of drama in England that Sidney did not live to witness. The careers of Kyd and Marlowe were over and Shakespeare's early plays had been performed. From the point of view of drama, the writing and publication of the *Defence* could hardly have been less opportunely timed.

For further reading

Dowlin 1944; Gilbert 1940; Herrick, 1947; Myrick 1965; Spingarn 1908b; Symmes 1903; Weinberg 1961.

---

[4] Sidney may be recalling some academic production of Seneca or Sophocles. The method of staging is lightly mocked but staging is not the issue here.

[5] *The School of Abuse, containing a pleasant invective against Poets, Pipers, Players, Jesters and such like Caterpillars of the Commonwealth* (1579). A playwright, whose plays have not survived, Stephen Gosson (1554–1624) turned against the theatre and joined its Puritan opponents. He defended his *School of Abuse* in *Ephemerides of Phialo* (1579) and in *Plays Confuted in Five Actions* (1582).

From *The Defence of Poesy*

29–33   ... By these, therefore, examples and reasons, I think it may be manifest that the poet, with that same hand of delight, doth draw the mind more effectually than any other art doth; and so a conclusion not unfitly ensue[s], that as virtue is the most excellent resting place for all worldly learning to make his end of, so poetry, being the most familiar to teach it, and most princely to move towards it, in the most excellent work, is the most excellent workman. But I am content not only to decipher him by his works[6] (although works, in commendation or dispraise, must ever hold an high authority), but more narrowly will examine his parts, so that (as in a man) though all together may carry a presence full of majesty and beauty, perchance in one defectious piece we may find a blemish. Now in his parts, kinds, or species (as you list to term them), it is to be noted that some poesies have coupled together two or three kinds, as the tragical and comical, whereupon is risen the tragicomical ⟨In/170; Gu/149⟩. Some in the [like] manner have mingled prose and verse, as Sanazzar and Boethius.[7] Some have mingled matters heroical and pastoral. But that cometh all to one in this question, for if severed they be good the conjunction cannot be hurtful. Therefore, perchance forgetting some, and leaving some as needless to be remembered, it shall not be amiss, in a word to cite the special kinds, to see what faults may be found in the right use of them.

Is it then the pastoral poem which is misliked, ... the lamenting elegiac, ... the bitter but wholesome iambic, ... the satiric ... ? No, perchance it is the comic, whom naughty playmakers and stage-keepers have justly made odious. To the argument of abuse I will after answer. Only thus much now is to be said, that the comedy is an imitation of the common errors of our life, which he representeth in the most ridiculous and scornful sort that may be; so as it is impossible that any beholder can be content to be such a one.

Now, as in geometry the oblique must be known as well as the right, and in arithmetic the odd as well as the even, so in the actions of our life who seeth not the filthiness of evil wanteth a great foil to perceive the beauty of virtue. This doth the comedy handle so in our private and domestical matters as, with hearing it, we get as it were an experience what is to be looked for of a niggardly Demea, of a crafty Davus, of a flattering Gnato, of a vainglorious Thraso ⟨Hw/203⟩;[8] and not only to know what effects are

---

[6] Sidney is playing on the religious sense of "works" as associated with "faith" and "grace."

[7] The Italian poet Jacopo Sanazzaro (1458–1530) was the author of *Arcadia*, a pastoral romance. *Of the Consolation of Philosophy*, by the renowned theologian and scholar Boethius (A.D. 470–525), is also a work mixing prose and verse.

[8] The characters cited are from Terence's plays: Demea from *Adelphi*; Davus, the slave, from *Andria*; Gnatho and Thraso from *Eunuchus*. Thomas Lodge, in his *Defence of Poetry, Music and Stage Plays* (1579), had written:

Terence will not report the abuse of harlots under their proper style, but he can finely gird them under the person of Thais. He dare not openly tell the rich of their covetousness

to be expected but to know who be such, by the signifying badge given them by the comedian. And little reason hath any man to say that men learn evil by seeing it so set out since, as I said before, there is no man living but, by the force truth hath in nature, no sooner seeth these men play their parts but wisheth them *in pistrinum:*[9] although perchance the sack of his own faults lie so behind his back that he seeth not himself to dance the same measure; whereto yet nothing can more open his eyes than to see his own actions contemptibly set forth. So that the right use of comedy will (I think) by nobody be blamed; and much less of the high and excellent tragedy, that openeth the greatest wounds and showeth forth the ulcers that are covered with tissue; that maketh kings fear to be tyrants, and tyrants manifest their tyrannical humours; that with stirring the affects of admiration ⟨Cn/138⟩ and commiseration, teacheth the uncertainty of this world ⟨Sg/109; Cv/135⟩,[10] and upon how weak foundations gilden roofs are builded . . . .

55–60   Our tragedies and comedies, not without cause cried out against, observing rules neither of honest civility nor of skilful poetry, excepting *Gorboduc*[11] (again, I say, of those that I have seen), which notwithstanding as it is full of stately speeches and well-sounding phrases, climbing to the height of Seneca his style, and as full of notable morality, which it doth most delightfully teach, and so obtain the very end of poesy,

and severity towards their children, but he can control them under the person of Durus Demeas. He must not show the abuse of noble young gentlemen under their own title, but he will warn them in the person of Pamphilus. Will you learn to know a parasite? Look upon his Davus. Will you seek the abuse of courtly flatterers? Behold Gnato. (Smith 1904, 1:82)

The accusation that comedies taught rather than cured vice was a common one, as was the response made by Sidney.

9   *in pistrinum* = punished by being set to work in the mill (as slaves were both in actuality and in the plays of Terence and Plautus).

10   Sidney succinctly transforms a familiar idea of catharsis into an original one: tragic surgery is something done as a painful necessity ("a sweet violence") to the body politic. Aristotle's fear has become, as commonly in the Renaissance, the rational response of a royal spectator who applies the tragic example to his own situation, as in Sidney's immediately following illustration from Seneca.

That the lesson of tragedy is the fickleness of fortune is also a commonplace (with the strong implication here that virtue and faith in God are thereby made more compelling). So also is the Scaligerian notion that tragedy teaches by moving the emotions. But the *substitution* of admiration for fear (for which he has already found another place) appears to be Sidney's own thought. His application of the word is quite different from Corneille's, though the word itself means something similar in both: "awe" or "wonder."

Sidney's idea of admiration is close to that of *meravigli* – "the which engenders and intensifies pity and fear" – in Castelvetro. Sidney's "admiration" makes the audience emotionally receptive, particularly to "commiseration," a word which is free from the possible connotations of weakness in "pity." To admit "pity" when stern action is required might be thought inappropriate: "commiseration" is never out of place, even in battle. See Gilbert 1940, 459–61, and Herrick 1947, 222–26.

11   *Gorboduc*, by Thomas Sackville and Thomas Norton, was written in imitation of Seneca and was the first English tragedy to use blank verse. It was played before Queen Elizabeth in 1561.

yet in truth it is very defectious in the circumstances, which grieves me because it might not remain as an exact model of all tragedies. For it is faulty both in place and time, the two necessary companions of all corporal actions ⟨Ed/147; Wh/166⟩.[12] For where the stage should always represent but one place and the uttermost time presupposed in it should be, both by Aristotle's precept and common reason, but one day, there is both many days and many places, inartificially[13] imagined ⟨Ar/41⟩. But if it be so in *Gorboduc*, how much more in all the rest; where you shall have Asia of the one side and Afric of the other, and so many under-kingdoms that the player, when he comes in, must ever begin with telling where he is or else the tale will not be conceived? Now ye shall have three ladies walk to gather flowers and then we must believe the stage to be a garden. By and by, we hear news of shipwreck in the same place and then we are to blame if we accept it not for a rock. Upon the back of that, comes out a hideous monster, with fire and smoke and then the miserable beholders are bound to take it for a cave. While, in the meantime, two armies fly in, represented with four swords and bucklers and then what hard heart will not receive it for a pitched field? Now of time they are much more liberal, for ordinary it is that two young princes fall in love. After many traverses, she is got with child, delivered of a fair boy; he is lost, groweth a man, falleth in love, and is ready to get another child; and all this in two hours space ⟨Wh/166; Lp/187⟩ – which how absurd it is in sense even sense may imagine, and art hath taught, and all ancient examples justified and, at this day, the ordinary players of Italy will not err in. Yet will some bring in an example of *Eunuchus* in Terence, that containeth matter of two days, yet far short of twenty years. True it is, and so it was to be played in two days, and so fitted to the time set forth.[14] And though Plautus have in one place done amiss, let us hit with him and not miss with him. But they will say, how then shall we set forth a story, which contains both many places and many times? And do they not know that a tragedy is tied to the laws of poesy, and not of history – not bound to follow the story but, having liberty, either to feign a quite new matter or to frame the history to the most tragical conveniency? Again, many things may be told which cannot be showed, if they know the difference betwixt reporting and representing. As, for example, I may speak (though I am here) of Peru and in speech digress from the description of that to the description of Calicut; but in action I cannot represent it without Pacolet's horse:[15] and so was the manner the Ancients took, by some

---

[12] Sidney is the first English writer to refer explicitly to the "unities" (though he does not use this word) of place and time.

[13] "inartificially" = inartistically.

[14] Scaliger (*Poetices* 6.3) suggests that *Heautontimorumenos* was played over two days and that this justifies the time scheme of the plot. Sidney apparently substituted *Eunuchus* in error.

[15] In the early French romance *Valentine and Orson*, Pacolet is a dwarf who has a little wooden horse that magically transports him wherever he wishes to go.

Nuntius ⟨Gd/127; Dd/280–81⟩[16] to recount things done in former time or other place. Lastly, if they will represent an history, they must not (as Horace saith ⟨Hr/68:147⟩) begin *ab ovo*, but they must come to the principal point of that one action which they will represent. By example this will be best expressed. I have a story of young Polydorus, delivered for safety's sake, with great riches, by his father Priamus to Polymestor, King of Thrace, in the Trojan war time. He, after some years, hearing the overthrow of Priamus, for to make the treasure his own, murdereth the child. The body of the child is taken up [by] Hecuba; she the same day findeth a slight to be revenged most cruelly of the tyrant. Where now would one of our tragedy writers begin but with the delivery of the child? Then should he sail over into Thrace and so spend I know not how many years, and travel numbers of places. But where doth Euripides?[17] Even with the finding of the body, the rest leaving to be told by the spirit of Polydorus. This need no further to be enlarged; the dullest wit may conceive it.

But besides these gross absurdities, how all their plays be neither right tragedies, nor right comedies; mingling kings and clowns ⟨Wh:166⟩, not because the matter so carrieth it, but thrust in clowns by head and shoulders, to play a part in majestical matters, with neither decency nor discretion: so as neither the admiration and commiseration, nor right sportfulness, is by their mongrel tragicomedy obtained ⟨Gu/151; Lp/187⟩.[18] I know Apuleius did somewhat so, but that is a thing recounted with space of time, not represented in one moment: and I know the Ancients have one or two examples of tragicomedies, as Plautus hath *Amphitruo*.[19] But, if we mark them well, we shall find that they never, or very daintily, match hornpipes and funerals. So falleth it out that, having no right comedy, in that comical part of our tragedy we have nothing but scurrility, unworthy of any chaste ears; or some extreme show of doltishness, indeed fit to lift up a loud laughter and nothing else; where the whole tract of a comedy should be full of delight, as the tragedy should be still maintained in a well-raised admiration. But our comedians think there is no delight without laughter; which is very wrong, for though laughter may come with delight yet cometh it not of delight, as though delight should be the cause of laughter. But well may one thing breed both together: nay, rather in themselves they have, as it were, a kind of

16 Sidney emphasizes the use of the Nuntius or Messenger as a means of preserving the unities of time and place without fragmenting the plot. He may also be hinting that playwrights who are not aware of this function will also be unaware of the importance of the Nuntius in terms of the preservation of decorum.

17 In his *Hecuba*.

18 This is not entirely inconsistent with Sidney's remark above on tragicomedy.

19 The prologue to *Amphitryon*, which refers to the mixture of gods and men in the play and humorously adopts the term "tragicomedy" was often cited by defenders of the genre in the sixteenth century.

contrariety. For delight we scarcely do but in things that have a conveniency to ourselves or to the general nature; laughter almost ever cometh of things most disproportioned to ourselves and nature. Delight hath a joy in it, either permanent or present. Laughter hath only a scornful tickling. For example, we are ravished with delight to see a fair woman and yet are far from being moved to laughter. We laugh at deformed creatures, wherein certainly we cannot delight. We delight in good chances; we laugh at mischances. We delight to hear the happiness of our friends, or country, at which he were worthy to be laughed at that would laugh. We shall, contrarily, laugh sometimes to find a matter quite mistaken and go down the hill against the bias, in the mouth of some such men, as for the respect of them one shall be heartily sorry, yet he cannot choose but laugh; and so is rather pained than delighted with laughter. Yet deny I not that they may go well together; for as in Alexander's picture well set out we delight without laughter and in twenty mad antics[20] we laugh without delight, so in Hercules, painted with his great beard and furious countenance, in a woman's attire, spinning at Omphale's commandment, it breeds both delight and laughter. For the representing of so strange a power in love procures delight; and the scornfulness of the action stirreth laughter. But I speak to this purpose, that all the end of the comical part be not upon such scornful matters as stir laughter only but mix with it that delightful teaching which is the end of poesy. And the great fault even in that point of laughter, and forbidden plainly by Aristotle, is that they stir laughter in sinful things, which are rather to be pitied than scorned ⟨Ar/41⟩. For what is it to make folks gape at a wretched beggar or beggarly clown? Or, against law of hospitality, to jest at strangers because they speak not English so well as we do? What do we learn? Sith it is certain, *Nil habet infelix paupertas durius in se / Quam quod ridiculos homines facit.* ["Miserable poverty has nothing harder in it than that it makes men ridiculous," Juvenal, *Satire* 3.152–53.] But rather a busy-loving courtier, a heartless threatening Thraso, a self-wise-seeming schoolmaster, and a wry transformed traveller: these if we saw walk in stage names, which we play naturally, therein were delightful laughter, and teaching delightfulness: as in the other, the tragedies of Buchanan[21] do justly bring forth a divine admiration. But I have lavished out too many words of this play matter. I do it because as they are excelling parts of poesy, so is there none so much used as in England, and none can be more pitifully abused – which, like an unmannerly daughter, showing a bad education, causeth her mother Poesy's honesty to be called in question.

---

[20] "antics" = grotesque people or performers.
[21] George Buchanan (1506–82), scholar and poet, translated the *Medea* and *Alcestis* of Euripides and was the author of two Latin plays on biblical themes.

19

FELIX LOPE DE VEGA
(1562–1635)

The author of hundreds of plays, Lope de Vega Carpio was also an accomplished novelist, poet, and sonneteer. He certainly had no pretensions to being a systematic theorist, yet his *Arte nuevo de hacer comedias en este tiempo*, which was first printed in 1609, in a collection of his poems, is a penetrating deconstruction of certain basic assumptions about the idea of art as applied to the theatre. The verse form of the work is important, not least in conveying subtle ironies and ambiguities. These can be approximated in a prose translation, but the tone of the original, which modulates between an insinuating humility and a jaunty assurance, is difficult to capture.

Two key words in the *New Art* are used ambivalently. One of these is the first word of the title, *arte*, which is often preceded by the indefinite article. This suggests that, like his contemporaries throughout Europe, Lope means by "an art" a specific prescriptive genre ⟨In/4⟩, but he may also be making a deliberate transition to a modern meaning for the word. The title of the address may imply this: that what is meant by the very word "art" is new.

Also ambivalent is the word *comedia*. Lope uses it to designate the genre traditionally paired with tragedy, but he also demonstrates the inapplicability of the classical generic categories to the popular drama of Spain, and so uses *comedia* to designate the specifically Spanish form. The subtle elisions of these distinct senses of the same word tend to produce a third meaning somewhat equivalent to the English "play"; a usage that implicitly avoids or denies the classical generic categories.

As the document itself declares, it is addressed to the Madrid Academy, one of several in that city in the early seventeenth century. Lope probably wrote and delivered his verse address in, or shortly before, 1608, in order to oblige somebody or other, but the circumstances are unknown. Like Corneille after him, Lope appears to be sincerely, but not unironically, respectful of classical and scholastic theory but, unlike the French playwright, he did not feel the need to reconcile his practice with the precepts he endorsed. Instead, he drew attention to the great gulf between classical standards and the demands of the public and pointedly declined to resolve (theoretically) some of the major contradictions between theory and practice.

For further reading
Montesinos 1964; Parker 1966; Pérez and Escribano 1961; Rozas 1976.

New Art of Making Comedies at the Present Time: addressed to the Academy of Madrid

You noble minds, flower of Spain, who in this assembly and renowned academy will shortly surpass not only the academies (as they were likewise called) of Italy, which, in envy of Greece, Cicero dwelling beside the Avernian lake, described,[1] but [will surpass] also Athens, where such an exalted assembly of philosophers was seen in the Lyceum[2] of Plato – you command me to write for you an art of [making] comedies which is cognizant of the popular taste.

This topic seems easy, and it would [indeed] be easy for whoever among you has written fewer of them and knows more about the art of writing them and is generally better informed [than I am]. For my liability in this matter is to have written them without [using] the art [in question].

Not because I was ignorant of the [classical] precepts, thanks be to God, for I covered the books that dealt with the subject while I was still a novice as a scholar, before I had seen the sun travel ten times from Aries to Pisces.[3] [Not because I was ignorant] but because, in short, I discovered that in Spain at that time comedies were not [examples of] how their first originators thought they should, universally, be written, but were [in keeping with] the way they were handled by many barbarians, who taught the common people their own crude manners; and thus they were introduced [into Spain] in such a way that whoever writes them now according to the [principles of] art dies unknown and unrewarded, for among those who lack their light, habit counts for more than reason and strength [of intellect].

The truth is that I have sometimes written in accordance with the art that few are acquainted with. But after seeing monstrosities,[4] replete with painted flats, emerge from another quarter to which the common people are drawn, and the women who canonize this lamentable practice, I [too] revert to that barbarous custom; and, when I have to write a comedy, I lock up the precepts with six keys. I eject Terence and Plautus from my study, to prevent them from howling at me, since the truth in dumb books has a way of crying out; and I write guided by the art[5] invented by those who aspire to the applause of the common people; for since the people pay for them [i.e. plays] it is fitting to address them in an idiotic way to give them pleasure.

---

[1] Cicero had a villa at Pozzuoli, near Lake Averno. Lope is apparently alluding to the *Academica*, in which Cicero described the evolution of the academy from its origins in the grove sacred to Academus, where Plato taught.

[2] Lope confuses Plato's "Academy" with Aristotle's "Lyceum."

[3] I.e., "before I was ten years old."

[4] Because they mix genres these comedies are "monstrous" in the way that the Minotaur (referred to below) is.

[5] The word *arte* is here used in a boldly assertive and paradoxical way. The art he adopts ignores the precepts of "art."

Now true comedy,[6] like every kind of poem or poetry, has its intended objective, and this has been to imitate men's actions and to depict the customs of its age. Moreover, any poetic imitation is constituted of three elements ⟨Ar/37; Rb/87⟩,[7] which are: discourse, melodious verse, harmony – music, one might say – which it [comedy, like other imitations] has in common with tragedy; [comedy] being differentiated only in that it deals with actions of common people, of no great consequence, and tragedy with exalted and royal ones. Just look at ours and see if they do not have a few flaws!

[These old comedies] went by the name *actus*[8] because they imitate the actions and affairs of common people. In Spain, Lope de Rueda[9] was the example for these precepts, and today his prose comedies are seen in print. They are so lowbrow that he introduces into them the concerns of artisans and the love of a blacksmith's daughter; consequently the custom has been adopted of calling the old comedies *entremeses*,[10] in which the art [of comedy] is in its [first] strength, being a single action involving common people, for an *entremés* involving the king has never been seen. And from this it is seen that the art [of constructing comedies] came to be held in such poor esteem, on account of lowness of style; and that [the introduction of] the king in comedy was for the sake of ignoramuses.

In his *Poetics* Aristotle sketches ⟨Ar/38⟩, though obscurely, its beginning: the dispute of Athens and Megara over which of them was the first inventor. The Megarians say Epicarmus was, although Athens would have it that it was Magnetes. Aelius Donatus ⟨Dn/80⟩ says that they [plays] began with the ancient sacrifices; and he makes Thespis the author of tragedy (following Horace, who asserts the same thing ⟨Hr/72:275⟩), Aristophanes of comedy in the same way. Homer composed the *Odyssey* in imitation of comedy but the *Iliad* was a renowned example of tragedy, in imitation of which I called my *Jerusalem* "epic" and added [the adjective]

---

[6] Having finished his preamble, Lope now turns, brusquely, to the classical precepts. For these he draws (at first very closely) on Robortello. Lope's differentiation of "true" comedy from the kind that he (mostly) writes is consistent with the whole argument.

[7] Lope's "discourse" *platéa* corresponds with Robortello's *sermone* for Aristotle's *logos*; and Lope's "melodious verse" (*verso dulce*) with Robortello's *rhythmo*, Aristotle's *rytmos*. Using the same term as Robortello and Aristotle, Lope distinguishes "harmony," as music, from the internal harmony of the verse.

[8] Lope translates Robortello's *actus*, meaning the whole comedy, as *acto*. He is not speaking about idiomatic Spanish usage but about the way in which scholars (i.e., Robortello) referred to comedy. As used here, the word *acto* (deliberately close to the Latin) is not the equivalent of the Spanish form *auto*, though this has been assumed.

[9] Lope de Rueda (c. 1505–65) was a highly esteemed actor, manager, and writer of comedies. There is a blacksmith's daughter in his *Armelina*. He is supposed to have been the first in Spain to use the trope of the woman disguised as a man. Cervantes praised both his acting and his interludes.

[10] *Entremeses* (side-dishes) are interludes, often dealing with low life, performed between the acts of full-length plays.

"tragic."[11] And similarly everybody generally calls the *Inferno*, *Purgatorio*, and *Paradiso* of the celebrated poet Dante Alighieri comedy, and Manetti in his prologue regretfully acknowledges this.[12]

Now everyone knows that for a time comedy, as something suspect, went silent, and that satire also was then born, which being crueller came to an end faster, and made way for New Comedy. Choruses came first, after which the complement of characters was introduced; but Menander, whom Terence followed, despised choruses as tiresome. With respect to the [accepted] precepts, Terence was better informed,[13] since he never raised the style of comedy to a tragic height, something that many have faulted as a vice in Plautus; for, in this respect, Terence was cannier.

Tragedy has history for plots and comedy has the fictitious; for this reason [comedy], having a low-life plot, was called "planipedia," since the actor did it without buskin or stage. The kinds of comedies were the *palliata*, *mimes*, the *togata*, the *atellana*, the *tabernaria* ⟨Dn/80; Nh/112⟩, which were as various then as now.

With Attic elegance the Athenians castigated vices and habits by means of comedies and awarded their prizes to the two authors of [respectively] the words and the staging. For this reason Tully called them [comedies] "mirror of customs and a live image of truth" ⟨Dn/79⟩, a very high tribute which makes them keep pace with history. See if it [comedy] is worthy of a crown and glory!

But I suppose you are saying that to sketch this tangled business is [but] to translate books and weary you. Believe me, there has been compelling reason for having you recall to mind something of these things; because, you see, you ask me to write an art of making comedies in Spain, where whatever has been written is opposed to [the principles of] art; to say what they [Spanish plays] are now like, in contrast to [the practice of] antiquity and to what is founded in reason, is to ask me to draw on my experience, not on [the principles of] art, since art declares a truth that the ignorant populace contradicts.

If, men of acumen, you want an art [a theoretical treatise], I implore you to read the learned Robortello of Udine and you will see [in his commentary] on Aristotle, and in what he writes separately in *De Comoedia*, as much as is scattered throughout many books; for everything contemporary is in a state of confusion.[14]

If you are asking for an opinion of those [kinds of comedy] that are now in possession [of the stage], since the common people inevitably establish,

---

[11] Whether deliberately or otherwise Lope misconstrues Robortello by taking Homer's epics as imitations of comedy and tragedy rather than their distant models.

[12] Both Gianozzo Manetti (1396–1454) and Antonio Tuccio Manetti (1423–97) wrote on Dante but no specific source for this allusion has been discovered.

[13] The word "informed" translates the word *visto* in the printed text, but Prades speculates that *justo* ("right") was intended (José Prades, 1971).

[14] Having summarized the classical tenets, Lope now offers his own advice.

in conformity with their laws [of playmaking], the base chimera that is this monstrous [kind of] comedy, I would say – forgive me – what I hold fast to: that I have to obey those who can command me. I would like to tell you how, gilding the vulgar error, and given that there is no alternative to following [the principles of] the art, I would like them [comedies] to provide a middle way between two extremes.

Choose the subject and do not be put out – grant these precepts pardon – if it should be about kings; though, in this respect, I understand that our sovereign, the wise King Philip of Spain, seeing a king in them [comedies] would get annoyed; whether it was at the spectacle of art being contradicted or because royal authority ought not to be imagined as consorting with base plebeians. This is to revert to ancient comedy, into which Plautus, as we see, put the gods; as is demonstrated by Jupiter in his *Amphitryon*. God knows that I would hesitate to approve this since Plutarch, speaking of Menander, did not think highly of ancient comedy; however, since we have so far distanced ourselves from art and, in Spain, do it a thousand injuries, for this once let the learned seal their lips.

The tragic mixed with the comic, and Terence with Seneca, even though it be like another Minotaur of Pasiphae,[15] will make one part serious, the other ridiculous; for this variety is very delightful. Nature gives us a good example, for from such variety she derives beauty.

Note that the [chosen] subject should have only one action, with care taken that the plot be in no way episodic, that is, [by] the inclusion of other matters that digress from the primary objective, and [note] that it should not be able to withstand the removal of any part without the destruction of the whole, with which it is integral. It is unnecessary to note that it [the action] should take place within the passage of a day, though this is Aristotle's advice, since we have already abandoned respect for him when we mix tragic high seriousness with the baseness of low comedy. Make [the duration of the action] as short as may be, if it is not a question of the poet writing history in which several years have to pass, which may be included in the time between one act and another ⟨Cn/250⟩, [during which also] if necessary, a character may go on a journey, something which deeply offends whoever notices it. But let whoever is offended not go to see [such plays].

Oh what a lot of people nowadays are horrified to see that years are to elapse in an affair that the course of an artificial day once had to bring to a conclusion, who do not even want to concede the mathematical day to it ⟨Cn/249⟩. But considering that the peevishness of a seated Spaniard will not be abated if everything from Genesis to the Last Judgment is not represented for him in two hours, I hold that, if one has to give pleasure here, the right way to do it is with what works best.

15　The Minotaur, or Bull of Minos, was the son of Pasiphae and a bull. He had the body of a man and the head of a bull and was confined in the labyrinth built by Daedalus.

Having chosen the subject, write [a draft] in prose and divide it into three acts [as units] of time, contriving, if possible, not to overshoot the end of the day in each act. Captain Virués,[16] a notable intelligence, arranged comedy in three acts. Before him it went on all fours, baby-footed, for comedies were infants then. And I myself wrote them at the age of eleven and twelve in four acts on four sheets of papers (for each sheet contained an act) and at that time it was customary to give, in the three intermissions, three little *entremeses* – while now we scarcely have one – followed by a dance, dance being so much a part of comedy that Aristotle approves ⟨Ar/61⟩ it, and Athenaeus, Plato, and Xenophon discuss it, although he [Xenophon] reproves the improper kind and for this reason is upset by Callipides, who in this way appears to imitate the antique Chorus.[17] Having divided the subject into two parts, make the connection from the beginning to the point at which the action is running down, but do not admit the resolution until you reach the last scene, for if the common people know how it ends they will turn their faces towards the door and their backs away from what they waited for for three hours, cheek by jowl, since there is nothing more to know than what appears [in the resolution].

The theatre should seldom be left in the state in which no character is speaking, since in these intervals the common people get restless and the plot unfolds at [too] great length. Apart from this being itself a serious fault, [the avoidance of it] greatly increases the charm and ingenuity [of the play].

Begin, then, with a chaste diction and without spending deep thoughts and ideas on domestic matters, which have only to imitate the small-talk of two of three people. But when the character enters who persuades, advises or dissuades this is the moment that calls for maxims and ideas, for in this [instance] truth is undoubtedly imitated; for a man adopts a different style of speech, [a style] out of the ordinary, when he is giving advice, persuading, or analyzing something. Aristides,[18] the rhetorician, gave us the touchstone, since he wants the language of comedy to be unadorned, limpid, simple, and he adds that it is taken from the usage of the man in the street ⟨Jn/199⟩, making a distinction from deliberated discourse, for then the diction will be splendid, sonorous, and elaborate. Neither drag in scripture nor let the language cause offense with precious diction, since if

---

[16] Cristobál de Virués (c. 1550–c.1614) wrote Senecan tragedies. He was also an epic poet, a soldier, and Lope's friend.

[17] The reference to Aristotle, Athenaeus, Plato, Xenophon, and Callipides are taken directly from Robortello. Athenaeus (born c. 170 B.C.) was the author of *Deipnosophistae* (*Doctors at Dinner*), the supposed record of a conversation which includes extracts from many authors, including those of Greek Middle Comedies. Plato thought that dancing should be confined to religious celebrations (by contrast with Aristotle for whom it is a mode of imitation and a constituent of tragedy). Xenophon (born c. 431 B.C.), the historian, was a follower and friend of Socrates.

[18] Aristides (died c. A.D. 189) was the author of two well-known treatises on rhetoric.

you are to imitate actual speakers, it will not be by [talk about] Panchaian islands, Metauran rivers, hippogrifs, *semones*, and centaurs.[19]

If the king should speak, imitate, as far as you can, royal gravity; if the old man should speak contrive a sententious kind of modesty; portray lovers with feelings that profoundly move whoever listens to them; present soliloquies in such a way that the actor is altogether transformed and, by changing himself, changes the auditor. Let him question himself and answer himself and, if he is to utter a lover's complaints, let him always preserve the decorum due to women. Do not let ladies be unworthy the name and if they switch [from female] attire, let it be in a way that is excusable, for masculine disguise is usually very pleasing. Avoid things impossible, for it is a maxim that only the verisimilar is suitable for representation; do not let the lackey concern himself with lofty matters nor deliver himself of ideas, as we have seen in some foreign comedies; and by no manner of means let the character contradict himself, with respect to what he has already stated. I mean do not let his memory fail the way that in Sophocles it is blameworthy that Oedipus is not made to recall that he has killed Laius with his own hand. Let the scenes be finished off with maxims, with grace, with elegant lines, so that the character having entered who is to speak, he does not [then] leave with the audience displeased. In the first act present the situation, in the second knot the succeeding events in such a way that, up to the middle of the third act, nobody can tell, hardly, how it will end. Always defeat expectation and, when it appears that something should be left obscure, focus [on something] very remote from what is [ultimately] intended. Fit your verse considerately to the matter being dealt with; *décimas* [ten-line, octosyllabic stanzas] are right for lovers' complaints; the sonnet is good for those who are in a state of expectation; narrative passages call for *romances* [octosyllabics with alternating assonance] although they [also] stand out brilliantly in octaves; triplets are for serious subjects; and for those concerning love, *redondillas* [heptasyllabic quatrains]. Rhetorical figures such as repetition or anadiplosis are important; and in the beginning of these same lines those [passages] concerning varieties of anaphora, ironies, and interrogatives, also apostrophe and exclamations.

To deceive with the truth, in the way that Miguel Sánchez[20] (worthy of this reminder of his inventiveness) made a practice of doing in his comedies, is something that has been thought well of. The common people have always cherished equivocal speech and amphibological uncertain-

---

[19] Panchaia is a mythical island. On the bank of the Metauro, an Italian river, the Romans defeated the Carthaginians. Hippogrifs are fabulous creatures, half dragons, half horses. The *semones* were Roman demigods. In dramatic dialogue, such allusions are precious and to be avoided, says Lope.

[20] Miguel Sánchez (born c. 1545) is best known for his religious poetry but he also wrote at least two plays.

ty,[21] since they think that only they understand what the other person is saying. The best subjects are questions of honor because everybody is powerfully moved by them, and, along with them, virtuous deeds, since virtue is universally loved. Thus we see that if, as it happens, an actor plays a traitor, he is so hateful to everybody that they do not sell him what he goes to buy and the people fly from him when they meet him; and if he is loyal, they lend to him, invite him out, and even distinguished people honor and love him, fête him, and acclaim him.

Let each act have only four folios since twelve [folios – for the whole play] are the measure of the time and the patience of the auditor.[22] In the satirical part do not be plain and open, since it is known for this reason comedies were prohibited by law in Greece and Italy; sting without hatred, for if by chance you slander neither hope for applause nor aspire to fame.

You may take as aphorisms matters herein that do not come to you from the art of antiquity, for which the present occasion allows no more room. As to what to do with the three kinds of staging that Vitruvius mentions,[23] with their scene-drops and trees, huts and houses, and illusions of marbles, as described by Valerius Maximus, Pietro Crinito, Horace in his *Epistles*, and others;[24] that is the business of the producer. About costumes Julius Pollux[25] would tell us, if it were necessary, for in Spain, the comedy of the time admits barbarous things: a Turk wearing a Christian's ruff and a Roman in tight breeches.

But there is no one at all whom I can call more barbarous than I am myself, since I am so bold as to lay down precepts that violate art and allow myself to drift in the stream of popular taste, for which reason Italy and France call me ignorant; but what am I to do, if I have written four hundred and eighty-three plays, including one finished this week! For, with only six exceptions, all of them seriously offend against the principles of art. But after all, I stand by what I have written and I know that, though done otherwise they might have been better, they would not have pleased as they have for, at times, what runs counter to good judgment for the same reason pleases the fancy.

---

[21] An amphibology is an ambiguity, usually one depending on a grammatical construction.

[22] This probably means that a play that would not strain the time and patience of the audience would be printed, in quarto format, on ninety-six pages: that is, on twelve folios each folded to make four leaves.

[23] In his *De Architectura*, begun in about 16 B.C., Pollio Vitruvius discusses the architectural practice of the Greeks and its relation to modern techniques. Book v of this ten-volume work describes the building of theatres and the settings appropriate for tragedy, comedy, and satire.

[24] Valerius Maximus compiled *Memorable Deeds and Words*, a work in nine volumes, dedicated to the emperor Tiberius; the collection, arranged according to such topics as "social customs," includes illustrative anecdotes and extracts from many authors. Petrus Crinitus (born c. 1465) was a professor of Latin rhetoric in Florence.

[25] Julius Pollux (living in A.D. 180), a Greek born in Egypt, was the author of *Onomasticon*, an explanatory dictionary of Greek words and technical terms, including those having to do with the theatre.

Why should comedy be the mirror of human life
And what good does it do for the young and the old?
What do you look for in it except pleasing conceits, refined
    words and a noble purity of eloquence?
[Comedy –] in which grave matters arise in the midst of smiles
    and in which merry jests are mixed with solemnity!
How treacherous the servants are, how shameless the woman,
    how fraudulent and full of every kind of deceit!
How wretched, unhappy, foolish and inept the lover! How
    tortuously do those things fall out that you think well
    begun![26]

Listen attentively, and do not enter into disputation about the theory of art, for it will be found in the comedy [itself] so that, in listening to it, all can be revealed.

---

[26] The source of this (Latin) verse is unknown. It may be by Lope himself.

20

BEN JONSON
(1573–1637)

Jonson had no doubt that there was an art of drama with principles that could be articulated and, indeed, taught. This being so, it was more effective, he said, "to show the right way to those that come after" than to point out the errors in existing works. Less interested in criticism than in theory, and less in theory than in example, he attempted, he said, to bring his "precepts into practice," adding that "rules are ever of less force and value than experiments" (Jonson/Herford and Simpson 1925–52, VII: 617).

"Something of art was wanting to the drama till he came," Dryden said of Jonson ⟨Dd/286⟩ and, indeed, there was no English precedent for Jonson's combination of theory and practice. The "comic laws" that he "first did teach the age,"[1] are frequently advanced in prologues, epilogues, and dedications and are also to be found embedded in "inductions," interludes, and the dialogue of his plays. But Jonson never attempted a comprehensive statement about drama, unless in the lost dialogue that was intended as the introduction to his translation of Horace's *The Art of Poetry*.

Some of his precepts of art are to be found in *Timber; or Discoveries*. This commonplace-book, in which Jonson made entries drawn from his reading, and his own reflections, was published after his death as an unorganized collection of notes, mostly concerned with men and manners but including some trenchant remarks on the art of drama. Another, but unreliable, source is the report of his conversation by the Scottish poet William Drummond. It was Drummond who attributed to Jonson the opinion "that Shakespeare wanted art." Drummond gave no context for the remark but an extract from *Discoveries*, printed below, may explain it. Jonson (like Lessing after him) supposed that to invoke genius (even Shakespeare's) as an *alternative* to art was as wrongheaded as to substitute a pedantic obedience to rules for art's discipline.

Inartistic and commercial approaches to the theatre, whether by practitioners or audiences, exasperated Jonson, as did the ephemerality of its real achievements. And, while a number of his contemporaries deprecated the printing of plays, Jonson became the first English playwright to supervise the systematic publication of his dramatic works. His attachment to print, his insistence on the supremacy of the poet (even in devising the spectacular elements of masque), and his fierce condemnations of the shortcomings of the theatre have been taken as signs of "a deeply inherent non-dramatic principle in him" or "a deeply rooted antitheatricalism" (Barish 1981, 132). Be that as it may, Jonson was convinced that there was a dramatic principle in life itself and that any meretricious theatrical exploitation of it

---

[1] Commendatory poem from Richard Brome's *The Northern Lass*, 1632. Jonson/Herford and Simpson 1925–52, VIII: 409.

was a danger to be resisted.

Jonson's attachment to the idea of an art of drama that might be practiced and articulated runs deeper than his reliance on any existing canons. His attitude to classical dramatic theory was one of respectful independence. Though he never dissents from the *Poetics* (which he approaches through the work of the Dutch scholar Daniel Heinsius), he ignores such major topics as tragic catharsis and says nothing about the contrast between his own practice and Aristotle's theory. Jonson tends, in fact, to arrogate to comedy the effective power usually associated with tragedy and to concern himself chiefly with questions of style, plot structure, and characterization. With respect to the last, his theory and practice, which related observation of individuals to a typology of "humours," put the English comic playwrights who followed him in his debt.

For further reading

Barish 1960, 1981; Enck 1957; Sweeney 1985.

From *Timber; or Discoveries*[2]

129[3]   I know nothing can conduce more to letters than to examine the writings of the ancients and not to rest in their sole authority or take all on trust from them; provided the plagues of judging and pronouncing against them be away; such as are envy, bitterness, precipitation, impudence and scurrile scoffing. For to all the observations of the ancients we have our own experience, which, if we will use and apply, we have better means to pronounce. It is true they opened the gates and made the way, that went before us; but as guides, not commanders ... .[4]

647   I remember the players have often mentioned it as an honour to Shakespeare that in his writing (whatsoever he penned) he never blotted out a line. My answer hath been, 'Would he had blotted a thousand', which they took for a malevolent speech. I had not told posterity this but for their ignorance, who choose that circumstance to commend their friend by wherein he most faulted. And to justify my own candour, for I loved the man, and do honour his memory (on this side idolatry) as much

---

[2] *Timber; or Discoveries: Made upon Men and Matter as they have Flowed Out of His Daily Readings or Had their Reflux to his Peculiar Notion of the Times*. This collection of notes and short essays was first published in the 1640 folio edition of Jonson's *Works*. It was begun after 1623, the date of the fire in his lodging which destroyed, among other books and documents, his introduction to Horace's *Art of Poetry*. Jonson's marginal inscriptions, which are not glosses but labels (often the repetition of a single name used in the adjoining text), have been omitted.

[3] Line numbers at the beginnings of the extracts from *Discoveries* correspond to the text in Jonson/Herford and Simpson 1925–52, vol. VIII.

[4] The above passage is based on *In Libros de Disciplinis Praefatio* by Juan Luis Vives (1492–1540), the Spanish philosopher notable for his opposition to Aristotelian scholasticism and for the independence of his thought.

as any. He was, indeed, honest and of an open and free nature, had an excellent fantasy, brave notions and gentle expressions, wherein he flowed with that facility that sometime it was necessary he should be stopped. . . . Many times he fell into those things could not scape laughter, as when he said, in the person of Caesar, one speaking to him, 'Caesar thou dost me wrong.' He replied, 'Caesar never did wrong but with just cause.'[5] And such like, which were ridiculous. But he redeemed his vices with his virtues. There was ever more in him to be praised than to be pardoned. . . .

772   The true artificer will not run away from nature as he were afraid of her, or depart from life and the likeness of truth, but speak to the capacity of his hearers. And though his language differ from the vulgar somewhat, it shall not fly from all humanity, with the Tamerlanes and Tamer-Chams of the late age, which had nothing in them but the scenical strutting and furious vociferation to warrant them to the ignorant gapers.[6] He knows it is his only art so to carry it as none but artificers perceive it. An other age, or juster men, will acknowledge the virtues of his studies . . . .

2095   Nothing is more ridiculous than to make an author a dictator, as the schools have done Aristotle.[7] The damage is infinite knowledge receives by it. For to many things a man should owe but a temporary belief and a suspension of his own judgement, not an absolute resignation of himself or a perpetual captivity. Let Aristotle and others have their dues but if we cannot make farther discoveries of truth and fitness than they, why are we envied? Let us beware, while we strive to add, we do not diminish or deface. We may improve but not augment. By discrediting falsehood, truth grows in request. We must not go about like men anguished or perplexed, for vicious affectation of praise, but calmly study the separation of opinions, find the errors have intervened, awake antiquity, call former times into question; but make no parties with the present nor follow any fierce undertakers; mingle no matter of doubtful credit with the simplicity of truth, but gently stir the mold about the root of the question . . . .

2555   I am not of that opinion to conclude a poet's liberty within the narrow limits of laws, which neither the grammarians nor the philosophers prescribe. For, before they found out those laws there were many excellent poets that fulfilled them. Amongst whom none is more perfect than Sophocles, who lived a little before Aristotle. Which of the Greeklings durst ever give precepts to Demosthenes? Or to Pericles (whom the age

---

[5] *Julius Caesar* 3.1.47–48 reads "Know, Caesar, doth not wrong; nor without cause / Will he be satisfied." It is possible that the words quoted by Jonson were spoken on the stage.

[6] An allusion to Marlowe's *Tamburlaine the Great* (1590–92) and to a lost play apparently echoing Marlowe's. The sentences that follow are derived from Quintilian's *Institutio Oratoria*.

[7] In this extract Jonson is drawing on Francis Bacon's *Of the Advancement of Learning*, Book 1, Chapter 4, where Bacon attacks what he calls the "degenerate learning" of the Schoolmen who made "Aristotle their dictator."

surnamed *heavenly* because he seemed to thunder and lighten with his language)? Or to Alcibiades, who had rather Nature for his guide than Art for his master?

But whatsoever Nature, at any time, dictated to the most happy, or long exercise to the most laborious, that wisdom and learning of Aristotle hath brought into an Art, because he understood the causes of things and what other men did by chance or custom he doth by reason; and not only found out the way not to err but the short way we should take not to err. ...[8]

2625   The parts of a comedy are the same with a tragedy and the end is partly the same. For they both delight and teach. The comics are called *didaskaloi*[9] of the Greeks, no less than the tragics.

Nor is the moving of laughter always the end of comedy, that is rather a fowling for the people's delight, or their fooling. For, as Aristotle says rightly ⟨Ar/41⟩, the moving of laughter ⟨Sy/182⟩ is a fault in comedy, a kind of turpitude that depraves some part of man's nature without a disease; as a wry face without pain moves laughter, or a deformed vizard, or a rude clown ⟨Wh/166⟩ dressed in a lady's habit and using her actions. ...

So that what, either in the words or sense of an author, or in the language or actions of men, is awry, or deprived, doth strangely stir mean affections and provoke for the most part to laughter. And therefore it was clear that all insolent and obscene speeches, jests upon the best men, injuries to particular persons, perverse and sinister sayings (and the rather unexpected) in the Old Comedy did move laughter; especially where it did imitate any dishonesty. And scurrility came forth in the place of wit, which who understands the nature and genius of laughter cannot but perfectly know.

Of which Aristophanes affords an ample harvest, having not only outgone Plautus, or any other in that kind, but expressed all the moods and figures of what is ridiculous, oddly. In short, as vinegar is not accounted good until the wine be corrupted, so jests that are true and natural seldom raise laughter with the beast, the multitude. They love nothing that is right and proper. The farther it runs from reason or possibility, with them, the better it is. What could have made them laugh like to see Socrates presented – that example of all good life, honesty and virtue – to have him hoisted up with a pulley and there play the philosopher, in a basket? Measure just how many foot a flea could skip geometrically by just such a scale and edify the people from the engine ⟨Dd/288⟩?[10] This was theatrical wit, right stage-jesting and relishing a playhouse

---

[8] This passage, drawn from Daniel Heinsius' *De Tragoediae Constitutions* (published in 1611), does not contradict Bacon's view in the extract above, but the divergence is a caution against taking the notes in *Discoveries* as Jonson's unqualified opinions. In the next extract also, Jonson is drawing on Heinsius.

[9] *didaskaloi* = teachers. They were so called because they trained the Chorus.

[10] See Aristophanes' *Clouds*, lines 144ff. and 218f.

invented for scorn and laughter; whereas, if it had savoured of equity, truth, perspicuity and candour, to have tasted a wise or a learned palate, spit it out presently: this is bitter and profitable; this instructs and would inform us. What need we know anything that are nobly born more than a horse race or a hunting match, our day to break with citizens and such innate mysteries? This is truly leaping from the stage to the tumbrel again, reducing all wit to the original dung-cart ⟨Hr/72:276⟩.[11]

Of the magnitude and compass of any fable, epic or dramatic
To the resolving of this question, we must first agree in the definition of the fable. The fable is called the imitation of one entire and perfect action, whose parts are so joined and knit together as nothing in the structure can be changed or taken away without impairing, or troubling, the whole; of which there is a proportionable magnitude in the members. As for example: – if a man would build a house he would first appoint a place to build it in, which he would define within certain bounds. So, in the constitution of a poem, the action is aimed at by the poet which answers place in a building, and that action hath his largeness, compass and proportion.[12] But as a court or king's palace requires other dimensions than a private house, so the epic asks a magnitude from other poems. Since what is place in the one [buildings] is action in the other [poems] the difference is in space. ... So the space of the action may not prove large enough for the epic fable yet be perfect for the dramatic, and whole.

Whole we call that, and perfect, which hath a beginning, a midst and an end. So the place of any building may be whole and entire for that work though too little for a palace. As to a tragedy and a comedy, the action may be convenient and perfect that would not fit an epic poem in magnitude. So a lion is a perfect creature in himself though it be less than an elephant. The head of a lion is whole though it be less than that of a buffalo or a rhinoceros. They differ – but in *specie*; either in the kind is absolute. Both have their parts and either the whole. Therefore, as in every body so in every action which is the subject of a just work there is required a certain proportionable greatness, neither too vast nor too minute. ... Too vast oppresseth the eyes and exceeds the memory: too little scarce admits either.

Now, in every action it behooves the poet to know which is his utmost bound, how far with fitness and a necessary proportion he may produce and determine it. That is, till either the good fortune change into the worse or the worse into the better. For, as a body without proportion cannot be goodly, no more can the action, either in comedy or tragedy, without his fit bounds. And every bound, for the nature of the subject, is esteemed best

[11] Jonson is alluding to the supposed origins of drama in performances mounted on carts ("dung" being his own extrapolation!).
[12] In Heinsius' extended metaphor "action" corresponds to the site on which the building is to be erected (the "place"), "fable" to the erected building itself.

that is largest, till it can increase no more. So, it behooves the action in tragedy or comedy to be let grow till the necessity ask a conclusion; wherein, two things are to be considered: first, that it exceed not the compass of one day; next, that there be place left for digression and art ⟨Dd/282⟩.[13] For the episodes and digressions in a fable are the same that household stuff and other furniture are in a house. And so far for the measure and extent of a fable dramatic.

Now, that it should be one and entire. One, is considerable two ways: either as it is only separate and by itself; or as being composed of many parts it begins to be one as those parts grow, or are wrought, together. That it should be one the first way, alone and by itself, no man that hath tasted letters ever would say; especially having required before a just magnitude and equal proportion of the parts in themselves. Neither of which can possibly be if the action be single and separate, not composed of parts which laid together in themselves, with an equal and fitting proportion, tend to the same end; which thing, out of antiquity itself, hath deceived many; and more this day it doth deceive.

So many there be of old that have thought the action of one man to be ⟨Ar/44⟩ one – as of Hercules, Theseus, Achilles, Ulysses and other heroes – which is both foolish and false, since by one and the same person many things may be severally done, which cannot be fitly referred or joined to the same end; which not only the excellent tragic poets but the best masters of the epic, Homer and Virgil, saw. ...

From the Induction to *Every Man out of his Humour*[14]

ASPER: ... in every human body
The choler, melancholy, phlegm and blood
By reason that they flow continually
In some one part, and are not continent,
Receive the name of humours.[15] Now thus far

---

13 The common Renaissance tenet that the time scheme of a play should not exceed a day is coupled with the notion dear to Jonson (and found in Heinsius) that the plot should allow for the entwining of various strands.

14 *Every Man out of his Humour* was performed at the Globe and at court in 1599. It was published in the following year. It contains the first and fullest of Jonson's "inductions." Before the beginning of the play proper, Asper, the supposed author of the play, Cordatus, its presenter, and Mitis, their friend, discuss Asper's approach to comedy. Asper is committed to the exposure of vice and folly at whatever cost. The superficial affectation of real, psychological "humours" is one of his targets.

15 Jonson is adapting to literary use the medieval medical science of "humours." Its foundation was Aristotle's theory of four primary qualities of matter – cold, hot, wet, and dry – that combined to form the four elements of earth, air, fire, and water. In Hippocratic medical science this theory had been developed and applied to human physiology and psychology, and it was thus used by Galen (2nd century A.D.) and his medieval successors. Corresponding to the four elements were four bodily fluids and their associated humors:

It may, by metaphor, apply itself
Unto the general disposition:
As when some one peculiar quality
Doth so possess a man that it doth draw
All his affects,[16] his spirit and his powers,
In their confluctions, all to run one way,
This may be truly said to be a humour.
But that a rook, in wearing a pied feather,
The cable hat-band or the three-piled ruff,
A yard of shoe-tie or the Switzer's knot
On his French garters, should affect a humour!
O, 'tis then most ridiculous.

CORDATUS: He speaks pure truth. Now, if an idiot
Have but an apish or fantastic strain,
It is his humour.

ASPER: Well I will scourge those apes;
And to these courteous eyes oppose a mirror
As large as is the stage whereon we act,
Where they shall see the times' deformity
Anatomised in every nerve and sinew,
With constant courage and contempt of fear.[17] ...

Prologue to *Every Man in his Humour*[18]

Though need make many poets, and some such
As art, and nature have not bettered much;

blood (the sanguine); black bile (the melancholic); yellow bile (the choleric); and phlegm (the phlegmatic). The particular blend of these fluids in any individual constituted his complexion and determined his humor. An individual with excess of black bile, for instance, would be of a melancholic humor. Seizing on this old-fashioned science as a potentially elaborate and refined system of characterization, Jonson distinguishes sharply between two related methods of comedy: the portrayal of real humors and satirical depiction of the affectation of them as, for instance, by someone of a quite sanguine temperament attempting to make himself more interesting by affecting a melancholy humor.

[16] "affects" = passions.

[17] The "courteous eyes" looking at the mirror are those of the audience. The observation and representation of vice and folly in order to correct them is as fundamental to Jonson's understanding of comedy as it was general among his contemporaries. The notion that the better sort of spectators would approve such "physic of the mind" while the worse sort utterly rejected it is especially intense and pervasive in Jonson's work.

[18] *Every Man in his Humour* was performed at the Curtain Theatre in 1598. The play was printed in 1601 and, in a considerably revised form, in 1616. The Prologue did not appear in the earlier version. Shakespeare's plays, especially the histories (or *The Tempest* as a play which has been graced by the audience's pleasure in the portrayal of a monster), would supply prime examples of most of the faults mentioned; but so would many plays by other dramatists, e.g., Heywood's *The Four Prentises of London*.

Yet ours, for want, hath not so loved the stage,
As he dare serve th'ill customs of the age,
Or purchase your delight at such a rate,
As, for it, he himself must justly hate.
To make a child, now swaddled, to proceed
Man, and then shoot up, in one beard, and weed ⟨Wh/166; Sy/180⟩,
Past threescore years; or, with three rusty swords,
And help of some few foot and half-foot words,
Fight over York and Lancaster's long jars,
And in the tiring house bring wounds, to scars.
He rather prays, you will be pleased to see
One such, today, as other plays should be.
Where neither *Chorus* wafts you o'er the seas;
Nor creaking throne comes down, the boys to please;
Nor nimble squib is seen, to make afeard
The gentlewomen; nor rolled bullet heard
To say, it thunders; nor tempestuous drum
Rumbles, to tell you when the storm doth come;
But deeds, and language, such as men do use;
And persons, such as *Comoedie* would choose,
When she would show an image of the times ⟨Dn/79⟩,
And sport with human follies, not with crimes⟨Ar/41⟩.
Except, we make 'hem such by loving still
Our popular errors, when we know th'are ill.
I mean such errors, as you'll all confess
By laughing at them, they deserve no less;
Which when you heartily do, there's hope left, then,
You, that have so graced monsters, may like men.

From *The Magnetic Lady*[19]: Chorus

BOY: Now, Gentlemen, what censure you of our *protasis*, or first *act*?

PROBEE: Well, Boy, it is a fair presentment of your actors. And a hand-
          some promise of somewhat to come hereafter.

DAMPLAY: But, there is nothing done in it, or concluded: therefore I say no
          act.

BOY: A fine piece of logic! Do you look, Mr. Damplay, for conclusions
          in a *protasis*? I thought the law of comedy had reserv'd 'hem to

[19] *The Magnetic Lady* was performed in 1632 and published in 1640. In the induction to the
play, Probee and Damplay, representatives of the people, inquire after the playwright. The
Boy, a general assistant in the theatre, invites them to see the play from the stage and to
make a critical commentary on it. This they do, after each act, their comments and the
Boy's keen responses constituting a critical dialogue on the play and on the theory of
comedy. The extract is from the critical "Chorus" following Act 1.

the *catastrophe*; and that the *epistasis* (as we are taught) and the *catastasis* had been intervening parts to have been expected ⟨Sg/102⟩.[20] But you would have them all together, it seems: the clock should strike five, at once, with the acts.

DAMPLAY: Why, if it could be so, it were well, Boy.

BOY: Yes, if a child could be born, in a play, and grow up to a man i' the first scene, before he went off the stage; and then after to come forth a squire, and be made a knight; and that knight to travel between the act, and do wonders in the holy land, or elsewhere; kill paynims, wild boars, dun cows and other monsters; beget him a reputation, and marry an emperor's daughter for his mistress; and convert her father's country; and at last come home, lame, and all to be laden with miracles.

DAMPLAY: These miracles would please ⟨Lp/187⟩, I assure you, and take the people! For there be more of the people that will expect miracles, and more than miracles, from this pen.

BOY: Do they think this pen can juggle? ... who expect what is impossible, or beyond nature, defraud themselves. ...

[20] From Horace, Renaissance theorists derived the idea of a dramatic structure that modified Aristotle's description and was applicable to the theatre of the time. The *protasis*, *catastrophe*, and *epitasis* were the commonly accepted elements of this structure. *Catastasis* is the term used by Scaliger for a second catastrophe in which all the complications in the plot are resolved. In Jonson's usage, the *catastasis* brings the "digressions" or "underplot" to a resolution.

21

THOMAS HEYWOOD
(c. 1574–1641)

A playwright who, by his own account, wrote or collaborated in 220 plays, a poet, a translator, a deviser of pageants, and an actor, Thomas Heywood was well qualified for the task of defending the English theatre against those who abhorred and sought to suppress it. But *An Apology for Actors* (1612) was an ineffectual response to the attacks on the theatre that were mounted with increasing intensity through the late sixteenth and earlier seventeenth centuries, and no hindrance to the more ferocious ones that would bring about the prohibition of 1642. Unfortunately, the accusation that Heywood's *Apology* "repeatedly betrays the cause it is attempting to serve" (Barish 1981, 117) is well founded. Heywood's examples of a performance being used as the occasion for the kidnapping of the Sabine women, and of the thespian Caesar so involved in his role that he killed his fictional antagonist on the stage, are scarcely such as to allay misgivings about the effects of theatre.[1] Heywood is so enthusiastic about the power, in itself, of theatrical illusion to influence the spectators' conduct that he scarcely discriminates between good and bad results, though he does argue that the abuse of theatre is not a sufficient reason to abolish an essentially useful and pleasurable institution.

The axiom stated in his introductory verses to *An Apology* underlies his whole defense: since human life is inescapably theatrical, the art of theatre is necessary to life. *Theatrum mundi* is thus more than a metaphor for Heywood. Its reality is what, for him, makes actors (to borrow Grotowski's word) "holy." But he does not pursue the complexities and dangers inherent in the fusion of theatre and actuality (as Massinger would, so brilliantly, in *The Roman Actor*).[2] Instead, Heywood defends and celebrates the dignity of the actor's calling on the understanding that drama itself must be seen to be useful, as well as potent and pleasurable, if the profession of actor is to be given its due.

For further reading

Barish 1981; Boas 1950.

---

[1] But the "rape" of the Sabine women (captured in the course of a religious celebration by the Romans, who needed wives) was often represented in heroic terms. Plutarch, in his life of Romulus, uses it as an instance of "the greatness of Rome ... that she did always unite and incorporate those whom she conquered into herself."

[2] Massinger's play (1626) includes examples very much like those offered by Heywood. In *The Roman Actor*, however, the "real" miser is by no means cured by the stage portrayal of one, and the "real life" performances (culminating in an "actual" death on a stage) are sordid, bloody affairs that compete with, and destroy, the arts of acting and imitation proper.

The Author to his Book[3]

The world's a theatre, the earth a stage,
Which God, and nature, doth with actors fill,
Kings have their entrance with due equipage,
And some their parts play well and others ill.
The best no better are (in this theatre),
Where every humour's fitted in his kind,
This a true subject's acts, and that a traitor,
The first applauded and the last confined.
This plays an honest man, and that a knave,
A gentle person this, and he a clown.
One man is ragged, and another brave.
All men have parts and each man acts his own.
She a chaste lady acteth all her life,
A wanton courtesan another plays.
This covets marriage love, that, nuptial strife,
Both in continual action spend their days.
Some citizens, some soldiers, born to adventure,
Shepherds and seamen; then our play's begun,
When we are born and to the world first enter,
And all find *Exits* when their parts are done.
If then the world a theatre present,
As by the roundness it appears most fit,
Built with star-galleries of high ascent,
In which Jehovah doth as spectator sit.
And chief determiner t'applaud the best,
And their endeavours crown with more than merit,
But by their evil actions dooms the rest,
To end disgraced, whilst others praise inherit.
    He that denies then theatres should be,
    He may as well deny a world to me.

From *An Apology for Actors*, Book III

... To proceed to the matter: first, playing is an ornament to the City, which strangers of all nations, repairing hither, report of in their countries, beholding them here with some admiration: for what variety of entertainment can there be in any city of Christendom more than in London? ... Secondly, our English tongue, which hath been the most harsh, uneven and broken language of the world, part Dutch, part Irish, Saxon, Scotch,

---

[3] These verses by Heywood himself come at the end of a series of verse commendations of *An Apology* by his friends.

Welsh and, indeed, a gallimaufry of many but perfect in none, is now by this secondary means of playing continually refined, every writer striving in himself to add a new flourish to it; so that, in process, from the most rude and unpolished tongue it is grown to a most perfect and composed language and many excellent works and elaborate poems writ in the same, that many nations grow enamoured of our tongue (before despised). ... Thirdly, plays have made the ignorant more apprehensive, taught the unlearned the knowledge of many famous histories, instructed such as cannot read in the discovery of all our English chronicles: and what man have you now of that weak capacity that cannot discourse of any notable thing recorded even from William the Conqueror, nay from the landing of Brute, until this day, being possessed of their true use? For, or because, plays are writ with this aim, and carried with this method: to teach the subjects obedience to their king; to show the untimely end of such as have moved tumults, commotions and insurrections; to present them with the flourishing estate of such as live in obedience, exhorting them to allegiance; dehorting them from all traitorous and felonious stratagems. *In gravity, tragedy outdoes every kind of writing* [Ovid, *Tristia* 2.287–88].

If we present a tragedy, we include the fatal and abortive ends of such as commit notorious murders, which is aggravated and acted with all the art that may be, to terrify men from the like abhorred practices. If we present a foreign history, the subject is so intended that, in the lives of Romans, Grecians, or others, either the virtues of our countrymen are extolled or their vices reproved . . . .

If a comedy, it is pleasantly contrived with merry accidents and inter-mixed with apt and witty jests, to present before the prince at certain times of solemnity or else merrily fitted to the stage. And what is then the subject of this harmless mirth? Either in the shape of a clown to show others their slovenly and unhandsome behaviour that they may reform that simplicity in themselves, which others make their sport, lest they happen to become the like subject of general scorn to the auditory, else it treats of love, deriding foolish inamorates, who spend their ages, their spirits, nay them-selves in the servile and ridiculous employments of their mistresses. And these are mingled with sportful accidents to recreate such as of themselves are wholly devoted to melancholy, which corrupts the blood; or to refresh such weary spirits as are tired with labour or study, to moderate the cares and heaviness of the mind, that they may return to their trades and faculties with more zeal and earnestness after some small soft and pleasant retirement ⟨Gu/157⟩. Sometimes they discourse of Pantaloons, usurers that have unthrifty sons, which both the fathers and sons may behold to their instructions; sometimes of courtesans, to divulge their subtleties and snares, in which young men may be entangled, showing them the means to avoid them. If we present a pastoral, we show the harmless love of shepherds, diversely moralised, distinguishing betwixt the craft of the city and the innocence of the sheepcote. Briefly, there is neither tragedy, history, comedy, moral or pastoral from which an infinite use cannot be gathered. I speak not in defence of any lascivious shows, scurrilous jests or scandalous invectives ⟨Sy/181⟩. If there be any such, I banish them quite from my patronage . . . .

22

TIRSO DE MOLINA (FRAY GABRIEL TÉLLEZ) (1583?–1648)

The battle between the supporters of the Spanish *comedia*[1] and those who attacked it as a degenerate form of classical comedy ⟨Lp/185⟩ was still being fought when Tirso de Molina published *The Country Houses of Toledo* (*Los Cigarrales de Toledo*) in 1624. This miscellany, modeled on Boccaccio's *Decameron*, includes the texts of three of Tirso's plays, one of which is made the occasion for the defense of the *comedia nueva* and of its supreme exponent, Lope de Vega.

The very form of *The Country Houses* throws into relief a highly significant feature of Tirso's theory in that the texts of the plays are presented in a fictional context of imagined performances. The whole process of the writing of the playscript and its embodiment by the actors is more a *bringing to* life than an *imitation of* life. In this respect, Tirso's fiction anticipates Diderot's similar use of a mixture of narrative, dialogue, and drama in his *The Natural Son* (*Le Fils naturel*) and its context of the fictional discussion of the play and its origins.

The *cigarrales* of Tirso's title are a group of country estates, noted for the beauty of their orchards and houses. Their residents, having retired from the city to escape the heat of summer, agree among themselves to mount, each in turn, a series of entertainments, which include presentations of plays by Tirso. In this fictional context, the critical attack on *The Bashful Man at Court* (*El Vergonzoso en palacio*) is not only discourteous and disruptive but it may be detrimental to a whole order of civility and artistic refinement. And Tirso's defense of the *comedia* is by no means as limited as might at first appear. What is at stake is the possibility of *progress* in the arts (and society) – an idea fraught with far-reaching theological and philosophical, as well as aesthetic, implications.

If Tirso's tribute to Lope de Vega as the master of the modern *comedia* gives the latter no more than his due, it also acknowledges that such a disciple as Tirso (who wrote some 400 plays, over 80 of them extant) may improve on the master's art as, in his Don Juan play, at least, he surely did.

Ezra Pound claimed that Lope de Vega "gave Spain her dramatic literature, and that from Spain Europe derived her modern theatre" (Pound 1970, 181). Pound exaggerated, but the forms of the *comedia* are probably more pertinent to modern drama than are the classical genres of tragedy and comedy. Tirso saw clearly the place of the *comedia* in the shaping of a modern dramatic form, and he refused to underrate the importance of either Lope de Vega's work or his own in this development.

---

[1] In Tirso, as elsewhere, *comedia* may mean "play" or "comedy" or *comedia* (the distinctively Spanish genre). The choice of word in this version depends on context, but it should be remembered that in this document the Spanish word is always *comedia* and that its use is highly ambivalent.

For further reading

Darst 1974; Nougué 1962; Pound 1970; Sullivan 1976.

From *The Country Houses of Toledo*

"THE FIRST HOUSE"[2]

It was four hours since the greatest of the planets began to take aboard in the Indies the cargo of gold[3] that, like a prodigal, it scatters among us every day – indeed, if it did not return with new treasures it would be tedious to see it behaving so repetitively – when, in the biggest of *Buenavista*'s lovely rooms,[4] that preserve the memory of its renowned former owner, there gathered, waiting for the play to begin, the most splendid and illustrious audience that ever conferred a glory on the River Tagus .... A tribunal of beauty, of all that was worthy and adorned with nobility in the imperial city [of Toledo] was ranged on one side. On the other, the chairs were honored to bear the pick of the valor of Toledo, in whose differing aspects time made a parade of the ages of man; in some endowing youth with gold, in others collecting, in silver, the interest due from age.

The play was called *The Bashful Man at Court*, a play received (years ago)[5] with general applause and commendations for its author not only in all the Spanish theatres but in those most renowned in Italy and both the Indies.[6] It was, indeed, found worthy enough for one of the greatest potentates of Castile to honor the muses of the theatrical profession and ennoble it by himself taking the part of the Bashful Man, so that all the professionals witnessed him in one moment of this fitting recreation transcend their many years of study.

The men who appeared in it were the best qualified in the nation, and the women, Anarda, Narcissa, Lucinda, and Doña Leocadia, were miracles of beauty and as illustrious as beautiful. So the performance was authoritative, as it deserved to be; for, if the subject matter embodied in it does not tarnish it, it is worthy in itself of the highest regard and praise; in the first place emerging so unscathed from [the scrutiny] of those who, dispassionately and knowledgeably, have the responsibility (nowadays) of ridding plays of indecent words and actions.

Six singers entered with various instruments: four musicians and two women. Not to make this book tiresomely bulky and to avoid breaking the

---

[2] Translated from Armesto 1913.
[3] I.e., it was four hours after sunset.
[4] "Buenavista" is the house in which the first entertainment takes place.
[5] The play was written before 1611.
[6] From 1616 to 1618 Tirso was in Hispaniola (the present Dominican Republic) attached to the mission of the Mercedarian order to which he belonged. The two "Indies" are the West Indies and the American mainland.

thread for those who find pleasure in reading their plays without interruption, I shall not set down here – nor shall I later – the lyrics, dances, and interludes. To establish that they were excellent it is enough to record that the musical contributions were by Juan Blas, unmatched for this kind of thing; by Alvaro who, if not first, does not come second either; and by the university wit, Pedro Gonzalez, his equal in every way, who, after having for some years refined human melodiousness in order to make it better, took the redemptive habit of Our Lady of Mercy; in which order he, if anyone, was the swan of melody, supreme and unrivaled in the age. The interludes were by Don Antonio de Mendoza, whose wit and inventions were equal to his gentleness and nobility, and the dances by Benavente, that relish of the spirit, delight of nature, and, in short, prodigy [from the region] of our Tagus. And if they achieved fame for their patrons, they did not disgrace those who sponsored them in *Buenavista* now. This taken as given, and the musicians being already in, the [actor] who delivered the prologue came in, and this is how it went . . . .[7]

Following the prologue was an intricate and harmonious dance, at the end of which began the play, which is as follows . . . .[8]

The naturalness of the players, the finery of the characters, and the variety of the incidents, were such that, this same play having wound to its calm conclusion ⟨Cn/248⟩, the time had passed so quickly for them that although [the audience] had spent nearly three hours [watching it] they found no other fault with it than the brevity of the treatment; that is with respect to those auditors who were open-minded and were present on this occasion for the sake of refreshing the soul with the poetic entertainment rather than in order to find fault with it. However, the drones, who do not know how to make the honey that they steal from the productive bees, could not refrain from their old habits and with a buzz of detraction had to pick away at the delightful honeycombs of art. Some such said it was too long and some that it was inappropriate. There was the historical pedant who insisted that the poet deserved censure since, in defiance of the truth of the annals of Portugal, he had turned Don Pedro, the Duke of Coimbra – who [historically] died without leaving a son and heir in a battle against his nephew King Alonso – into a shepherd [who has a son], in a manner derogatory to the House of Avero and its Grand Duke, whose daughters he portrayed as so free and easy that (contrary to the rules of decorum that applied to them) they made the privacy of their garden into a theatre for [the display of] their lack of modesty. As if the art of Apollo were to be confined to the historical record and were not allowed to build, on the basis of actual persons, the imagined structures of the inventive wit! Defenders of the absent poet were not lacking. Replying on behalf of the poet's repu-

---

[7] The prologue follows.
[8] The complete text of the play follows.

tation, they would have silenced the Zoilistic[9] arguments had those con-
tumacious understandings – narcissistically attached to their own views
and more penetrating in their censure of others' productions than in their
awareness [of the faults] of their own – been open to persuasion.

"Among the many faults," said one presumptuous fellow – a native of
Toledo, which would willingly deny the connection if it were not a matter
of small consequence that one malicious monster should emerge from
among so many sons [of the city], who, wise and well-disposed, add luster
to its benign atmosphere – "the one that most exhausts my patience is to
see how cavalierly the poet transgresses the limits and rules by which the
first originators of comedy endowed this genre with artistic principle; for
although such a work must consist of an action of which the beginning,
middle, and end transpire within twenty four hours at the most ⟨Lp/187⟩,
without imposing on us a change of place, this one has stuffed in at least a
month and a half of amorous incidents for us. But even within this period
of time, it seems impossible that a lady so illustrious and prudent could
bring herself to love a shepherd so blindly, make him her secretary, declare
her feelings to him in riddles, and finally gamble her reputation on the rash
decision of a man so lowly ⟨Cd/215⟩ that, in the opinion of both, the most
distinguished armorial bearings of his lineage were a pair of peasant's
sandals, his ancestral home a hut, and his vassals a poor herd of goats and
oxen. I refrain from criticizing the ignorance of Doña Serafina (otherwise
depicted as so prudent) who, falling in love with her own picture and with
no further assurance about its original than Don Antonio gives her, stoops
lower even than would be worthy of the most plebeian belle – as indeed it
was to let in, in the dark, someone whom she might, by the light of a
candle, have left to punishment and correction.[10] And over and above this,
I do not know why something that mixes among its characters dukes and
counts has to be called a comedy ⟨Gu/150–51; Lp/187⟩,[11] being such
that the most serious characters admitted in similar plots do not rise above
[the rank of] citizens, patricians,[12] and ladies of middling status."

The malicious disputant was about to proceed when, interrupting him,
Don Alexis – who since the entertainment was his idea thought it his
business to defend it – replied:

"You are not right in the slightest; for – apart from the obligation on the
guest that courtesy imposes not to slight his host by speaking ill of the
dishes that are put before him (however ill-seasoned they may be) – the

---

[9] Zoilos was the fourth-century B.C. Greek rhetorician who criticized the works of Homer.
    Tirso uses the name adjectivally to mean carpingly critical.
[10] In the play Doña Serafina fancies herself as a thespian. Her suitor, Don Antonio, has her
    portrait painted secretly as she rehearses a male role. Rejecting Don Antonio, Serafina
    narcissistically falls in love with the supposed subject of the portrait and Don Antonio
    deceives her by arranging an assignation between her and that imaginary man.
[11] Here, the word *comedia* is being taken to mean "comedy," in the classical sense.
[12] I.e., not royalty or major aristocracy.

play in question has abided by the rules of what is now customary.[13] And it seems to me – placing myself in the position of those who judge dispassionately – that the favor rightly accorded to the comedies that are presented in this Spain of ours, compared with those of antiquity, is due to their well-known advantages although they run counter to what was first laid down by the originators. For if they established [the rule] that a play should represent only an action that, in all decency, can be accomplished within twenty-four hours, how much more undesirable would it be that, in such a short time, a suitor in his senses should fall in love with a sensible lady, make his addresses, entertain and woo her, and before even a day has passed get her to commit herself and be disposed to favor his attentions in such a way that beginning his suit in the morning he marries her that night? What room is there to build up zeal, intensify moments of despair, be consoled with hope, and depict the other feelings and occurrences without which love is of no account? Or how could one appreciate that the suitor be true and faithful if a few days, months, or even years do not elapse, during which his constancy may be tried?

"In the judgment of somebody of [even] moderate understanding, these drawbacks are more serious than the consequences of having the auditors, without their moving from the one place, see and hear things happening over the course of many days. So just as the reader of a history discovers the course of events over long periods and in different places in a few brief pages and without many hours spent, comedy, which is an image and representation of its plot,[14] must, when it takes as its plot the career of two lovers, give a living portrayal of what could have happened to them. And this, not being lifelike when done in a day, it is obliged to imagine that those days pass that are required for the specific action to be brought to its completion. For it was not for nothing that poetry was called "live painting." The latter [painting], imitating lifelessly, portrays on the confined space of a yard and a half of canvas background perspective and long views, which make the eye consent to the representation; and it is incorrect to deny to the pen the license that is conceded to the pencil since the former is richer in meaning than the latter to the degree that he who speaks, articulating syllables in our language, makes himself better understood than the one who, being mute, explains his ideas by means of signs. And if, Sir, you argue that we who lay claim to their profession, ought to uphold the precepts of the first originators – on pain of being supposed ambitious

---

13 The ambivalence in the use of the word "rules" (*leyes*) shrewdly compresses the sense, which can be interpreted thus: the "rules" exist in order to ensure that the comedy will accurately reflect the customs of the time, and this comedy, in so doing, must therefore be regular; and since the "rules" also *derive* from the customs of the time, matters that concern a modern audience (such as psychological probability) must be included among them.

14 Not an image and representation *of* life but a really living representation (as a painting is not) of the subject or plot.

and ungrateful for the light they shed to enable us to follow their artistry – I reply thus, Sir: that although veneration is owed to such precursors for having done well in face of the difficulty that attends all things in their beginnings, nevertheless it is certain that in adding refinements to their invention (a necessary, though easy matter), the accidentals must be changed, improving them with experience while the essence is preserved. Would it not be splendid if because the first musician produced from the chime of the hammers on the anvil the difference between high and low pitches and the harmony of music those who now practice it had to go about burdened with the tools of Vulcan; and if those who were busy adding strings to the harp deserved chastisement rather than reward; and if they left everything of antiquity in the perfection that we now recognize, denouncing whatever is additional to or unusable by it! Between nature and art there is this difference: that what constituted nature from the moment of its creation cannot be altered; thus the pear tree will always produce pears, and the oak its coarse fruit. Yet despite this, variation in the habitat and the different influence of atmosphere and climate to which it [the particular species] is subject very often differentiates it from its own kind and almost reconstitutes it into other, varied, ones.[15] For if we are to give credit to Antonio de Lebrija, in the prologue to his *Vocabulario*, in the beginning of the world God created only one kind of melons, from which so many, and among them such varied kinds have developed, as may be seen in pumpkins, cucumbers, and gherkins, all of which, in their beginnings, bore one and the same crop. Beyond which, the gardener can variegate these things, at least in part, though not in every respect, by means of the grafting process. From two different species a third is developed, as is observed when the peach tree grafted on to the quince produces the quince-peach, in which the golden color and tartness of the one are cross-bred with the sweetness and redness of the other ⟨Gu/152⟩.[16] But with the products of art, the usage, the treatment, and the incidentals change every day while the main thing, which is the essence, remains intact. The first tailor who cut clothes for our first parents was God – if it is proper that such a humble office should be attributed to such illustrious artistry. But would that be a reason for us – I speak of the decent and God-fearing: I am not concerned with profane and lascivious persons, for such are a law unto themselves – to go covered in skins like them and to censure [the wearing of] clothes because they are as different in material as

[15] Tirso's tentative suggestion that nature itself may be changed and developed by art and that art and nature are involved in a mutually determining process may be compared with the more developed (but inconclusive) discussion in Shakespeare's *The Winter's Tale* 4.4.79–103.
[16] A cross between the quince and the peach is unknown to modern horticulture and would not be produced by grafting, anyway. The "quince-peach" was known in the seventeenth century and the word is adopted to indicate the differentiation made in the Spanish text between two words for "peach."

they are in their varied forms from theirs [Adam's and Eve's]? Obviously you would say not. So if "in products of art," whose being consists solely in human and mutable shaping, usage can change with respect to the trappings and functions only stopping short of what is essential; and "in what is natural" different fruits are produced every day by means of cross-grafting, why is it such an enormity that the *comedia*, imitating both things [art and nature], should modify the rules of its antecedents and industriously cross-graft the tragic with the comic, producing a harmonious mixture of these two existing genres; and that, making use of both, it [*comedia*] should present serious characters as in the one and humorous and ridiculous ones as in the other? Moreover, if the excellence of Aeschylus and Euripides[17] in Greece, like that of Seneca and Terence among the Romans, sufficed to establish the rules that are so insistently defended by those who propound them, the excellence of our Spanish *Vega*[18] – the honor of Manzanares, the Cicero of Castile, and the Phoenix[19] of our nation – made such advances in both genres so well known (through the quantity as well the quality of his studies, never properly recognized, though much envied and reviled) that the authority with which he puts them forward is sufficient to repeal their old laws.

"And Lope de Vega having brought the *comedia* to the perfection and subtlety that it now enjoys, it is enough *to go to school to him alone* and for those of us who pride ourselves on being his disciples to regard ourselves as fortunate in having such a master and firmly defend his teaching against whoever might with animosity impugn it. For if, in many places in his writings, he says that it is in order to conform to the popular taste that he abandons the art of antiquity – for he never assented to the restraint of rules and precepts – he said so out of his natural modesty and so that ignorant malice should not ascribe to arrogance what is, in fact, the perfection of good manners. As practitioners of the *comedia*, on the one hand and, on the other, for the reasons I have proposed (apart from many others that remain in the armory of the understanding) – it is right we should esteem both Lope de Vega as reformer of the new *comedia* and the *comedia* itself as more attractive and entertaining, so delighting the age that it does not forget him."

---

[17] The name in the printed text is actually *Enio* (Quintus Ennius, the Latin poet and tragedian of the third and second centuries B.C., who wrote in imitation of the Greeks and may have been born on Greek territory). Tirso apparently intended Euripides.

[18] Tirso is playing on the name "Vega," linking the playwright with the brightest star in the constellation of Lyra.

[19] The honorific *Fénix* is a tribute paid to Lope de Vega by his admirers.

23

TWO SEVENTEENTH-CENTURY VIEWS OF CORNEILLE'S *LE CID*

The great popular success of Corneille's *Le Cid* in January 1637 opened a debate which lasted until the following October, when Cardinal Richelieu ordered that it be discontinued (Corneille/Barnwell 1965, xiii–xiv). Critics and playwrights took part in the fray, which engendered many publications for and against Corneille's play. Among the most important was *Observations on* Le Cid (published in April 1637) by Georges de Scudéry, a successful dramatist, whose aim was to point out the flaws in the play that had so dazzled its audience. Claiming to attack "*Le Cid*, and not its author," whom he never names, Scudéry sets out to prove:

> That the subject is completely worthless;
> That it violates the principal rules of dramatic poetry;
> That it lacks judgment in its composition;
> That it has many bad verses;
> That almost all of its good qualities are plagiarized;
> And thus the admiration it has received is undeserved.
> (Corneille/Marty-Laveaux 1862, XII:442)

His tone is by turns vituperative, mocking, or pitying and, despite claims to the contrary, the personal bias of a rival dramatist comes through.

To lend credence to his argument, he quotes extensively from Aristotle's *Poetics*, which he interprets in conventional neo-classical ways.[1] This accounts for the central position he gives to *vraisemblance* (here translated "verisimilitude" or "plausibility"), which he holds to be the most important of the rules of dramatic art.[2] Having chided Corneille for not abiding by the "rules," Scudéry proceeds to fault him for preserving unity of time (the twenty-four-hours rule), since it leads to a mockery of both truth and verisimilitude. Of even greater importance is the supposed offense against decency (*bienséance*), which is inextricably linked with the moral purpose of drama. Scudéry, like most of those opposed to *Le Cid*, claims that plays should be morally instructive. Corneille fails to provide exemplary characters or poetic justice at the end of the play.

Another well-known document in this literary dispute is *The Opinion of the French Academy concerning* Le Cid, which appeared in December 1637. It was drawn up by

---

[1] Scudéry is aware, but unconcerned, that he is applying Aristotle's remarks on tragedy to a tragicomedy.

[2] See Morgan 1986. Morgan argues that in seventeenth-century French theory "*vraisemblance* ... emerged as a literary concept in relation to two separate critical issues: one is the rhetorical concern for the credibility of the poetic artefact as an essential condition of its capacity to stir the audience's emotions; the other is the use of the Aristotelian theory of mimesis to justify an elevated conception of poetry in general and of tragic and heroic poetry in particular" (p.293).

Jean Chapelain and a committee of fellow academicians, and was probably intended to put an end to the debate, although in the preamble the authors note that "poetry would not have reached its present state of perfection, without the disputes that have arisen over the works of the most celebrated authors of recent years" (Corneille/Marty-Laveaux 1862, XII:464).

This is a more balanced and better-reasoned argument than Scudéry's, which it follows closely, considering each of his points in turn, and either supporting or refuting them. The Academy's intervention in the debate is clearly explained:

> The Academy thought that in an age when people flock to the theatre, considering it the most delightful form of entertainment to be found, it should remind them of that most noble and perfect purpose conceived by those who formulated the rules of this art.
> (Corneille/Marty-Laveaux 1862, XII:465)

In the attempted reconciliation of utility and pleasure, proper pleasure is strictly defined as being of an elevated kind, compatible with reason and good sense. Like Scudéry, the academicians believe that this double purpose of drama is best served by a verisimilitude, which may be, as they explain, of an ordinary or extraordinary (but plausible) kind, and which applies to both plot and character.

This first official publication of the Academy was drawn up at the behest of Cardinal Richelieu. His influence may perhaps be seen in the suggestion that a form of censorship is required, and that the people are to be "protected" from certain dangerous ideas which might have repercussions in both private and public life. Both the playwright's choice of subject and his treatment of it have, according to these views, serious political implications as well as artistic ones.

For further reading

Corneille/Barnwell 1965; Corneille/Marty-Laveaux 1862; Morgan 1986; Sweetser 1962.

From *Observations on* Le Cid[3]

... The opinion of Aristotle and of all the learned men who have followed him establishes as an incontestable maxim that invention is the chief quality of both the poet and the poem ⟨Cv/133–34⟩. This is such an undoubted truth, that the very words for poetry and poet come from a Greek word which simply means fabrication. Therefore, since the plot of *Le Cid* was taken from a Spanish author, if it were a well-conceived plot, Guillén de Castro[4] should receive the credit for it, rather than his French translator. But far from agreeing that it is well conceived, I maintain that it is completely without merit. A tragedy composed according to the rules of art should have only one main action, around which are centered all the other actions, just as all the lines drawn from the circumference of a circle

---

[3] Translated from Corneille/Marty-Laveaux 1862, XII:441–61.
[4] Guillén de Castro y Bellvis (1569–1631) was the Spanish dramatist whose play about the Cid was Corneille's source.

converge at the center. Since the plot must be taken from history or well-known stories, in accordance with the rules handed down to us, it is not the author's intention to surprise the audience, for they already know what is to be represented. But this does not apply to tragicomedy, for although this genre was hardly known in antiquity, nevertheless, since it is a kind of composite of tragedy and comedy, and its ending makes it even more like comedy, in the first act the plot must become sufficiently complicated to keep the minds of the spectators in suspense until the very end of the play, when everything is unraveled.

This Gordian knot does not require an Alexander to untie it in *Le Cid*. Chimène's father dies quite near the beginning, and throughout the play she and Rodrigue express only a single passion; there is no diversity, no complexity, no knot to be untangled. From the beginning, the least perceptive member of the audience can guess, or rather see, what the outcome will be. Thus I believe I have shown very clearly that the subject has no merit at all ... I shall just as easily prove that [*Le Cid*] offends against the principal rules of dramatic art, and ... of all the rules to which I refer, undoubtedly the most important and most fundamental to the whole work is the rule of verisimilitude. Without it we cannot be taken in by that pleasant deception which makes us become involved in the fate of these imaginary heroes. The poet whose aim is to touch the emotions of his audience by the passions of his characters, no matter how strong, intense and well expressed they may be, will never be able to succeed if what he is depicting is not plausible.[5]

Those great masters of the past who taught me what I am expounding here, for those unfamiliar with it, have always told us that the poet and the historian should not use the same methods, and that it is better for the poet to treat a plausible subject that is not true than one that is true but implausible ⟨Ar/45⟩. ... It is true that Chimène married the Cid, but it is not at all plausible that a daughter with a sense of honor would marry the man who killed her father ⟨Cn/240⟩. This event was good for the historian, but of no value to the poet ....

[Aristotle] shows that it is much more difficult to be a poet than a historian, since the latter merely relates things as they actually happened, whereas the poet portrays them not as they are, but as they ought to be ⟨Ar/45⟩. This the author of *Le Cid* failed to do; when he discovered an episode in Spanish history in which this daughter married her father's murderer, he ought to have concluded that it was not a fit subject for a perfect poem, since it was historical and therefore true, but implausible, especially since it offends against reason and decency .... But this first error in judgment led to another; in order to observe the twenty-four-hours rule, an excellent precept when properly understood, the French author

[5] An example of the rhetorical interpretation of *vraisemblance*.

compounded the faults of his Spanish model .... The rule of verisimilitude is not observed, although it is absolutely necessary. And truly, all of the magnificent exploits accomplished by the Cid over a number of years are so compressed in this play to fit into twenty-four hours, that the characters seem like *dei ex machina* coming down from the sky. For in the short space of a natural day, a tutor is chosen for the Prince of Castile, there is a quarrel and a duel between Don Diègue and the Count, another duel between Rodrigue and the Count, Rodrigue's battle against the Moors, a duel between Rodrigue and Don Sanche, and arrangements are made for the marriage of Chimène and Rodrigue. I leave you to decide whether this was a day well spent, and whether these people could justly be accused of laziness.

... we must realize that dramatic poetry was invented to teach by entertaining, and in this pleasant guise is concealed philosophy, lest it appear too austere in the eyes of the world. Sweetened by pleasure, the medicine of instruction is more easily swallowed, and one is cured almost without being aware of the treatment. Thus the poet never fails to let us see virtue rewarded and evil punished ⟨Ar/50; Rm/293; Cn/238⟩. If we sometimes see wicked people prosper and good people persecuted, there is always a complete reversal of the situation at the end, and we are also shown the triumph of the innocent and the torments of the guilty. In this way, our minds are imperceptibly inculcated with the hatred of vice and the love of virtue.

But far from following this model, *Le Cid*, sets a very bad example. In this play we see an unnatural daughter who talks only of her obsessive love, when she should be talking about her grief; who laments the loss of a lover, when she should be thinking only of the loss of her father; who continues to love the one she should abhor; who tolerates the presence of her father's killer in the same house with her father's corpse; and, as the crowning insult to her father's memory, marries the man who shed his blood. ...

It was because of plays like this that Plato banished from his Republic all poetry, but especially mimetic poetry ⟨Pl/30⟩, because it represented to the mind all kinds of conduct, vices as well as virtues, crimes as well as noble actions .... But, in order to modify the stringency of Plato's ban, Aristotle ... recommends in his *Poetics* that the majority of actions represented on stage should be good, and that if wicked characters must be introduced, they should be outnumbered by virtuous characters. ... If the author in question had been aware of these precepts, as well as the others we have already pointed out, he would certainly not have allowed wickedness to triumph in his play, and his characters would have been motivated by more admirable intentions ....

... In the short time it takes to say 140 lines, the author has Rodrigue go home and arm himself, go to the place appointed for the duel, fight the duel, win it, disarm Don Sanche, give him back his sword, order him to present it to Chimène, and this also allows time for Don Sanche to arrive at the home of Chimène, all while 140 lines are spoken on stage. This is absolutely impossible and should be considered a serious error in dramatic composition.

When we want to allow for the passage of time, this should be done with music or a chorus between the acts, so that offstage actions can be presumed to take place in this interval ⟨Lp/187⟩; otherwise, events can only be shown in the same way they may happen naturally. . . .

. . . Since the same place represents the King's chamber, the Infanta's chamber, the house of Chimène, and the street, with almost no change of décor, most of the time the spectators do not know where the actors are. . . .

From *The Opinion of the French Academy concerning Le Cid*[6]

[The Academy] was indeed of the opinion that [*Le Cid*] might be a good play, but that it was not to be considered good merely because it was enjoyable. Since it was a matter of judging its artistic merit rather than its popularity, it was more important to weigh the arguments in its favor than to count up the numbers of its supporters, being less concerned whether the audience liked it, than whether they ought to have liked it. Nature and truth have put a certain value on things, which cannot be altered by the value assigned by chance or opinion. Those who pass judgment on these things on the basis of what they seem to be rather than on what they are in reality are laying themselves open to blame. It is true that there is some disagreement on this point among those who have formulated the rules of the art. Some, apparently too susceptible to sensual delight, claim that pleasure is the true aim of dramatic poetry ⟨Cv/131⟩; others, more mindful of the value of other people's time, considering it too precious to waste on entertainments that give only pleasure without profit, maintain that its true aim is to be useful. Although both sides use such different terms, on careful examination it becomes apparent that they are actually saying the same thing. For to give them their due, those who espoused the cause of pleasure were surely too reasonable not to advocate a form of pleasure in keeping with reason. It must be assumed, if one is not to do them an injustice, that the pleasure they meant is not the enemy, but the instrument of virtue, imperceptibly and without disgust purging men of their vices. . . . We are not concerned here with satisfying libertines and dissolute men who only laugh at stories of adultery and incest and do not care whether the laws of nature are violated, as long as they are entertained. We are not concerned with pleasing those without knowledge or

6 Translated from Corneille/Marty-Laveaux 1862, XII:463–501.

discernment, who would be equally touched by the suffering of Clytemnestra and of Penelope. Bad examples have a dangerous influence, even when only performed in the theatre. All too many real crimes are caused by seeing them acted out on stage, and it is very dangerous to titillate the common people with pleasures which could one day cause public affliction. They should be carefully protected from seeing or hearing actions that they would be better off not knowing about. Nor should we let them see examples of cruelty or tyranny, without at the same time showing them the punishment of these crimes, so that on leaving the theatre, they take away with them some fear at least, mingled with much pleasure. Moreover, it is almost impossible to give pleasure to anyone at all with disorder and confusion, and if it happens that plays not written according to the rules sometimes please an audience, it is only because they are in some way regular. The mind is so carried away by a few truly beautiful and extraordinary passages, that for a long time it is incapable of seeing the surrounding flaws, which slip by imperceptibly while the mind's eye is still dazzled by the flashes of brilliance. On the other hand, if some regular plays give little pleasure, it is not the rules that are to blame, but the authors, whose infertile minds could not provide a subject worthy of the art. ...

... From what we can judge of Aristotle's opinion about verisimilitude, he recognizes only two kinds, ordinary and extraordinary. The first includes things that ordinarily happen to people, according to their rank, age, character, and passions. Thus it is plausible for a merchant to be motivated by profit, for a child to act unwisely, for a spendthrift to become destitute, and for an angry man to seek vengeance, with all of the usual attendant results. Extraordinary verisimilitude comprises things which seldom happen and go beyond the bounds of what is commonly plausible, such as when a clever villain is outwitted, or a strong man defeated. In this category are included all unexpected events attributed to fortune, provided that they are the result of a plausible sequence of common events. ... But both ordinary and extraordinary verisimilitude must have this particular characteristic, that when shown to the audience, whether they grasp it intuitively or by reflection on all the elements from which it derives, it will make them believe, without further proof, that it contains nothing but truth, since they see nothing in it that is inconsistent with truth. The reason why verisimilitude rather than truth is assigned as the subject matter of epic and dramatic poetry, is that since the aim of these genres is useful enjoyment, the audience is more likely to experience this with verisimilitude, which they accept more readily, than with truth, which might be so strange and incredible that they would refuse to be convinced on the strength of truth alone ⟨Cn/247⟩. Several elements are required to make an action plausible, and it is essential to observe the decorum [*bienséance*] of time, place, rank, character, and emotion, but above all, it is important to make sure that each person in the play acts in accordance with the character that has been attributed to him, so that, for example, a wicked man will not contemplate good actions. The reason for observing these laws so carefully is that there is no other way for the poet to achieve the marvelous ⟨Cn/241–42⟩, which delights the soul with wonder and with pleasure, providing the perfect means for good poetry to be useful.

For these reasons, we find the subject of *Le Cid* defective in its most essential element, because it lacks both ordinary and extraordinary verisimilitude. For the poet fails to observe the decorum of character for a daughter portrayed as virtuous, when Chimène decides to marry the man who has killed her father. The poet also fails to observe the rules of extraordinary verisimilitude, since the dénouement is not brought about by an unforeseen occurrence, resulting from a series of plausible events. On the contrary, Chimène consents to the marriage, impelled only by the force of her passion, and the outcome of the plot depends solely on the unexpected injustice of the King who orders the marriage to take place, when by all the laws of reason he ought not even to suggest it. We do indeed admit that the fact that this story is historically true argues in the poet's favor, and makes it easier to excuse him than if it were an invented subject. But we maintain that not all true subjects are suitable for the theatre, and that some of them deserve the same fate as the trial records of heinous crimes, which the judges condemn to be burned with the criminals. There are abominable truths, which should either be suppressed for the good of society, or if they cannot be concealed, should merely be noted as strange occurrences. It is mainly under these circumstances that the poet is entitled to prefer verisimilitude to truth and to work on a subject that is fictitious but reasonable, rather than one that is true but contrary to reason. If he is obliged to treat this kind of historical subject, he must then make it fit within the bounds of decency, without consideration for truth. It would be better for him to change it completely than to leave anything that is incompatible with the rules of his art. For poetry takes as its model the universal Ideas of things ⟨Ar/45⟩, purging them of their flaws and particular irregularities, which history, by the rigor of its laws, is obliged to tolerate . . . .

. . . One of the principal rules of mimetic poetry is to avoid the inclusion of too many incidents, which prevent the poet from using the necessary embellishments and from giving the action to be imitated its proper magnitude . . . . But although we consider that [the author of *Le Cid*] was justly criticized for the large number of incidents used in this play, we believe there was even greater reason to censure him for having made Chimène agree to marry Rodrigue on the very day when he had killed the Count. That is completely beyond all credence, and would be unlikely to occur to even the most depraved and heartless creature, let alone to a dutiful daughter. In this case it is not merely a question of crowding several varied and lengthy episodes into such a short time, but of putting into the same mind, in less than twenty-four hours, two such contradictory thoughts as the desire for justice for the death of a father and the wish to marry his murderer. Two actions which could not be reconciled in the course of an entire lifetime are brought together in a single day. The Spanish author showed more respect for the rules of decency, since he allowed several days to elapse between these two events. But the French poet wanted to conform to the twenty-four hours rule, and in trying to avoid one error, committed another. For fear of violating the rules of art, he preferred to defy the laws of nature. ... We also believe that the author of the *Observations* would have had reason to blame the poet for giving the opening speeches of the play to a servant; we consider this scarcely in keeping with the seriousness of the subject, and only to be tolerated in comedy. ...

24

FRANÇOIS HÉDELIN, ABBÉ D'AUBIGNAC
(1604–76)

François Hédelin, abbé d'Aubignac, was a member of the household of Cardinal Richelieu, responsible for the education of the Cardinal's nephew. The author of four tragedies,[1] he shared Richelieu's interest in the reformation and rehabilitation of the theatre,[2] and was widely admired for his expertise in the history and theory of ancient drama. *The Practical Art of the Theatre* (*La Pratique du théâtre*), which was begun in 1640, at the instigation of Cardinal Richelieu, was to have been a more ambitious work, but strained relations between d'Aubignac and Richelieu (who died two years later) prevented its completion as originally planned and it was not published until 1657.[3]

The Practical Art consists of four books, of which the first contains a defense and history of drama, touching on its purpose. The dramatist's art, training, use of décor and setting, responsibility, and attitude to the audience are then discussed, along with the parodox of reality and representation in the theatre. The second book sets forth the traditional rules, including the unities of action, time and place, to which d'Aubignac adds his own precept of continuity of action. The quantitative parts of drama, acts, scenes, intervals, choruses, and monologues are covered in the third book, while the fourth deals with characters and the different sorts of discourse or dialogue.

In his discussions of the rules of drama or problems facing the dramatist, d'Aubignac usually gives the theoretical background, and then proceeds to suggest "practical" ways of making the precepts work. This was what, in his opinion, constituted the originality of *The Practical Art*. He gives many examples from ancient plays (particularly the tragedies of Euripides and Sophocles), but also uses French dramatists as his models, especially Corneille, whom he calls "the master of the stage." This admiration was later qualified, in response to Corneille's silent but hostile treatment of d'Aubignac in the *examens* and *discours* of 1660.[4]

Unlike Corneille, d'Aubignac held that the main goal of the theatre was to teach – "It provides a subtle instruction on things which the people most need to know,

---

[1] *Cyminde* and *La Pucelle d'Orléans* (1642), *Sainte Catherine* (now lost), and *Zénobie* (1647).

[2] At the request of Richelieu, d'Aubignac drew up a plan for a general reform of French theatre, entitled *Project pour le rétablissement du théâtre françois*, which was not published until 1657. It contained suggestions for improving the quality of plays, theatrical facilities, and productions, as well as for bettering the moral and economic situation of the actors.

[3] An anonymous English translation, which takes considerable liberties with both the sense and structure of the French original, was published under the title *The Whole Art of the Stage* in 1684.

[4] Corneille admitted in a letter to the abbé de Pure that in the *discours* he was refuting criticisms by d'Aubignac and the members of the Academy without naming them (Corneille/Barnwell 1965, 000).

and are most reluctant to accept" (1,3) – but he never forgot that the theatre is also to delight and entertain.

For further reading

Arnaud 1888; Morgan 1986.

From *The Practical Art of the Theatre*[5]

1,3 On what is meant by the practical art of the theatre ...

... Much has been written about the excellence of the dramatic poem, its origins, its development, its definition, its types, the unity of action, the appropriate length, well-constructed incidents, passions, character, language, and many other such matters, but always in general terms, which I call the theory of drama. But as for the observations that needed to be made about these principal rules, as well as how to prepare for events and maintain the unity of time and place, continuity of action, the connection between scenes, intervals after the acts, and many other particular details, nothing has come down to us from antiquity, and modern writers have hardly touched on the subject. That is what I call the practical art of the theatre.

1,6 On the audience

... I refer to the audience solely from the poet's point of view, to show how he must have them in mind when he is writing for the theatre.

Here I shall make a comparison with painting, as I have decided to do often in this treatise, and I maintain that it may be considered in two ways. First, it may be seen as painting, that is, as an artefact made by a painter, in which there are only appearances, and not things, shadows, and not figures, artificial light, false elevations, distances in perspective, the illusion of foreshortening, and mere semblances of everything that is not. Secondly, it may be seen as containing a thing that is depicted, either real, or supposed to be real, in a definite place, with natural qualities, indubitable actions, and all the circumstances compatible with order and reason.

Similarly, in a play one may first consider the spectacle and mere performance, in which art creates nothing but images of things that do not actually exist. These are princes in outward appearance, palaces painted on canvas, feigned deaths, and in short, everything is a facsimile of something else. Thus the actors are made to look like those they represent, and the stage decoration depicts the place where they are supposed to be. An audience is present, the characters speak the common language, and everything must be clearly perceptible. . . .

Or, on the other hand, a play may be considered from the point of view

---

[5] This is a new translation. The numbers in the margin refer to the book and chapter numbers of d'Aubignac's original publication.

of the story, which is true, or taken to be true, with all its events that actually happen, in that order, at that time and place ... as they appear to us. The characters are considered by the signs of their status, their age and sex; their words are taken as having actually been spoken, their deeds as really having been done, and all things exactly as we see them. I know full well that the playwright is behind all of this. He arranges the order and structure of his play, according to his fancy; he lengthens or shortens time, as he sees fit; he chooses whatever place he wants in the whole world; and he invents the complications of the plot, depending on the strength and vividness of his imagination. In short, he changes the subject matter and gives it form as he wishes. Nevertheless, all of these things must fit so well together, that their beginning, middle, and end seem to come about naturally and spontaneously. And although he is their author, he must handle them so skillfully that they do not appear to have been written at all.

... Therefore, when we wish to judge the plays performed in our theatres, we suppose that the story is true, or at least could have happened, and based on this assumption we approve of all the words and deeds which could be said or done by those who are speaking and acting .... And on the contrary, we find fault with everything that is out of keeping with the characters, place, or time ... because we do not believe that it happened in this way. ...

When he considers the spectacle or representational aspect of his tragedy, the playwright does everything in his power, with the aid of art and imagination, to make it admirable to the audience, for his only goal is to please them. He will retain all the most illustrious incidents of an historical subject. He will strive to depict the characters in as pleasing a way as possible; to use the most brilliant rhetorical figures and the strongest passions of moral philosophy; to conceal nothing that needs to be known and can give pleasure to the spectators, and to show nothing that is unfit to be seen or shocking. Finally, he will try every means to win the approval of the audience, who at that moment are his only concern.

But when he considers the reality of the tragedy as a true story, or one that he supposes to be true, his only concern is to make sure that everything is plausible, and to compose all of the actions, dialogue, and incidents as if they actually had occurred. He suits thoughts to character, time to place, and effects to causes. He adheres so closely to reality that he is unwilling to go against its conditions, its order, its effects, or its decorum. In short, verisimilitude is his only guide, and he rejects anything which is incompatible with it. Everything is done as if there were no spectators; this means that all of the characters must act and speak as if they were really kings, and not Bellerose or Montdory;[6] as if they were in the place of the

---

[6] Bellerose, or Pierre Le Messier (c. 1600–70), was a well-known actor and leader of the company at the Hôtel de Bourgogne. Montdory, or Guillaume Desgilberts (1594–1651),

Horatii in Rome, and not at the Hôtel de Bourgogne in Paris;[7] and as if they were not seen or heard by anyone except those who are on stage acting, and appear to be in the place that is represented. They often say that they are alone and no one can see or hear them ... despite the fact that all this is said and done in front of two thousand people .... This convention must be carefully observed, and anything which seems to be directed towards the audience is reprehensible. ...

Here is how the playwright must distinguish between these two ways of considering a play. He studies everything that he wants and needs to communicate to the audience either aurally or visually, and decides what is to be spoken or shown to them, for he must keep them in mind, in considering the action as represented. But these narrations or visual spectacles must not be contrived merely for the audience's benefit. ... Considering the action as real, he must look for a motive or a plausible reason, which is called a pretext [*couleur*], for these narrations and these spectacles really to have happened in this way. I dare say that the greatest art in writing for the theatre lies in finding all these pretexts. A character must come on stage and speak, because the audience has to know his intentions and his feelings. Past events must be revealed through narration ⟨Sy/180–81⟩, otherwise the audience would fail to understand the rest of the play. A spectacular scene must be shown, because it will move the audience to sorrow or admiration. This is what it means to work on the representative aspect of the action, and that is part of the playwright's duty and even his prime intention. It must, however, be concealed by some pretext which stems from the action considered as real. Thus the actor who is to speak comes on stage because he is looking for someone or has to meet someone. There will be a narration of past events in order to help with present decisions or to obtain necessary aid. A spectacular scene will be shown because it is to incite someone to vengeance. That means working on the realistic aspect of the action, without thought for the audience, because all of these things could plausibly happen in this way, considering the events in and for themselves. ... In a word, the audience is not the concern of the playwright when the play is considered as a true action, but only when it is seen as a representation ....

1,7 On the mixture of representation and reality of dramatic action

... I call the reality of dramatic action the story of the play to the extent that it is viewed as true, considering that all the events in the story really

was another renowned actor and head of the company at the Théâtre du Marais. A friend of Corneille, he produced and starred in *Le Cid*. He and his company enjoyed the encouragement and support of Cardinal Richelieu.

7 The Hôtel de Bourgogne, the first and most important theatre in Paris, was built in the mid sixteenth century in the ruins of the palace of the dukes of Burgundy. Its company later formed the basis for the Comédie-Française, founded in 1673.

occurred or should have occurred. But representation is the totality of elements that contribute to the performance of a play, and considered in and for themselves are necessary to it, for example, the actors, the scene painters, the scenery, the musicians, the audience, etc.

... It is important never to confuse the representational aspect of a play with the true action of the story that is being performed. ...

1,8   How the playwright must indicate the scenery and actions that are required in a play

... In a play the author's intentions must be expressed in the words spoken by the actors; he has no other means available to him, and would not dare mingle with them to furnish additional information that is lacking in the dialogue ... . Since the playwright has no opportunity to explain them himself, everything that is seen on stage, and every action that is to be performed there, must be indicated by the actors. ... All of the playwright's ideas about the setting, or about the movements, costumes, and gestures of the characters, that are necessary for understanding the story, must be expressed in the lines that are spoken ⟨Sg/108⟩. ... In a play written according to the rules, everything must be as easily understood by reading it as by seeing it. And any play which cannot be comprehended in this way is certainly deficient.

Nonetheless, to write plays well, it is not enough merely to put necessary information into the dialogue; it must be done skillfully, giving the actor who reveals the information a valid reason for doing so, that is completely in keeping with the character he is portraying. ... The playwright must never forget to make clear the time of a dramatic action and the place where it occurs ⟨Cn/247⟩. These two details are essential to the understanding of a play. ... Thus we see the necessity of indicating the scenery in the dialogue, to connect the story with its setting, the actions with their objects, and with artistry to create a well-ordered whole, by the perfect harmony of all its component parts.

2,1 On the subject

... There is still some debate about the extent to which a playwright is allowed to change a story to make it suitable for the stage. There are various opinions on this subject among both the ancients and the moderns, but in my view he may make changes, not only in the circumstances, but also in the main action, as long as he writes a good play ... . Drama does not show things as they have been, but as they ought to have been. And the playwright must correct any part of the subject which does not fit in with the rules of his art, just as a painter does with an imperfect model. ...

... It must be remembered (and this may be one of my most important observations about plays) that if the subject is not in keeping with the customs and opinions of the audience, it will never be successful, in spite of all the playwright's attention to structure and use of ornamentation. For plays must be different depending on the nationality of the people for whom they are to be performed.... Thus the Athenians enjoyed seeing plays about the cruelties and misfortunes of kings, the disasters that befell illustrious families, and the rebellion of the people against wrong-doing on the part of a sovereign. Because they lived in a democratically governed state, they wished to foster the belief that monarchy is always tyrannical, so that those with ambitions of seizing power would be discouraged, for fear of just retaliation by an entire nation. On the other hand, in our country, the love and respect that we have for our monarchs means that such horrid spectacles could not be shown to an audience. We do not wish to believe that kings can be wicked, nor would we allow their subjects, even despite apparent ill-treatment, to raise a hand against their sacred persons, or rebel against their power ....

At the French court tragedies are preferred to comedies, and among the common people comedies, and even farces and the crude buffoonery of our theatres, are considered more entertaining than tragedies. In this kingdom, those born into the nobility or accustomed to their society, are sustained only by noble feelings and inclined only to lofty intentions, motivated by either virtue or ambition, so that their life bears a close relationship to tragedy. But the common people, raised in the gutter and used to unseemly feelings and language, accept very readily the vile clowning of our farces, and always take pleasure in seeing in them the images of their own daily lives. ...

2,2 On verisimilitude

... Verisimilitude is ... the essence of drama, without which nothing reasonable can be said or done on stage. ...

... I have observed, however, that few people have understood how far verisimilitude should be taken. It is generally believed that it must be observed in the main action of a play and in the incidents that are obvious to the least intelligent members of the audience, but no one has gone any further than this. In fact the most insignificant actions represented on the stage must be plausible, or else they are completely worthless and have no place in the play. All human actions, however simple, are made up of several attendant circumstances, such as time, place, person, status, intentions, means, and the reason for acting. Since the theatre must reflect a perfect image of this action, it must represent it completely, and verisimilitude must be observed in all its parts. ... But to maintain this verisimilitude in all of the aspects of a dramatic action requires a thorough knowledge and practice of the rules of drama. Their sole purpose is to make all the parts of an action plausible, in bringing it to the stage, to create a complete and perfect image of that action. ...

2,3 On the unity of action

... It is certain that drama is nothing more than an image, and since it is impossible to make a single perfect image from two different models, it is therefore impossible for two different actions (that is, main actions) to be reasonably represented in one play. ...

Our poet will therefore select from among the extensive range of subject matter a remarkable action ⟨Cn/247⟩, and ... a critical moment, made striking by the happiness or misfortune of some illustrious person, within which he can briefly encompass the rest of the story. By representing just one part, he will cleverly make the audience relive the whole thing, without either enlarging the main action or sacrificing anything essential to the perfection of his work. ...

... A play must contain no more than one main action ⟨Cn/248⟩, which must be shown in its entirety, with its consequences, without leaving out any of the circumstances which naturally must be appropriate to it. ... It might be useful for the playwright to know that if the main action upon which his play is to be based included in reality too many incidents, he should exclude the less important, and particularly the less moving episodes. But if he finds there are too few incidents, his imagination must make up for this lack. This can be done in two ways, either by inventing a few complications which could reasonably be part of the main action ... or else by finding historical events that happened before or after the main action of the play, and skillfully weaving them into the plot, eliminating the differences of time and place as indicated in the following chapters ....

But here it should be noted that the playwright must always select the simplest action possible, because he will always be more in control of the passions and other embellishments of his work when he gives them only as much subject matter as he thinks necessary to achieve their full effect, than when he uses historical incidents, which are always more difficult to adapt, and may ruin the desired effect ....

2,4 On continuity of action

Once the playwright has chosen the subject or story that he considers likely to make a good play, and has selected the crucial moment which will determine the unity of dramatic action, he must bear in mind that in addition to unity this action must also have continuity. This means that from the beginning of the play to the very end of the catastrophe, from the first actor's entrance on stage until the last one makes his final exit, the main characters must always be in action, and the stage must constantly be occupied by the representation of schemes, undertakings, passions, turmoil, anxiety, and various agitations of this kind, which keep the audience from thinking that the action of the play is finished. ... It is for this reason that good dramatists always make the actors say where they are going and what their intentions are when they leave the stage, so that the audience may know that they will not be idle, and will not stop playing their roles, even though they are no longer seen.

But when we say that the main characters must always be in action, this does not necessarily mean the protagonists, who often have the most to bear and the least to do. As far as the continuity of action is concerned, the main characters are those responsible for the complications of the plot, for instance, a slave, a maidservant, or some clever knave. It is enough for even the least important character to act, as long as this action is necessary, and the audience can expect some change or some important turn of events. ...

2,5 On unity of place

... Since drama consists of actions rather than narration, and the place is a natural adjunct of the action, it is absolutely essential that the place where an actor appears is an exact image of the actual surroundings of the character he is portraying.

If this is properly understood, we see that the place may not be altered later in the play, since it does not change in the remainder of the represented reality. A single unaltered image cannot represent two different things . . . .

Once a site has been chosen in which to represent an action, it must be presumed to remain stationary throughout the play, as indeed it does. This does not apply to the back and sides of the stage; for since they represent merely the things which in reality surround those doing the actions, and could be subject to change, they could therefore be changed in the representation. This is what constitutes scene changes and the variety of stage design which always delights the common people, and when well executed, appeals even to people of discernment. ...

Not only must the proscenium represent a fixed place but this space must also be presumed to be open in reality, as it appears in the representation. For since the actors move about freely in the entire space, there certainly must not be any solid obstacle in the way to prevent them from being seen or from moving about. Thus the ancient dramatists usually chose as the scene of a tragedy the space in front of a palace, and for comedies a crossroads overlooked by the houses of the main characters. These places could be plausibly represented by the empty space of the stage, and the palaces and houses by painted scenery at the back and sides. ...

It should therefore be taken as a precept that the proscenium may only represent an open space of reasonable size, where those portrayed by the actors could be in reality. And when we read in stage directions, "The scene is set in Aulis, Eleusis, Chersonese, or Argos,"[8] this does not mean that the particular place where the characters appear includes the entire city or region. It implies instead that all of the action and intrigues of the play, what happens both off-stage and in front of the audience, takes place in that place, only the smallest part of which is occupied by the stage. . . .

Those then are the theoretical considerations; here are my reflections on the practical aspects. The playwright does not want to show the audience all of the ordinary details of the story, but only the most important and the most striking. . . . He must therefore determine, above all, exactly which characters he needs on the stage and choose a place where the necessary characters could plausibly be found. . . .

Further, he must consider whether there is some well-known incident in his plot which is necessary because it clarifies the story or adds to its beauty, and which could only happen in a particular place. In that case, he must make the rest of the events fit into this setting. . . . After choosing the place, the playwright must decide what parts of the story would give pleasure by being seen, so that he can show them on the stage, and what parts should not be shown, but must only be narrated. Such events are presumed to have taken place nearby, or at least close enough that the actor who is telling about them could easily have had time to come back from there since his last exit. Otherwise, it must be assumed that he left before the beginning of the play . . . .

Again it is essential for the dramatist to know that none of the characters should come on stage without a reason, since otherwise it is not plausible for them to be there. The ancient dramatists always motivate the presence of all characters on the stage, either by the requirements of the action, which could not happen elsewhere, or by some other words cunningly worked into the dialogue. . . .

2,7 On the length of the dramatic action, or On the proper time and duration for a play

No other question has been more debated in our time than the one I am about to treat now . . . . To talk about it intelligently, it must be considered that there are two kinds of duration in a play, each of which has its own appropriate time.

The first is the actual length of the performance. For although a play, as we have often indicated, is . . . merely an image, and hence ordinarily to be considered only in its representative aspect, nevertheless it must not be forgotten that there is reality even in things that are represented. In reality the actors are seen and heard; the lines are really spoken, and the audience

---

[8] Aulis, a port of Boeothia, where the Greek fleet gathered before sailing to Troy, is the setting for *Iphigenia in Aulis* by Euripides; Eleusis for his *The Suppliant Women*; and Chersonese, a peninsula in Thrace, for his *Hecuba*. Aeschylus' *Agamemnon* takes place in Argos.

actually experiences pleasure or pain while watching these performances. Real time passes while the minds of the audience are occupied for a certain duration, that is, from the beginning of the play to the end. This time is what I call the actual length of the performance.

This length of time can only be measured in terms of how long the audience's patience can reasonably be expected to last. Since plays are intended to give pleasure, they must not go on so long that they finally become boring and tiresome. Nor must they be so short that the spectators leave feeling they have not been sufficiently entertained.... But the proper length must be determined by ordinary opinion, and, as I have said, in keeping with reasonable patience. Experience is the best guide in these matters, for it teaches us that comedies more than three hours long are tiresome, and those that are much shorter seem unsatisfying. ...

The second duration of a play is the length of the represented action considered as real, which includes all the time necessary to do everything shown to the audience, from the moment the first actor makes his entrance, until the last one exits. This is the most important length of time, not only because it is naturally part of the content and nature of the play, but also because it is entirely dependent on the mind of the playwright; it proceeds from his imagination and is revealed in the words of his characters ....

Aristotle said that one of the chief differences between epic poetry and tragedy is that the former is not limited in time, and the latter must be contained within a revolution of the sun ⟨Ar/41⟩. ... This means its movement in the course of a day; but a day can be considered in two ways, either by the movement of the sun ... which is called the natural or twenty-four hour day, or by the presence of its light between sunrise and sunset, which is called artificial day ⟨Cn/249⟩. It must be observed that Aristotle is referring only to artificial day, within which the dramatic action is to be confined .... The reason behind the correct interpretation is clear and based on the nature of drama, which, as we have said before, consists not of narration, but of human actions, and must convey a perceptible image of these actions. It is not customary to see people doing things before daybreak, or continuing their activities after nightfall. ...

... First, the dramatist should carefully choose the day ⟨Cn/250⟩; ⟨Dd/289⟩ on which all the events of his play are to take place, and this choice will usually be determined by the most striking incident of the whole story. This will constitute the catastrophe, to which all the other events lead, just as all the lines from the circumference of a circle come together in the center. And if he is free to choose whatever day he wants, he should fix upon the day on which all the incidents of the play could most easily be brought together. ...

Once this choice has been made, the most expedient device is to make the play begin as close as possible to the catastrophe, in order to use less time for stage business, and to have more scope to develop the passions and other speeches which are likely to please the audience. . . .

2,9 On the dénouement or catastrophe and outcome of the play

. . . For me the word "catastrophe" means merely a reversal of the original situation of the play, the final peripety, and a turn of events that changes all the intrigues to the opposite of what one ought to expect. Comedies almost always have a happy ending . . . . But serious tragedies . . . always end either with the misfortune of the main characters, or with their long-awaited prosperity . . . . This second type of ending was not as common in antiquity as it is nowadays. . . .

Incidents which are not properly prepared in advance are often implausible, because they happen too precipitously. This fault is greater and more obvious in the catastrophe than in any other part of the play . . . . Since it is the most important event, to which all the others lead, it is therefore the one that requires the greatest and most careful preparation. Aristotle and all those who followed him require that the catastrophe should arise from the heart of the play itself ⟨Ar/54⟩, and that the various complications, with which the playwright seems to obstruct his plot, are in fact so many devices to help in its unraveling. This is why they have always admired this type of ending for tragedies, rather than those that depended on the presence or intervention of some divinity . . . . However, in the case of plays in which the outcome is already known . . . everything in the play should contribute to convincing the audience, in their own minds, that this character, whose life and destiny are at stake, ought not to die . . . . And the more reasons the audience finds to believe that he should not die, the more sorrow they will feel, to know that he must die . . . .

If the outcome is not known ⟨Cn/244⟩, and the success of the play depends on unraveling all of the complications by some unexpected new element, care must be taken that it is not revealed too soon, and that all of the things that are to prepare it do not give it away . . . .

It is also essential to see that the catastrophe brings the play to a satisfactory end, so that the audience are not left with questions about things they should know or want to hear . . . .

However, in avoiding one trap, the dramatist must not fall into another, that is, adding to the catastrophe unnecessary lines and superfluous actions which contribute nothing to the dénouement . . . .

2,10 On tragicomedy

Because tragedies often had unhappy endings . . . a number of people imagined that the word *tragic* only referred to a disastrous or ill-fated incident, and that a play could not be called a tragedy if the ending did not result in the death or misfortune of the main characters. This was certainly an error, since this term merely means an action which is exalted, serious, and befitting the perturbations and vicissitudes of the destinies of princes. A play is called a tragedy only in consideration of the events and characters whose lives are portrayed, and not because of its ending. ...

But for no reason at all we have removed the name of tragedy from plays whose ending is happy even though the subject and characters are tragic, that is to say, heroic, calling them instead *tragicomedies*. ... Now I am not entirely opposed to this word, but I contend that it is unnecessary, since tragedy can also refer to plays that end happily ⟨Gd/127⟩, when the lives of illustrious characters are depicted. Moreover, "tragicomedy" has no real meaning in the way we apply it, for the plays we designate with this term, composed of the words tragedy and comedy, have no comic elements. Everything in them is serious and marvelous, with no trace of everyday life or buffoonery.

In addition, this name alone can spoil the whole effect of a play, which lies in the peripety or reversal of fortune. For it is always all the more enjoyable when an apparently disastrous situation is completely reversed and turns out to have a happy ending, contrary to the audience's expectations. But as soon as a play is called a tragicomedy, the ending is given away. ...

4,2 On dialogue in general

If we consider tragedy according to its nature and strictly as a kind of dramatic poetry ... we may say that it is so bound up with actions that discourse does not seem to belong to it. It is called *drama*, which means *action*, and not *narrative*. Those who perform it are called *actors*, and not *orators*. The people for whom it is performed are called *spectators* and not *auditors*. Lastly, the place where it is performed is not an *auditorium* but a *theatre*, meaning *a place where one watches what is done*, not *where one listens to what is said*. Therefore the speeches in a tragedy must be like actions of those who appear on the stage; for there *to speak* is *to act* ... . In short, speeches in drama are secondary to action, although the entire tragedy as it is represented consists solely of dialogue ⟨Sg/108⟩. That is the playwright's whole task, requiring all the strength of his imagination. If he depicts some actions on the stage, this affords him the opportunity to write some excellent dialogue; everything he imagines is meant to be spoken; he does everything in his power to give tongue to love, hate, sorrow, joy, and the other human passions ... . Finally, if we take the trouble to examine this kind of play carefully, we will find that the actions exist merely in the audience's imagination, and are brought to life by the playwright's skill, although there is nothing tangible beyond the dialogue ... . People would not flock to the theatre in such great numbers, if it were merely to see actors in dumb-show.

... The plays of M. Corneille give palpable proof of the importance of dialogue. What makes them so much superior to other plays of our time is not the plot, but the speeches. Their excellence does not depend on the actions, which are more numerous in the plays of other dramatists, but in the way the characters express their intensity of passion. In fact, even implausible actions are so well surrounded by scenes of emotional beauty and power, that only the most knowledgeable people notice these flaws. The brilliance of his dialogue dazzles and enchants us, giving us no opportunity to judge the rest impartially ... .

4,5 On didactic speeches or instructions

... I am certainly of the opinion that plays should teach, but it is important to understand how this should be done. The playwright must show the audience the action he is depicting in its entirety and in all its details ... . He must represent it as it is, and in all its magnitude, so that the audience understands it completely. For since drama is the imitation of human actions, it imitates them merely to teach them, and this must be done directly. But as for moral standards, that is, the maxims pertaining to moral conduct, which can lead us to love virtue and hate vice, drama teaches these only indirectly, and by means of actions ⟨Sg/109⟩. This can be done in two ways. First, if the dramatic action is clear and well-constructed, it will show the power of virtue shining out even in the midst of persecution; virtue is often rewarded, and even when overcome, it always remains admirable. The dramatic action always points out the deformities of vice, which is often punished, and even when it triumphs by violence, never ceases to be abominable. Hence the spectators draw their own conclusion, quite naturally, that it is better to embrace virtue at the risk of suffering injustice, than to give in to vice, even with the hope of impunity. ... I have often noticed that it is less convincing in a play when someone who has strayed from the narrow path of virtue is recalled to his duty by high-flown moral precepts, than when he is brought to his senses by some misfortune that befalls him ... . As for the other type of moral instruction, it entirely depends on the playwright's skill in supporting his dramatic action with various strong and daring maxims, imperceptibly woven into the fabric of his play ... . These general precepts ... must be connected to the subject, and made applicable to the characters and actions of the play, so that the person who is speaking appears to be more attentive to the business at hand than to the fine truths he is expressing ... .

4,6 On moving speeches

... It is not sufficient to awaken a passion by a remarkable incident and a few stirring lines, but it must be developed to the point at which it is fully realized. The audience should not merely be moved, they should be enraptured. This may be accomplished by the grandeur of the subject, or the various surrounding causes, but particularly by the power of the imagination, which must be kindled and forced to endure the same kind of pain and pressure as the pangs of giving birth, if it is to produce a work worthy of admiration. . . .

PIERRE CORNEILLE
(1606–1684)

Pierre Corneille began to write plays, he said, before he was properly aware that "there was an art of tragedy and that Aristotle had laid down its precepts."[1] But the controversy over the production of *Le Cid* in 1637 ⟨Cd/212⟩ got him thoroughly involved in issues concerning the relation of practice to precept, and this remained a major concern throughout his career. The publication of d'Aubignac's *Practical Art of the Theatre* at a time when Corneille was writing critical *examens* of his individual plays and revising them may have been a stimulus for a more extended theoretical work ⟨Db/220⟩.[2] This took the form of the series of three treatises, which appeared (one in each volume) in the collected edition of his plays published in 1660: "On the Purpose [*utilité*] and the Parts of a Play," "On Tragedy and the Means of Treating It according to Verisimilitude or 'the Necessary,'" and "On the Three Unities: of Action, of Time, and of Place." These treatises constitute a defense against the critical attacks of his contemporaries, a justification of his own practice, and an attempt to codify the contributions that he, as a modern playwright of genius, has made to the development of dramatic art.

It is significant that Corneille starts his first treatise by asserting that pleasure is the sole end of tragedy. Long before, in 1645, in his prefatory epistle to *The Sequel to the Liar* (*La Suite du Menteur*), he had declared all dramatic art to be a "divertissement" from the greyness of everyday life (Corneille/Barnwell 1965, 183), and throughout his career he had repudiated the moralizing theories of such influential contemporaries as Chapelain ⟨Cd/212–13, 216⟩.

Rejecting crudely didactic objectives, Corneille proposes instead a kind of spiritual enlightenment which leads the mind of the spectator to a state of serenity. Though this may be brought about by such conventional means as an instructive theme, poetic justice, and the awakening of the audience's conscience, it is most fully achieved through the evocation of admiration for the hero's greatness of soul.[3]

Corneille's insistence that the "only goal is to please the spectator" would long remain a minority opinion. Lessing, arguing in 1767 for the importance of drama's moral influence on the audience, would sharply criticize Corneille's contrary view and his attribution of it to Aristotle.[4] To give the spectators what Aristotle calls "appropriate" pleasure, Corneille advises, "one must follow the precepts of art." He

---

[1] From a letter of 6 March 1649; see Corneille/Barnwell 1965, xxiii.
[2] Some of the most significant differences (and agreements) between Corneille and d'Aubignac are indicated below, but a detailed comparison of the texts printed here will reveal many more.
[3] See the *examen* to *Nicomède*, Corneille/Barnwell 1965, 152.
[4] See the twenty-ninth essay in G. E. Lessing's *Hamburg Dramaturgy* (1769).

accepts the necessity of certain rules but he interprets them freely, guided by his particular understandings of verisimilitude and of the sublime.

Verisimilitude was often contrasted with historicity (*le vrai*) in terms of *choice* of subject; and in relation to the *treatment* of the subject was commonly equated with the "probable" in Aristotle (and thus with the pseudo-Aristotelian "unities").[5] D'Aubignac ⟨Db/224–25⟩ and Chapelain ⟨Cd/217⟩ privilege verisimilitude over historical truth in plays: if historical events are so far removed from the common experience of reasonable men as to seem incredible, they should not be portrayed on stage. Corneille, on the other hand, insists upon the powerful testimony of history, because what has already happened is necessarily possible; historical truth is sufficiently convincing in itself and does not need to be represented with verisimilitude. What attracts Corneille to history (which is taken to include the great myths of antiquity) is its "great subjects," which open the way to the sublime and which are often so extraordinary (Medea killing her children, for example) that they require the authority of history to give them the credibility essential to dramatic art.

Corneille knows full well that public approval depends less on the regularity of the play than on what catches the audience's imagination. But though he is in the tradition of the great crowd-pleasers, he is also convinced that pleasing the spectators is not only a high art but one with principles that can be articulated.

For further reading
Barnwell 1965; Chapelain 1936; Schérer 1950; Sellstrom 1986.

From "On the Purpose and the Parts of a Play"

Although, according to Aristotle, the only end of dramatic poetry should be to please the audience and most of these plays[6] have pleased them, nevertheless I maintain that many of them have not reached the goal of art. "One must not claim," says this philosopher, "that dramatic poetry gives us every kind of pleasure, but only that pleasure which is proper to it" ⟨Ar/50⟩; and to find this appropriate pleasure and to give it to the audience one must follow the precepts of art and please in accordance with them. It is axiomatic that there are precepts, since there is an art; but it is not established what the precepts are. We agree about the name without agreeing about the thing, and we agree about the words only to argue about their meaning. No one denies that we must observe the unity of action, place, and time, but it is no small problem to know what unity of action is and what the limits of this unity of time and place are. The poet must treat his subject with verisimilitude and in accordance with "the necessary."[7] This is what Aristotle said ⟨Ar/46⟩ and all his interpreters

---

[5] See Corneille/Barnwell 1965, 295–96.

[6] I.e., Corneille's own plays.

[7] Verisimilitude: "something having the semblance of truth, what we would accept as the truth: the norm is provided by the sum of our experience, not by individual, often exceptional, cases" (Corneille/Barnwell 1965, xvi–xvii).

repeat the same words, which seem to them so clear and so intelligible that not one of them has deigned to tell us, any more than Aristotle himself did, what exactly this verisimilitude and this "necessary" are. "The necessary" is accompanied by verisimilitude in this philosopher's work with one sole exception – where he speaks of comedy ⟨Ar/45–46⟩ – but despite this, many have so ignored "the necessary" that a very false maxim has come into being: that "the subject of a tragedy must have verisimilitude." In this way, they apply only half of what he says about how to treat the subject.[8] This is not to say that one cannot make a tragedy of a subject which merely has verisimilitude.[9] Aristotle ⟨Ar/46⟩ gives us as an example *The Flower* of Agathon, in which both names and events are purely fictitious, as in comedy. But the great subjects which stir our passions and oppose impetuosity with duty or human feelings must always go beyond verisimilitude and would not be believed by the audience were they not supported either by the authority of historical fact which is very persuasive, or by a commonly held belief which gives us an already convinced audience. It hardly seems "probable" that Medea kills her children, that Clytemnestra assassinates her husband, that Orestes stabs his mother, but history tells us it is so and no one finds the representation of these great crimes incredible.[10] Nevertheless it is not permitted to invent examples such as these. That which truth or public opinion makes acceptable would be rejected were there no other basis for a play than a resemblance to this truth or public opinion. That is why our authority says "subjects come from chance" which makes things happen "and not from Art" which imagines them ⟨Ar/51⟩. Chance is the mistress of events, and the choice she allows us among those events she presents to us contains a secret defense against our attacking her and producing on stage events not to her liking. Also "the old tragedies dwell only on a few families, because it is only to a few families that things worthy of tragedy happened" ⟨Ar/49, 51⟩. The following centuries have supplied us with enough subjects to overstep these limits without walking in the footsteps of the Greeks any longer, but I do not think we have been given the liberty to set aside their rules. It is necessary to adapt these to ourselves, if possible, and make them applicable to what we do. Having cut out the role of the Chorus we are obliged to fill our plays with more episodes than the Greeks had; this is something extra we have added but which should not go beyond their precepts, even though it may go beyond their practices.

So we have to know, then, what these rules are; but it is our misfortune that Aristotle and Horace after him wrote so obscurely that they need

---

[8] The subject need not be verisimilar but the treatment of it should be, and should comply with "the necessary."

[9] That is, without its being historical or mythical.

[10] *Medea*, by Euripides and by Seneca; *Agamemnon*, by Aeschylus; *Electra*, by Sophocles and by Euripides.

interpreters and that until now those who tried to act as such have often interpreted these writers from the point of view of grammarians and philosophers. As they had more experience in scholarship and in theory than in the theatre, reading them may make us more learned, but will not give us any deep insights into how to succeed in the theatre. I shall risk a few remarks on the strength of fifty years of theatre work, and shall simply state my thoughts on this matter, without any desire for an argument which would put me in a position of defending them and without claiming that anybody should renounce his concepts in favor of mine.

Thus, what I have proposed from the beginning of this treatise – that "dramatic poetry's only goal is to please the spectators" – is not, in a stubborn way, to get the better of those who think that they are ennobling art by making its purpose profit as well as pleasure. This argument would be of no use, since it is impossible to please according to the rules, without at the same time providing much that is useful. It is true that Aristotle in all of his *Poetics* never once used this word. . . . But it is no less true that Horace teaches us that we cannot please everybody if we do not add an element of the useful. Solemn and serious people, old people, and lovers of virtue will be bored if they find nothing to profit them in the play: "Old people rail at what contains no serviceable lesson" ⟨Hr/74:341⟩. Thus, although the useful comes in only under the guise of pleasure, it is nonetheless necessary. It is more valuable to examine the manner in which it fits into a play than to debate, as I have already said, a useless question concerning the usefulness of a dramatic poem. I am of the opinion that there are four categories of the useful.

The first consists of maxims and morally instructive statements that can be scattered almost throughout the work, but they have to be used moderately, rarely put into general dialogue or if they are, then very unobtrusively, especially when put into the mouth of an impassioned man or when another character replies to him; for he would have neither the patience to listen to them [these maxims] nor the serenity of spirit to think of them and to utter them. In matters of state where a man of importance consulted by a king explains himself in a sane, well-balanced manner, these kinds of speeches may justifiably be more extended; but in the end it is always good to reduce them – often from a thesis to a hypothesis. I prefer to make an actor say "love gives you many anxieties" than "love gives many anxieties to those under its spell."

It is not that I would like to eliminate entirely this last way of enunciating moral or political maxims. All my plays would be severely crippled if those I have mixed in were cut out; but again they must not be used extensively when not applied to something specific. Otherwise they always become platitudes which never fail to bore the audience because the action languishes ⟨Lp/188; Db/232⟩. . . . The only rule one can establish about these speeches is that they must be placed judiciously and above all only given to characters with clear minds who will not be carried away by the heat of the action.

The second category of the useful in a dramatic poem lies in the simple depiction of vices and virtues, which never fails to make its effect when it is well done and when the traits are so recognizable that they cannot be confused with each other, nor vice taken for virtue. Virtue, however unhappy, always makes itself loved; vice, although triumphant, always makes itself hated. The ancients were often content merely to depict them without taking the trouble to have good deeds recompensed and bad ones punished ⟨Rm/293; Cd/215; Db/232⟩. Clytemnestra and her lover [Aegisthus] kill Agamemnon with impunity . . . .[11]

It is this interest that we love to take in the virtuous which has obliged us to accept this other manner of ending the dramatic poem – punishing bad actions and rewarding good ones – which is not a precept of art, but a practice that we have espoused from which anybody may depart at his peril. It is a custom that has been in existence since the time of Aristotle and perhaps this philosopher did not care for it very much as he said, "it was only in vogue because of the poor judgments of the spectators, and those who practice it yield to the taste of the populace and write according to the wishes of their audience" ⟨Ar/50⟩. Indeed, it is certain that we could not see an honest man in the theatre without wishing him prosperity and getting angry at his misfortunes. This means that when he is overwhelmed by them we leave the theatre with our hearts filled with sorrow, and take away a sort of indignation against the author and the actors. But when the outcome fulfills our wishes and virtue is rewarded, we leave full of joy and go away completely satisfied with the play and those who performed it ⟨Cd/215⟩. The happy outcome of virtue, in spite of its setbacks and perils, makes us want to embrace it. The tragic result of crime or of injustice is capable of augmenting the natural horror within us out of fear of a similar misfortune.

This constitutes the third category of the useful in the theatre, as the fourth lies in the purgation of the passions through the medium of pity and of fear. But as this fourth category is peculiar to tragedy I will explain it further in the second volume, where I shall treat tragedy in particular, and pass on to the parts that Aristotle attributes to the dramatic poems. Although in his treatment of this subject Aristotle speaks only of tragedy, I am speaking of dramatic poems in general, because everything he says about it applies also to comedy, and because the difference between these two types of dramatic poem consists only in the high rank of the characters ⟨Rb/87; Cv/140⟩ and the actions they imitate and not in the manner in which they imitate these actions nor in the things which contribute to this imitation ⟨Ar/41⟩.

---

[11] In *Agamemnon*, by Aeschylus.

The dramatic poem is composed of two sets of parts. One set is called quantitative, or parts of quantity or extent. Aristotle names four of them: the prologue, the episode, the *exodos*, and the chorus ⟨Ar/48⟩. The other set can be called the integral parts which are to be found in each of the first types and together with the first set they form the whole. The philosopher found six of these parts: plot, character, thought, diction, music, and spectacle ⟨Ar/42⟩. In considering the proper criteria of these six, only the plot rightly depends upon the art of poetry. The others need other subsidiary arts: character[12] needs moral judgment; thought needs rhetoric; diction needs grammar, and the other two parts each have their own art which the playwright does not need to know as they can be supplied by others, which is why Aristotle does not deal with them. But as it is necessary that he [the playwright] himself should carry out everything concerning the first four, a knowledge of the arts they depend on is absolutely necessary, unless he has received from nature a sufficiently strong and profound common sense which can make up for this lack.

The requirements of the plot are different for tragedy and comedy. At present I will touch on the latter only, which Aristotle simply defines as "an imitation of low and rascally persons" ⟨Ar/41⟩. I cannot help saying that this definition does not satisfy me at all. Since many scholars believe that Aristotle's *Poetics* has not come down to us in its entirety, I wish to believe that in the version of which time has robbed us there would be a more complete definition.

... Whatever one makes of it, this definition agreed with the usage of his times, where in comedy only characters of a lower rank would speak. But this definition is not entirely correct for our times when even kings can be introduced into comedy ⟨Lp/187⟩, when their actions are not at all above it.[13] When one puts on stage a simple love intrigue between royal personages, and they run no risk, either to their lives or to the State, I do not think that, although the characters are illustrious, the action is sufficiently so to be elevated to the rank of tragedy. The dignity of tragedy requires some great interest of state, or some passion more noble or more manly than love, such as ambition or revenge and which inspires a fear of misfortunes greater than the loss of a mistress. It is fitting to mix love into it, because love is a source of much pleasure and may serve as a basis for these interests and for these other passions of which I speak, but it [love] must be content with a secondary role in the play and leave them the primary one.

This maxim will at first seem new. It is, nonetheless, a practice of the ancients, where we see no tragedy based solely on a love interest which

---

12 Corneille's word, *moeurs*, means "character," "characterization," "humor," or "disposition." It has, that is to say, a range of connotations similar to *ethos*, Aristotle's word for "character."

13 Corneille had introduced royal persons in *Don Sanche d'Aragon* (1650), and later in *Tite et Bérénice* (published in 1671) and *Pulchérie* (1673).

has to be untangled. On the contrary they often exclude it, and those who wish to consider my own plays will recognize that following their example I have never let love occupy the first place and that even in *Le Cid* (which is, without doubt, more concerned with love than any play that I have written) the duties of rank and the protection of honor prevail over all the tenderness that love inspires in my lovers ⟨Cd/215⟩.

I have more to say. Although there may be great interests of state in a play, and the care that a royal person must feel about his reputation will silence his passion (as in *Don Sanche*), as long as the play contains no peril to their lives, or loss of their estates, I do not think it can be called anything more elevated than a comedy. But to correspond in some way to the dignity of the people whose actions are represented in the play, I have risked adding the epithet "heroic" to distinguish it from ordinary comedies. There is no example of this in ancient times; but there is also no example in those times of having kings in a play who were not exposed to one of these great perils. We should not imitate their example so slavishly that we do not dare try something of our own, as long as it does not completely reverse the rules of art . . . .

Comedy, thus, differs from tragedy in that the latter needs for its plot an illustrious, extraordinary, and serious action. The former restricts itself to common and playful actions. Tragedy demands great dangers for its heroes; comedy satisfies itself with the worry and discontent of its protagonists. Both have this in common, that this action has to be complete and finished, that is to say that in the final outcome, the spectator must be so well informed about the feelings of all those who have had a part in it that he leaves with his mind at rest and not doubting anything ⟨Db/230; Ar/42⟩. . . .

I know of discerning people and those most knowledgeable in poetic art who reproach me for having neglected to finish *Le Cid* (and several other of my plays), because I do not conclude it precisely with the marriage of the protagonists and because I do not send them off to get married at the end of the play. To which one can easily reply that marriage is not a necessary ending for a happy tragedy, nor even for comedy. It is the danger to the hero which constitutes tragedy and when the hero has escaped the danger, the action is finished. Although there is love involved it is absolutely unnecessary that he [the hero] speak of marrying his mistress when propriety does not allow it. It is sufficient to indicate the idea after all the obstacles have been removed, without having him name the day ⟨Cd/215⟩. It would be intolerable that Chimène should agree to marry Rodrigue on the very day after he kills her father, and Rodrigue would be ridiculous if he were to make the slightest demonstration of desiring it. . . . For comedy, Aristotle imposes only one obligation for the conclusion, "to turn enemies into friends" ⟨Ar/50⟩. This must be understood in slightly more general terms than the words seem to carry, and to extend it to the reconciliation of all sorts of disagreements, such as the return of a son into the good graces of his father who has been angry with him for his debaucheries. This is quite an ordinary ending for ancient comedies. Or two lovers separated by some trick played on them, or by some dominant force, are reunited by the shedding of light on this trick or by the consent of those who planted the obstacle.[14] This is what happens nearly always in our comedies, which very rarely have an ending other than marriage. We must be careful, however, that this consent does not result from a simple change of will, but from an event which provides the occasion. There would be no great art in the dénouement of a play if the author, on the contrary, having sustained the play for four acts on the basis of the authority of a father who disapproves of the amorous inclinations of his son or daughter, suddenly has him consent in the fifth act solely because it is the fifth and would not dare to write a sixth. There needs to be a considerable effect which forces him to consent, as, for instance, if his daughter's lover were to save his life when he were on the point of being assassinated by his enemies, or if by some unhoped-for accident he [the lover] were to be recognized as being of higher rank and greater fortune than he had appeared.

Since it is necessary that the action be complete, nothing further should be added because when the effect is achieved the spectator desires nothing more and is bored by all the rest. Thus the feelings of joy experienced by the two lovers who are reunited after overcoming large obstacles must be very short . . . .

I come to the second part of a play, characterization. Aristotle prescribes four requirements for it, "that they be good, suitable, lifelike and consistent" ⟨Ar/52⟩. He said so little about these terms that he leaves much room for doubt about what he meant.

I cannot see how one could come to understand the word "good" as meaning virtuous. Most plays, ancient as well as modern, would be left in a pitiful state if one were to cut out everything which concerns the evil or vicious characters or characters stained by some weakness which does not harmonize with virtue. Horace took great care to describe in general the character of every age, and attributes to them more imperfections than perfections ⟨Hr/67:120–24; 68–69:158–74⟩. He does not provide us with great virtues to express, since he makes us portray Medea as proud and indomitable, Ixion as treacherous, and Achilles carried away by anger to the point of declaring that he was beyond the law and only accepted force of arms as the right. Thus one must find a "goodness" compatible with these kinds of manners. If I may give my conjectures on what Aristotle wants from us regarding this ["goodness"], I believe that it is the character who is outstanding and elevated whether of a virtuous temper or a

[14] As in Corneille's *Mélite* (1629/30).

criminal one, according to what is proper and suitable to the person portrayed. Cléopâtre in *Rodogune* is very wicked. No act of parricide[15] instills horror in her, as long as it keeps her on the throne, which she prefers above everything, so violent is her attachment to power. But all her crimes are accompanied by a greatness of soul which has something so elevated about it that one simultaneously despises her actions and admires the source from which they spring. ...

Another conjecture comes to mind, concerning what Aristotle means by this "goodness in the portrayal of character" which he imposes as a first condition. They must be as virtuous as possible, so that we do not depict the vicious or the criminal on stage, if the subject in hand does not require it. He himself leads us to this thought when, wishing to point out an example breaking this rule, he uses that of Menelaus in *Orestes* by Euripides, whose fault consists not in being unjust but in being unjust without necessity ⟨Ar/52⟩. ...

Secondly, the characterization must be suitable. This condition is easier to understand than the first. The playwright must consider the age, the rank, the birth, occupation, and country of those he depicts. He must know what one owes to one's country, parents, friends, and king. He must know what are the duties of a magistrate or general so that he can portray accordingly those whom he wants the spectators to love, and portray in a contrary way those whom he wants them to hate. It is an infallible maxim that to be successful one must interest the audience in the protagonists. It is worth noting that what Horace said about the character of each age is not a rule which one can dispose of without scruples ⟨Hr/73:312ff.⟩. He makes young people spendthrifts and old ones misers: the contrary is seen every day without causing surprise, but the one must not act in the character of the other, even though there are sometimes habits and passions which would be better suited [in a particular play] to the other. It is suitable for a young but not an old man to be in love; this does not prevent an old man from falling in love: one often sees examples of it, but it would be considered insane, if he wanted to make love like a young man and if he claimed that he was loved for the fine quality of his personal appearance. He can hope that his [addresses] are listened to, but this hope has to be based on his wealth or his position and not on his merits. His claims cannot be reasonable if he does not believe that he is dealing with a soul [a woman] sufficiently ambitious to put aside everything for the glitter of wealth or ambition of rank.

Lifelikeness, a quality which Aristotle requires in the portrayal of character, particularly concerns people whom we know through history or fable and we must always portray them as we find them. That is what Horace means by the following verse: "Make Medea wild and intractable ... "

---

[15] "Parricide" is used here in its broadest sense of the murder of any near relative.

⟨Hr/67:123⟩. He who would portray Ulysses as a great warrior or Achilles as a great speaker or Medea as a subservient woman would expose himself to public ridicule.

Thus these two qualities [of "suitability" and "lifelikeness"], which some interpreters have difficulty in differentiating according to the unstated distinctions that Aristotle wants to make between them, easily harmonize, provided that they are separated and that fitting qualities are given to the imaginary characters who have never lived except in the mind of the playwright. The other qualities are reserved for those characters who are known to us through history or fable, as I have already said.

I still have to speak of consistency, which obliges us to have our persons keep the same character at the end of the play that we gave them at the beginning: "let it [a new character] remain to the end as it was when introduced, and keep it true to itself" ⟨Hr/68:126–27⟩. Inconsistency can, nonetheless, be present without being a defect, not only when we introduce characters of a light and inconsistent temper but also when, in conserving an interior consistency, we give an external inconsistency, according to the occasion. Such is the case with Chimène in the matter of her love. She still strongly loves Rodrigue in her heart, but this love acts differently in the presence of the King, differently again before the Infanta, and differently yet again before Rodrigue. This is what Aristotle calls inconsistently consistent character ⟨Ar/52⟩.[16] ...

After character comes thought, by which the actor lets us know what he wants or does not want and in which he can content himself with a simple statement of what he intends to do, without supporting it with moral reasoning, as I have just said. This part needs rhetoric to paint the passions and the agitations of the mind, to consult, deliberate, exaggerate, or extenuate; but there is the difference in this respect between the playwright and the orator, that the latter can display his art and make it remarkable with full freedom, while the other must hide it with care, because it is never he himself who speaks and those he makes speak are not orators ⟨Ar/43⟩. ...

To end this treatise, I still have to speak of the quantitative parts which are the prologue, the episode, the *exodos*, and the chorus. "The prologue is what is spoken before the first chorus; the episode is spoken between the choruses; and the *exodos* is spoken after the last chorus" ⟨Ar/48⟩. That is all that Aristotle tells us about it. ...

I equate this prologue with our first act in accordance with Aristotle and in some way to supply what he has not said or what we have lost over time, I would say that the prologue must contain the seed of all that has to happen, with respect to both the principal action and minor events, so that no character who was not introduced in the first act (or at least mentioned

---

[16] Aristotle actually speaks of a consistently inconsistent character, not an inconsistently consistent one!

by somebody who was introduced in the first act) can appear in the following ones ⟨Db/227⟩. This is a new and rather strict rule and I have not always kept it;[17] but I believe that it greatly helps to achieve a true unity of action by linking all actions that are found in the play. ...

The equivalent to the "episode" in Aristotle is our three middle acts. But as he applies this name elsewhere to actions which are outside the main action and he designates them as a dispensable ornament, I would say that although these three acts are called the "episode," that is not to say that they should only be composed of episodes. ...

I shall say nothing about the *exodos*, which is nothing other than our fifth act. I think that I explained its main use when I said that the action of a play must be complete. I shall add only this word: one must, if one can, keep the entire catastrophe for it, and even hold it back as near to the end as possible. The more it is deferred, the more the mind remains in suspense and the impatience to know what turn it will take is a reason why it is received with greater pleasure. This does not happen when this [fifth] act begins with the catastrophe. The spectator who knows it [the ending] too early has no more curiosity, and his attention languishes during the rest, which teaches him nothing new ⟨Lp/188⟩. ...

I seek no modern examples but those from my own work, partly because I know my own works better than those of others and I am more the master of them, and partly because I do not want to run the risk of displeasing those whom I would criticize for something or whom I would not praise sufficiently for the excellent work they have done. I have already stated that I write without ambition and without contentiousness. I strive always to follow Aristotle's opinion in the subject he has treated, and since I perhaps understand it in my own way, I do not object if somebody else understands it in his way. The commentary I use most is my experience of the theatre and my thoughts about what I have seen audiences like or dislike. ...

From "On Tragedy and the Means of Treating It according to Verisimilitude or 'the Necessary'"

Apart from the three purposes of a play of which I spoke in the discourse which serves as a preface to the first part of this collection [i.e. "On the Purpose and the Parts of a Play," above], tragedy has this special use that "through pity and fear, it purges similar emotions" ⟨Ar/42⟩. These are the terms Aristotle uses in his definition and which teach us two things: one that tragedy arouses pity and fear; two, that by means of pity and fear, it purges similar emotions. ...

[17] See Schérer 1950, 51–61.

"We pity," he says, "those whom we see suffering an undeserved misfortune and we fear that the same may happen to us when we see people similar to ourselves suffering" ⟨Ar/49⟩. Thus pity includes a concern for the person whom we see suffering, the fear which follows concerns us, and just this passing from one to the other gives us enough of an opening to find the manner in which the purgation of the emotions in tragedy takes place. Pity for a misfortune into which we see people like ourselves fall brings us to the fear of something similar happening to us, this fear leads to the desire to avoid it, and this desire leads us to purge, moderate, rectify, and even to root out in ourselves this passion, which before our very eyes plunges into misfortune the people we pity. The reason for this is ordinary, but natural and indubitable: to avoid the effect, we have to eliminate the cause. ... It is true that, ordinarily, only kings are the leading characters in a tragedy and that the audience, not having royal power, has no reason to fear the misfortunes that happen to them. But these kings are men just like the audience and fall into their misfortunes through a transport of passion, of which the spectators themselves are capable. They even give a rationale which easily stretches from the greatest to the least; and the spectator can readily conceive that if a king gives himself up to an excess of ambition, love, hate, or vengeance and falls into a misfortune so great that one pities him, he [the spectator] who is only a commoner has all the more reason to bridle such passions for fear that they may sink him in a similar misfortune. Moreover, it is not necessary to show only the misfortunes of kings in the theatre. Those of other men could find a place there if they were sufficiently illustrious and sufficiently extraordinary to merit it and if history cared enough to inform us about them. ...

If the purgation of emotions is achieved in tragedy, I insist that it must be done in the manner that I am going to explain. But I doubt that it is ever achieved even in those [tragedies] which fulfill the conditions Aristotle demanded. They are to be found in *Le Cid* and are the reason for its great success: Rodrigue and Chimène have this integrity subject to passions and these passions cause their misfortune since they are only unhappy inasmuch as they are passionate for each other. They fall into unhappiness through this human weakness of which we, like them, are capable. Their misfortune invariably arouses pity and it has cost the spectators enough tears that it cannot be disputed. This pity must [if Aristotle is correct] make us fear falling into the same misfortune and purge in us this excess of love which causes their misfortune, and makes us pity them. But I do not know if pity either instills fear or purges love and I am very much afraid that Aristotle's reasoning on this point is only a beautiful idea which never has its effect in reality. ...

Nevertheless, whatever difficulty there might be in finding this effective and palpable purgation of passions by means of pity and fear, it is easy for us to agree with Aristotle. We have only to say that in this way of expressing himself he did not mean that these two means [pity and fear] always act together; and that according to him[18] one of the two is sufficient to produce this purgation, with the difference, however, that pity cannot occur without fear and that fear can occur without pity. The death of the Count in Le Cid causes no pity, and can, nevertheless, better purge in us this sort of arrogance that is envious of the glory of others than all the compassion we feel for Rodrigue and Chimène can purge the emotions attached to this violent love which arouses pity for both of them. ...

To oppose the feelings of one's nature to the raptures of passion or to the severity of duty will create a powerful agitation, which will please the audience. ...

In the tragic actions which take place between people who are close to each other, it is necessary to consider if he who wishes to kill the other knows him or does not know him, or if he carries out the deed or fails to do so. The diverse combinations of these two ways to act form four sorts of tragedies to which our philosopher attributes various degrees of perfection. The least perfect is the play in which "one knows whom one wishes to kill, and in fact has him killed, as in the case of Medea who kills her children, Clytemnestra her husband, Orestes his mother" ⟨Ar/51⟩. And the second type has something more elevated than the first according to [Aristotle]. "One character has another die without knowing him, and recognizes him with profound pain after having slain him; and this happens," he says, "either before the tragedy as with Oedipus, or during the tragedy .... The third kind has a high degree of excellence; [it is] to be found "when one is ready to kill someone close to oneself without knowing it, and when one recognizes this person soon enough to save him, such as when Iphigenia recognizes Orestes as her brother just as she is going to sacrifice him to Diana, and escapes with him" ⟨Ar/51⟩. ... He entirely condemns the fourth type which consists of those who knowingly undertake the deed and do not carry it through, which he says "are rather unsuccessful and not at all tragic" ⟨Ar/51⟩. He gives as an example Haemon in Antigone, who pulls his sword on his father and only uses it to kill himself ⟨Ar/51⟩. But if this condemnation were not modified it would be taken too far and would include not only Le Cid but Cinna, Rodogune, Héraclius, and Nicomède.

Let us then say that [the condemnation] applies only to those [characters] who know the person they want to be rid of, and fail to act, by a simple change of mind, without there being any important event which obliges them to do so and without any loss of power on their part. I have already classed this sort of ending as faulty. But when the characters do all they can and are prevented from arriving at a result by some superior

---

[18] Corneille is boldly distorting Aristotle.

power or by some change in fortune which makes them perish themselves, or puts them under the power of those whom they would like to ruin, there is no doubt that this creates a tragedy of a type perhaps even more sublime than the three types that Aristotle admits; and if he did not speak of it, it is because he saw no examples of it in the theatre of his own time, where it was not the fashion to save good people through the death of bad ones unless one tarnished them with some crime, as with Electra, who frees herself from oppression by the death of her mother, which she encourages her brother to bring about and for which she helps him to find the means. . . .

The poet's goal is to please according to the rules of his art. In order to please he sometimes has to heighten the brilliance of great actions and to extenuate the horror of fatal ones. These are necessities of embellishment in which he can violate the particular verisimilitude by some alteration of history, but he cannot do without the general verisimilitude, except rarely, and then for things which are of the utmost beauty and so brilliant that they dazzle. Above all, he must never push them [the embellishments] beyond an extraordinary verisimilitude, because these ornaments which he adds from his own invention are not absolutely necessary and it is better to dispense with them completely than to adorn his play with them contrary to all types of verisimilitude. In order to please according to the rules of his art he has to confine his action to unity of time and place; and as this is an absolute and indispensable necessity, he has much greater freedom in these two items than in those of embellishments.

Given the difficulty of finding in history or human imagination enough of these illustrious events worthy of tragedy, whose resolutions and effects could happen at the same place and on the same day, without slightly violating the usual order of things, I cannot believe that this kind of violation is completely condemnable, provided it does not extend to the impossible. There are excellent subjects where one cannot avoid it; and a scrupulous playwright would deprive himself of a fine opportunity for fame, and the public of a great deal of satisfaction, if he did not dare to be bold enough to put them on stage, for fear of having to make them move faster than verisimilitude permits. In this case I will give him some advice which he might perhaps find beneficial: he should not specify a fixed time in his play, nor any specific place where he puts his characters.[19] The imagination of the spectator will have more liberty to let itself drift with the flow of the action, if it is not fixed by these boundaries; and he might not notice this haste, if the boundaries did not remind him and focus his attention on it despite himself. I have always regretted having made the King say, in *Le Cid*, that he wanted Rodrigue to wait an hour or two after the defeat of the Moors before fighting Don Sanche. I had done it to show

---

[19] Corneille very directly contradicts d'Aubignac's pervasive insistence on the unities of time and place.

that the play took place within twenty-four hours; and this only served to alert the audience to the constraint to which I submitted the action. If I had ended this fight without designating the time, perhaps no one would have noticed it.

I do not think that in comedy the playwright has this liberty to compress the action, out of the necessity of reducing it to fit the unity of time. Aristotle wants all actions included in it to be verisimilar, and he does not by any means add the words: "or necessary," as he does for tragedy ⟨Ar/45–46⟩. Also the difference is quite great between the actions of one and the other. Those of comedy stem from ordinary people and consist only of love intrigues and deceptions, which develop so easily in a day that quite often, in the plays of Plautus and Terence, the time of their duration scarcely exceeds that of their performance. But in tragedy public affairs are usually intermingled with the private interests of the illustrious people who appear in them. There are battles, the capture of cities, great dangers, revolutions of states; and all this is hard to reconcile with the promptitude that the rule obliges us to impose on what happens on stage. . . .

From "On the Three Unities: Of Action, of Time, and of Place"

. . . Thus I maintain, as I have already said, that in comedy unity of action consists of unity of intrigue or of hindrance to the schemes of the protagonists. In tragedy it consists of unity of danger, whether the hero succumbs to it or escapes from it. I do not claim that one cannot allow several dangers in the latter, and several intrigues or obstacles in the former, provided that one leads necessarily into the other . . . .

. . . There must be only one complete action, which leaves the spectator with a calm mind; but it can only evolve through several other incomplete actions, which serve as progressions, and keep the spectator in an agreeable state of suspense. This is what must be done at the end of every act in order to render the action continuous. It is not necessary to know precisely everything the characters do in the intervals between the acts, nor what they are doing when they do not appear on stage, but it is necessary that every act leave an expectation of something that must happen in the following act. . . .

This leads me to remark that the playwright is not obliged to present to view all the particular actions which lead to the main one. He must choose those which for him are the most worthwhile to show, either because of the beauty of the spectacle, or because of the brilliance and vehemence of the passions which they produce, or because of some other charm which is attached to them; and he must hide the other [actions] backstage so as to reveal them to the spectator either through narration or through some other exercise of art.[20] Above all, he must bear in mind that particular actions and the main action have to be linked together in such a way that the last actions portrayed are produced by the preceding ones and that all actions have their origin in the protasis which must end with the first act ⟨Cn/243; Jn/199–200⟩. ...

The liaison between the scenes which unites all the particular actions of every act ... is a great ornament in a play which greatly serves to give continuity in the performance; but finally it is only an ornament and not a rule. ...

The rule regarding unity of time is founded on these words of Aristotle, "that a tragedy must contain the duration of its action within one revolution of the sun, or try not to go much beyond it" ⟨Ar/41⟩. These words give rise to this famous dispute as to whether they should be understood as meaning a natural day of twenty-four hours, or an artificial day of twelve: these are two opinions each of which has a considerable following ⟨Lp/187; Cd/215; Db/229⟩. For myself, I find that there are subjects so difficult to contain in so short a time, that not only would I give them a full twenty-four hours, but I would even permit myself the same licence that this philosopher gives in exceeding this a little, and without scruple would push it as far as thirty. There is a maxim in law that one must stretch favor and restrain rigor ... and I find that an author is rather bothered by this constraint, which has forced some of the writers of antiquity to go as far as the impossible. Euripides in *The Suppliant Women* has Theseus of Athens leave with an army, do battle before the walls of Thebes (which are about twelve or fifteen leagues away), and come back victorious in the following act. And from the moment he leaves until the arrival of the messenger, who comes to give an account of his victory, Aethra and the Chorus have only thirty-six lines to speak. That is a lot to do in so short a time.[21] ...

Many inveigh against this rule which they call tyrannical and they would be right if it were founded only on Aristotle's authority. But what must make it acceptable is the common sense that supports it. The play is an imitation or, more properly put, a portrayal of the actions of men, and there is no doubt that portraits are all the more excellent, the more they resemble the original. The performance lasts two hours, and if the action therein represented did not need more [time] in reality, it would resemble it perfectly. Thus we stop neither at twelve hours, nor at twenty-four, but contain the action of the play in the least amount of time possible, so that its performance better resembles reality and is more perfect. ...

Above all I would like to leave this duration [of the action] to the imagination of the spectators and never to fix the time needed, unless

---

[20] Compare Chapelain 1936, 125.

[21] In Greek convention, passage of time could be indicated by choral songs, as here. The passage (of forty-six, not thirty-six, lines) was probably divided into two *hemi-chori* rather than by Aethra and the Chorus.

required by the subject, principally when its verisimilitude is a little forced, as in *Le Cid*, because this [definiteness] only serves to warn the audience of this precipitateness. What need is there to remark at the beginning of a play that the sun is coming up, that it is midday in the third act, and that the sun is setting at the end of the last act, even when no violence is done to anything in a play by the necessity of obeying this rule? It is an affectation which merely serves to annoy an audience; it is sufficient to establish the possibility of the thing within the time that contains it, so that one may follow [the passage of time] easily if one wants to pay attention to it, without having to apply one's mind to it despite oneself. Even in actions which have no more duration than their actual performance, it would be tasteless to note from act to act that half an hour has passed between one and the other.

I repeat what I have said elsewhere,[22] that when we take a longer time, such as ten hours, I would like to see the eight that we have to lose be consumed in the intervals between acts ⟨Lp/187⟩, and that each of the acts contains only the time that the performance uses up, especially when there is a constant liaison between scenes; for this liaison does not tolerate a gap between two scenes. Nonetheless I think that the fifth act, because of a particular privilege, has the right to hurry time on a little, so that the part of the action that it represents takes more than is needed for its performance. The reason for this is that the spectator is impatient to see the ending, and when the ending depends on actors who have left the stage, all the conversation one gives to those who remain on stage awaiting news of the others only drags and seems to be without action. . . .

I cannot forget that although we must compress all the tragic action into the space of a day, this does not prevent the tragedy revealing what its heroes have been doing for several years through a narration or in some other more artful manner, since there are tragedies the crux of which consists in the obscurity of the hero's birth which needs to be explained, as in *Oedipus*. . . . But I cannot forget that the choice of an illustrious and much awaited day is a great ornament to any play. Occasions do not always present themselves and in all that I have done up to now you will only find four examples[23] of this type . . . .

As for unity of place, I can find no precept either in Aristotle or Horace ⟨Cv/137⟩.[24] This has led some people to believe that the rule was only established as a consequence of the unity of time, and they have consequently persuaded themselves that this unity extends as far as a man can come and go in twenty-four hours. This opinion is a little free, and if one made a character travel by coach the two sides of the stage could represent Paris and Rouen. . . .

---

[22] In the *examen* to *Mélite*.
[23] He cites *Horace*, *Rodogune*, *Andromède*, and *Don Sanche d'Aragon*.
[24] It appeared first in Castelvetro.

... To rectify in some fashion this duplication of places when it is unavoidable, I would like two things to be done: first, that the setting never change in the same act, but only between one act and another, as is done in the first three acts of *Cinna*; secondly, that the two places never need different sets and that neither of the two is ever named, but only the general place where both are contained, such as Paris, Rome, Lyon, Constantinople, etc. This will help to deceive the spectator who, seeing nothing that makes him notice the diversity of places, will not notice any (unless through a malicious and critical reflection, of which few are capable), the majority wholeheartedly following the action that they see presented. ...

CHARLES DE SAINT-EVREMOND
(1613–1703)

A member of the Norman aristocracy, Saint-Evremond was associated with such well-known figures as the Prince de Condé,[1] La Fontaine,[2] and Foucquet,[3] the wealthy and extravagant administrator of the nation's finances. His military career did not prevent him from taking an active interest in the important literary and philosophical questions of the day. He was part of the brilliant coterie of *libertins* or free-thinkers encouraged by Foucquet, and wrote letters, essays, and poems which were not published, but were probably widely circulated among his friends. In 1661, with the arrest of Foucquet, Saint-Evremond was obliged to flee to Holland to avoid imprisonment. From there he went to England, where he remained in exile for the rest of his life.

Living in London, he kept abreast of literary and intellectual trends in France and corresponded with his friends there. He was particularly interested in the theatre, and had new plays sent to him as soon as they were published. He himself wrote three comedies[4] and several of his essays deal with drama. These include one on Racine's *Alexander the Great*, in which he shows his preference for Corneille; "On English Comedy" ("De la comédie Angloise"), a reasonably balanced view of comedy in England; and "On Ancient and Modern Tragedy," a succinct presentation of some of his most essential ideas which is printed, in part, below.

In Saint-Evremond's view, Greek tragedy, which is unsuitable for modern French audiences for historical, psychological, and religious reasons, should not be imitated. French tragedy is as good in its own way as the Greek, he asserts, though its treatment of love is unsatisfactory. For Saint-Evremond, nobility and grandeur are essential qualities of the tragic hero, as they were for Corneille. His analysis of the psychological and emotional elements of tragedy is somewhat different from anything encountered in earlier French theorists. He contrasts the nature of pity and terror in ancient and in modern tragedy and underlines the differences in religion and morality, which previous theorists tended to ignore or minimize, in their quest for unity with antiquity. His ideal tragedy is human and heroic,

---

[1] Louis, Prince de Condé (1621–86), also known as "le Grand Condé," was one of the greatest generals of his time. Saint-Evremond served under him as a lieutenant from 1642 to 1649.

[2] Jean de La Fontaine (1621–95), celebrated for his *Fables* (1668–94), was also a member of Foucquet's coterie and a long-time friend of Saint-Evremond.

[3] Nicolas Foucquet (1615–80) gave generous protection to many writers, including Molière and La Fontaine.

[4] *La Comédie des académistes* in its first version (1638) was probably a collaboration. Saint-Evremond later reworked it, and it was included among his works, published in 1705. *Sir Politick Would-Be* (based on a character from Jonson's *Volpone*) was written between 1662 and 1665 in collaboration with the Duke of Buckingham and Lord d'Aubigny. *Les Opéra* was written in 1676.

portraying a nobility of soul that will inspire admiration and emulation in the audience.

For further reading

Furetière, 1690.

From "On Ancient and Modern Tragedy"[5]

Never have there been so many rules for writing good tragedies, but so few are written that all of the old ones must be revived. I recall that the abbé d'Aubignac wrote one according to all the laws he had imperiously laid down for the theatre. It was not a success, and as he boasted to all and sundry that he was the only one of our authors who had properly followed Aristotle's precepts, Monsieur le Prince[6] remarked: "I am grateful to M. d'Aubignac for having so carefully followed Aristotle's rules, but I cannot forgive those rules for having made M. d'Aubignac write such a bad tragedy."

It must be admitted that Aristotle's *Poetics* is an excellent work, but no book is so perfect that it can establish rules for all nations and every age. Descartes and Gassendi[7] have discovered truths that were unknown to Aristotle. Corneille has found forms of excellence for the stage that Aristotle did not dream of ⟨Cn/236–37⟩. Modern philosophers have noticed errors in the *Physics*, and modern poets have seen flaws in the *Poetics*, at least from our point of view, given that everything has changed as much as it has.

In the ancient dramas, gods and goddesses caused every momentous and extraordinary event that occurred, by their hatred, their friendship, their vengeance, and their protection. Nothing in these many supernatural occurrences seemed incredible to the people, who believed in a close relationship between gods and men. The gods almost always operated through human passions; men undertook no enterprise without seeking the advice of the gods, and accomplished nothing without their help. Thus, there was nothing unbelievable in this mixture of divinity and humanity. But today we find all of these marvels incredible. The gods have abandoned us and we have abandoned them. If an author wishing to imitate the

---

[5] The text is found in *Oeuvres mêlées* (Saint-Evremond/de Nardis 1966, 284–93). It may have been written in 1674 or shortly afterward, possibly in response to Boileau's *L'art poétique* of 1674. See discussion in Saint-Evremond/Ternois 1962–69, IV:166–68.

[6] The Prince de Condé.

[7] René Descartes (1595–1650) was a renowned French philosopher and mathematician, whose work inspired much debate in the seventeenth century. The abbé Pierre Gassend, known as Gassendi (1592–1650), was a philosopher and mathematician opposed to Aristotelian scholasticism and to the dogmatism of Descartes. He attempted to combine Christianity and the philosophy of Epicurus. Saint-Evremond was greatly influenced by him.

ancients in some way were to put saints and angels in his play, he would be considered sacrilegious by pious people, and simple-minded by free-thinkers. Preachers would not allow the theatre to impinge on the functions of the pulpit, and would object to people going to hear actors say the same words that are proclaimed with authority to all people in the churches.

Moreover, this would give the free-thinkers a great advantage, allowing them to ridicule, in the theatre, the same sermons they must listen to with feigned submission in church, out of respect for the place where they are given and for the people who give them.

But let us suppose that our theologians allowed dramatists to make free use of all sacred subjects, and that the less pious members of the audience were as docile as true believers. There is no doubt that the most sacred doctrine, the most Christian actions, and the most instructive truths result in the most boring tragedies.

The spirit of our religion is directly opposed to the nature of tragedy. The patience and compassion of our saints are completely at odds with the qualities required of dramatic heroes. ...[8]

If my reasoning is correct, we must be satisfied with things that are strictly natural, but extraordinary. The main actions of our heroes must be such that we can accept them as humanly possible and admire them as exceptional and truly heroic. In short, we require only what is great, but human; within the human we must avoid the mediocre; within what is great, we must shun the incredible. ...

To tell you my honest opinion, I believe ancient tragedy would have been much better off without its gods, oracles, and soothsayers.

It was because of them that the theatre was filled with an atmosphere of superstition and terror capable of leading humanity into countless errors and of further increasing its misfortunes. And considering the influence that Athenian tragedy was wont to have on the minds of the audience, one could say that Plato had more reason for banning it than Aristotle had for recommending it. For since tragedy did in fact consist in arousing excessive emotions of terror and pity, was this not tantamount to making the theatre into a school of fear and compassion, where people learned to be terrified of every danger and to grieve over every misfortune? ...

Our modern plays do not have the same drawbacks as those of antiquity, since they never inspire that superstitious terror which had such a detrimental effect on courage. Our fear is usually no more than a titillating

---

[8] There follows a passage on Corneille's tragedy *Polyeucte* (1641), which dealt with Polyeucte and Néarque, two early Christian martyrs in Rome. Saint-Evremond observes that "what would have made an excellent sermon was a poor tragedy, except for the conversations between Pauline and Severus, animated by other [i.e., non-religious] feelings and passions, which saved the author's reputation from being destroyed by the Christian virtues of his martyrs" (Saint-Evremond/de Nardis 1966, 286).

agitation that accompanies the suspension of the spirits.[9] It proceeds from the warm concern we feel for the characters whose fate becomes important to us.

Much the same may be said about pity in our plays. We strip it of all its weakness, leaving intact all of its charitable and humane elements. I like to see pity for the misfortune of a great man in adversity. I like him to win compassion and sometimes to command our tears. But I want these tender, noble feelings to consider both his misfortunes and his virtue, so that as well as the same emotion of pity, we feel a strong admiration, which kindles in our soul an eager desire to imitate him.

It remained for us to add a little love to the new tragedy, to better rid us of the black thoughts caused by the superstition and terror of the ancient tragedy. And in truth, there is no other passion that awakens in us more noble and generous impulses than an honorable love. ... But ... our authors have misused this fine passion as much as the ancient writers abused their fear and pity. For, with the exception of eight or ten plays in which it has been treated with great skill, in our plays both lovers and love are equally distorted.

We portray an affected tenderness where we should have the noblest feelings. What should be most moving becomes weak and ineffectual. And sometimes, when we think we are being natural and unaffected, we are in fact lapsing into petty foolishness.

In trying to make kings and emperors who are perfect lovers, we make them ridiculous. By making them sigh and moan, when there is no reason to do either, we make them ineffectual, both as lovers and as monarchs.[10] ...

I hope that one day we shall find the proper way to use this passion, which has become too commonplace. Love, which should temper whatever is either too barbaric or too tragic, and should nobly stir the soul, quicken the heart, and uplift the mind, will not always be the subject of a mere feigned attachment or besotted foolishness. Then we shall have no need to envy the ancients; if we are neither too enamored of antiquity nor too disparaging of our own age, we will not model our plays on the tragedies of Sophocles and Euripides.

I do not deny that these tragedies had qualities that were in keeping with the tastes of the Athenians. But if the *Oedipus* itself, that masterpiece of ancient tragedy, could be translated into French, without losing any of its power, I venture to say that we would find it completely barbaric, appalling and immoral. ...

[9] These are the "animal spirits" described by Descartes. They were thought to be "very subtle and constantly moving bodies contained in the brain and in the nerves: they are the cause of thought and emotions" (Furetière 1690).

[10] In his essay on *Alexander the Great*, Saint-Evremond criticized Racine for depicting Alexander and Porus, an Indian monarch, as lovesick swains. See Saint-Evremond/ Niderst 1970, 115–17.

Today we see people shown on stage without the intervention of the gods, which is much more beneficial to the public and to private individuals. For in our tragedies there is no villain who is not detested and no hero who is not admired. Few crimes go unpunished and few virtues are not rewarded. By providing the audience with good examples on the stage, by discreetly adding these pleasurable feelings of love and admiration to fear and pity adjusted to suit our age, we shall achieve in our theatre that perfection desired by Horace: "everyone votes for the man who mixes wholesome and sweet" ⟨Hr/74:343⟩, which could never be according to the rules of ancient tragedy.

I shall end with a thought that is new and daring. In tragedy we must seek above all else the clear expression of nobility of soul, which stirs in us an affectionate admiration ⟨Cn/242⟩. This kind of admiration has the power to enrapture our minds, uplift our hearts, and touch us to the soul.

27

JEAN RACINE
(1639–1699)

Almost all Racine's theoretical writing is to be found in the prefaces which offer critical justifications for his plays. There is considerable arrogance (especially in the prefaces to the earlier plays) in Racine's attitude towards his critics. Not limiting himself to withering remarks about their ignorance, he indulges in diatribe, as in the first preface to *Britannicus*, in which he attacks Corneille and his style of playwriting.

In almost every preface Racine proclaims his sources in a way calculated to enhance his reputation as a dramatist knowledgeable enough to be capable of intelligent imitation of the ancients. He is meticulous in providing references from historians, even when dealing with mythological subjects, but he firmly claims the artist's right to depart from history or from his ancient models, as in *Iphigenia*, *Mithridates*, and *Phaedra*.

Thanks to his tutors at Port-Royal, Racine had a thorough grounding in Greek and was thus much more familiar with Greek tragedy than other dramatists of his day. He not only took subjects from the Greek, as in *Phaedra*, *Iphigenia*, and *Andromache*, but also experimented, in *Esther* and *Athaliah*, with the use of a Chorus and music, after the Greek model. Racine's choice of subject in his one venture into comedy was also from a Greek source. Instead of imitating Terence or Plautus, as most comic playwrights since the Renaissance had done, he took Aristophanes as his model, but protested that he would rather have imitated Menander or Terence "who followed the rules." His knowledge of Greek theatre may also account for the preoccupation, in most of his prefaces, with simplicity of plot coupled with intensity of emotion. In the preface to *Phaedra* he also speaks emphatically of the moralizing function of tragedy but its main purpose, he holds, is to give pleasure to the audience and to touch their emotions.

Racine's prefaces are entirely different in tone and purpose from his translation and interpretation (not published during his lifetime) of parts of Aristotle's *Poetics*. These "principles of tragedy" are in the form of marginal notes with additional words and clarifications of Racine's own. His interpretation of catharsis is that the specified emotions are purified, not eliminated: the performance, "by arousing pity and terror, purifies and *tempers* emotions of this kind." There are also some interesting variations on Aristotle's *hamartia*, which is interpreted by Racine as a failing (though not an "*excessive*" one) inherent in the human frailty of the hero, whose misfortune is thus made to seem not altogether unjust.[1] He does not translate the sections on the length or magnitude of tragedy or on unity of plot, which had been of great interest to Chapelain, Corneille, and d'Aubignac. Instead, he concentrates

---

[1] For a detailed discussion of this concept, see Vinaver 1955, ch. 4, "Tragic Error," esp. 99–102.

on the qualitative parts of tragedy, as described by Aristotle, on the nature of the tragic hero, on recognitions, on the nature of the tragic action and the kind of characters involved in it, and especially on the emotions this intimate and necessary relation between characters and action produces in the audience.

For further reading

Barnwell 1982; Knight 1974; Vinaver 1955.

From Racine's translation and interpretation of Aristotle's *Poetics*[2]

Definition of tragedy ⟨Ar/41–42⟩

Tragedy is the imitation of a complete action, serious in nature and of *appropriate* magnitude. This imitation uses language, *a style* composed for pleasure, so that each of the component parts has a distinct identity and function.

The action is not imitated by narration, but by a *live performance*, which by arousing pity and terror, purifies and *tempers* emotions of this kind. *This means, that in kindling these passions, tragedy removes what is excessive and corrupt in them, and restores them to a state that is moderate and in keeping with reason. . . .*

Poetry and history ⟨Ar/45⟩

Poetry is something more philosophic and more complete than history; the poet is concerned with the general, and the historian considers only the particular. By general I mean what is appropriate for a certain kind of person to do or say, according to verisimilitude or necessity. And that is the subject of poetry, which clothes its idea with whatever *name it pleases, that is, adopting the names of certain characters, to make them act or speak according to its idea.*

History, on the other hand, deals only with particular circumstances, for example, what Alcibiades did, or what happened to him. . . .

Plot structure ⟨Ar/44⟩

Since it is by imitation that the poet may produce in us *the pleasure inspired by* pity and fear, clearly this pleasure must come from the action and, so to speak, the heart of the story ⟨Db/232⟩. . . . Let us now see what kinds of incidents can bring about this fear and this pity.

---

[2] For the French text and a commentary see Racine/Vinaver 1951. These marginal notes were in Racine's copy of Pietro Vettori's commentary on the *Poetics* (1573). Vettori (1499–1585) was a Florentine scholar and humanist. Racine's additions and clarifications have been italicized here for easy identification.

They must of necessity be actions involving people who are friends, or enemies, or neither.

If an enemy kills an enemy, we feel no pity, either in seeing the deed committed or in the contemplation of it. Only at the very moment when we see him do the deed, *are we able to feel that simple emotion common to human nature on seeing a man killed*. Nor will we have much pity for mutually indifferent people *who want to kill one another*. There remains therefore only those incidents that occur between people connected by ties of family or *friendship*, as for example when a brother kills, or is about to kill his brother, a son his father, a mother her son, or a son his mother. These are the kind of incidents the poet should try to find. ...

... But *by far* the best treatment is when someone commits some *horrible* deed, without *knowing what he or she is doing*, and after the action comes to realize *what has been done*. For there is nothing *wicked* or monstrous about such a deed, and the discovery is *horrifying* and makes us shudder. ...

Character ⟨Ar/52⟩

Let us now discuss character. There are four points to bear in mind. First, the character should be good. A *person* has character when we discover, either by his actions or his words, his inclination or *disposition to vice or virtue*. His character will be bad if his inclination is bad, and will be good if his inclination is good. Character can be seen in people of every *station*, for a woman may be good, and a slave may also be good, although usually a woman has less goodness than a man, and a slave is *almost* entirely worthless.

The second *requirement* of character is to be appropriate, for courage is an element of character, but it is inappropriate to the character of a woman, since women are not *by nature* brave and intrepid.

Thirdly, the character must have verisimilitude ⟨Ar/52; Cn/242⟩, (*this means that the persons imitated by the playwright must behave the same way on the stage as they are known to have behaved in real life*). This quality of verisimilitude is different from the two previously mentioned qualities of goodness and appropriateness.

In the fourth place, character must remain consistent. For although the character who is represented occasionally may appear to change *his mind and way of speaking*, nonetheless he must always *remain fundamentally the same, motivated by a single principle*, and he must be inconsistently consistent ⟨Ar/52; Cn/243⟩ and uniform.[3] ...

Nor must there be anything absurd or implausible in the action. That is only permissible in things which lie outside the tragedy, as can be seen in Sophocles' *Oedipus*. (*Perhaps Aristotle means that is was unlikely that there had not been a more thorough search for the murderers of Laius. This lack of*

---

[3] Aristotle says "consistently inconsistent." Racine's misreading is the same as Corneille's.

verisimilitude was permitted, according to Aristotle, because it preceded the actual events of the tragedy.)

Since the tragedy is an imitation of people of *most excellent character*, we must be like good artists who, while keeping the likeness in their portraits, improve on the appearance of the subject. In the same way, when the poet depicts people who are irascible, mild-mannered, or of any other tempera-ment, he must not only show them as they are, but he must represent them *to such a degree of excellence* that they could serve as models of anger or gentleness *or some other disposition*. This is how Agathon and Homer succeeded in representing Achilles.

The poet must observe all these things and must take care above all not to offend those senses by which we judge poetry – *the eyes and ears*. For there are several ways of offending them. This subject has been discussed in some of my other writings.

Discovery 1 ⟨Ar/53⟩

Discovery has already been defined; there are several different types. ...

For example, because of his scar, Ulysses was recognized in one way by his nurse and in another by the swineherds. There is less art *in this latter instance where Ulysses deliberately shows them his scar to prove his identity and support his story*, whereas in the other case, *his nurse recognizes him herself when she sees the scar. Thus this is not an intentional discovery*. Instead, there is an *element of surprise which makes it* a peripety. Spontaneous discoveries are much better than those that are *intentional*. ...

From the Preface to *Alexander the Great*[4] (1666)

... Finally, the most important objection to my play is that the subject is too simple and too sterile. I will not remind these critics of the prevailing taste in antiquity; it is clear they are only dimly aware of it. But their complaints are without foundation, for I have filled all the scenes with action, have made them seem linked together as if by necessity, have given every character an obvious reason for being on stage, and, using few incidents and within a brief compass, have succeeded in writing a play that kept them enthralled, perhaps in spite of themselves, from beginning to end. ...

From the Preface to *Andromache* (1668)

... the public has been too well-disposed to me, to be concerned with the particular displeasure of two or three people who would like all the heroes of antiquity to be reformed and made into perfect heroes. I admire their intention of wanting us to show only blameless characters on the stage.

---

[4] From the first preface, 1666.

But I beg them to remember that it is not my place to change the rules of drama. Horace advises us ⟨Hr/67:120–22⟩ to make Achilles wild, unyielding, and violent, just as he was, and as his son is also portrayed. And Aristotle, far from requiring heroes who are perfect, suggests, on the contrary, that tragic characters, that is, those whose misfortune makes the catastrophe of the tragedy, should be neither completely good nor completely bad. He does not want them to be extremely good, because the punishment of a good person would make the spectators feel indignation rather than pity. Nor should the characters be excessively bad, because we do not pity a villain. Their goodness must therefore be moderate, that is, virtue capable of weakness, and they must be reduced to misfortune by some failing which makes them worthy of pity without being detestable. ...

From the Preface to *The Litigants* (*Les Plaideurs*, 1669)

When I read *The Wasps* by Aristophanes, I little dreamed that I would turn it into *The Litigants*. Admittedly I found it very entertaining and full of humor, and I was tempted to introduce it to the public, but I had intended to write it for the Italians,[5] since I felt it was theirs by right. A judge who jumps out of windows, a dog accused of crimes, and the lamentations of his family, all seemed to me incidents worthy of a renowned actor like Scaramouche. My plan was cut short by the departure of this actor, but some of my friends expressed the desire to see a sample of Aristophanes performed. I did not at first accede to their suggestion, maintaining that for all Aristophanes' wit, I would not be inclined to take him as a model if I were to write a comedy. I would much prefer to imitate Menander and Terence, who followed the rules, rather than Plautus and Aristophanes, who did not. I was told that I was not required to write a comedy, and that they merely wanted to see whether Aristophanes' witticisms would still be entertaining in our language. Thus, partly by encouraging me and partly by putting their hands to the task, my friends made me start a play which did not take long to finish.

Most people, however, pay no heed to an author's efforts or intention. What I wrote as a diversion was at first examined as if it had been a tragedy. Even those who found it most entertaining were afraid of having laughed against the rules, and reproached me for not being more serious about making them laugh. A few others imagined that it was proper for them to be bored, and that matters of justice could not be fit entertainment for people at court. Shortly afterward the play was performed at Versailles. There they had no qualms about showing their enjoyment. Those who had

---

[5] The troupe of Italian actors under Tiberio Fiorillo, the famous Scaramouche. They shared the Petit-Bourbon stage with Molière's troupe.

felt they were dishonoring themselves by laughing in Paris were perhaps obliged to laugh in Versailles to maintain their honor. ...

For my part, I think Aristophanes was right to go beyond what is plausible. ... It was appropriate to exaggerate the characters a little, to prevent them from recognizing themselves. The audience did not fail to discern the truth in the midst of the ridiculous, and I am convinced that the misplaced eloquence of two orators was better exercised on behalf of a canine defendant than if a real criminal had been in the dock and the audience had been concerned with a man's life.

Be that as it may, I can say that our age is no more out of humor than the age of Aristophanes, and if the purpose of my comedy was to make people laugh, no comedy was ever more to the purpose. I do not expect to receive any great honor for having entertained people for quite some time. But I take some satisfaction in having done so without using one of those base *double entendres* or indecent jokes which most of our writers use so readily, causing our theatre to sink back into the depravity from which it had been rescued by some more modest authors.

From the Preface to *Britannicus* (1670)

... Critics also found fault with Junia. ... It was considered strange that she should appear on stage after the death of Britannicus. They objected to her saying, in four rather touching lines, that she was going to see Octavia.[6] They claimed it was unnecessary to have her come back for that; someone else could have told what she intended to do. They do not know that one of the rules of drama is to tell only those things that cannot be shown; all of the ancient dramatists often have characters come on stage merely to say where they have been or where they are going.

All of that is redundant, say my critics. The play ends with the account of Brittanicus' death, and the audience should not have to listen to the rest. They do listen to it, however, just as attentively as to the end of any other tragedy. For my part, I have always understood that since tragedy is an imitation of a complete action, involving several characters, this action is not finished until we know what has become of these same characters. Sophocles almost always does this. Thus, in *Antigone*, he uses as many lines to show the rage of Haemon and the punishment of Creon after the death of Antigone, as I did for the imprecations of Agrippina, Junia's departure, the punishment of Narcissus, and Nero's despair, after the death of Britannicus.

How could one ever satisfy critics who are so hard to please? It would be easy, if one were willing to go against good sense. One would merely have to abandon what is natural, and plunge into the extraordinary. Instead of

---

[6] This was in Act v, scene vi. Racine later removed the offending scene.

a simple action, with few incidents, as an action which takes place in a single day and gradually moves towards its end should be, sustained only by the motivations, thoughts, and passions of the characters, it would have to be filled with numerous events requiring at least a month, with a great deal of stage business, as surprising as it is implausible, with an infinite number of long-winded speeches, in which characters say just the opposite of what they should say.[7] ...

From the Preface to *Berenice* (1671)

... "Titus, who loved Berenice passionately, and was even believed to have promised to marry her, sent her away from Rome, against his will and hers, in the first days of his rule as emperor."[8] This action is very famous in history, and I found it very fitting for the theatre, because of the intensity of the feelings it could arouse in the audience. ... Death and bloodshed are not necessary in a tragedy; all it requires is an important action, heroic characters, intense emotions, and an atmosphere of majestic sadness, which is the essential pleasure of tragedy.

I thought I could find all of these requirements in my subject. But what delighted me even more was its extreme simplicity. For a long time I had been wanting to try my hand at writing a tragedy with that simplicity of action so prized by the ancients. ...

... In a tragedy, only what is plausible is touching. How can there be plausibility when the events of one day could scarcely fit into several weeks? There are those who think this simplicity betrays a lack of imagination. They do not realize that, on the contrary, the entire task of the imagination is to make something out of nothing, and that those poets who resorted to a multiplicity of incidents always did so because they knew that they lacked the richness and strength of imagination to keep an audience engrossed for five acts in a simple action, sustained by the intensity of the emotions, by the beauty of the thoughts and the elegance of the expression. ...

... The principal rule is to give pleasure and to touch the emotions. All of the other rules are intended only to help us succeed in this first one. ...

From the Preface to *Bajazet* (1697)

... Some readers may be surprised that we have dared to put on the stage a story that happened so recently. But I have seen nothing in the rules of dramatic art to deter me from my undertaking. In truth, I would not advise

---

[7] This is an obvious reference to the plays of Corneille.
[8] Suetonius, *The Lives of the Twelve Caesars*, "Titus," ch. 7.

an author to select as the subject of a tragedy an action as contemporary as this one, if it has occurred in the same country where he intended to have his tragedy performed. ... Distance between countries to some extent makes up for too great a proximity in time. For the common people I daresay what happens a thousand miles away is almost as remote as what happened a thousand years ago. This is why Turkish characters, for example, however modern they may be, command respect in our theatres. We already consider them venerable. Their manners and customs are completely different from ours. We have so few dealings with princes and other people who live in the Seraglio, that we consider them, so to speak, like people living in another century. ...

From the Preface to *Mithridates* (1673)

There is hardly a more famous name than that of Mithridates. His life and death occupy a considerable part of Roman history. ... I included every-thing which could reveal the character and thought of this prince, for instance his violent hatred of the Romans, his great courage, his cleverness, his cunning, and lastly that jealousy which was so natural to him and which so often led to the deaths of his mistresses. The one fact which may not be as well known as the rest, was his plan to march on Italy. ...

... I have linked this plan even more closely with my subject. I used it to let Mithridates discover the secret thoughts of his two sons. One cannot be too careful about making everything that happens on stage absolutely necessary. Even the best scenes may become tedious, the moment they can be separated from the action, and begin to slow it down instead of advancing it toward its conclusion. ...

From the Preface to *Phaedra* (1677)

Here is yet another tragedy whose subject is taken from Euripides. Although I have differed somewhat from him in the conduct of the action, I have enriched my play with everything that seemed most striking in his. If I owed him nothing more than the mere idea for the character of Phaedra, I might say I owe him perhaps the most reasonable thing I have written for the stage. I am not surprised that this character was so successful in Euripides' time, nor that it is again well received in our own, since it has all the qualities Aristotle requires of the tragic hero, in order to arouse compassion and fear. Indeed Phaedra is neither completely guilty, nor completely innocent. By her destiny and the anger of the gods, she is entrapped in an illicit passion, whose horror she is the first to recognize.

She makes every effort to overcome it, preferring to succumb to death rather than disclose it to anyone. And when she is forced to reveal it, she speaks with a confusion that shows clearly that her crime is a punishment from the gods and does not proceed from her own will. I even took care to make her a little less odious than she is in the tragedies of the ancient dramatists, where she decides of her own accord to accuse Hippolytus. I thought that calumny was too base and too heinous a crime to attribute to a princess whose sentiments are otherwise so noble and virtuous. Such baseness seemed to me more suited to the character of a nurse, who nevertheless only makes this false accusation to save her mistress' life and honor. Phaedra only agrees to this because she is beside herself with agitation, and a moment later she comes on stage with the intention of upholding Hippolytus' innocence and telling the truth.

In Euripides and Seneca, Hippolytus is accused of actually raping his stepmother ... but here he is accused merely of having the intention to do so. I wanted to spare Theseus embarrassment, which could have made him less acceptable to the audience.

As for the character of Hippolytus, I had observed that writers in antiquity had a tendency to criticize Euripides for having depicted him as a philosopher, without any faults. This meant that his death caused much more indignation than pity. I thought I should give him some weakness which would make him somewhat guilty towards his father, but without detracting from the magnanimity which prompts him to spare Phaedra's honor, and go to his death without accusing her. By weakness I mean his involuntary passion for Aricia, who is the daughter and the sister of his father's mortal enemies. ...

It was in Plutarch that I found that what had given rise to the belief that Theseus had descended into the underworld to carry off Proserpine was a journey he took into Epirus, towards the source of the Acheron where a king, whose wife Pirithous[9] wanted to abduct, kept Theseus prisoner after having slain Pirithous. Thus I tried to keep the verisimilitude of history, without sacrificing any of the embellishments of fable, which adds so much richness to poetry. And the rumor of Theseus' death, based on this mythical journey, leads Phaedra to make a declaration of love, which becomes one of the principal causes of her misfortune, and which she never would have made as long as she believed her husband was still alive.

For the rest, I do not yet venture to say that this play is indeed my best tragedy. I will leave it to my readers and to time to decide its true worth. I can, however, state that in none of my other plays was virtue shown so clearly as in this one. The least faults are severely punished. The mere thought of crime is looked on with as much horror as the crime itself. The weaknesses of love are held to be real weaknesses. The passions are

---

[9] Theseus' friend.

displayed only to show that disruption they cause, and vice is painted throughout in colors that reveal its deformities and make them abhorrent. And that is the proper aim that every dramatist should strive for. The earliest tragic poets had this in mind above all else. Their stage was a school where virtue was as well taught as in the schools of the philosophers. Thus Aristotle was willing to set down the rules for dramatic poetry, and Socrates, the wisest of all philosophers, did not consider it beneath him to put his hand to the tragedies of Euripides. It might be hoped that our plays were as well constructed and as full of useful instruction as the works of those dramatists. Perhaps this might make tragedy acceptable to many people known for their piety and their knowledge, who have recently condemned it. They might judge it more favorably if dramatists gave as much thought to edifying their audiences as to entertaining them thus fulfilling the true aim of tragedy.

28

JOHN DRYDEN
(1631–1700)

In 1665–66, when the London theatres were closed by the plague, Dryden retired to the country and there wrote *An Essay of Dramatic Poesy*. Couched in the form of a dialogue, which allows for a certain irresolution, the *Essay* is an attempt to take stock of the fundamental principles of drama, and to assess the English contribution to the art. The "memorable day" on which the supposed dialogue takes place is in key with its nationalist tendency: at sea, the English defeat the Dutch; on the river, the four-character dialogue tends to demonstrate the superiority of the best (but not the most recent) English over French drama.

The cultural conflict represented in the *Essay* was not an isolated engagement. English pride had been wounded by a French critique of the state of drama in England, English theatrical practice had been vigorously defended, and the French theatre had been counter-attacked before Dryden's intervention.[1] In his "Defense of an Essay of Dramatic Poesy" (1668), Dryden declared that the original *Essay* was designed "to vindicate the honour of our English writers from the censure of those who unjustly prefer the French before them."[2] This appears to be the case with respect to English drama of the *previous* age and, more tenuously, current plays, but the statement also obscures Dryden's indebtedness to Corneille for the theoretical perspectives of the *Essay*.[3]

Of the four speakers, Lisideius would follow the French entirely but Neander, his particular disputant, does not go to the opposite extreme. Crites and Eugenius represent another set of polarities: Crites is the (rather casual) representative of a (rather archaic) scholasticism and Eugenius of an enthusiastic modernism. In the course of the discussion some errors and confusions are dispelled but many issues remain open and charged with ambivalence. Crites is careless in attributing the formulation of the "rules" to the Ancients (and also to the French) and this prop of his argument is smartly knocked aside. But his historical and social interpretation of the growth and decline of poetry through ages and nations is forcefully made and accepted by the others. All four speakers are made to cite Paterculus as a

---

[1] Samuel Sorbière had visited England in 1663 and, in the following year, published his *Relation d'un voyage en Angleterre*, in which he crudely attacked English culture, including the theatre. In 1665, Thomas Spratt responded with *Observations on Mons. Sorbier's Voyage into England*, asserting the superiority of contemporary English drama, in which he found as much regularity as in the French, and more natural development of plot and character. As a supplement to the controversy, Dryden's essay is remarkable for its moderation. See Williamson 1946.

[2] Dryden/Watson 1962, II:124.

[3] Particular borrowings are indicated by cross-references in the text but the influence is fundamental and pervasive. Dryden apparently used the first edition of Corneille's three treatises, published in 1660 (see chapter 25, above), not one of the later, revised, editions. See Aden 1955 and LeClercq 1970.

classical authority for the idea that discernment of the particular genius of ages and people is a major function of criticism. Eugenius' defense of the Moderns brings us closer to the central concerns of the *Essay*, on which Neander will ultimately focus. These concerns tend to be referred to two presiding geniuses often invoked: Ben Jonson and Pierre Corneille. The discussants could almost be described as, at times, the delegates of these ambivalently used super-powers.

Jonson is the dramatist who not only acknowledges the incomparable greatness of the Ancients but also stands on their shoulders. Again, Jonson's respect for artistic principles, even "rules," rivals that of the French. That he uses them to such brilliant effect, moreover, constitutes an endorsement of their validity, but his work also exhibits a "copiousness" (which might otherwise be supposed to be fatally inhibited by the rules) in which English and Spanish drama excel, by contrast with the French.

Yet it is not Jonson but Corneille, the practicing dramatist deeply concerned with the principles of his art, who seems to be the chief inspiration of the *Essay*. Neander gives him some hard knocks but also discriminates between Corneille's actual opinions and the rigidly neo-classical ones attributed to him. At the climax of the *Essay*, Neander's commentary on Jonson's *Epicoene* is a tribute not only to Jonson but to Corneille's method and approach, as the word "examen" immediately suggests. The "examen" is neither abstract and prescriptive nor merely pragmatic. It is not a critique of a particular work in isolation but an attempt to discover the generally applicable principles operative in an exemplary play. At the end of his career, Corneille had set out to vindicate his work and elucidate his art: near the beginning of his, Dryden embarks on a similar program, which was to be continued largely through critical prefaces on the lines of Corneille's *examens*.

Two other presences in the *Essay* are Dryden himself and Shakespeare. The narrative keeps us mindful that Neander is only a limited projection of a Dryden who is the architect of the whole dialogue, the one who defines the attitudes and places the emphases of all the speakers. He is a powerfully motivated inquirer who may become a candidate for admission to the pantheon of great dramatists and critics alluded to in the *Essay*. And above the battle hovers Shakespeare, as a reminder of the transcendence of great art over all theory.

Throughout the *Essay*, there is perceptible effort to establish and define an English critical vocabulary. It includes such key terms as "concernment," "relations," "Nature," "passions," and "imagination," which the speakers use with a consistency that indicates the single intelligence from which they all stem. Dryden places a particular emphasis on "concernment," meaning the degree to which the audience's attention and sympathy is aroused and sustained, and on the ways in which drama may succeed and fail in this respect. Dryden's later theoretical views, it is worth noting, became rather less liberal than those that emerge from the dialogue of the *Essay*.[4]

For further reading

Aden 1955; Hume 1970; Huntley 1948; LeClercq 1970; Sherwood 1950; Swedenberg 1966; Trowbridge 1946; Williamson 1946.

---

[4] His 1679 preface to his adaptation of Shakespeare's *Troilus and Cressida*, which is the occasion for an essay on "The Grounds of Criticism in Tragedy," is a notable example of his relatively rigid later views.

From *An Essay of Dramatic Poesy*[5]

It was that memorable day,[6] in the first summer of the late war, when our navy engaged the Dutch; a day wherein the two most mighty and best appointed fleets which any age had ever seen, disputed the command of the greater half of the globe, the commerce of nations, and the riches of the universe. While these vast floating bodies, on either side, moved against each other in parallel lines, and our countrymen, under the happy conduct of his Royal Highness, went breaking, by little and little, into the line of the enemies; the noise of the cannon from both navies reached our ears about the city, so that all men being alarmed with it, and in a dreadful suspense of the event, which they knew was then deciding, everyone went following the sound as his fancy led him; and leaving the town almost empty, some took towards the park, some cross the river, others down it; all seeking the noise in the depth of silence.

Among the rest it was the fortune of Eugenius, Crites, Lisideius and Neander, to be in company together; three of the persons whom their wit and quality have made known to all the town; and whom I have chosen to hide under these borrowed names,[7] that they may not suffer by so ill a relation as I am going to make of their discourse. . . .

Taking then a barge which the servant of Lisideius had provided for them, they made haste to shoot the bridge, and left behind them that great fall of waters which hindered them from hearing what they desired: after which, having disengaged themselves from many vessels which rode at anchor in the Thames, and almost blocked up the passage towards Greenwich, they ordered the watermen to let fall their oars more gently; and then, everyone favouring his own curiosity with a strict silence, it was not long ere they perceived the air to break about them like the noise of distant thunder, or of swallows in a chimney: those little undulations of sound, though almost vanishing before they reached them, yet still seeming to retain somewhat of their first horror, which they had betwixt the fleets. After they had attentively listened till the sound by little and little went from them, Eugenius, lifting up his head, and taking notice of it, was the

---

[5] The *Essay* was first published in 1668. Dryden revised the text, mostly for style and grammar, in the second edition of 1684; there was a third edition in 1693. The present text is based on the first edition, with some readings from the second edition silently incorporated.

[6] 3 June, 1665. The Second Dutch War ended in July 1667 with the Treaty of Breda.

[7] Malone identified Eugenius (meaning "well born") as Charles Sackville, Lord Buckhurst, to whom the *Essay* is dedicated; Crites (the "critical" or "censorious" one) as Dryden's brother-in-law, Sir Robert Howard; Lisideius (possibly a pun on "*Le Cid*" and/or "Sedley") as Sir Charles Sedley, author of the play *The Mulberry Garden* (1668); and Neander (the "new man") as Dryden himself. Not only the accuracy of these identifications but the relevance of any such have been challenged, and it is worth noting that in his Preface to *Four New Plays* (1665), reprinted in Spingarn 1908a, II.97–104, Howard, unlike Crites, asserts the *superiority* of the modern over the ancient playwrights. See Huntley 1948.

first who congratulated to the rest that happy omen of our Nation's victory: adding that we had but this to desire in confirmation of it, that we might hear no more of that noise, which now was leaving the English coast. When the rest had concurred in the same opinion, Crites, a person of sharp judgement, and somewhat too delicate a taste in wit, which the world have mistaken in him for ill-nature, said, smiling to us, that if the concernment of this battle had not been so exceeding great, he could scarce have wished the victory at the price he knew he must pay for it, in being subject to the reading and hearing of so many ill verses as he was sure would be made on that subject. Adding, that no argument could scape some of those eternal rhymers, who watch a battle with more diligence than the ravens and birds of prey; and the worst of them surest to be first upon the quarry: while the better able, either out of modesty writ not at all, or set that due value on their poems, as to let them be often desired and long expected! ...

'If your quarrel', said Eugenius, 'to those who now write, be grounded only on your reverence to antiquity, there is no man more ready to adore those great Greeks and Romans than I am: but on the other side, I cannot think so contemptibly of the age in which I live, or so dishonourably of my own country, as not to judge we equal the Ancients in most kinds of poesy, and in some surpass them .... .

'But I see I am engaging in a wide dispute, where the arguments are not like to reach close on either side; for Poesy is of so large an extent, and so many both of Ancients and Moderns have done well in all kinds of it, that in citing one against the other, we shall take up more time this evening than each man's occasions will allow him: therefore I would ask Crites to what part of Poesy he would confine his arguments, and whether he would defend the general cause of the Ancients against the Moderns, or oppose any age of the Moderns against this of ours?'

Crites, a little while considering upon this demand, told Eugenius that if he pleased, he would limit their dispute to Dramatic Poesy; in which he thought it not difficult to prove, either that the Ancients were superior to the Moderns, or the last age to this of ours.

Eugenius was somewhat surprised, when he heard Crites make choice of that subject. 'For aught I see', said he, 'I have undertaken a harder province than I imagined; for though I never judged the plays of the Greek or Roman poets comparable to ours, yet, on the other side, those we now see acted come short of many which were written in the last age: but my comfort is, if we are o'ercome, it will only be by our own countrymen ... as for the Italian, French, and Spanish plays, I can make it evident that those who now write surpass them, and that the Drama is wholly ours.' ...

Eugenius was going to continue this discourse, when Lisideius told him that it was necessary, before they proceeded further, to take a standing measure of their controversy; for how was it possible to be decided who writ the best plays, before we know what a play should be? But, this once agreed on by both parties, each might have recourse to it, either to prove his own advantages, or to discover the failings of his adversary.

He had no sooner said this, but all desired the favour of him to give the definition of a play; and they were the more importunate, because neither Aristotle, nor Horace, nor any other, who had writ of that subject, had ever done it. Lisideius, after some modest denials, at last confessed he had a rude notion of it; indeed, rather a description than a definition; but which served to guide him in his private thoughts, when he was to make a judgement of what others writ: that he conceived a play ought to be, *A just and lively image of human nature, representing its passions and humours, and the changes of fortune to which it is subject, to the delight and instruction of mankind.*

This definition, though Crites raised a logical objection against it; that it was only *a genere et fine* [according to general class and purpose],[8] and so not altogether perfect; was yet well received by the rest: and after they had given order to the watermen to turn their barge, and row softly, that they might take the cool of the evening in their return, Crites, being desired by the company to begin, spoke on behalf of the Ancients . . . .

' . . . Those Ancients have been faithful imitators and wise observers of that Nature which is so torn and ill represented in our plays; they have handed down to us a perfect resemblance of her; which we, like ill copiers, neglecting to look on, have rendered monstrous and disfigured. But, that you may know how much you are indebted to those your masters, and be ashamed to have so ill requited them, I must remember you, that all the rules by which we practise the Drama at this day, (either such as relate to the justness and symmetry of the plot, or the episodical ornaments, such as descriptions, narrations, and other beauties, which are not essential to the play) were delivered to us from the observations which Aristotle made, of those poets, who either lived before him, or were his contemporaries: we have added nothing of our own, except we have the confidence to say our wit is better; of which none boast in this our age, but such as understand not theirs. Of that book which Aristotle has left us, *peri tes Poietices*, Horace his *Art of Poetry* is an excellent comment, and, I believe, restores to us that Second Book of his concerning *Comedy*, which is wanting in him.

'Out of these two have been extracted the famous Rules, which the French call *des trois unités* ⟨Cn/248⟩, or, the three unities, which ought to be observed in every regular play; namely, of time, place, and action. . . .

'If by these rules (to omit many other drawn from the precepts and practice of the Ancients) we should judge our modern plays, 'tis probable that few of them would endure the trial: that which should be the business of a day, takes up in some of them an age; instead of one action, they are the epitome of man's life; and for one spot of ground (which the stage

---

[8] That the definition does not concern drama in particular but literature – or even art – in general, is the essence of Crites' objection.

should represent) we are sometimes in more countries than the map can show us.

'But if we will allow the Ancients to have contrived well, we must acknowledge them to have written better .... I must desire you to take notice, that the greatest man of the last age (Ben Jonson) was willing to give place to them in all things: he was not only a professed imitator of Horace, but a learned plagiary of all the others; you track him everywhere in their snow ... and whether you consider the bad plays of our age, or regard the good plays of the last, both the best and the worst of the modern poets will equally instruct you to admire the Ancients.'

Crites had no sooner left speaking, but Eugenius, who had waited with some impatience for it, thus began:

'I have observed in your speech, that the former part of it is convincing as to what the Moderns have profited by the rules of the Ancients; but in the latter you are careful to conceal how much they have excelled them; we own all the helps we have from them, and want neither veneration nor gratitude while we acknowledge that to overcome them we must make use of the advantages we have received from them: but to these assistances we have joined our own industry; for, had we sat down with a dull imitation of them, we might then have lost somewhat of the old perfection, but never acquired any that was new. We draw not therefore after their lines, but those of Nature; and having the life before us, besides the experience of all they knew, it is no wonder if we hit some airs and features which they have missed. I deny not what you urge of arts and sciences, that they have flourished in some ages more than others; but your instance in philosophy makes for me: for if natural causes be more known now than in the time of Aristotle, because more studied, it follows that poesy and other arts may, with the same pains, arrive still nearer to perfection; and, that granted, it will rest for you to prove that they wrought more perfect images of human life than we; which seeing in your discourse you have avoided to make good, it shall now be my task to show you some part of their defects, and some few excellencies of the Moderns. ...

'Be pleased then in the first place to take notice, that the Greek poesy, which Crites has affirmed to have arrived at perfection in the age of the Old Comedy, was so far from it, that the distinction of it into acts was not known to them; or if it were, it is yet so darkly delivered to us that we cannot make it out.

'All we know of it is, from the singing of their Chorus; and that too is so uncertain, that in some of their plays we have reason to conjecture they sung more than five times. Aristotle indeed divides the integral parts of a play into four ⟨Ar/48; Sg/102; Jn/200⟩.[9] First, the *protasis*, or entrance, which gives light only to the characters of the persons, and proceeds very

---

[9] These structural divisions are not Aristotle's (for which see *Poetics*, Book 12) but Scaliger's.

little into any part of the action. Secondly, the *epitasis*, or working up of the plot; where the play grows warmer, the design or action of it is drawing on, and you see something promising that it will come to pass. Thirdly, the *catastasis*, called by the Romans *status*, the height and full growth of the play: we may call it properly the counterturn, which destroys that expectation, imbroils the action in new difficulties, and leaves you far distant from that hope in which it found you; as you may have observed in a violent stream resisted by a narrow passage, – it runs round to an eddy, and carries back the waters with more swiftness than it brought them on. Lastly, the *catastrophe*, which the Grecians called *lusis*, the French *le dénouement*, and we the discovery or unravelling of the plot: there you see all things settling again upon their first foundations; and, the obstacles which hindered the design or action of the play once removed, it ends with that resemblance of truth and nature, that the audience are satisfied with the conduct of it. Thus this great man delivered to us the image of a play; and I must confess it is so lively, that from thence much light has been derived to the forming it more perfectly into acts and scenes: but what poet first limited to five the number of acts, I know not; only we see it so firmly established in the time of Horace, that he gives it for a rule in comedy: *Neu brevior quinto, neu sit productior actu* [Neither shorter nor longer than five acts] ⟨Hr/69:189⟩. So that you see the Grecians cannot be said to have consummated this art; writing rather by entrances, than by acts, and having rather a general indigested notion of a play, than knowing how and where to bestow the particular graces of it.

'But since the Spaniards at this day allow but three acts, which they call *jornadas* ⟨Nh/113⟩, to a play, and the Italians in many of theirs follow them, when I condemn the Ancients, I declare it is not altogether because they have not five acts to every play, but because they have not confined themselves to one certain number: it is building an house without a model; and when they succeeded in such undertakings, they ought to have sacrificed to Fortune, not to the Muses.

'Next, for the plot, which Aristotle called *to* [= *ho*] *mythos* and often *ton pragmaton synthesis* [the arrangement of incidents] ⟨Ar/42⟩, and from him the Romans *fabula*, it has already been judiciously observed by a late writer, that in their tragedies it was only some tale derived from Thebes or Troy, or at least something that happened in those two ages; which was worn so threadbare by the pens of all the epic poets, and even by tradition itself of the talkative Greeklings (as Ben Jonson calls them) that before it came upon the stage, it was already known to all the audience: and the people, so soon as ever they heard the name of Oedipus, knew as well as the poet, that he had killed his father by a mistake, and committed incest with his mother, before the play; that they were now to hear of a great plague, and oracle, and the ghost of Laius: so that they sat with a yawning kind of expectation, till he was to come with his eyes pulled out, and speak a hundred or more verses in a tragic tone, in complaint of his misfortunes. But one Oedipus, Hercules, or Medea, had been tolerable: poor people, they scaped not so good cheap; they had still the *chapon bouillé* [leftovers] set before them, till their appetites were cloyed with the same dish, and, the novelty being gone, the pleasure vanished; so that one main end of dramatic poesy in its definition, which was to cause delight, was of consequence destroyed.

'In their comedies, the Romans generally borrowed their plots from the Greek poets; and theirs was commonly a little girl stolen or wandered from her parents, brought back unknown to the city, there got with child by some lewd young fellow, who, by the help of his servant cheats his father; and when her time comes, to cry *Juno Lucina, fer opem* [Juno, Goddess of Childbirth, help me!], one or other sees a little box or cabinet which was carried away with her, and so discovers her to her friends, if some god do not prevent it, by coming down in a machine, and taking the thanks of it to himself.

'By the plot you may guess much of the characters of the persons. An old father, who would willingly, before he dies, see his son well married; his debauched son, kind in his nature to his mistress, but miserably in want of money; a servant or slave, who has so much wit to strike in with him, and help to dupe his father; a braggadochio captain, a parasite, and a lady of pleasure.

'As for the poor honest maid, on whom the story is built, and who ought to be one of the principal actors in the play, she is commonly a mute in it: she has the breeding of the old Elizabethan way, which was for maids to be seen and not to be heard; and it is enough you know she is willing to be married, when the fifth act requires it.

'These are plots built after the Italian mode of houses; you see through them all at once: the characters are indeed the imitations of Nature, but so narrow, as if they had imitated only an eye or an hand, and did not dare to venture on the lines of a face, or the proportion of a body.

'But in how strait a compass soever they have bounded their plots and characters, we will pass it by, if they have regularly pursued them, and perfectly observed those three unities of time, place, and action; the knowledge of which you say is derived to us from them. But in the first place give me leave to tell you, that the unity of place, however it might be practised by them, was never any of their rules: we neither find it in Aristotle, Horace, or any who have written of it, till in our age the French poets first made it a precept of the stage ⟨Cv/132; In/6⟩.[10] The unity of time, even Terence himself (who was the best and most regular of them) has neglected: his *Heautontimorumenos*, or *Self-Punisher*, takes up visible two days, says Scaliger,[11] the two first acts concluding the first day, the

[10] Not the French but Castelvetro.
[11] Scaliger, *Poetics* 6.3.

three last the day ensuing ⟨Sy/180⟩; and Euripides, in tying himself to one day, has committed an absurdity never to be forgiven him; for in one of his tragedies[12] he has made Theseus go from Athens to Thebes, which was about forty English miles, under the walls of it to give battle, and appear victorious in the next act; and yet, from the time of his departure to the return of the Nuntius, who gives the relation of his victory, Aethra and the Chorus have but thirty-six verses; which is not for every mile a verse ⟨Cn/249⟩.

'The like error is evident in Terence his *Eunuch*, when Laches, the old man, enters by mistake into the house of Thais; where, betwixt his exit and the entrance of Pythias, who comes to give ample relation of the disorders he has raised within, Parmeno, who was left upon the stage, has not above five lines to speak. *C'est bien employer un temps si court* [That is a lot of business for such a short time], says the French poet ⟨Cn/249⟩, who furnished me with one of the observations: and almost all their tragedies will afford us examples of like nature.

''Tis true, they have kept the continuity, or, as you called it, *liaison des scènes* ⟨Cn/249⟩, somewhat better: two do not perpetually come in together, talk, and go out together; and other two succeed them, which the English call by the name of single scenes; but the reason is, because they have seldom above two or three scenes, properly so called, in every act; for it is to be accounted a new scene, not only every time the stage is empty; but every person who enters, though to others, makes it so; because he introduces a new business. Now the plots of their plays being narrow, and the persons few, one of their acts was written in a less compass than one of our well-wrought scenes; and yet they are often deficient even in this. ...

'But as they have failed both in the laying of their plots, and in the management of them, swerving from the rules of their own art by misrepresenting Nature to us, in which they have ill satisfied one intention of a play, which was delight; so in the instructive part they have erred worse: instead of punishing vice and rewarding virtue, they have often shown a prosperous wickedness, and an unhappy piety: they have set before us a bloody image of revenge in Medea, and given her dragons to convey her safe from punishment; a Priam and Astyanax murdered, and Cassandra ravished, and the lust and murder ending in the victory of him who acted them: in short, there is no indecorum in any of our modern plays, which if I would excuse, I could not shadow with some authority from the Ancients. ...

' ... for love-scenes, you will find few among them; their tragic poets dealt not with that soft passion, but with lust, cruelty, revenge, ambition, and those bloody actions they produced; which were more capable of raising horror than compassion in an audience: leaving love untouched,

---

12 *The Suppliant Women*, ⟨Cn/249, n. 21⟩.

whose gentleness would have tempered them, which is the most frequent of all the passions, and which, being the private concernment of every person, is soothed by viewing its own image in a public entertainment.

'Among their comedies, we find a scene or two of tenderness, and that where you would least expect it, in Plautus; but to speak generally, their lovers say little, when they see each other, but *anima mea, vita mea; zoe kai psyche* [my life, my love],[13] as the women in Juvenal's time used to cry out in the fury of their kindness. Any sudden gust of passion (as an ecstasy of love in an unexpected meeting) cannot better be expressed than in a word and a sigh, breaking one another. Nature is dumb on such occasions; and to make her speak, would be to represent her unlike herself. But there are a thousand other concernments of lovers, as jealousy, complaints, contrivances, and the like, where not to open their minds at large to each other, were to be wanting to their own love, and to the expectation of the audience; who watch the movement of their minds, as much as the changes of their fortunes. For the imaging of the first is properly the work of a poet; the latter he borrows from the historian.'

Eugenius was proceeding in that part of his discourse, when Crites interrupted him. 'I see', said he, 'Eugenius and I are never like to have this question decided betwixt us; for he maintains the Moderns have acquired a new perfection in writing; I can only grant they have altered the mode of it. ... So in their love-scenes, of which Eugenius spoke last, the Ancients were more hearty, we more talkative: they writ love as it was then the mode to make it .... '

This moderation of Crites, as it was pleasing to all the company, so it put an end to that dispute; which Eugenius, who seemed to have the better of the argument, would urge no farther: but Lisideius, after he had acknowledged himself of Eugenius his opinion concerning the Ancients, yet told him, he had forborne, till his discourse were ended, to ask him why he preferred the English plays above those of other nations? and whether we ought not to submit our stage to the exactness of our next neighbours?

'Though', said Eugenius, 'I am at all times ready to defend the honour of my country against the French, and to maintain, we are as well able to vanquish them with our pens, as our ancestors have been with their swords; yet, if you please', added he, looking upon Neander, 'I will commit this cause to my friend's management; his opinion of our plays is the same with mine: and besides, there is no reason that Crites and I, who have now left the stage, should re-enter so suddenly upon it; which is against the laws of comedy.'

'If the question had been stated', replied Lisideius, 'who had writ best, the French or English, forty years ago, I should have been of your opinion, and adjudged the honour to our own nation; but since that time' (said he,

---

[13] Juvenal, *Satire* 6.195.

turning towards Neander) 'we have been so long together bad Englishmen, that we had not leisure to be good poets. Beaumont, Fletcher, and Jonson (who were only capable of bringing us to that degree of perfection which we have) were just then leaving the world;[14] as if (in an age of so much horror) wit, and those milder studies of humanity, had no farther business among us. But the Muses, who ever follow peace, went to plant in another country: it was then that the great Cardinal of Richelieu began to take them into his protection; and that, by his encouragement, Corneille, and some other Frenchmen, reformed their theatre, which before was as much below ours, as it now surpasses it and the rest of Europe ⟨Cd/213⟩. But because Crites in his discourse for the Ancients has prevented[15] me, by observing many rules of the stage which the Moderns have borrowed from them, I shall only, in short, demand of you, whether you are not convinced that of all nations the French have best observed them? In the unity of time you find them so scrupulous, that it yet remains a dispute among their poets, whether the artificial day of twelve hours, more or less, be not meant by Aristotle, rather than the natural one of twenty-four ⟨Lp/187; Cn/249⟩; and consequently, whether all plays ought not to be reduced into that compass. This I can testify, that in all their dramas writ within these last twenty years and upwards, I have not observed any that have extended the time to thirty hours: in the unity of place they are full as scrupulous; for many of their critics limit it to that very spot of ground where the play is supposed to begin; none of them exceed the compass of the same town or city. The unity of action in all plays is yet more conspicuous; for they do not burden them with under-plots, as the English do: which is the reason why many scenes of our tragi-comedies carry on a design that is nothing of kin to the main plot; and that we see two distinct webs in a play, like those in ill-wrought stuffs; and two actions, that is, two plays, carried on together, to the confounding of the audience; who, before they are warm in their concernments for one part, are diverted to another; and by that means espouse the interest of neither. From hence likewise it arises, that the one half of our actors are not known to the other. They keep their distances, as if they were Montagues and Capulets, and seldom begin an acquaintance till the last scene of the fifth act, when they are all to meet upon the stage. There is no theatre in the world has any thing so absurd as the English tragi-comedy; 'tis a drama of our own invention, and the fashion of it is enough to proclaim it so; here a course of mirth, there another of sadness and passion, a third of honour, and a duel: thus, in two hours and a half, we run through all the fits of Bedlam. The French affords you as much variety on the same day, but they do it not so unseasonably, or *mal propos*, as we: our poets present you the play and the farce together; and our stages still retain somewhat of the original civility of the Red

---

[14] All died before the Civil War: Beaumont in 1616; Fletcher in 1625; Jonson in 1637.
[15] "prevented" = anticipated, preceded.

Bull:[16] *Atque ursum et pugiles media inter carmina poscunt* [And even demand a bear and boxers in the middle of a song].[17] The end of tragedies or serious plays, says Aristotle ⟨Ar/42⟩, is to beget admiration, compassion, or concernment;[18] but are not mirth and compassion things incompatible ⟨Sy/181⟩? and is it not evident that the poet must of necessity destroy the former by intermingling of the latter? that is, he must ruin the sole end and object of his tragedy, to introduce somewhat that is forced into it, and is not of the body of it. Would you not think that physician mad, who, having prescribed a purge, should immediately order you to take restringents?

'But to leave our plays, and return to theirs. I have noted one great advantage they have had in the plotting of their tragedies; that is, they are always grounded upon some known history: according to that of Horace, *Ex noto fictum carmen sequar* [A song made from the familiar is what I aim for] ⟨Hr/71:240⟩; and in that they have so imitated the Ancients, that they have surpassed them. For the Ancients, as was observed before, took for the foundation of their plays some poetical fiction, such as under that consideration could move but little concernment in the audience, because they already knew the event of it. But the French goes farther: *Atque ita mentitur, sic veris falsa remiscet, / Primo ne medium, medio ne discrepet imum* [And he feigns and mixes true and false in such a way that the beginning is not discordant with the middle, nor the middle with the end] ⟨Hr/68:151–52⟩. He so interweaves truth with probable fiction, that he puts a pleasing fallacy upon us; mends the intrigues of fate, and dispenses with the severity of history, to reward that virtue which has been rendered to us there unfortunate. ... On the other side, if you consider the historical plays of Shakespeare, they are rather so many chronicles of kings, or the business many times of thirty or forty years, cramped into a representation of two hours and a half; which is not to imitate or paint Nature, but rather to draw her in miniature, to take her in little; to look upon her through the wrong end of a perspective, and receive her images not only much less, but infinitely more imperfect than the life: this, instead of making a play delightful, renders it ridiculous. ...

'Another thing in which the French differ from us and from the Spaniards, is, that they do not embarrass, or cumber themselves with too much plot; they only represent so much of a story as will constitute one whole and great action sufficient for a play; we, who undertake more, do but multiply adventures; which, not being produced from one another, as effects from causes, but barely following, constitute many actions in the drama, and consequently make it many plays.

[16] A London theatre notorious for coarse presentations and disorder.

[17] Horace, *Epistles* 2.1.185–86.

[18] In the Renaissance, admiration was often made an equal third with Aristotle's pity and fear. "Compassion" here corresponds with "pity," but "concernment" is a more inclusive term than "fear," embracing other kinds of audience involvement.

'But by pursuing closely one argument, which is not cloyed with many turns, the French have gained more liberty for verse, in which they write; they have leisure to dwell on a subject which deserves it; and to represent the passions (which we have acknowledged to be the poet's work), without being hurried from one thing to another, as we are in the plays of Calderón, which we have seen lately upon our theatres, under the name of Spanish plots.[19] . . .

'But . . . the French writers . . . do not burden themselves too much with plot, which has been reproached to them by an *ingenious person*[20] of our nation as a fault; for, he says, they commonly make but one person considerable in a play; they dwell on him, and his concernments, while the rest of the persons are only subservient to set him off. . . .

'But, if he would have us to imagine, that in exalting one character the rest of them are neglected, and that all of them have not some share or other in the action of the play, I would desire him to produce any of Corneille's tragedies, wherein every person, like so many servants in a well-governed family, has not some employment, and who is not necessary to the carrying on of the plot, or at least to your understanding of it.

'There are indeed some protatic[21] persons in the Ancients, whom they make use of in their plays, either to hear or give relation: but the French ⟨Cn/248⟩ avoid this with great address, making their narrations only to, or by such, who are some way interested[22] in the main design. And now I am speaking of relations, I cannot take a fitter opportunity to add this in favour of the French, that they often use them with better judgement and more *propos* than the English do. Not that I commend narrations in general, – but there are two sorts of them. One, of those things which are antecedent to the play, and are related to make the conduct of it more clear to us. But 'tis a fault to choose such subjects for the stage as will force us on that rock, because we see they are seldom listened to by the audience, and that is many times the ruin of the play; for, being once let pass without attention, the audience can never recover themselves to understand the plot: and indeed it is somewhat unreasonable that they should be put to so much trouble, as that, to comprehend what passes in their sight, they must have recourse to what was done, perhaps, ten or twenty years ago.

'But there is another sort of relations, that is, of things happening in the

---

[19] Sir Samuel Tuke (d. 1674) based his very popular *The Adventures of Five Hours* on *Los Empeños de seis horas* by Antonio Coello y Ochoa (1611–82) and Calderón de la Barca (1600–81). Tuke's play, performed in January 1663, was followed by a number of adaptations of Spanish plays by other hands. Dryden's own *An Evening's Love, or the Mock-Astrologer* (1668) itself derives from Calderón's *El Astrólogo fingido* via a French adaptation by Thomas Corneille (see n. 25, below, this chapter).

[20] Thomas Spratt in his *Observations* (1665), pp. 249–50: "The French, for the most part, take only one, or two great men, and chiefly insist on some one remarkable accident of their story."

[21] Scaliger (*Poetices* 1.13) uses this term for characters appearing only in the *protasis* or exposition. Dryden, who spells it "protatick," probably took the term from Corneille.

[22] "interested" = interested; having a concern with or right in.

action of the play, and supposed to be done behind the scenes; and this is many times most convenient and beautiful; for by it the French avoid the tumult to which we are subject in England, by representing duels, battles and the like; which renders our stage too like the theatres where they fight prizes. For what is more ridiculous than to represent an army with a drum and five men behind it; all which the hero of the other side is to drive in before him; or to see a duel fought, and one slain with two or three thrusts of the foils, which we know are so blunted, that we might give a man an hour to kill another in good earnest with them.

'I have observed that in all our tragedies, the audience cannot forbear laughing when the actors are to die; it is the most comic part of the whole play. All *passions* may be lively represented on the stage, if to the well-writing of them the actor supplies a good commanded voice, and limbs that move easily, and without stiffness; but there are many *actions* which can never be imitated to a just height: dying especially is a thing which none but a Roman gladiator could naturally perform on the stage, when he did not imitate or represent but do it; and therefore it is better to omit the representation of it.

'The words of a good writer, which describe it lively, will make a deeper impression of belief in us than all the actor can insinuate into us, when he seems to fall dead before us; as a poet in the description of a beautiful garden, or a meadow, will please our imagination more than the place itself can please our sight. When we see death represented, we are convinced it is but fiction; but when we hear it related, our eyes, the strongest witnesses, are wanting, which might have undeceived us; and we are all willing to favour the sleight, when the poet does not too grossly impose upon us. They therefore who imagine these relations would make no concernment in the audience are deceived by confounding them with the other, which are of things antecedent to the play: those are made often in cold blood, as I may say, to the audience; but these are warmed with our concernments, which were before awakened in the play. What the philosophers say of motion, that, when it is once begun, it continues of itself, and will do so to eternity, without some stop put to it, is clearly true on this occasion: the soul, being already moved with the characters and fortunes of those imaginary persons, continues going of its own accord; and we are no more weary to hear what becomes of them when they are not on the stage, than we are to listen to the news of an absent mistress. But it is objected, that if one part of the play may be related, why not all ⟨Hr/ 69:180–84⟩?[23] I answer, some parts of the action are more fit to be

---

[23] " ... [Horace] directly declares his judgement that everything makes more impression presented than related: nor, indeed, can anyone rationally assert the contrary; for if they affirm otherwise, they do by consequence maintain, that the whole play might as well be related as acted" (Sir Robert Howard, Preface to *Four New Plays* [1665], in Spingarn 1908a, II:100).

represented, some to be related. Corneille says judiciously, that the poet is not obliged to expose to view all particular actions which conduce to the principal; he ought to select such of them to be seen, which will appear with the greatest beauty, either by the magnificence of the show, or the vehemence of passions which they produce, or some other charm which they have in them; and let the rest arrive to the audience by narration ⟨Cn/248⟩. 'Tis a great mistake in us to believe the French present no part of the action on the stage; every alteration or crossing of a design, every new-sprung passion, and turn of it, is a part of the action, and much the noblest, except we conceive nothing to be action till the players come to blows; as if the painting of the hero's mind were not more properly the poet's work than the strength of his body. . . .

'But I find I have been too long in this discourse, since the French have many other excellencies not common to us; as that you never see any of their plays end with a conversation, or simple change of will, which is the ordinary way in which our poets use to end theirs ⟨Cn/241⟩.' . . .

Lisideius concluded . . . and Neander, after a little pause, thus answered him:

'I shall grant Lisideius, without much dispute, a great part of what he has urged against us; for I acknowledge that the French contrive their plots more regularly, and observe the laws of comedy, and decorum of the stage (to speak generally), with more exactness than the English. Farther, I deny not but that he has taxed us justly in some irregularities of ours, which he has mentioned; yet, after all, I am of opinion that neither our faults nor their virtues are considerable enough to place them above us.

'For the lively imitation of Nature being in the definition of a play, those which best fulfil that law ought to be esteemed superior to the others. 'Tis true, those beauties of the French poesy are such as will raise perfection higher where it is, but are not sufficient to give it where it is not: they are indeed the beauties of a statue, but not of a man, because not animated with the soul of Poesy, which is imitation of humour and passions: and this Lisideius himself, or any other, however biassed to their party, cannot but acknowledge, if he will either compare the humours ⟨Jn/197; Cg/298⟩ of our comedies, or the characters of our serious plays with theirs. He who will look upon theirs which have been written till these last ten years, or thereabouts, will find it an hard matter to pick out two or three passable humours amongst them. Corneille himself, their arch-poet, what has he produced except *The Liar*, and you know how it was cried up in France; but when it came upon the English stage, though well translated,[24] and that part of Dorant acted to so much advantage by Mr. Hart as I am confident it never received in its own country, the most favourable to it would not put

---

[24] *Le Menteur* was anonymously translated as *The Mistaken Beauty, or the Liar*. In the 1684 edition of the *Essay*, Dryden omitted the name of the actor, Charles Hart, who had died in 1683.

it in competition with many of Fletcher's or Ben Jonson's. In the rest of Corneille's comedies you have little humour; he tells you himself, his way is, first to show two lovers in good intelligence with each other; in the working up of the play to embroil them by some mistake, and in the latter end to clear it, and reconcile them ⟨Cn/241⟩.

'But of late years Molière, the younger Corneille, Quinault,[25] and some others, have been imitating afar off the quick turns and graces of the English stage. They have mixed their serious plays with mirth, like our tragi-comedies, since the death of Cardinal Richelieu; which Lisideius and many others not observing, have commended that in them for a virtue which they themselves no longer practise. . . .

' . . . As for their new way of mingling mirth with serious plot, I do not, with Lisideius, condemn the thing, though I cannot approve their manner of doing it. He tells us, we cannot so speedily recollect ourselves after a scene of great passion and concernment, as to pass to another of mirth and humour, and to enjoy it with any relish: but why should he imagine the soul of man more heavy than his senses? Does not the eye pass from an unpleasant object to a pleasant in a much shorter time than is required to this? and does not the unpleasantness of the first commend the beauty of the latter? The old rule of logic might have convinced him, that contraries, when placed near, set off each other. A continued gravity keeps the spirit too much bent; we must refresh it sometimes, as we bait[26] in a journey,[27] that we may go on with greater ease. A scene of mirth, mixed with tragedy, has the same effect upon us which our music has betwixt the acts; and which we find a relief to us from the best plots and language of the stage, if the discourse have been long. I must therefore have stronger arguments, ere I am convinced that compassion and mirth in the same subject destroy each other; and in the mean time cannot but conclude, to the honour of our nation, that we have invented, increased, and perfected a more pleasant way of writing for the stage, than was ever known to the ancients or moderns of any nation, which is tragi-comedy.

'And this leads me to wonder why Lisideius and many others should cry up the barrenness of the French plots, above the variety and copiousness of the English. Their plots are single; they carry on one design, which is pushed forward by all the actors, every scene in the play contributing and moving towards it. Our plays, besides the main design, have underplots or by-concernments, of less considerable persons and intrigues, which are

---

[25] Thomas Corneille (1625–1709) was the younger brother of Pierre, and a prolific playwright, some of whose comedies were adapted from the Spanish. Philippe Quinault (1635–88) wrote tragedies, very successful comedies and opera libretti. Dryden, in his adaptation of Molière's L'Etourdi, drew also on Quinault's L'Amant indiscret.

[26] "bait" = abate (our efforts).

[27] Both the phrase "bait in a journey" and the example of music between the acts suggest that Dryden has in mind an elaboration of the Spanish term jornada, which is used earlier in the Essay.

carried on with the motion of the main plot; as they say the orb of the fixed stars, and those of the planets, though they have motions of their own, are whirled about by the motion of the *Primum Mobile*, in which they are contained. That similitude expresses much of the English stage; for if contrary notions may be found in Nature to agree; if a planet can go east and west at the same time, one way by virtue of his own motion, the other by the force of the First Mover, it will not be difficult to imagine how the under-plot, which is only different, not contrary to the great design, may naturally be conducted along with it.

'Eugenius[28] has already shown us, from the confession of the French poets, that the unity of action is sufficiently preserved, if all the imperfect actions of the play are conducing to the main design; but when those petty intrigues of a play are so ill ordered, that they have no coherence with the other, I must grant that Lisideius has reason to tax that want of due connection; for co-ordination in a play is as dangerous and unnatural as in a state. In the mean time he must acknowledge our variety, if well ordered, will afford a greater pleasure to the audience.

'As for his other argument, that by pursuing one single theme they gain an advantage to express and work up the passions, I wish any example he could bring from them would make it good; for I confess their verses are to me the coldest I have ever read. Neither, indeed, is it possible for them, in the way they take, so to express passion, as that the effects of it should appear in the concernment of the audience, their speeches being so many declamations, which tire us with the length; so that instead of persuading us to grieve for their imaginary heroes, we are concerned for our own trouble, as we are in tedious visits of bad company; we are in pain till they are gone. When the French stage came to be reformed by Cardinal Richelieu, those long harangues were introduced, to comply with the gravity of a churchman. Look upon the *Cinna* and the *Pompey*; they are not so properly to be called plays, as long discourses of reason of state; and *Polieucte* in matters of religion is as solemn as the long stops upon our organs.[29] Since that time it is grown into a custom, and their actors speak by the hour-glass like our parsons;[30] nay, they account it the grace of their parts, and think themselves disparaged by the poet, if they may not twice or thrice in a play entertain the audience with a speech of an hundred lines. I deny not that this may suit well enough with the French; for as we, who are a more sullen people, come to be diverted at our plays, so they, who are of an airy and gay temper, come thither to make themselves more serious: and this I conceive to be one reason why comedies are more pleasing to us, and tragedies to them. But to speak generally: it cannot be

28 Crites, in fact.
29 The three plays are by Pierre Corneille.
30 An hour-glass was the artificial means sometimes used to control the length of sermons in the seventeenth century.

denied that short speeches and replies are more apt to move the passions and beget concernment in us, than the other; for it is unnatural for anyone in a gust of passion to speak long together, or for another in the same condition to suffer him, without interruption. Grief and passion are like floods raised in little brooks by a sudden rain; they are quickly up; and if the concernment be poured unexpectedly in upon us, it overflows us: but a long sober shower gives them leisure to run out as they came in, without troubling the ordinary current. As for Comedy, repartee is one of its chiefest graces; the greatest pleasure of the audience is a chace of wit, kept up on both sides, and swiftly managed. And this our forefathers, if not we, have had in Fletcher's plays, to a much higher degree of perfection than the French poets can, reasonably, hope to reach. . . .

'But to . . . pass to the latter part of Lisideius his discourse, which concerns relations: I must acknowledge with him, that the French have reason to hide that part of the action which would occasion too much tumult on the stage, and to choose rather to have it made known by narration to the audience. Farther, I think it very convenient, for the reasons he has given, that all incredible actions were removed; but, whether custom has so insinuated itself into our countrymen, or Nature has so formed them to fierceness, I know not; but they will scarcely suffer combats and other objects of horror to be taken from them. And indeed, the indecency of tumults is all which can be objected against fighting: for why may not our imagination as well suffer itself to be deluded with the probability of it, as with any other thing in the play? For my part, I can with as great ease persuade myself that the blows are given in good earnest, as I can, that they who strike them are kings or princes, or those persons which they represent. . . . But for death, that it ought not to be represented, I have, besides the arguments alleged by Lisideius, the authority of Ben Jonson, who has forborne it in his tragedies; for both the death of Sejanus and Catiline are related . . . . To conclude this subject of relations; if we are to be blamed for showing too much of the action, the French are as faulty for discovering too little of it: a mean betwixt both should be observed by every judicious writer, so as the audience may neither be left unsatisfied by not seeing what is beautiful, or shocked by beholding what is either incredible or undecent.

'I hope I have already proved in this discourse, that though we are not altogether so punctual as the French, in observing the laws of Comedy, yet our errors are so few, and little, and those things wherein we excel them so considerable, that we ought of right to be preferred before them. But what will Lisideius say, if they themselves acknowledge they are too strictly bounded by those laws for breaking which he has blamed the English? I will allege Corneille's words, as I find them in the end of his "Discourse of the Three Unities": – *Il est facile aux speculatifs d'estre severes, etc.* " 'Tis easy for speculative persons to judge severely; but if they would produce to public view ten or twelve pieces of this nature, they would perhaps give more latitude to the rules than I have done, when, by experience, they had known how much we are limited and constrained by them, and how many beauties of the stage they banished from it."[31] To illustrate a little of what he has said: by their servile observations of the unities of time and place, and integrity of scenes, they have brought on themselves that dearth of plot, and narrowness of imagination, which may be observed in all their plays. ...

' ... I dare boldly affirm these two things of the English drama; – first, that we have many plays of ours as regular as any of theirs, and which, besides, have more variety of plot and characters; and secondly, that in most of the irregular plays of Shakespeare or Fletcher (for Ben Jonson's are for the most part regular) there is a more masculine fancy and greater spirit in the writing, than there is in any of the French. I could produce, even in Shakespeare's and Fletcher's works, some plays which are almost exactly formed; as *The Merry Wives of Windsor*, and *The Scornful Lady*: but because (generally speaking) Shakespeare, who writ first, did not perfectly observe the laws of Comedy, and Fletcher, who came nearer to perfection, yet through carelessness made many faults, I will take the pattern of a perfect play from Ben Jonson, who was a careful and learned observer of the dramatic laws, and from all his comedies I shall select *The Silent Woman*; of which I will make a short examen, according to those rules which the French observe.'

As Neander was beginning to examine *The Silent Woman*, Eugenius, earnestly regarding him, 'I beseech you, Neander', said he, 'gratify the company, and me in particular, so far, as before you speak of the play, to give us a character of the author; and tell us frankly your opinion, whether you do not think all writers, both French and English, ought to give place to him.'

'I fear', replied Neander, 'that in obeying your commands I shall draw some envy on myself. Besides, in performing them, it will be first necessary to speak somewhat of Shakespeare and Fletcher, his rivals in poesy; and one of them, in my opinion, at least his equal, perhaps his superior.

'To begin, then, with Shakespeare. He was the man who of all modern, and perhaps ancient poets, had the largest and most comprehensive soul. All the images of Nature were still present to him, and he drew them, not laboriously, but luckily; when he describes any thing, you more than see it, you feel it too. Those who accuse him to have wanted learning, give him the greater commendation: he was naturally learned; he needed not the spectacles of books to read Nature; he looked inwards, and found her there. I cannot say he is every where alike; were he so, I should do him injury to compare him with the greatest of mankind. He is many times flat, insipid;

[31] See Corneille/Barnwell 1965, 79.

his comic wit degenerating into clenches, his serious swelling into bombast. But he is always great, when some great occasion is presented to him; no man can say he ever had a fit subject for his wit, and did not then raise himself as high above the rest of the poets . . . .

'Beaumont and Fletcher, of whom I am next to speak, had, with the advantage of Shakespeare's wit, which was their precedent, great natural gifts, improved by study . . . . Their plots were generally more regular than Shakespeare's, especially those which were made before Beaumont's death; and they understood and imitated the conversation of gentlemen much better; whose wild debaucheries, and quickness of wit in repartees, no poet before them could paint as they have done. Humour, which Ben Jonson derived from particular persons, they made it not their business to describe: they represented all the passions very lively, but above all, love. I am apt to believe the English language in them arrived to its highest perfection: what words have since been taken in, are rather superfluous than ornamental. Their plays are now the most pleasant and frequent entertainments of the stage; two of theirs being acted through the year for one of Shakespeare's or Jonson's: the reason is, because there is a certain gaiety in their comedies, and pathos in their more serious plays, which suits generally with all men's humours. Shakespeare's language is likewise a little obsolete, and Ben Jonson's wit comes short of theirs.

'As for Jonson, to whose character I am now arrived, if we look upon him while he was himself (for his last plays were but his dotages), I think him the most learned and judicious writer which any theatre ever had. He was a most severe judge of himself, as well as others. One cannot say he wanted wit, but rather that he was frugal of it. In his works you find little to retrench or alter. Wit, and language, and humour also in some measure, we had before him; but something of art was wanting to the Drama, till he came. He managed his strength to more advantage than any who preceded him. You seldom find him making love[32] in any of his scenes, or endeavouring to move the passions; his genius was too sullen and saturnine to do it gracefully, especially when he knew he came after those who had performed both to such an height. Humour was his proper sphere; and in that he delighted most to represent mechanic[33] people. He was deeply conversant in the Ancients, both Greek and Latin, and he borrowed boldly from them: there is scarce a poet or historian among the Roman authors of those times whom he has not translated in *Sejanus* and *Cataline*. But he has done his robberies so openly, that one may see he fears not to be taxed by any law. He invades authors like a monarch; and what would be theft in other poets, is only victory in him. With the spoils of these writers he so represents old Rome to us, in its rite, ceremonies and customs, that if one of their poets had written either of his tragedies, we had seen less of it than in

[32] "making love" = dramatizing courtship or wooing.
[33] "mechanic" = vulgar, crude.

him. If there was any fault in his language, 'twas that he weaved it too closely and laboriously, in his comedies especially: perhaps too, he did a little too much Romanize our tongue, leaving the words which he translated almost as much Latin as he found them: wherein, though he learnedly followed their language, he did not enough comply with the idiom of ours. If I would compare him with Shakespeare, I must acknowledge him the more correct poet, but Shakespeare the greater wit. Shakespeare was the Homer, or father of our dramatic poets; Jonson was the Virgil, the pattern of elaborate writing; I admire him, but I love Shakespeare. To conclude of him, as he has given us the most correct plays, so in the precepts which he has laid down in his *Discoveries*, we have as many and profitable rules for perfecting the stage, as any wherewith the French can furnish us.

'Having thus spoken of the author, I proceed to the examination of his comedy, *The Silent Woman*.

Examen of the Silent Woman

'To begin first with the length of the action; it is so far from exceeding the compass of a natural day, that it takes up not an artificial one. 'Tis all included in the limits of three hours and a half, which is no more than is required for the presentment on the stage. A beauty perhaps not much observed; if it had, we should not have looked on the Spanish translation of *Five Hours* with so much wonder. The scene of it is laid in London; the latitude of place is almost as little as you can imagine; for it lies all within the compass of two houses, and after the first act, in one.[34] The continuity of scenes[35] is observed more than in any of our plays, except his own *Fox* and *Alchemist*. They are not broken above twice or thrice at most in the whole comedy; and in the two best of Corneille's plays, the *Cid* and *Cinna*, they are interrupted once. The action of the play is entirely one; the end or aim of which is the settling Morose's estate on Dauphine. The intrigue of it is the greatest and most noble of any pure unmixed comedy in any language; you see in it many persons of various characters and humours ⟨Jn/197; Cg/298⟩, and all delightful: at first, Morose, or an old man, to whom all noise but his own talking is offensive. Some who would be thought critics, say this humour of his is forced: but to remove that objection, we may consider him first to be naturally of a delicate hearing, as many are, to whom all sharp sounds are unpleasant; and secondly, we may attribute much of it to the peevishness of his age, or the wayward authority of an old man in his own house, where he may make himself obeyed; and to this the poet seems to allude in his name Morose. Besides this, I am assured from divers persons, that Ben Jonson was actually

---

[34] There are actually three houses and six locations.
[35] *Liaison des scènes* is not evident in this play, though it is in parts of the other two plays mentioned.

acquainted with such a man, one altogether ridiculous as he is here represented. Others say, it is not enough to find one man of such an humour; it must be common to more, and the more common the more natural. To prove this, they instance the best of comical characters, Falstaff: there are many men resembling him; old, fat, merry, cowardly, drunken, amorous, vain and lying. But to convince these people, I need but tell them, that humour is the ridiculous extravagance of conversation, wherein one man differs from all others. If then it be common, or communicated to many, how differs it from the other men's? or what indeed causes it to be ridiculous so much as the singularity of it? As for Falstaff, he is not properly one humour, but a miscellany of humours or images, drawn from so many several men: that says *praeter expectatum*, unexpected by the audience; his quick evasions, when you imagine him surprised, which, as they are extremely diverting of themselves, so receive a great addition from his person; for the very sight of such an unwieldy old debauched fellow is a comedy alone. And here, having a place so proper for it, I cannot but enlarge somewhat upon this subject of humour into which I am fallen. The Ancients had little of it in their comedies; for the *to geloion* [the laughable] of the Old Comedy, of which Aristophanes was chief, was not so much to imitate a man, as to make the people laugh at some odd conceit, which had commonly somewhat of unnatural or obscene in it. Thus, when you see Socrates brought upon the stage, you are not to imagine him made ridiculous by the imitation of his actions, but rather by making him perform something very unlike himself; something so childish and absurd, as by comparing it with the gravity of the true Socrates, makes a ridiculous object for the spectators ⟨Jn/195⟩.[36] In their New Comedy which succeeded, the poets sought indeed to express the *ethos*, as in their tragedies the *pathos* of mankind. But this *ethos* contained only the general characters of men and manners; as old men, lovers, serving-men, courtesans, parasites, and such other persons as we see in their comedies; all which they made alike: that is, one old man or father, one lover, one courtesan, so like another, as if the first of them had begot the rest of every sort: *Ex homine hunc natum dicas?* [Do you say he is of human birth?].[37] The same custom they observed likewise in their tragedies. As for the French, though they have the word *humeur* among them, yet they have small use of it in their comedies or farces; they being but ill imitations of the *ridiculum*, or that which stirred up laughter in the Old Comedy. But among the English 'tis otherwise: where by humour is meant some extravagant habit, passion, or affection, particular (as I said before) to some one person, by the oddness of which, he is immediately distinguished from the rest of men; which being lively and naturally represented, most frequently begets that malicious pleasure in the audience which is testified by laughter; as all

[36] As in Aristophanes' *The Clouds* (218ff.).
[37] Terence, *Eunuch*, line 460.

things which are deviations from customs are ever the aptest to produce it: though by the way this laughter is only accidental, as the person represented is fantastic or bizarre; but pleasure is essential to it, as the imitation of what is natural. The description of these humours, drawn from the knowledge and observation of particular persons, was the peculiar genius and talent of Ben Jonson; to whose play I now return.

'Besides Morose, there are at least nine or ten different characters and humours in *The Silent Woman*; all which persons have several concernments of their own, yet are all used by the poet, to the conducting of the main design to perfection. I shall not waste time in commending the writing of this play; but I will give you my opinion, that there is more wit and acuteness of fancy in it than in any of Ben Jonson's. Besides, that he has here described the conversation of gentlemen in the persons of True-Wit, and his friends, with more gaiety, air and freedom, than in the rest of his comedies. For the contrivance of the plot, 'tis extreme elaborate, and yet withal easy; for the *lusis*, or untying of it, 'tis so admirable, that when it is done, no one of the audience would think the poet could have missed it; and yet it was concealed so much before the last scene, that any other way would sooner have entered into your thoughts. But I dare not take upon me to commend the fabric of it, because it is altogether so full of art, that I must unravel every scene in it to commend it as I ought. And this excellent contrivance is still the more to be admired, because 'tis comedy, where the persons are only of common rank, and their business private, not elevated by passions or high concernments, as in serious plays. Here every one is a proper judge of all he sees, nothing is represented but that with which he daily converses: so that by consequence all faults lie open to discovery, and few are pardonable. 'Tis this which Horace has judiciously observed: *Creditur, ex medio quia res arcessit, habere / Sudoris minimum; sed habet Comedia tanto / Plus oneris, quanto veniae minus* [It is supposed that because it draws on actuality, it is less laborious; but comedy is that much more onerous since less is forgiven it].[38] But our poet, who was not ignorant of these difficulties, has made use of all advantages; as he who designs a large leap takes his rise from the highest ground. One of these advantages is that which Corneille ⟨Cn/250⟩ has laid down as the greatest which can arrive to any poem, and which he himself could never compass above thrice in all his plays; viz. the making choice of some signal and long-expected day, whereon the action of the play is to depend. This day was that designed by Dauphine for the settling of his uncle's estate upon him; which to compass he contrives to marry him. That the marriage had been plotted by him long before-hand, is made evident by what he tells True-Wit in the second act, that in one moment he had destroyed what he had been raising many months.

[38] *Epistles* 2.1.168–70.

'There is another artifice of the poet, which I cannot here omit, because by the frequent practice of it in his comedies he has left it to us almost as a rule; that is, when he has any character or humour wherein he would show a *coup de maistre*, or his highest skill, he recommends it to your observation by a pleasant description of it before the person first appears. Thus, in *Bartholomew Fair* he gives you the pictures of Numps and Cokes, and this those of Daw, Lafoole, Morose, and the Collegiate Ladies; all which you hear described before you see them. So that before they come upon the stage, you have a longing expectation of them, which prepares you to receive them favourably; and when they are there, even from their first appearance you are so far acquainted with them, that nothing of their humour is lost to you.

'I will observe yet one thing further of this admirable plot; the business of it rises in every act. The second is greater than the first; the third than the second; and so forward to the fifth. There too you see, till the very last scene, new difficulties arising to obstruct the action of the play; and when the audience is brought into despair that the business can naturally be effected, then, and not before, the discovery is made. But that the poet might entertain you with more variety all this while, he reserves some new characters to show you, which he opens not till the second and third act. In the second Morose, Daw, the Barber, and Otter; in the third the Collegiate Ladies: all which he moves afterwards in by-walks, or under-plots, as diversions to the main design, lest it should grow tedious, though they are still naturally joined with it, and somewhere or other subservient to it. Thus, like a skilful chess-player, by little and little he draws out his men, and makes his pawns of use to his greater persons.

'If this comedy and some others of his were translated into French prose (which would now be no wonder to them, since Molière has lately given them plays out of verse, which have not displeased them), I believe the controversy would soon be decided betwixt the two nations, even making them the judges. ... '[39]

---

[39] In the last part of the dialogue, Crites attacks the use of rhyme in serious plays since "a play is an imitation of nature; and since no man without premeditation speaks in rhyme, neither ought he to do it on the stage."

29

THOMAS RYMER
(1643?–1713)

Thomas Rymer made a grave error when he published his unperformed heroic tragedy, *Edgar*. The play was a constant theme for mockery and did much to undermine its author's intellectual standing. But Dryden treated Rymer's critical writings with circumspection[1] and even Rymer's detractors were rather in awe of his learning and his method, which owed much to Scaliger, and which he used against some of the most esteemed English plays of the preceding generation.

After the seventeenth century, Rymer was either forgotten or dismissed as a neo-classical extremist.[2] Dr. Johnson called him a "tyrant"; Macaulay, in passing, "the worst critic that ever lived." Ezra Pound, however, praised[3] his method, which was to quote, scrutinize, and compare specific passages, and T. S. Eliot went out of his way to note that he had "never . . . seen a cogent refutation of Thomas Rymer's objections to *Othello*."[4]

Rymer's approach to drama begins with a systematic application of the Aristotelian categories of plot, characterization, and thought. With respect to plot, logical development (and hence probability) is paramount; in characterization he demands decorum; and his discussions of thought occasion some of his wittiest demonstrations of the dubious, or trivial, moral implications of some popular tragedies. Rymer scorns all departures from what he calls "common sense"; he deplores (as Maeterlinck would two centuries later) the English taste for multiple deaths and bloody violence in tragedy; and he insists on the necessity of "poetical justice," a term that he, apparently, originated.[5]

For further reading

Eliot 1975; Saintsbury [1902–04] 1934.

---

[1] In his copy of Rymer's *The Tragedies of the Last Age*, Dryden jotted down his "Heads of an Answer to Rymer." These notes were later used as the basis for the much less antagonistic essay "The Grounds of Criticism in Tragedy," with which Dryden prefaced his adaptation of Shakespeare's *Troilus and Cressida* in 1679. See Rymer/Zimansky 1956, xxxiii and ff.

[2] He is, however, given credit for the contribution he made to historiography with his *Foedera*, a collection of historical treaties between English and other nations, of which Rymer completed fifteen volumes before his death and which was continued afterwards.

[3] See Rymer/Zimansky 1956, lxviii and ff. and 226.

[4] In a footnote to "Hamlet" (1919). Eliot was endorsing E. E. Stoll's remark that seventeenth- and eighteenth-century critics "were nearer in spirit to Shakespeare's art; and . . . nearer in their old-fashioned way, to the secret of dramatic art in general" (Eliot 1975, 45).

[5] See Spingarn 1908a, I.lxxiii–lxxiv.

From *The Tragedies of the Last Age, Considered and Examined by the Practice of the Ancients, and by the Common Sense of all Ages, in a Letter to Fleetwood Shepheard, Esq.*[6]

... I would not examine the proportions, the unities and outward regularities, the mechanical part of tragedies: there is no talking of beauties where there wants essentials.[7] 'Tis not necessary for a man to have a nose on his face, nor to have two legs: he may be a true man, though awkward and unsightly, as the Monster in *The Tempest*.

Nor have I much troubled their phrase and expression. I have not vexed their language with the doubts, the remarks and eternal triflings of the French grammaticasters. Much less have I cast about for jests and gone quibble-catching.

I have chiefly considered the fable or plot, which all conclude to be the soul of a tragedy, which with the Ancients is always found to be a reasonable soul but with us, for the most part, a brutish and often worse than brutish.

And certainly there is not required much learning, or that a man must be some Aristotle and Doctor of Subtleties, to form a right judgement in this particular: common sense suffices. And rarely have I known women-judges mistake in these points, when they have the patience to think and (left to their own heads) they decide with their own sense. But if people are prepossessed, if they will judge of *Rollo* by *Othello* and one crooked line by another, we can never have a certainty.

Amongst those who will be objecting to the doctrine I lay down may peradventure appear a sort of men who have remembered so and so and value themselves upon their *experience*. I may write by the *book* (say they) but they know what will *please*. These are a kind of stage-quacks or empirics in poetry, who have got a recipe to please and no *collegiate*[8] like 'em for purging the passions. ...

... a distinction is to be made between what pleases naturally in itself and what pleases on account of the machines, actors, dances and circumstances which are merely *accidental* to the tragedy.

Aristotle observes ⟨Ar/60⟩ that, in his time, some who (wanting talent

---

[6] In *The Tragedies of the Last Age* (1677), which may be the first critical essay of its kind in English, Rymer sets out to make extended analyses of a number of plays, scrutinizing particular passages and features of their construction.

    The epistolary form of the essay is, perhaps, something of an affectation and excuse for the lack of organization and system that Rymer so freely admits. Fleetwood Shepheard was a very minor poet and a follower of Charles Sackville, Earl of Dorset.

[7] In discriminating between the "beauties" and the "essentials," and not including the "unities" among the latter, Rymer moderates the conventional neo-classical position. The "essentials" have to do with plot (supremely), characterization and thought.

[8] *collegiate* = academic.

to write what might please) made it their care that the actors should help out where the Muses failed.

These objectors urge that there is also another great accident; which is that Athens and London have not the same meridian.

Certain it is that *nature* is the same and *man* is the same. He loves, grieves, hates, envies, has the same affections and passions in both places and the same springs that give them motion. What moved pity there will here also produce the same effect. . . .

Say others: poetry and reason, how come these to be cater-cousins? Poetry is the child of fancy and is never to be schooled and disciplined by reason. Poetry, they say, is blind inspiration, is pure enthusiasm, is rapture and rage all over.

But fancy, I think, in poetry, is like the faith in religion: it makes far discoveries and soars above reason but never clashes or runs against it. Fancy leaps and frisks and away she's gone; whilst reason rattles the chains and follows after. Reason must consent and ratify whatever by-fancy is attempted in its absence or else 'tis all null and void in law. However, in the contrivance and economy of a play, reason is always to be consulted. Those who object against reason are like the fanatics in poetry and never to be saved by their good works. . . .

In former times, poetry was another thing than history, or than the law of the land. Poetry discovered crimes that law could never find out and punished those the law had acquitted. The Areopagus cleared Orestes but with what furies did the poets haunt and torment him; and what a wretch made they of Oedipus, when the casuist excused his invincible ignorance!

The poets considered that naturally men were affected with pity when they saw others suffer more than their fault deserved; and vice, they thought, could never be painted too ugly and frightful. Therefore, whether they would move pity or make vice detested, it concerned them to be somewhat of the severest in the punishments they inflicted. Now, because their hands were tied that they could not punish beyond such a degree, they were obliged to have a strict eye on their malefactor that he transgressed not too far, that he committed no *two* crimes when but responsible for *one*; nor, indeed, be so far guilty as by the law to deserve death. For though *historical justice* might rest there yet *poetical justice* could not be so content.[9] It would require that the satisfaction be complete and full before the malefactor goes off the stage and nothing be left to God Almighty and to another world. Nor will it suffer that the spectators trust the poet for a hell behind the scenes: the fire must roar in the conscience of the

---

[9] The ultimate source of Rymer's idea of "poetic justice" seems to be Plato's accusation that poets "tell us that the wicked are often happy, and the good miserable . . . such things we shall forbid them to speak, and require them to recount the opposite" (*Republic* 392.B). By the time Joseph Addison disputed the idea of "poetic justice," in number 40 of *The Spectator*, it was widely accepted.

criminal; the fiend and the furies be conjured up to their faces with a world of machines and horrid spectacles; and yet the criminal could never move pity. Therefore, amongst the Ancients, we find no malefactors of this kind. . . .

We are to presume the greatest virtues where we find the highest rewards; and though it is not necessary that all heroes should be kings yet, undoubtedly, all crowned heads, by *poetical right*, are heroes. This is a flower, a prerogative, so certain, so inseparably annexed to the crown as by no poet, no parliament of poets, ever to be invaded. . . .

In framing a character for tragedy, a poet is not to leave his reason and blindly abandon himself to follow fancy, for then his fancy might be monstrous, might be singular and please nobody's maggot but his own; but reason is to be his guide: reason is common to all people and can never carry him from what is natural.

Many are apt to mistake *use* for *nature*, but a poet is not to be an historiographer but a philosopher. He is not to take nature at second hand, soiled and deformed as it passes in the customs of the unthinking vulgar. . . .

Some would laugh to find me mentioning *sacrifices*, *oracles* and *goddesses* – old superstitions, say they, not practicable but more than ridiculous on our stage. These have not observed with what art Virgil has managed the gods of Homer, nor with what judgement Tasso and Cowley employ the heavenly powers in a Christian poem. The like hints from Sophocles and Euripides might also be improved by modern tragedians; and something thence devised suitable to our faith and customs. 'Tis the general reason I contend for; nor would I have more oracles and goddesses on the stage than hear the persons speak Greek. They are apes and not men that imitate with so little discretion.

Some would blame me for insisting and examining only what is apt to *please*, without a word of what might profit.

1. I believe the end of all poetry is to please.
2. Some sorts of poetry please without profiting.
3. I am confident whoever writes tragedy cannot please but must also profit; 'tis the physic of the mind that he makes palatable.

And besides the purging of the passions, something must stick by observing that constant order, that harmony and beauty of Providence, that necessary relation and chain, whereby the causes and the effects, the virtues and rewards, the Vices and their punishments are proportioned and linked together; how deep and dark soever are laid the springs and however intricate and involved their operation. . . .

I have thought our poetry of the last age as rude as our architecture. One cause thereof might be that *Aristotle's treatise of poetry* has been so little studied amongst us. It was, perhaps, commented upon by all the great men in Italy before we well knew (on this side of the Alps) that there was such a book in being. And though Horace comprises all in that small epistle of his, yet few will think long enough together to be masters and to understand the reason of what is delivered together in so short. . . .

From *A Short View of Tragedy: its Original Excellency and Corruption. With some Reflections on Shakespeare and other Practitioners for the Stage*[10]

CHAPTER I

. . . Aristotle tells us of two senses that must be pleased – our *sight* and our *ears* – and it is vain for a poet (with Bayes in *The Rehearsal*)[11] to complain of injustice, and the wrong judgement in his audience, unless these two senses be gratified.

The worst on it is that most people are wholly led by these two senses and follow them upon content, without ever troubling their noddle farther.

How many plays owe all their success to a rare *show*? Even in the days of Horace, enter on the stage a person in a costly, strange habit – Lord, what clapping, what noise and thunder, as heaven and earth were coming together! Yet not one word spoken. . . .

The eye is a quick sense, will be in with our fancy and prepossess the head strangely. Another means whereby the eye misleads the judgement is the action. We go to see a play *acted*; in tragedy is represented a memorable *action*; so the spectators are always pleased to see *action* and are not often so ill-natured to pry into and examine whether it be proper, just, natural, in season or out of season. . . .

Many, peradventure, of the tragical scenes in Shakespeare cried up for the action might yet do better without words. Words are a sort of heavy baggage that were better out of the way at the push of action; especially in his bombast circumstance, where the words and action are seldom akin, generally are inconsistent, at cross-purposes, embarrass or destroy each other; yet to those who take not the words distinctly, there may be something in the buzz and sound, that like the drone to a bagpipe may serve to set off the action. . . . For 'What ship? Who is arrived?' the answer is:

> 'Tis one Iago, ancient to the General,
> He has had most favourable and happy speed;

---

[10] *A Short View* was published in 1692. The eight chapters comprise a brief history of Greek and Roman tragedy and its theory; an account of ecclesiastical attacks on the stage; commentary on tragedy in Europe; an account of the development of drama in England; and a (lengthy) critique of *Othello*.

[11] *The Rehearsal* (1671), a comedy by George Villiers, Duke of Buckingham (1628–87), satirizes heroic drama, particularly that of Dryden, who figures (along with William D'Avenant) in the characterization of Bayes. Rymer uses the play as a touchstone for critical good sense.

> Tempests themselves, high seas and howling winds,
> The guttered rocks and congregated sands,
> Traitors ensteep'd, to clog the guiltless keel,
> As having sense of beauty, do omit
> Their common natures, letting go safely by
> The divine Desdemona.   [*Othello* 2.1.66–73]

Is this the language of the Exchange, or the Insuring Office? Once in a man's life, he might be content at Bedlam to hear such a rapture. In a play, one should speak like a man of business, his speech be *politikos* ⟨Ar/57⟩, which the French render *agissante*; the Italians, *negotiosa* and *operativa*; but, by this Gentleman's talk one may guess he has nothing to do. ...

CHAPTER IV

... Grant there [be], in a tragedy, the felicity of invention, the novelty of the fictions, the strength of the verse, the easiness of expression, the solid reason, the warmth of passion, still heightened and rising from act to act; together with the richness of figures, the pomp of the theatre, the habits, gesture and voice of the actors, at the same instant charming both the eyes and the ears; so the senses being won, the judgement is surprised, and the whole man led at once captive: a body must be of brass or stone to resist so many charms and be master of himself amidst so much allurement and temptation.

Grant all this, I say, where is the hurt? What is the danger? If *the end* of all is to show *virtue in triumph?* The noblest thoughts make the strongest impression, and the juster passions find the kindest reception amongst us. The medicine is not less wholesome for the honey or the gilded pill. Nor can a moral lesson be less profitable when dressed and set off with all the advantage and decoration of the theatre.

This is, indeed, of all diversions the most bewitching; and the theatre is a magazine, not to be trusted but under the special eye and direction of a virtuous government; otherwise, according to the course of the world, it might, possibly, degenerate to deserve the aspersions and ill names whereby the Jesuits would render it odious, calling it the *School of Vice*, and *Sanctuary of Venus*, the *Temple of Impiety*, the *Furnace of Babylon*, the *Consistory of Impurity*, the *Shop of Lewdness*, the *Pest of Commonwealths*, the *Seminary of Debauchery, Satan's Festival* and the *Devil's Dancing School*. ...

CHAPTER VII

... Whatever rubs or difficulty may stick on the bark, the moral of this fable [of *Othello*] is very instructive.

First: this may be a caution to all maids of quality how, without their parents' consent, they run away with blackamoors. ...

Secondly: this may be a warning to all good wives that they look well to their linen.

Thirdly: this may be a lesson to husbands that before their jealousy be tragical the proofs may be mathematical. ...

So much ado, so much stress, so much passion and repetition about an handkerchief! Why was this not called the *Tragedy of the Handkerchief?* ...

CHAPTER VIII

... We want a law for acting *The Rehearsal* once a week, to keep us in our senses and secure us against the noise and nonsense, the farce and fustian which, in the name of tragedy, have so long invaded, and usurp, our theatre. ...

30

WILLIAM CONGREVE
(1670–1729)

Congreve's first play, *The Old Bachelor*, was very well received when it was produced in 1693, John Dryden being foremost among those who praised it. Dryden's esteem for the younger playwright's work grew and could hardly have mounted higher than in his "Commendatory Verses" to *The Double-Dealer* (1694), in which he declared:

> So bold, yet so judiciously you dare,
> That your least praise is to be regular.
> Time, place, and action, may with pains be wrought,
> But genius must be born, and never can be taught.
> This is your portion, this your native store;
> Heaven that but once was prodigal before,
> To Shakespeare gave as much; she could not give him more.

To be "judiciously ... regular" and yet to equal Shakespeare's genius was to demonstrate that the standards of the time were not incompatible with a supreme and timeless art.

Congreve himself made light of his accomplishments as a dramatist and (offensively in Voltaire's view) of the profession of writer in general. But, like Jonson, he was also disposed to scorn what he called "the general taste which seems now to be predominant in the palates of our audience." The author of a mediocre tragedy and of four comedies that seemed, even to his contemporaries, to have achieved the status of classics, Congreve retired prematurely from the stage, one of the reasons for this being the poor reception, in 1700, of his masterpiece, *The Way of the World*.

Though he referred to his comedies as "trifles," Congreve was concerned that the regularity of their art and their essential morality should be recognized, as is seen in the dedication of *The Double Dealer*:

> Yet I must take the boldness to say, I have not miscarried in the whole; for the mechanical part of it is regular. That I may say with as little vanity, as a builder may say he has built a house according to the model laid down before him; or a gardener that he has set his flowers in a knot of such or such a figure. I designed the moral first, and to that moral I invented the fable, and do not know that I have borrowed one hint of it anywhere. I made the plot as strong as I could, because it was single; and I made it single, because I would avoid confusion, and was resolved to preserve the three unities of the drama.

Among Congreve's few discussions of drama and theatre, the least persuasive is, perhaps, his response to *A Short View of the Profaneness and Immorality of the English Stage* (1698), Jeremy Collier's influential attack on the licentiousness of the drama of the time. Some years earlier, however, the critic John Dennis had drawn out the playwright's most penetrating observation on comedy. In the following letter to Dennis, first published (as was no doubt always intended) in 1696, Congreve defines what he takes to be the foundations of characterization, dialogue, and also morality, in comedy. Obviously, Congreve's starting point for the discussion of humors is Jonson. He also owes much to Dryden, whose classical temper and theoretical concerns he shares. But he goes beyond both in evolving his more modern understanding of humor in comedy and of characterization in general.

For further reading

Barnard 1972.

"On Humour in Comedy": a letter to John Dennis[1]

July 10, 1695

Dear Sir,

You write to me that you have entertained yourself two or three days with reading several comedies of several authors; and your observation is that there is more of *humour* in our English writers ⟨Dd/281⟩ than in any of the other comic poets, ancient or modern. You desire to know my opinion, and at the same time my thought, of that which is generally called *humour* in comedy.

I agree with you in an impartial preference of our English writers in that particular. But if I tell you my thoughts of *humour*, I must at the same time confess that what I take for true *humour* has not been so often written, even by them, as is generally believed: and some who have valued themselves, and have been esteemed by others, for that kind of writing, have seldom touched upon it. To make this appear to the world would require a long and laboured discourse and such as I neither am able nor willing to undertake. But such little remarks as may be contained within the compass of a letter, and such unpremeditated thoughts as may be communicated between friend and friend, without incurring the censure of the world, or setting up for a *dictator*, you shall have from me, since you have enjoined it.

To define *humour*, perhaps, were as difficult as to define *wit*; for like that, it is of infinite variety. ... And, since I have mentioned *wit* and *humour* together, let me make the first distinction between them and observe to you that *wit is often mistaken for humour.*

---

[1] This letter was first published in *Letters on Several Occasions: written by and between Mr. Dryden, Mr. Wycherley, Mr. –, Mr. Congreve and Mr. Dennis* (1696). Congreve's punctuation and spelling have been modernized but his use of italics (except for names of characters) has been retained.

John Dennis (1657–1734) was a follower of Dryden and one of the most important critics of the early eighteenth century. He wrote a defense of the theatre and was the author of a few mediocre plays. His reputation never recovered from Pope's inclusion of him among the "dunces" but Congreve, a friend of both Pope and Dennis, respected the latter's acumen and his considered neo-classical views.

I have observed that when a few things have been wittily and pleasantly spoken by any character in a comedy, it is very usual for those who make their remarks on a play while it is acting, to say: *Such a thing is very humorously spoken. There is a great deal of humour in that part.* Thus the character of the person speaking, maybe surprisingly and pleasantly, is mistaken for a character of humour, which indeed is a character of *wit*. But there is a great difference between a comedy wherein there are many things *humorously*, as they call it – which is *pleasantly* – spoken; and one where there are several characters of *humour*, distinguished by the particular and different humours, appropriated to the several persons represented, and which naturally arise from the different constitutions, complexions,[2] and dispositions of men. The saying of humorous things does not distinguish characters; for every person in a comedy may be allowed to speak them. From a witty man they are expected and even a fool may be permitted to stumble on them by chance. Though I make a difference between *wit* and *humour*, yet I do not think that humorous characters exclude wit: no, but the manner of wit should be adapted to the *humour*. As, for instance, a character of a splenetic and peevish *humour* should have a satirical wit. A jolly and sanguine humour should have a facetious wit. The former would speak positively,[3] the latter, carelessly; for the former observes and shows things as they are; the latter rather overlooks nature and speaks things as he would have them; and his *wit* and *humour* have both of them a less alloy of judgement than the other's.

As *wit*, so its opposite, *folly, is sometimes mistaken for humour.*

When a poet brings a *character* on the stage, committing a thousand absurdities, and talking impertinencies,[4] roaring aloud, and laughing immoderately on every, or rather upon no, occasion, that is a character of humour.

Is anything more common than to have a pretended comedy, stuffed with such grotesques, figures, and farce fools? Things that either are not in nature or, if they are, are monsters, and births of mischance .... As I don't think *humour* exclusive of wit, neither do I think it inconsistent with folly, but I think the follies should only be such as men's humours may incline them to; and not follies entirely abstracted from both humour and nature.

Sometimes, *personal defects are misrepresented for humours.*

I mean, sometimes characters are barbarously exposed on the stage, ridiculing natural deformities, casual defects in the senses, and infirmities of age. Sure the poet must both be very ill-natured himself, and think his audience so, when he proposes by showing a man deformed, or deaf, or blind, to give them an agreeable entertainment; and hopes to raise their

---

2 The "complexion" is the physical constitution that determines temperament and also the physical appearance that indicates both constitution and temperament.

3 "positively" = deliberately.

4 "impertinencies" = irrelevancies.

mirth by what is truly an object of compassion. But much need not be said upon this head to anybody, especially to you, who in one of your letters to me concerning Mr. Jonson's *Fox*, have justly excepted against this immoral part of ridicule in Corbaccio's character; and there I must agree with you to blame him, whom otherwise I cannot enough admire for his great mastery of true humour in comedy.[5]

External habit of body is often mistaken for humour.

By *external habit* I do not mean the ridiculous dress or clothing of a character, though that goes a good way in some received characters. (But undoubtedly a man's humour might incline him to dress differently from other people.) But I mean a singularity of manners, speech, and behaviour peculiar to all, or most, of the same country, profession, or education. I cannot think that a humour which is only contracted by use or custom; for, by disuse, or compliance with other customs, it may be worn off, or diversified. *Affectation is generally mistaken for humour.*

These are, indeed, so much alike that, at a distance, they may be mistaken, one for the other. For what is humour in one may be *affectation* in another; and nothing is more common than for some to affect particular ways of saying, and doing, things peculiar to others whom they admire and would imitate. *Humour* is the life, *affectation* the picture. He that draws a character of *affectation* shows *humour* at the second hand; he at best but publishes a translation and his pictures are but copies.

But, as these two last distinctions are the nicest,[6] so it may be most proper to explain them by particular instances from some author of reputation. *Humour* I take either to be born with us, and so of a natural growth; or else grafted into us by some accidental change in the constitution, or revolution of the internal habit of body; by which it becomes, if I may so call it, naturalized.

Humour is from nature, *habit* from custom; and *affectation* from industry.

Humour shows us as we are.

Habit shows us as we appear, under a forcible impression.

Affectation shows us what we would be, under a voluntary disguise.

Though here I would observe, by the way, that a continued affectation may, in time, become a habit. ...[7]

I should be unwilling to venture even upon a bare description of humour, much more to make a definition of it but, now my hand is in, I'll tell you what serves me instead of either. I take it to be: *A singular and unavoidable manner of doing, or saying, anything, peculiar to and natural to*

---

[5] Of Jonson's characterization of Corbaccio, in *Volpone, or The Fox*, Dennis had said that: "he is exposed for his deafness, a personal defect; which is contrary to the end of comedy instruction."

[6] "nicest" = most subtle and intricate.

[7] Congreve here discusses characterization in Jonson, particularly that of Morose in *Epicoene, or The Silent Woman*. His method, as well as his choice of play, is reminiscent of Dryden's "examen" in his *Essay of Dramatic Poesy*.

one man only; by which his speech and actions are distinguishable from those of other men ⟨Dd/288⟩.

Our *humour* has relation to us, and to what proceeds from us, as the accidents have to a substance.[8] It is a colour, taste, and smell diffused through all; though our actions are never so many, and different in form, they are all splinters of the same wood and have naturally one complexion, which, though it may be disguised by art, yet cannot wholly be changed. We may paint it with other colours but we cannot change the grain. So the natural sound of an instrument will be distinguished though the notes expressed by it are never so various and the divisions never so many. Dissimulation may, by degrees, become more easy to our practice but it can never absolutely transubstantiate us into what we would seem: it will always be in some proportion a violence upon nature.

A man may change his opinion but I believe he will find it a difficulty to part with his *humour*, and there is nothing more provoking than the being made sensible of that difficulty. Sometimes one shall meet with those who, perhaps, innocently enough, but at the same time impertinently, will ask the question: *Why are you not merry? Why are you not gay, pleasant, and cheerful?* Then, instead of answering, I could ask such a one: *Why are you not handsome? Why have you not black eyes and a better complexion?* Nature abhors to be forced.

Two famous philosophers, of Ephesus and Abdera, have their different sects at this day. Some weep and others laugh, at one and the same thing.[9]

I don't doubt but that you have heard several men laugh when they are angry; others who are silent; some that are loud: yet I cannot suppose that it is the passion of *anger* which is in itself different or more or less in one than t'other; but that it is the *humour* of the man that is predominant and urges him to express it in that manner. Demonstrations of pleasure are as various. One man has a humour of retiring from all company when anything has happened to please him beyond expectation; he hugs himself alone and thinks an addition to the pleasure to keep it secret. Another is on thorns 'til he has made a proclamation of it, and must make other people sensible of his happiness before he can be so himself. So it is in grief and other passions. Demonstrations of love and the effects of that passion upon several humours are infinitely different; but here the ladies who abound in servants[10] are the best judges. Talking of the ladies, methinks something should be said of the humour of the fair sex, since they are sometimes so kind as to furnish out a character for comedy.

But I must confess I have never made any observation of what I

---

[8] Congreve is using "accident" and "substance" in the philosophical senses of a non-essential attribute of something, and its essence.

[9] Democritus of Abdera (5th century B.C.) was called the "laughing philosopher," Heraclitus of Ephesus (6th century B.C.) the "weeping philosopher."

[10] "servants" = admirers or lovers.

apprehend to be true humour in women. Perhaps passions are too powerful in that sex to let humour have its course; or maybe, by reason of their natural coldness, humour cannot exert itself to that extravagant degree which it often does in the male sex. For if ever anything does appear comical or ridiculous in a woman, I think it is little more than an acquired folly, or an affectation. We may call them the weaker sex, but I think the true reason is because our follies are stronger and our faults are the more prevailing.

One might think that the diversity of humour, which must be allowed to be diffused throughout mankind, might afford endless matter for the support of comedies. But, when we come to closely consider that point, and nicely to distinguish the difference of humours, I believe we shall find the contrary. For, though we allow every man something of his own and a peculiar humour, yet every man has it not in quantity to become remarkable by it: or, if many do become remarkable by their humours, yet all those humours may not be diverting. Nor is it only requisite to distinguish what humour will be diverting but also how much of it, what part to show of it in light and what to cast in shades; how to set it off by preparatory scenes and by opposing other humours to it in the same scene. Through a wrong judgement, sometimes, men's humours may be opposed when there is really no specific difference between them; only a greater proportion of the same in one than t'other, occasioned by his having more phlegm, or choler, or whatever the constitution is from whence their humours derive their source ⟨Jn/197⟩.

There is infinitely more to be said on this subject, though perhaps I have already said too much; but I have said it to a friend who, I am sure, will not expose it, if he does not approve of it. I believe the subject is entirely new and was never touched upon before and, if I would have anyone see this private essay it should be someone who might be provoked by my errors in it to publish a more judicious treatise on the subject. Indeed, I wish it were done, that the world being a little acquainted with the scarcity of true humour, and the difficulty of finding it and showing it, might look a little more favourably on the labours of them who endeavour to search into nature for it and lay it open to the public view.

I don't say but that very entertaining and useful characters, and proper for comedy, may be drawn from affectations and those other qualities which I have endeavoured to distinguish from humour: but I would not have such imposed on the world for humour, nor esteemed of equal value with it. It were, perhaps, the work of a long life to make one comedy true in all its parts and to give every character in it a true and distinct humour. Therefore, every poet must be beholding to other helps to make out his number of ridiculous characters. But I think such a one deserves to be broke who makes all false musters;[11] who does not show one true humour

---

[11] The playwright who makes nothing but untruthful collections of characters (like fictional names on a military payroll – "false musters") deserves to be broken on the wheel.

in a comedy but entertains his audience to the end of the play with everything out of nature.

I will make but one observation to you more and have done; and that is grounded on an observation of your own that, and which I mentioned at the beginning of my letter, viz: that there is more of humour in our English comic writers than in any others. I do not wonder at it, for I look upon humour to be almost of English growth; at least, it does not seem to have such increase on any other soil. And what appears to me to be the reason of it is the great freedom, privilege, and liberty which the common people of England enjoy. Any man that has a humour is under no restraint or fear of giving it vent. They have a proverb among them, which maybe, will show the bent and genius of the people as well as a longer discourse: *He that will have a maypole shall have a maypole*. This is a maxim with them and their practice is agreeable to it. I believe something considerable, too, may be ascribed to their feeding so much on flesh, and the grossness of their diet in general. But I have done; let the physicians agree that. Thus you have my thoughts of *humour*, to my power of expressing them in so little time and compass. You will be kind to show me wherein I have erred; and, as you are very capable of giving me instruction so, I think, I have a very just title to demand it from you, being, without reserve,

Your real friend and humble servant,
William Congreve

BIBLIOGRAPHY

The names of authors whose works appear in this volume are in bold type.

Aden, John M. 1955. Dryden, Corneille and the *Essay of Dramatic Poesy*. *Review of English Studies* n.s. 6:147–56.
Aristotle
   Butcher, S. H., trans. 1895. *Aristotle's Theory of Poetry and the Fine Arts*. London.
   Bywater, Ingram, trans. 1909. *Aristotle on the Art of Poetry*. Oxford.
   Dorsch, T. S., trans. 1965. *Classical Literary Criticism: Aristotle On the Art of Poetry, Horace On the Art of Poetry, Longinus On the Sublime*. Harmondsworth.
   Else, Gerald F., trans. 1967. *Aristotle's Poetics*. Ann Arbor.
   Golden, Leon, and O. B. Hardison, trans. and eds. 1968. *Aristotle's Poetics: a Translation and Commentary*. Englewood Cliffs, NJ.
   Grube, George M., trans. 1958. *Aristotle on Poetry and Style*. Indianapolis, IN.
   House, Humphrey, trans. 1956. *Aristotle's Poetics*. Rev. Colin Hardie. London
   Lucas, D. W., ed. 1968. *Aristotle's Poetics*. Oxford.
   McKeon, R. P., ed. 1941. *The Basic Works of Aristotle*. New York.
   Telford, Kenneth A., trans. 1961. *Aristotle's Poetics, Translation and Analysis*. South Bend, IN.
Armstrong, William A. 1958. *Damon and Pithias* and Renaissance theories of tragedy. *English Studies* 39:200–7.
Arnaud, Charles, 1888. *Étude sur la vie et les oeuvres de l'abbé d'Aubignac*. Paris.
Artaud, Antonin. 1958. *The Theater and its Double*. Trans. Mary Caroline Williams. New York.
d'Aubignac, François Hédelin, the abbé
[1715] 1971. *La Pratique du théâtre*. Repr. of the three-vol. edn, Amsterdam 1715. Introductory commentary by Hans-Jörg Neuschäfer. Munich.
   Martino, Pierre, ed. 1927. *La Pratique du théâtre*. Paris.
Barilli, Renato. 1984. *Poetica e retorica*. Rev. edn. Milan.
Barish, Jonas A. 1960. *Ben Jonson and the Language of Prose Comedy*. Cambridge, MA.
   1981. *The Antitheatrical Prejudice*. Berkeley, CA
Barnard, John. 1972. Passion, "poetical justice," and dramatic law in *The Double Dealer* and *The Way of the World*. In *William Congreve*, ed. Brian Morris, 95–112. London.
Barnwell, H. T. 1965. Some reflections on Corneille's theory of *vraisemblance* as formulated in the *Discours*. *Forum for Modern Language Studies* 1(4):295–310.
   1982. *The Tragic Drama of Corneille and Racine*. Oxford.
Beare, W. 1946. Horace, Donatus and the five-act law. *Hermanthena* 67:53–57.
   1950. *The Roman Stage. A Short History of Latin Drama in the Time of the Republic*. London.
Benjamin, Walter. 1968. The work of art in the age of mechanical reproduction. In his *Illuminations*, trans. Harry Zohn. New York.
Bilancini, Pietro. 1890. *Giambattista Giraldi e la tragedia italiana nel sec. XVI*. Aquila.
Blanchard, Alain. 1983. *Essai sur la composition des comédies de Ménandre*. Paris.
Boal, Augusto. 1976. *Theatre of the Oppressed*. New York.
Boas, F. S. 1950. *Thomas Heywood*. London.
Bradner, Leicester. 1927. *The Life and Poems of Richard Edwards*., New Haven.
Bray, René. 1927. *La Tragédie cornélienne devant la critique classique, d'après la querelle de Sophonisbe*. Paris.
   1931. *La Formation de la doctrine classique en France*. Lausanne.
Bremer, J. M. 1969. *Hamartia*. Amsterdam.
Brink, C. O. 1963. *Prolegomena to the Literary Epistles*. Vol. 1 of *Horace on Poetry*. Cambridge.

1971. *The Ars Poetica*. Vol. II of *Horace on Poetry*. Cambridge.

1982. *Epistles Book II: The Letters to Augustus and Florus*. Vol. III of *Horace on Poetry*. Cambridge.

Brock, D. Heywood. 1983. *A Ben Jonson Companion*. Bloomington.

Bullough, Geoffrey. 1958. *Narrative and Dramatic Sources of Shakespeare*. Vol. II: *The Comedies*. London.

Castelvetro, Ludovico

Bongiorno, Andrew, trans. 1984. *Castelvetro on the Art of Poetry: an Abridged Translation of Lodovico Castelvetro's Poetica d'Aristotele Vulgarizzata et Sposta*. Medieval & Renaissance Texts & Studies, 29. Binghamton, NY.

Romani, Werther, ed. 1978. *Poetica d'Aristotile vulgarizzata e sposta*. 2 vols. Rome and Bari.

Chapelain, Jean. [1637] 1936. *Lettres sur la règle des 24 heures*. In *Opuscules critiques*, ed. A. C. Hunter, 113–26. Paris.

Charlton, H. B. 1913. *Castelvetro's Theory of Poetry*. Manchester.

Cicero. *De Republica*. 1960. Ed. K. Ziegler. Leipzig.

Clubb, Louise George. 1974. The making of the pastoral play: some Italian experiments between 1573 and 1590. In *Petrarch to Pirandello: Studies in Italian Literature in Honour of Beatrice Corrigan*, ed. Julius A. Molinaro, 45–72. Toronto.

Collingwood, R. G. 1938. *The Principles of Art*. Oxford.

Congreve, William

Davis, Herbert, ed. 1967. *The Complete Plays of William Congreve*. London.

Hodges, John C., ed. 1964. *Letters and Documents*. London.

Copeau, Jacques. 1923. *Etudes d'art dramatique. Critiques d'un autre temps*. Paris.

Corneille, Pierre

Barnwell, H. T., ed. 1965. *Writings on the Theatre*. Oxford.

Mantero, R., ed. 1964. *Corneille critique*. Paris.

Marty-Laveaux, Charles, ed. 1862. *Oeuvres de Pierre Corneille*. 12 vols. Paris.

Corrigan, Beatrice. 1934. Sforza Oddi and his comedies. *PMLA* 49:718–42.

Crane, R. S., ed. 1952. *Critics and Criticism: Ancient and Modern*. Chicago.

Curtius, E. R. 1953. *European Literature and the Latin Middle Ages*. Trans. W. R. Trask. London.

Dale. A. M. 1969. Ethos and "Dianoia": "Character" and "Thought" in Aristotle's *Poetics*. In his *Collected Papers*, 139–55. Cambridge.

Darst, David, H. 1974. *The Comic Art of Tirso de Molina*. Madrid.

Della Casa, Giovanni. [1558] 1958. *Il Galateo*. Trans. R. S. Pine-Coffin. Penguin.

Della Valle, Daniela. 1973. *Pastorale barocca: Forma e contenuti del Pastor Fido al Dramma Pastorale Francese*. Ravenna.

Della Volpe, Galvano. 1956. *Poetica del cinquecento*. Bari. (Repr. 1973 in vol. V of his *Opere*, 103–94. Rome.)

Dilke, O. A. W. 1958. When was the *Ars Poetica* written? *Bulletin of the Institute of Classical Studies* 5:49–57.

Donatus

Wessner, Paul, ed. 1962–63. *Donatus, Commentum Terenti*. Vols. I; II; and III, part I. Stuttgart.

Doran, Madeleine. 1954. *Endeavors of Art: a Study of Form in Elizabethan Drama*. Madison, WI.

Dryden, John

Monk, Samuel Holt, *et al.*, eds. 1971. *The Works of John Dryden*. Vol. XVII. Berkeley and Los Angeles CA.

Watson, George, ed. 1962. *Of Dramatic Poetry and other Critical Essays*. 2 vols. London.

Dowlin, C. M. 1944. Sidney and other men's thought. *Review of English Studies* 20:257–71.

Duckworth, George E. 1952. *The Nature of Roman Comedy. A Study in Popular Entertainment*. Princeton.

Eco, Umberto. 1983. *The Name of the Rose*. Trans. William Weaver. New York.

Edwards, Richard

White, Jerry D., ed. 1980. *Richard Edwards' "Damon and Pithias": a Critical Old-Spelling Edition*. New York.

Eliot, T. S. 1975. *Selected Prose*. Ed. Frank Kermode. New York.

Else, Gerald F. 1965. *The Origin and Early Form of Greek Tragedy*. Cambridge, MA
    1969. *Aristotle's Poetics: the Argument*. Cambridge, MA.

Enck, John J. 1957. *Jonson and the Comic Truth*. Madison.

Esslin, Martin. 1977. *An Anatomy of Drama*. London.

Euripides. 1984. *Cyclops*. Introduction and commentary by Richard Seaford. Oxford.

Evanthius. 1979. *De Fabula*. Ed. Giovanni Cupaiuolo. Naples.

Fantham, Elaine. 1984. Roman experience of Menander in the late republic and early empire. *Translations and Proceedings of the American Philological Association* 114:299–309.

Fergusson, Francis. [1949] 1968. *The Idea of a Theater*. Princeton.

Ferraro, Rose Mary. 1971. *Giudizi critici e criteri estetici nei "Poetices Libri Septem" (1561) di Giulio Cesare Scaligero rispetto alla teoria letteraria del Rinascimento*. Chapel Hill, NC.

Fletcher, John. [1610] 1893. *The Faithful Shepherdess*. In *Beaumont and Fletcher*, ed. J. St. Loe Strachey. 1949–50. 2 vols. London.

Friedrich, Rainer. 1983. Drama and ritual. In *Theories of Drama* vol. V: *Drama and Ritual*, 159–223. Cambridge.

Furetière, A. 1690. *Dictionnaire universel*. 3 vols. The Hague.

Gasté, Armand. 1898. *La Querelle du Cid. Pièces et Pamphlets*. Paris.

Giacomini, Lorenzo
    De la purgazione de la tragedia. In Weinberg 1970–74, III:345–72.

Gilbert, Allan H. 1940. *Literary Criticism from Plato to Dryden*. Detroit.

Giraldi, Giambattista ("Cinthio")
    1554. *Discorsi di M. Giovanni Battista Giraldi Intorno al Comporre de I Romanzi, delle Commedie delle Tragedie e Altre Maniere di Poesie*. Venice.
    Prologo all'Altile. In Weinberg 1970–74, I:487–92.
    Crocetti, Camillo Guerrieri, ed. 1973. *Scritti critici*. Milan.

Goggio, Emilio. 1943. Dramatic theories in the prologues to *commedie erudite* of the sixteenth century. *PMLA* 58:322–36.

Grazzini, Antonfrancesco ("Il Lasca")
    Plaisance, Michel, ed. 1976. *La Strega*. Paris.

Greene, William Chase. 1918. Plato's view of poetry. *Harvard Studies in Classical Philology*. 29:1–76.

Greg, Walter W. 1906. *Pastoral Poetry and Pastoral Drama*. London.

Grimal, Pierre. 1968. *Essai sur L'Art poétique d'Horace*. Paris.

Guarini, Giambattista
    Brognoligo, Gioacchino, ed. 1914. *Il* Pastor Fido *e Il Compendio della Poesia Tragicomica*. Bari.
    Staton, Walter F. and William E. Simeone. 1964. *A Critical Edition of Sir Richard Fanshawe's 1647 Translation of Giovanni Battista Guarini's* Il Pastor Fido. Oxford.

Hall, V. 1945. The preface to Scaliger's Poetics. *Modern Language Notes* 60:447–53.
    1948. Scaliger's defense of poetry. *PMLA* 63:1125–30.

Halliwell, Stephen. 1986. *Aristotle's Poetics*. London.

Hathaway, Baxter. 1962. *The Age of Criticism: the Late Renaissance in Italy*. Ithaca, NY.

Herrick, Marvin T. 1946. *The Fusion of Horatian and Aristotelian Literary Criticism, 1531–1555*. Illinois Studies in Language and Literature, 32, no. 1, Urbana.
    1947. Some neglected sources of *admiratio*. *Modern Language Notes* 52:222–26.
    [1950] 1964. *Comic Theory in the Sixteenth Century*. Urbana.
    [1955] 1962. *Tragi-Comedy: its Influence and Development in Italy, France and England*. Urbana.
    1965. *Italian Tragedy in the Renaissance*. Urbana.

Heywood, Thomas
    [1612, 1615] 1941. *An Apology for Actors*. With *A Refutation of the Apology for Actors* (1615) by I. G. Introductions and bibliographical notes by Richard H. Perkins. New York.
    Shepherd, R. H., ed. 1874. *The Dramatic Works of Thomas Heywood*. 6 vols. London.

Hirst, David L. 1984. *Tragicomedy*. London and New York.

Horace
    Bovie, S. P., trans. 1959. *The Satires and Epistles of Horace*. Chicago.

Rudd, Niall, trans. 1979. *Horace: Satires and Epistles / Persius: Satires: A Verse Translation with an Introduction by Niall Rudd*. Rev. edn. Penguin.

Russell, Donald Andrew, and Michael Winterbottom, eds. 1972. *Ancient Literary Criticism: the Principal Texts in New Translations*. Oxford.

Wilkins, A. S., ed. 1896. *The Epistles of Horace*. London.

Horne, P. R. 1962. *The Tragedies of Giambattista Cinthio Giraldi*. London.

Hume, Robert D. 1970. *Dryden's Criticism*. Ithaca.

Huntley, Frank L. 1948. On the persons in Dryden's *Essay of Dramatic Poesy*. *Modern Language Notes* 63:88–95. (Repr. in Swedenberg 1966.)

Ingegneri, Angelo

Marotti, Ferruccio, ed. 1974. *Della poesia rappresentativa e del modo di rappresentare le favole sceniche* [1598]. In his *Lo spettacolo dall'Umanesimo al Manierismo*, 271–308. Milan.

Izard, Thomas C. 1942. *George Whetstone: Mid-Elizabethan Gentleman of Letters*. New York.

Janko, Richard. 1984. *Aristotle on Comedy*. London.

Jonson, Ben

Herford, C. H., and Simpson, Percy and Evelyn, eds. 1925–52. *Works*. 11 vols. Oxford.

Redwine, James D., ed. 1970. *Ben Jonson's Literary Criticism*. Regents Critics Series. Lincoln, NB.

Knight, R. C. 1974. *Racine et la Grèce*. Paris.

Kramer, J. E. 1968. *Damon and Pithias*: an apology for art. *English Literary History* 35:475–90.

Latte, K. 1925. Reste frühellenistischer Poetik in Pisonem Brief des Horaz. *Hermes* 60:1–13.

LeClercq, R. V. 1970. Corneille and *An Essay of Dramatic Poesy*. *Comparative Literature* 22:319–27.

Lemaître, Jules. 1888. *Corneille et la poétique d'Aristote*. Paris.

Lisle, Jacques Alaric. 1852. *Essai sur les théories dramatiques de Corneille*. Paris.

Lope de Vega, Felix

Brewster, William, trans. 1957. The new art of writing plays. In *Papers on Playmaking*, ed. Brander Matthews, 1–19. New York.

José Prades, Juana de, ed. 1971. *El Arte nuevo de hacer comedias en este tiempo: edición y estudio preliminar de Juana de José Prades*. Madrid.

Lucas, Corinne. 1984. *De l'horreur au "lieto fine."* Rome.

Maggi, Vincenzo, and Lombardi, Bartolomeo. 1550. *Aristotelis librum de poetica communes explicationes*. Venice.

McKeon, R. P. 1952. Literary criticism and the concept of imitation in antiquity. In Crane 1952, 147–75.

McPherson, D. 1971. Some Renaissance sources for Jonson's early comic theory. *English Language Notes* 8:180–82.

Montesinos, José F. 1964. La paradoja del "Arte nuevo." *Revista del occidente* 2:302–30.

Montgomery, Robert L. 1979. *The Reader's Eye*. Berkeley.

Morgan, Janet. 1986. The meaning of *vraisemblance* in French classical theory. *Modern Language Review* 81:293–304.

Myrick, K. 1965. *Sir Philip Sidney as a Literary Craftsman*, 2nd edn, Lincoln, NB.

Nagler, Alois Maria. 1964. *Theatre Festivals of the Medici*. Trans. George Hickenlooper. New Haven.

Nettleship, R. 1891. *Lectures on the Republic of Plato*. London.

Nougué, Andre. 1962. *L'Oeuvre en prose de Tirso de Molina: Los Cigarrales de Toledo et Deleytar aprovechando*. Paris.

Oddi, Sforza

1572. *Erofilomachia ovvero il duello d'amore e d'amicizia*. Perugia.

1576. *I morti viv*. Perugia.

1591. *Prigione d'amore*. Venice.

Owen, A. S. 1931. *Aristotle on the Art of Poetry*. Oxford.

Parker, J. H. 1966. Lope de Vega's "Arte nuevo de hacer comedias": post-centenary reflections. In *Hispanic Studies in Honor of Nicholson B. Adams*, ed. John Keller and Karl Selig, 113–30. Chapel Hill, NC.

Perella, Nicolas J. 1973. *The Critical Fortune of Battista Guarini's* Il Pastor Fido. Florence.

Pérez, L. C., and F. Sánchez Escribano. 1961. *Afirmaciones de Lope de Vega sobre la precéptive dramática*. Madrid.

Pickard-Cambridge, A. C. 1927. *Dithyramb, Tragedy and Comedy*. Oxford.

[1927] 1962. *Dityramb, Tragedy and Comedy*. 2nd edn, rev. T. B. L. Webster. Oxford.

1968. *The Dramatic Festival of Athens*. Oxford.

Pierre, Grimal. 1968. *Essai sur l'Art poétique d'Horace*. Paris.

Plato

Adam, James, ed. 1938. *The Republic of Plato*. 2 vols. Cambridge.

Cornford, F. M., trans. 1941. *The Republic of Plato*. London.

Croiset, M., trans. 1946. *La République de Platon*. Paris.

Grube, G. M. A., trans. 1974. *Plato's Republic*. Indianapolis.

Hermann, Karl Friedrich, ed. 1855. *Rei Publicae Libri Decem*. Berlin.

Shorey, Paul, trans. 1937. *The Republic*. 2 vols. Loeb Classical Library.

Pound, Ezra. 1970. *The Spirit of Romance*. London.

Preminger, Alex, O. B. Hardison, Jr., and Kevin Kerrane, eds. 1974. *Classical and Medieval Literary Criticism: Translations and Interpretations*. New York.

Racine, Jean

Knight, R. C., and H. T. Barnwell, eds. 1977. *Andromaque*. Geneva.

McGowan, Margaret M., ed. 1968. *Bajazet*. London.

Picard, Raymond, ed. 1951. *Oeuvres complètes*. 2 vols. Paris.

Vinaver, Eugène, ed. 1951. *Principes de la tragédie en marge de la poétique d'Aristote*. Paris.

Ristine, F. H. 1910. *English Tragicomedy: its Origin and History*. New York.

Robortello, Francesco

1548. *In Librum Aristotelis De arte poetica explicationes*. Florence.

Rodini, Robert, J. 1970. *Antonfrancesco Grazzini*. Madison.

Rozas, Juan Manuel. 1976. *Significado y doctrina del "Arte Nuevo" de Lope de Vega*. Sociedad General Española de Librería, Colección "Temas," 9. Madrid.

Rymer, Thomas

Spingarn 1908a, II:163–255.

Zimansky, Curt A., ed. 1956. *The Critical Works of Thomas Rymer*. New Haven.

Saint-Evremond, Charles de

Carile, Paolo, ed. 1976. *La Comédie des Académistes et les académiciens*. Paris.

de Nardis, Luigi, ed. 1966. *Oeuvres mêlées [par] Saint-Evremond*. Rome.

Fau, Guy, ed. 1972. *Saint-Evremond; Textes*. Editions Nationalistes. Paris.

Finch, Robert, and Eugène Joliat, eds. 1978. *Sir Politick Would-Be*. Geneva.

Hayward, John, ed. 1930. *The Letters of Saint-Evremond*. London.

Niderst, Alain, ed. 1970. *Textes choisis*. Paris.

Ternois, René, ed. 1967–78. *Lettres*. 2 vols. Paris.

1962–69. *Oeuvres en prose de Charles de St.-Evremond*. 4 vols. Paris.

Saintsbury, George. [1902–04] 1934. *A History of Criticism and Literary Taste in Europe from the Earliest Texts to the Present Day*. 2nd edn. 3 vols. Edinburgh.

Sánchez Escribano, Federico, and Alberto Porqueras Mayo. 1972. *Preceptiva Dramática Española del Renacimiento al Barocco*. Madrid.

Sanesi, Ireneo. 1954. *La comedia*. 2nd edn. 2 vols. Milan.

Scaliger, Julius Caesar

[1561] 1964. *Poetices libri septem*. Facsimile reprint of the Lyon 1561 edition with an introduction by August Buck. Stuttgart and Bad Cannstatt.

Padelford, F. M., ed. 1905. *Selected Translations of Scaliger's Poetics*. Yale Studies in English. New York.

Schérer, Jacques. 1950. *La Dramaturgie classique en France*. Paris.

Sellstrom, A. Donald 1986. *Corneille, Tasso and Modern Poetics*. Columbus, OH.

Sherwood, John C. 1950. Dryden and the rules: the Preface to *Troilus and Cressida*. *Comparative Literature* 2:73–83.

Sidney, Sir Philip

[1595] 1968. *The Defence of Poesie*. Menston, England.

Duncan-Jones, Katherine, and Jan Van Dorsten, eds. 1973. *Miscellaneous Prose of Sir Philip Sidney*. Oxford.

Shepherd, G. ed. 1965. *An Apology for Poetry*. London

Smith 1904, I:148–207.

Soens, Lewis, ed. 1970. *Sir Philip Sidney's Defense of Poesy*. Lincoln, NB.

Sifakis, G. 1967. *Studies in the History of Hellenistic Drama*. London.

Smith, G. Gregory, ed. 1904. *Elizabethan Critical Essays*. 2 vols. London.

Somville, Pierre. 1974. *Essai sur la poétique d'Aristote et sur quelques aspects de la postérité*. Paris.

Spingarn, Joel E., ed. 1908. *Critical Essays of the Seventeenth Century*. 3 vols. Oxford.

   1908b. *A History of Literary Criticism in the Renaissance*. 2nd edn. New York.

Stinton, T. C. W. 1975. Hamartia in Aristotle and Greek Tragedy. *Classical Quarterly* 25:221–54.

Sullivan, Henry W. 1976. *Tirso de Molina and the Drama of the Counter Reformation*. Amsterdam.

Swedenberg, H. T., Jr., ed. 1966. *Essential Articles for the study of John Dryden*. Hamden, CT

Sweeney, John Gordon. 1985. *Jonson and the Psychology of Public Theater: To Coin the Spirit, Spend the Soul*. Princeton.

Sweetser, Marie-Odile. 1962. *Les Conceptions dramatiques de Corneille d'après ses écrits théoriques*. Geneva.

Syme, Sir Ronald. 1980. The sons of Piso the Pontifex. *American Journal of Philology* 101:333–41.

Symmes, Harold S. 1903. *Les Débuts de la critique dramatique en Angleterre jusqu'à la mort de Shakespeare*. Paris.

Teichmüller, G. 1867–69. *Aristotelische Forschungen*. Halle.

Tirso de Molina (Fray Gabriel Téllez)

   Armesto, Victor Said, ed. 1913. *Cigarrales de Toledo*. Madrid.

   Prieto, Antonio, ed. 1982. *El Vergonzoso en palacio / El Condenado por desconfiado*. Barcelona.

Todorov, Tzvetan. 1977. *The Poetics of Prose*. Oxford, and Ithaca, NY

Toffanin, Giuseppe. 1920. *La Fine dell'umanesmo*. Milan.

Torres Naharro, Bartolomé de

Gillet, Joseph E., ed. 1946–1951. *Propalladia and Other Works of Bartolomé de Torres Naharro*. 3 vols. Bryn Mawr, PA

   1961. *Torres Naharro and the Drama of the Renaissance*. Vol. IV of the above. Completed by Otis H. Green. Philadelphia.

Tracy, H. L. 1948. Horace's *Ars Poetica*: a systematic argument. *Greece and Rome* 17:104–15.

Trowbridge, Hoyt. 1946. The place of rules in Dryden's criticism. *Modern Philology* 44:84–96.

Vinaver, Eugène. 1955. *Racine and Poetic Tragedy*. Trans. P. Mansell Jones. Manchester.

Webster, T. B. L. 1950. *Studies in Menander*. Manchester.

Weinberg, Bernard. 1942. Scaliger versus Aristotle on poetics. *Modern Philology* 39:337–60.

   1952. Robortello on the *Poetics*. In Crane 1952. 319–48.

   1961. *A History of Literary Criticism in the Italian Renaissance*. 2 vols. Chicago.

   1970–74. *Trattie di poetica e retorica del Cinquecento*. 4 vols. Bari.

Whetstone, George

   [1578] 1910. *Promos and Cassandra*. Tudor Facsimile Texts. London.

Wiles, Timothy J. 1980. *The Theater Event: Modern Theories of Performance*. Chicago.

Williams, Gordon. 1964. Review and discussion of *Horace on Poetry*, by C. O. Brink. *Journal of Roman Studies* 54:186–96.

   1968. *Tradition and Originality in Roman Poetry*. Oxford.

Williamson, George. 1946. The occasion of *An Essay of Dramatic Poesy*. *Modern Philology* 44:1–9. (Repr. in Swedenberg 1966).

INDEX

Accademia degli alterati 172
Accademia degli umidi 115
Accius 71
Acro (Helenius) 112
action, 42–43, 92–93, 109–10, 125–26,
  137, 170–71, 187, 196, 231, 241,
  244, 280, 295; and passion 280; as
  instruction 110; in tragedy 135, 258,
  263
actors 2, 16, 35, 40, 48, 79–80, 83, 86,
  91, 113, 231, 295, 277
Addison, Joseph 293
admiration in tragedy 181, 182
Aeschylus 40, 45, 47, 56, 58, 72, 80, 103,
  106–07, 177, 211, 229, 236, 238
aesthetics 3, 10, 11
Agathon 46, 53, 56, 57, 236, 260
Alexamen of Teios 108
anagnorisis (*see also* recognition) 47, 48
anapaestic metre 48
Ancients versus Moderns controversy
  270ff.
apodeixin apo endiathetou (demonstration
  from thought) 85
Apuleius 181
archon 41
Ariosti, Flaminio 122
Ariosto, Ludovico 126
Aristarchus 74
Aristides 188
Aristophanes 14, 38, 99, 103, 106, 151,
  185, 195, 257, 261–62, 288
Aristotle 3, 5–8, 10, 12, 14, 17, 32ff.,
  62–64, 67, 70, 78, 84ff., 98–99,
  101, 108–09, 111, 119, 121, 123,
  125–29, 133–38, 141–43, 146, 149,
  152–54, 158, 172–75, 179–80, 182,
  184–88, 193–95, 200, 213–15, 217,
  229–30, 234–36, 238–47, 249–50,
  253–54, 257–61, 264, 266, 271–72,
  274, 277–78, 292, 295; *Poetics* 1–3,
  5, 7–8, 10, 32ff., 62–63, 78, 84ff.,
  121, 130ff., 154–55, 161, 172, 185,
  212, 215, 237, 253, 257, 258ff.,
  272, 294; *Rhetoric* 89, 93, 97
Armesto, Victor Said 206
Armstrong, William A. 146
Arnaud, Charles 221

ars (technique) 72
art 3, 4; and craft 4; and nature 107, 152,
  210–11; and philosophy 3; and science
  1, 4; and the state 15; as imitation
  108; of drama 192–93; aesthetic
  principles 2; function of 2; place in
  Greek society 14; origins of 2
Artaud, Antonin 3
Athenaeus 188
Attalus III 82
d'Aubignac, François Hédelin, the abbé 4,
  6, 8, 12, 220ff., 234–35, 247, 253,
  257
audience 79, 83–84, 86, 102, 113, 129,
  217, 221, 223–25, 232, 238, 273,
  280
D'Avenant 295

Bacon, Francis 194–95
Badius, Jodocus 111–12
Beaumont, Sir Francis 276, 286
Bellerose (Pierre Le Messier) 222
Benjamin, Walter 13
Boal, Augusto 4, 8
Boccaccio, Giovanni 115, 155, 205
Boethius 178
Bongiorno, Andrew 130–31
Brecht, Berthold 3–4, 55
Brome, Richard 192
Buchanan, George 182
Burbage, James 177
Butcher, S. H. 48, 55
Bywater, Ingram 56

Caecilius 65
Caldéron de la Barca, Pedro 279
Callipides 188
Carcinus 53–54
Castelvetro, Ludovico 3–7, 9–10, 129ff.,
  179, 250, 274
Castró, Guillén de 213
catastasis 99, 102, 200
catastrophe 78, 81, 102–03, 112, 200,
  229–30
categories of drama 237–39
catharsis 7–8, 42, 90, 101, 148, 172–73,
  179, 193, 257 (*see also* purgation)
Cato the Censor 65